Foragers on America's Western Edge

The Archaeology of California's Pecho Coast

Terry L. Jones
Brian F. Codding

THE UNIVERSITY OF UTAH PRESS
Salt Lake City

The Defiance House Man colophon is a registered trademark
of The University of Utah Press. It is based on a four-foot-tall
Ancient Puebloan pictograph (late PIII) near Glen Canyon, Utah.

LIBRARY OF CONGRESS CATALOGING-IN-PUBLICATION DATA

Names: Jones, Terry L., author. | Codding, Brian F., author.
Title: Foragers on America's western edge : the archaeology of California's
    Pecho Coast / Terry L. Jones, Brian F. Codding.
Description: Salt Lake City : The University of Utah Press, [2018] | Includes
    bibliographical references and index. |
Identifiers: LCCN 2018011928 (print) | LCCN 2018013435 (ebook) | ISBN
    9781607816447 () | ISBN 9781607816430 (cloth)
Subjects: LCSH: Chumash Indians—California—San Luis Obispo
    County—Antiquities. | Excavations (Archaeology)—California—San Luis
    Obispo County. | San Luis Obispo County (Calif.)—Antiquities. | Morro Bay
    (Calif.)—Antiquities. | Pismo Beach (Calif.)—Antiquities.
Classification: LCC F868.S18 (ebook) | LCC F868.S18 J65 2018 (print) | DDC
    979.4/78—dc23
LC record available at https://lccn.loc.gov/2018011928

Errata and further information on this and other titles available at UofUPress.com.

Printed and bound in the United States of America.

Contents

Figures

Tables

Acknowledgments

First and foremost we would like to recognize Roberta Greenwood for completing such impressive seminal research on the Pecho Coast nearly fifty years ago and for providing images from that early work. It has been an honor to try to add to her remarkable accomplishment.

The archaeological investigations described here are the results of a series of California Polytechnic State University–San Luis Obispo field and laboratory classes conducted between 2004 and 2017. Students whose efforts in the field were tremendously appreciated include Kay Abscher, Jennifer Alford, Alexandra Alvarez, Marrie Arrata, Lindsey Arrillaga, Roshanne Bakhtiary, Joel Barnard, Natalie Belton, Greg Benson, Trina Blanchette, Katie Campos, Alejandra Camacho, Jason Carr, Erica Cerles, Missie Cochran, Audrey Cody, Emma Cook, Matt Costello, Jessica Dell, Katie Dickson, Gina DiTommaso, Breda Doherty-Louie, Charles Dunlap, Lisa Eckart, Hannah Ehrlich, Jasmine Escalante, Colleen Ferguson, Matthew J. Fisher, Jennifer Flores, Lyudmilla Feldsher, Karlee Forbis, McKenna Friend, Carla Friddle, Sebastian Garza, Gary Gayer, Tyler Gibson, Kristina Gill, Isaac Gonzales, Camilla Greenbach, Kristina Greenwood, Frances Griffey, Xandie Groves, Alexis Hahn, Taylor Haight, Mike Harroch, Ashley Heath, Paige Hernandez, Savannah K. Hewes, Emily Hill, Madalyn Hosick, Justin Housman, Madalyn Hunt, Alessia Isolani, Chad Jackson, Eric Jenkins, Matthew Jordan, Mary Judkins, Nate Kleinsasser, Eden Knapp, Carly Koenig, Samantha Kuri, Chris Lascola, Samantha Law, Jacob Lerner, Paige Liss, Shandala Loving, Dan Knecht, Danielle Krauss, April Matthews, Lauren May, Hannah MacDonald, Kristen Meckel-Parker, Ann Mekis, Rebecca Miller, Nicole Morrisey, Leila Morrison, Mary Murphy, Elizabeth Murry, McKenzie Myers, Alma Munoz, Marissa Myres, Kristen Nelson, Erika Nielsen, Evin Newton, Madeleine Noet, Michelle L. Oga, Will Osselburn, Stephen Page, Kyle Palazzolo, Beatriz Pereira, Molly Pendley, Christiaan Petrie, Max Pirtle, Jay Prober, Hugh Radde, Madalyn Rainey, Lia Randazzo, Michael Rea, Angela Rezai, Brooke Richter, Chris Risse, Alex Roa, Torie Robinson, Kyleigh Rogers, Morgan Roth, Rachel Salsa, Janae Samano, Methi Satyanarayana, Jennifer Saunders, Tim Schamp, Darin Schmicking, Jason Segers, Abdul Sesay, Lucinda Simpson, Cassandra Smith, Riley Stevens, Meaghan Sullivan, Olivia Surnow, Georgia Suter, Elanna Tahan, Michael Tarantino, Elena Teare, Katy Templeton, Melissa Tew, Brianna Thomas, Allissa Torney, Jordan Traub, Blaize Uva, Kenneth Blake Vernon, Stefan Voge, Mikaela Vournas, Natasha Walstra, Caitlin Walsh, Jack Webb, Aaron Weisberg, Kaya Wiggins, Hilary Wighton, and Darren Wollrich, and Emma Wright.

Washing, sorting, cataloging, and preliminary analyses of materials recovered from the field class projects were completed by students in ANT-311 (Archaeological Laboratory Methods), typically taught during the fall and winter following spring field classes. Students who worked in the laboratory included Alexandra Alvarez, Dani Ashcraft, Roshanne Bakhtiary, Amber Barton, Lindsay Brown, Angeli Calinog, Hannah Buckingham, Ying-Ying Chow, Emma Cook, Breda Doherty-Louie, Jake Fahnhorst, Kelly Fischer, Molly Finch, Karlee Forbis, Raelyn Frederick, Carla Friddle, Shayna Gonzales, Madison Hames, Sara Hannigan, Aliza Herzberg, Emily Hill, Chad Jackson, Chris Lascola, Samantha Law, Rosalie Leborgne, Jacob Lerner, Paige Liss, April Matthews, Tori Mau, Kelley Nekota, Erika

Nielsen, Marley Ochoifeoma, Stephen Page, Kyle Palazzo, Christiaan Petrie, Shalini Quattlebaum, Maria Ramirez-Rieschick, Brooke Richter, Phil Roberts, Melissa Tew, Darin Schmicking, Tatiana Schwirblat, Lucinda Simpson, Brianna Thomas, Jack Webb, Rebecca Wheeler, Kaya Wiggins, Darren Wollrich, and Emma Wright.

Archaeologists who worked as field supervisors were Mark Linder, Bill Stillman, Nathan Stevens, Damon Haydu, and Kacey L. Hadick.

Professional archaeologists who volunteered on one or more of the excavations were Noah Arnold, Angela Barrios, Inne Choi, Dan Contreras, Sebastian Garza, Kristina Gill, Dan Knecht, Leroy Laurie, Dave Makar, Kate Magargal, Erik Martin, Wayne Mills, Barry Price, Bill Stillman, Kenneth Blake Vernon, Wendy Waldron, Elise Wheeler, Tom Wheeler, Brian Wood, and Peter Yaworsky.

Special studies and ancillary analyses were provided by Judy Porcasi (bird and mammal bone identification), Ken Gobalet (fish bone identification), Thad van Bueren (glass beads), Eric Wolgemuth and Angela Arpaia (paleobotany), Willamette Analytics (obsidian hydration), Northwest Obsidian Research Laboratory (obsidian sourcing), and Beta Analytic (radiocarbon dating). All artifact illustrations were completed by Rusty van Rossmann.

We also wish to thank our local Chumash representatives who consulted on the projects during the planning stages and who monitored field work: Matthew Goldman, McKenzie Goldman, Leilynn Odom, Peggy Odom, and Mona Tucker.

We are deeply indebted to Elise Wheeler from California State Parks who facilitated the first field classes at CA-SLO-9, and essentially helped launch our ongoing investigation of the Pecho Coast.

We would also like to express our appreciation to Maggie Trumbly, Sally Krenn, Kelly Kephart, and especially Mike Taggart from PG&E for their ongoing efforts to facilitate Cal Poly's work on the Pecho Coast. Thanks to their hard work, a great many Cal Poly students have had opportunities to participate in field and laboratory research, and to attend and participate in professional conferences. Applied Earthworks's Barry Price provided excellent professional field workers to help oversee students.

We also thank our two peer reviewers, Bill Hildebrandt and Clay Lebow, for providing us with detailed, thoughtful, and, in a few instances, challenging comments on earlier drafts of the book.

We wish to thank Reba Rauch from the University of Utah Press for her kind, careful encouragement throughout the process of publication.

Finally, we wish to express our love and appreciation to our life partners, Debbie Jones and Janeen Codding, who put up with much more than any wives should ever be asked to while we were pursuing the thirteen years of research reported here.

Thank you all.

CHAPTER 1

Introduction

In 1972 the San Luis Obispo County Archaeo-logical Society (SLOCAS) published a mono-graph in which Roberta Greenwood detailed the results of extensive excavations along a stretch of the central California shore known as "the Pecho Coast." Occupied by Chumash-speaking peoples at the time of contact, the Pecho Coast is a rugged, isolated 20-km-long peninsula between Point San Luis Obispo and Hazard Canyon (Figure 1.1) in San Luis Obispo County. It gets its name from a Mexican land grant (Cañada de los Osos y Pecho y Islay) es-tablished in 1842 although the ultimate deriva-tion is from a local Chumash village, *Tstyiwi* (the meaning of which, chest or breast, is the same as the Spanish, *pecho*). To the north of Pecho is Morro Bay, a small, shallow estuary adjacent to a community of the same name, while the vil-lage of Avila Beach is 6 km to the east. Pecho is distinguished by broad coastal terraces and a high-energy, wave-battered rocky shore fronted by extensive kelp forests (Figure 1.2). Low coastal hills that rise up from the eastern edges of the terraces are covered with coastal scrub, oak woodland, and small patches of grassland that provide habitat for the important terrestrial food resources of native California: acorns, seeds, rabbits, and deer.

Greenwood completed large-scale investiga-tions at six sites in 1968 in anticipation of con-struction of the Diablo Canyon Nuclear Power Plant (Figure 1.3). Her massive salvage project

(214 m³ hand recovery plus 30.0 m³ mechanical excavation) was conducted only two years after passage of the National Historic Preservation Act (NHPA) and predated both the National Environmental Policy Act (NEPA) and the California Environmental Quality Act (CEQA) (passed in 1970 and 1969, respectively). Effec-tive implementation of the cultural preservation mandates established in those laws would not occur in California until decades later as govern-ment agencies in the 1960s and 1970s struggled to acquire sufficient funding, create implement-ing regulations, and develop the technical ex-pertise to investigate and protect California's abundant, diverse archaeological record. Large-scale, government-mandated salvage operations were not unknown (many had been conducted in anticipation of reservoir construction in the 1950s and early 1960s), but successful, large-scale investigations of complex coastal sites were not common, and the legal pressure to conduct such work was not especially strong. In most parts of California site destruction in the face of devel-opment was still very much the norm (Moratto et al. 1970). In light of the nascent state of cul-tural resource management (CRM) compliance at the time, Greenwood's work at Diablo Can-yon represents the remarkable case of a private company (Pacific Gas and Electric) accepting their heritage stewardship responsibilities fully by supporting a large, well-designed investiga-tion (Greenwood 2004:1) that simultaneously

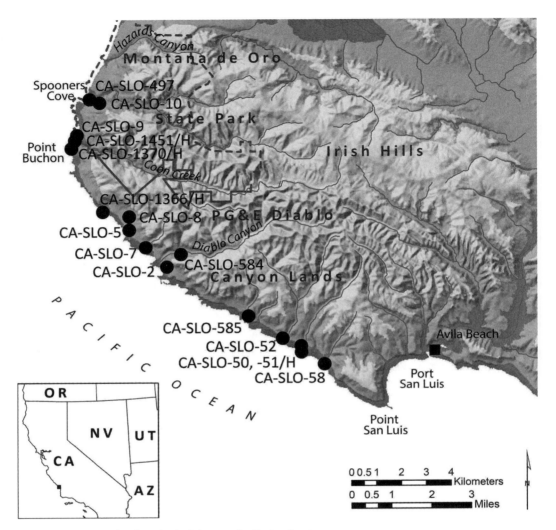

FIGURE 1.1. Excavated archaeological sites on the Pecho Coast.

accomplished salvage objectives while advancing regional and local archaeological research agendas. To this day, Greenwood's study remains one of the most impressive CRM projects ever completed in California.

More remarkable, however, were the actual archaeological findings from the project (Greenwood 1972), particularly those from CA-SLO-2, a large (320 × 400 m) shell midden situated within the footprint of the access road planned for the power plant. Shell-derived radiocarbon dates from the base of the 3.4 m deep deposit indicated that hunter-gatherers initiated a coastal adap-

tation here more than 9,000 years ago, while the overlying layers and findings from other sites showed that this marine-foraging lifeway had continued with some variations through to historic contact. At the time of reporting, CA-SLO-2 was one of the oldest coastal sites in the New World. It was, in fact, so much older than any other coastal site in California (the well-known San Francisco Bay shell mounds are no more than 5,000 years old) that it stood alone for decades as a seeming enigma.

Published in this rather obscure regional monograph and countering prevailing archae-

FIGURE 1.2. Overview of the Pecho Coast. © 2002–2017 Kenneth & Gabrielle Adelman, California Coastal Records Project, www.Californiacoastline.org.

FIGURE 1.3. Excavations beginning at CA-SLO-2, 1968 (photograph courtesy of Roberta Greenwood).

ological orthodoxy of the day that envisioned coastal adaptations as very recent developments (e.g., Cohen 1977; Osborn 1977; see review by Erlandson [2001]) Greenwood's findings did not attract serious attention until a decade later when Moratto (1984) and others began to consider the possibility of a coastal migration route into California—using the dates from CA-SLO-2 as support. Over the ensuing decades, evidence for the antiquity of coastal adaptations in California accumulated rapidly, especially from the northern (Erlandson 1991, 1994; Erlandson et al. 1996, 2007, 2011; Johnson et al. 2002, among others) and southern (Raab 1992; Raab et al. 2009) Channel Islands where many sites as old as, and several thousand years older than, Diablo Canyon have been reported (Erlandson 2013; Erlandson et al. 2008; Jones et al. 2007; Porcasi 2008). Indeed, the radiocarbon dates from the northern islands (ca 12,000 cal BP) are only slightly younger than Clovis, and most scholars accept that California was initially colonized by people traveling in watercraft along the coast at the same time that Clovis big-game hunters were settling the interior by foot (Erlandson et al. 2015; Raff and Bolnick 2014; Rasmussen et al. 2014).

Coincident with growing recognition for greater antiquity of coastal habitation came a steady growth in ecologically oriented method and theory—not only as a perspective that could improve understanding of the earliest adaptations in California but also to help explain variations in marine subsistence across space and over time. Early ecological models emphasized climate and demography (e.g., Glassow 1979, 1993a; Warren 1964) while more recent approaches have incorporated models from human behavioral ecology to examine economic intensification (Whitaker and Byrd 2014), resource overexploitation (Broughton et al. 2015), and settlement patterns (e.g., Jazwa et al. 2013; Winterhalder et al. 2010). Also following Greenwood's work, CRM came of age in California, establishing the legal, conservation-oriented framework for the vast majority of archaeological research in coastal and inland contexts that would be conducted throughout the state thereafter. The work described here is situated in both the ecologically oriented intellectual tradition and a CRM context.

The Pecho Coast as we define it here is controlled today by two institutions: Montaña de Oro State Park which encompasses 8,000 acres between Morro Bay and Coon Creek, and the Diablo Canyon Nuclear Power Plant property owned by Pacific Gas and Electric (PG&E) which encompasses 900 acres between Coon Creek and Point San Luis (Figure 1.1). Arnold Pilling, who completed the first true professional archaeological survey on the San Luis Obispo coast in the 1940s, defined the Pecho Coast as extending to and including Avila Beach (Pilling 1951). Because the latter is situated on a protected, south-facing shoreline and is adjacent to a paleo-estuary (Dills 1981; Jones et al. 2002), we excluded it from the current study. As we define it, the Pecho Coast is a 20 km stretch of rocky shore directly exposed to surf and storm action from the Pacific Ocean.

We present the results of research completed along the Pecho Coast in the decades following Greenwood's seminal 1972 study, primarily work completed by California Polytechnic State University–San Luis Obispo (Cal Poly) field classes between 2004 and 2017, but also CRM studies done by ourselves and others between 1972 and 2017. Seven Cal Poly field classes were conducted along this stretch, first in 2004 within Montaña de Oro State Park at CA-SLO-9 and -10, and, beginning in 2009, on PG&E property at CA-SLO-5, -51/H, -58, -1366/H, and -1370/H. Our research also included re-analyses and supplemental dating for two of Greenwood's original sites, CA-SLO-2 (Jones, Porcasi, Gaeta, et al. 2008), and -585 (Jones et al. 2011). Finally, Cal Poly assisted State Parks archaeologists in a modest salvage excavation at CA-SLO-497 in 2008. All of these projects were undertaken with a goal of recovering midden materials that either were naturally eroding from the edge of cliffs above the Pacific Ocean or were otherwise threatened.

The corpus of combined research provides a more detailed view of the 10,000-year sequence sketched out by Greenwood in 1972 that features variation attributable to both foraging efficiency and climatic flux. The earliest inhabitants of Pecho exploited a full complement of coastal resources (shellfish, fish, marine mammals, sea birds) but were not necessarily coastal specialists. Shoreline occupation was limited to seasonal camps, with longer-term residential sites situated slightly inland where subsistence was focused on terrestrial plant foods processed with choppers, core hammers, scraper planes, milling slabs, and handstones. This assemblage represents the distinctive Southern California Millingstone Culture (also known as the Millingstone Horizon [Wallace 1954]) that in today's parlance we refer to as the Millingstone/Lower Archaic Period. Various Millingstone manifestations have been recognized for more than 50 years as a vegetal resource–focused adaptation that was important during the early Holocene throughout most of central and southern California (Fitzgerald and Jones 1999; Kowta 1969; Moratto 1984; Wallace 1954). Animal foods emphasized in coastal settings were sea birds, rabbits, and deer, variation among which seems best explained with reference to habitat. Sea birds were heavily exploited when they were congregated in nesting colonies—typically located on remote headlands and nearshore rocks (requiring watercraft to exploit). Rabbits dominated the subsistence regime at many Millingstone/Lower Archaic sites reflecting the extent of their preferred vegetation habitat—coast scrub. Black-tailed deer, however, were abundant in the earliest (ca. 10,000–9000 cal BP) levels at CA-SLO-2 which is positioned adjacent to an expanse of interior oak woodland. Heavy exploitation of the apparently highly profitable, readily accessible seabirds is also seen at the earliest sites on Northern Channel Islands where it is linked to the "Paleo-Coastal Tradition" (Moratto 1984; Erlandson et al. 2011). While Pecho foragers show a linkage to the Paleo-Coastal tradition, their heavy involvement with Millingstone tools and plant resources also suggests cultural connections with the interior, despite the fact that direct evidence for trade or exchange with the interior (e.g., obsidian) is minimal at this time depth, implying that the Pecho population was rather isolated. The ethnolinguistic identity of these people is not clear, but it is likely that they were speakers of a Hokan language (Golla 2011).

Some cultural changes are apparent on the Pecho Coast mid-Holocene (ca. 5700 cal BP), including radiocarbon and other evidence for an increase in human population also seen on the south coast (Erlandson and Glassow 1997) and the broader central coast region as a whole

(Jones et al. 2007:142). People established a more serious footprint on the coast at this time when projectile points became more numerous and the first mortars and pestles appeared, suggesting greater investment in the use of acorns. The latter contributed to longer seasonal occupation of some settlements and a two-pronged settlement strategy involving long-term residential sites (where acorns were stored) and short-term camps. Technological changes notwithstanding, subsistence continued along previous lines with increased exploitation of sea birds. Large red abalones were exploited on the coast from the Millingstone/Lower Archaic through Early periods and show only slight size diminution, which is consistent with a highly productive California Current. In general, lifeways during the Millingstone/Lower Archaic and Early periods also seem consistent with a warmer, drier mid-Holocene climate. During the Early Period these climatic conditions seem to have encouraged higher populations along the coast (including Pecho) as some people abandoned the arid interior (Kennett et al. 2007; Mikkelsen et al. 2000; Warren 1968). However, intensification was limited to an increased exploitation of marine birds and greater reliance on acorns.

By the end of the Early Period (2550 cal BP), heavy exploitation of rookeries culminated in extinction of the flightless duck (*Chendytes lawi*) and an apparent suppression of onshore sea bird nesting colonies. Sea bird exploitation was never again a significant factor along the Pecho Coast after the highly vulnerable rookeries were overexploited. Consequently, Middle Period subsistence was characterized by distinct marine intensification that featured heavy exploitation of sea otters as replacements for the flightless duck, and increased fishing. Exploitation of otters seems to have been at least partially linked to increased extraregional exchange involving commodities like obsidian. While fishing intensified during the Middle Period (2550–950 cal BP), it never reached the level of intensity seen on the Channel Islands, nor is there much evidence for fishing far offshore. Pecho foragers never came close to reaching the carrying capacity of their shoreline habitat in light of the enormous untapped caloric potential of near-shore fisheries (Jones et al. 2016). Still, demographic pressures caused by population influx and climatic changes were felt.

Responses to droughts of the Medieval Climatic Anomaly are the most compelling examples of the latter. During the late Middle and Middle–Late Transition periods there, a serious reduction in numbers of deer bones is apparent (Codding et al. 2010), coeval with apogees in cottontail rabbits, marine mammals, and fish (Codding and Jones 2007). Foragers apparently took advantage of cool productive seas to offset reduced productivity in the terrestrial environment during the droughts at Pecho as they did at nearby Morro Bay (Jones et al. 2017). Red abalone shells show decreased mean diameter during this interval suggesting fairly frequent, intensive harvest. The bow and arrow made its way to the coast at this time as well (Codding and Jones 2007; Kennett et al. 2013), but it did not seem to have immediate effects on subsistence.

Amelioration of climate ca. 650–600 cal BP prompted cultural and subsistence changes. Most components dating to this time produced only very modest quantities of material suggesting ephemeral occupation. The exception to this was SLO-51/H, representing the ethnographic village of *Tstyiwi*, the only archaeologically documented Chumash village in San Luis Obispo County. This site shows evidence for use as a long-term residential base during the Late Period. It also produced a great quantity of *Olivella* and other beads which is similar to SBA-3404 in northern Santa Barbara County, which represents the Chumash village of *xonxon'ata* (Hildebrandt 2004). Other than beads, the Late Period marks a decline in almost all quantitative adaptive indices following an apogee during the Middle and/or Middle-Late Transition. These include reductions in fish-bone density (wet-screened samples), marine mammals, marine birds, and obsidian. Subsistence became slightly less marine-focused and long-distance interregional exchange ended. However, abundant shell beads, mostly Class E and K *Olivella* variants, seem not to have been produced locally but,

rather, originated from the Santa Barbara Channel. A striking increase in beads during the Late Period could represent the initial appearance of Chumash-speaking peoples, the second wave of linguistic expansion according to Golla's (2011) model, or the activities of powerful Chumashan leaders, like Buchon of the historic period, who were attempting to establish stronger alliances with northern communities through gifting, reciprocal exchange, and/or forced conquest. Historic accounts of Buchon consistently associate him with armed entourages and raiding/defensive activities.

Greenwood (1978a:523) suggested that northern Chumashan-speaking territory was already in decline when the Portolá expedition came through in 1769. While she did not elaborate on the basis for this opinion, it is not unlikely that an apparent drop-off in use of SLO-2 after the Middle Period was a contributing factor. Our investigations revealed a limited use of the Pecho Coast during the Late Period, with a substantive component only at SLO-51/H. Exactly when and why the focus of settlement shifted to this location is not clear, but there is a hint of a peak in the intensity of exploitation of the Pecho Coast and a decline prior to historic contact. Whether the decrease can be attributed to protohistoric diseases or the medieval droughts (or both) cannot at this point be resolved owing to poor chronological resolution.

After the arrival of Spanish explorers in 1769 and the establishment of Mission San Luis Obispo de Tolosa in 1772, Chumash-speaking peoples continued to reside at the village of *Tstyiwi* for several decades. Subsistence residues suggest that village inhabitants became fully sedentary for the first time, foraging within a limited radius in order to avoid contact with the Spanish. Charred plant remains from a feature indicate year-round site occupation, but the most important subsistence shift was a major increase in nearshore fishing. The volumetric density of fish remains in the postcontact component at SLO-51/H is the highest of any site in San Luis Obispo County. The postcontact matrix also showed the same high density of beads as the precontact component while the recovery of unfinished bead blanks and bead drills indicated that some beads were produced at the village after contact.

Between 1781 and 1803, 37 adults and 19 children from the village of *Tstyiwi* were baptized at Mission San Luis Obispo (Milliken and Johnson 2005). Nine glass beads recovered from SLO-51/H reflect interactions between the Spanish and inhabitants of *Tstyiwi* before 1800; however, two of the glass beads were most common in California between 1810 and 1820 (Appendix A), which raises the possibility of some type of activity at the village site after most inhabitants had been taken to the mission. During the Mexican Period in 1843 the property containing the village of *Tstyiwi* was part of the Pecho y Islay Rancho (10,300 acres), which was awarded to Francisco Padilla who was born in 1789 and came to California in 1825 (Green 2016:18). In 1845, Rancho Pecho y Islay was sold to Captain John Wilson and James G. Scott. Wilson moved his family to the land in 1845 and built an adobe house (Green 2016:19), remnants of which were still standing in the 1970s. Sometime between 1914 and 1916, Rosario Cooper, the last known Native speaker of the Northern Chumash language, told ethnographer John P. Harrington that the Pecho adobe was synonymous with the Chumash place name, *Tstyiwi* (Greenwood 1972:83).

Here we synthesize this record and evaluate these trends for the first time since Greenwood's seminal work. This monograph summarizes all the existing information on the prehistory of the Pecho Coast, providing a benchmark of comparison for existing syntheses to the north (e.g., Far Western Anthropological Research Group 2016; Jones 2003), to the south (e.g., Glassow 1996, 1997), and beyond. This monograph also offers an extended view of foragers on the western edge of North America, examining how local environmental factors shaped the emergence of these coastal societies through more than 10,000 years of prehistory.

CHAPTER 2

Contextual Background

Environment and Ethnohistory

To set the stage for our consideration of recent archaeological findings from the Pecho Coast, we here provide environmental and ethnographic background that establishes the context of the investigations. Under the heading of *environment* we describe the basic elements of the marine and terrestrial habitats that dominate the Pecho landscape, and we consider how they may have changed over time. Further, we identify the type, distribution, and ecology of subsistence resources and, to the degree possible, their potential processing costs and caloric yields in order to consider them within a framework of optimal foraging theory. For ethnography, we recount descriptions from the earliest Europeans to traverse the area near the Pecho Coast and later sources to draw general conclusions about the coastal adaptation that was pursued by Native people in this area around the time of historic contact.

Overviews of the prehistory, archaeology, and ethnohistory of San Luis Obispo County and the broader central California coastal region are also available from a variety of sources including Bertrando and Levulett (2004), Breschini and Haversat (1983, 1988), Greenwood (1972, 1978a), D. Jones (2012), D. Jones and colleagues (2002, 2004), T. Jones and colleagues (2007), Jones and Waugh (1995), Mikkelsen and colleagues (2000), Milliken and Johnson (2005), and Far Western Anthropological Research Group (2016), among others.

Environment

Situated within the central coast region (*sensu* Moratto 1984; see also Jones et al., 2007), the Pecho Coast is a 20-km-wide peninsula extending about 8 km into the Pacific Ocean between Morro (Estero) Bay and San Luis Obispo Bay in San Luis Obispo County, California. Just east of the coastal terraces that dominate the shoreline, low mountains known as the Irish Hills rise sharply to elevations of about 550 ft. With this increase in elevation, the landscape transitions from coastal scrub and chaparral to coastal oaks, chaparral, and grasslands bisected by a series of small, densely wooded drainages that flow to the Pacific Ocean. The mouths of these creeks form small, sandy beaches along a coastline otherwise dominated by exposed rocky shores, cliffs, and bluffs. The interface of nearshore, rocky littoral, and terrestrial environments abounds with a diversity of marine and land resources.

Geology

The geology of the Pecho Coast is summarized by Hall (1973) and Headlee (1966). Good descriptions of local rock units are also available from Chipping (1987). The coastal terraces that were most attractive for human settlement are Quaternary in age and are composed of alluvial and marine sediments. The hills that rise from the terraces are composed of a variety of primarily sedimentary rock formations. Here we describe these formations moving from south to north.

Between Point San Luis and Port San Luis the coastal escarpment is composed of meta-volcanic rocks of the Franciscan Complex that include basalt, diabase, and localized pockets of red chert. The latter is a raw material used for flaked-stone tool production throughout the central coast (referred to as "Franciscan chert"), although it is generally of poorer quality than other cherts. It is also unknown if the outcrops described geologically near Point San Luis were in fact the point source of toolstone recovered from Pecho archaeological sites. The Franciscan Complex dates to the Mesozoic, and lies un-comfortably beneath the Quaternary terrace sediments. Small Franciscan outcrops are also documented at the mouth and along the head-waters of Deer Canyon where Headlee (1966:34) noted "large chert bodies" within the area of the Franciscan complex at Deer Canyon.

Northwest of Deer Canyon to Diablo Canyon, the Obispo Formation dominates the slopes above the coastal terraces. Described as "pyro-clastic" and dominated by tuff (Chipping 1987: III-13; Surdam and Hall 1984:8), it dates to the Miocene and also contains interbedded mud-stones and siltstones in addition to andesites and basalt.

Northwest of Diablo Canyon, the Monterey Formation occurs in a 2–3 km wide swath that parallels the shoreline above ca. 400 ft elevation. The northeastern edge of the Monterey Forma-tion is Coon Creek which also serves as a bound-ary between Montaña de Oro State Park and lands of PG&E. Dating to the Middle Miocene, the Monterey Formation contains diatomaceous shale, porcelaneous shale, silty sandstone, cherty shale, and black interbedded cherts. The latter constitute the highest quality, most desirable toolstone used by prehistoric people in central and southern coastal California.

North of Coon Creek the Monterey Forma-tion gives way to the Pismo Formation, which dates to the Middle Miocene and contains clay-stone, siltstone, and porcelaneous shale. This formation dominates the coastal hills between Coon Creek and Islay Creek. On the north side of Islay Creek, marine terraces are covered by the dunes that extend all the way to Los Osos and ring the Morro Bay estuary.

The dunes have been studied by Cooper (1967) and most recently by Orme (1990) who designated them as the Morro Bay Dune Com-plex. They are the product of sand and other sediments deposited at the shoreline from major drainages, and represent a temporal range of development from late Pleistocene through the Holocene.

Soils

The majority of soils along the coastal terrace belong to loams of the Still series and Concep-cion series (United States Soil Conservation Service 1977). Still series soils were formed from weathered sedimentary rocks in an alluvial con-text; they are very deep and well drained with a slope ranging from 0 to 25 percent. Concepcion soils are very deep and moderately well drained with a slope from 2 to 30 percent; these soils are underlain by clay and sandy clay which repre-sent old marine terraces. Other coastal terrace soils include shaly clay in the Santa Lucia series and clay in the Cropley series (United States Soil Conservation Service 1977). Occurring mostly on the foothills sloping down to the terrace, soils in the Santa Lucia series are well drained, mod-erately deep, and formed in the residual from weathered acid shale. Cropley series soils are very deep, moderately well-drained alluvium weathered from sedimentary rock. These allu-vial fans spill on the coastal terrace with a slope between 0 and 9 percent. The northern portion of the study area, starting at Islay Creek, gives way to Dune Land soils as the terrace transitions to the sand spit extending into Morro Bay.

Climate

The Pecho Coast's Mediterranean climate is characterized by cool, moist winters and warm, dry summers with frequent fog between June and September. In a typical year the average daily temperature ranges around 56°F with a range between 27° in December and 101°F in September (Gerdes and Browning 1974:21). An-nual average precipitation is 37 cm (14.6 inches) per year with a range from 16 to 61 cm (Gerdes and Browning 1974:21). The prevailing winds are from the northwest which is the direction from which most of the winter storms approach.

Environmental Productivity

Conditioned by the combination of local soils and climate, environmental productivity measures the amount of biomass available. Based on the long-term average calculation of net primary productivity (NPP) by Running (2012), the overall environmental productivity of the Pecho Coast (as defined by Milliken and Johnson 2005) averages about 1.21 grams of carbon sequestered per cubic meter per day (calculation following Codding and Jones 2013).

Vegetation

Kuchler (1977) associates the Quaternary terraces of the Pecho Coast with coastal sagebrush shrub formation, and the Irish Hills with southern oak forest dominated by live oak (*Quercus agrifolia*). Today the terraces are occupied by agricultural fields and rangeland, with extensive grassland and some limited coastal sage scrub. Nonnative species dominate the vegetation of both complexes on the terraces today, but common species prior to contact included California sagebrush (*Artemesia californica*), coyote brush (*Baccharis pilularis*), poison oak (*Toxicodendron diversilobum*), and black sage (*Salvia mellifera*). The southern-oak forest is more intact in the hills above the terraces and would have been a source of acorns for Native inhabitants. As discussed below, California Indians likely burned this vegetation to increase subsistence yields, though the antiquity of such a practice is unknown.

Paleoenvironment

The degree to which past environments were divergent from current ones is a critical consideration in that a varied marine environment (particularly sea surface temperatures) and/or terrestrial climate could influence the nature of the resource base available to resident hunter-gatherers, and change through time in such ambient conditions could potentially cause changes in foraging practices. For our purposes, and given the available data, records of paleo sea surface temperature and variation in pollen are particularly relevant to marine and terrestrial reconstructions, respectively. For the most part, reconstructions of the paleoenvironment are reliant on findings from study sites outside the central coast proper including from the offshore varved sediments of Santa Barbara Channel (e.g., Heusser 1978, 1995, 1998; Kennett and Ingram 1995; Kennett and Kennett 2000, among others), the San Joaquin Valley (Davis 1999), and the Sierra Nevada (Anderson and Stillick 2013; Davis and Moratto 1988; Graumlich 1994; Stine 1994 [see review by West et al. 2007:26–30]), all with at least some applicability to the Pecho Coast. More directly relevant local studies are limited to an important recent pollen study by Anderson et al. (2015), discussed in detail below, an attenuated charcoal core (Mensing 1998), and a preliminary assessment of sea surface temperatures from the last 2,000 years based on oxygen isotope findings from archaeological mussel shells (Jones and Kennett 1999). For a more detailed review of regional paleoenvironmental studies, see Boone (2012), Kennett (2005), and West et al. (2007).

Sea Surface Temperatures and Marine Productivity

Long-term global variation in sea surface temperatures (SST) has been estimated from the Greenland Ice Sheet Project (GISP) ice core which revealed macro-patterns over the last 250,000 years (Dansgaard and Johnsen 1993). For the period of interest here (late Pleistocene and Holocene), the ice core shows a general trend of warming seas following a low point during the Last Glacial Maximum ca. 18,000 years ago. GISP also shows a strong signal from the Younger-Dryas event ca. 13,000 years ago when mean SST briefly plummeted to near glacial levels and then rebounded. However, the GISP core generally shows very little variation from 10,000 cal BP onward. A core reported from sediments offshore from Santa Cruz shows little if any Younger-Dryas signal (Pisias et al. 2001) and less short-term variability than in the Santa Barbara area. The Santa Cruz core also shows radiolarian evidence for seas slightly warmer than present during early Holocene with a modest decline thereafter. Importantly, these results support a study by Barron and Bukry (2007) based primarily on a northern California core, that shows reduced coastal upwelling between 9000 and 12,000 cal BP. Reduced upwelling intensity would be consistent with warmer SST. This study provides a Holocene history of the south-flowing California Current which is probably more relevant to the central coast than findings from the Santa Barbara Channel, which is influenced by the northerly flowing Southern California Countercurrent that causes higher SSTs and greater variability south of Point Conception. The Barron and Bukry (2007) study suggests the California Current was weak between 9000 and 12,000 cal BP and that it intensified between 9,000 and 8,000 years ago which increased upwelling intensity as far south as Point Conception. The current slackened between 4800 and 3600 cal BP when upwelling was reduced, after which time modern conditions appeared with enhanced spring upwelling and warm SST in the fall (Barron and Bukry 2007).

Variation in the California Current correlates only partially with an 11,000-year sequence of SST and inferred marine productivity from the Santa Barbara Channel (Kennett and Kennett 2000; Kennett 2005) (Figure 2.1). Kennett (2005) identified warm seas and lower marine productivity between 11,000–9600, 8200–6300, 5900–3800, 2300–1500, and post-500 cal BP, followed by cold seas from 9600–8200, 6300–5900, 3800–2300, and 1500–500 cal BP. Clearly this represents more variation than Barron and Bukry (2007) report for the California Current.

In one of the few studies from the central California coast, Jones and Kennett (1999) found that SST, inferred from oxygen isotopes from archaeological mussel shells, were about 1°C cooler than present and stable between 2,000 and 700 years ago. Between about 700 and 500 years ago, seasonal variation was greater than present, with extremes above and below historic levels. Water temperatures were 2–3°C cooler than today 500–300 years ago. This study also compiled historic sea temperature records from the Monterey Peninsula that clearly show that seas have warmed as much as 2°C just in the twentieth century.

Variation between the Santa Barbara Channel and the area influenced by the California Current (northern and central California) may be a product of different scales of resolution and/or stratigraphic integrity between the sequences as suggested by Pisias and colleagues (2001) or the lack of influence from the Southern California Countercurrent north of Point Conception. The latter would presumably cause more muted shifts and less variability in sea surface temperature and productivity on the central and northern California mainland including the Pecho Coast.

Terrestrial Climate

Intense interest in recent anthropogenic global warming has fueled a barrage of paleoenvironmental research worldwide in the last few decades that has established a reasonably secure global climatic history (Marcott et al. 2013), which is a composite of a multitude of regional sequences that vary from the global means in relative intensity and timing. The global record shows temperatures warmer than present during the early Holocene (the Holocene Maximum also once referred to as the Altithermal or Hypsithermal), followed by cooling through the middle to late Holocene culminating in the coolest temperatures of the Holocene during the Little Ice Age (600–150 years ago) (Figure 2.2). The Medieval Climatic Anomaly (MCA) shows as a minor return to warm temperatures between ca. 1,000 and 700 years ago (Marcott et al. 2013; West et al. 2007).

Marcott and colleagues's (2013) meta-study was preceded by a North America–only, continent-wide compilation of pollen core data by Viau and colleagues (2006) which shows similar but not identical trends. Specifically, that study suggests that the interval of highest July temperatures in North America was between 6000 and 3000 cal BP, with the latter date representing the peak in Holocene warmth. This is slightly later than most studies but it highlights difficulties in defining the precise duration and

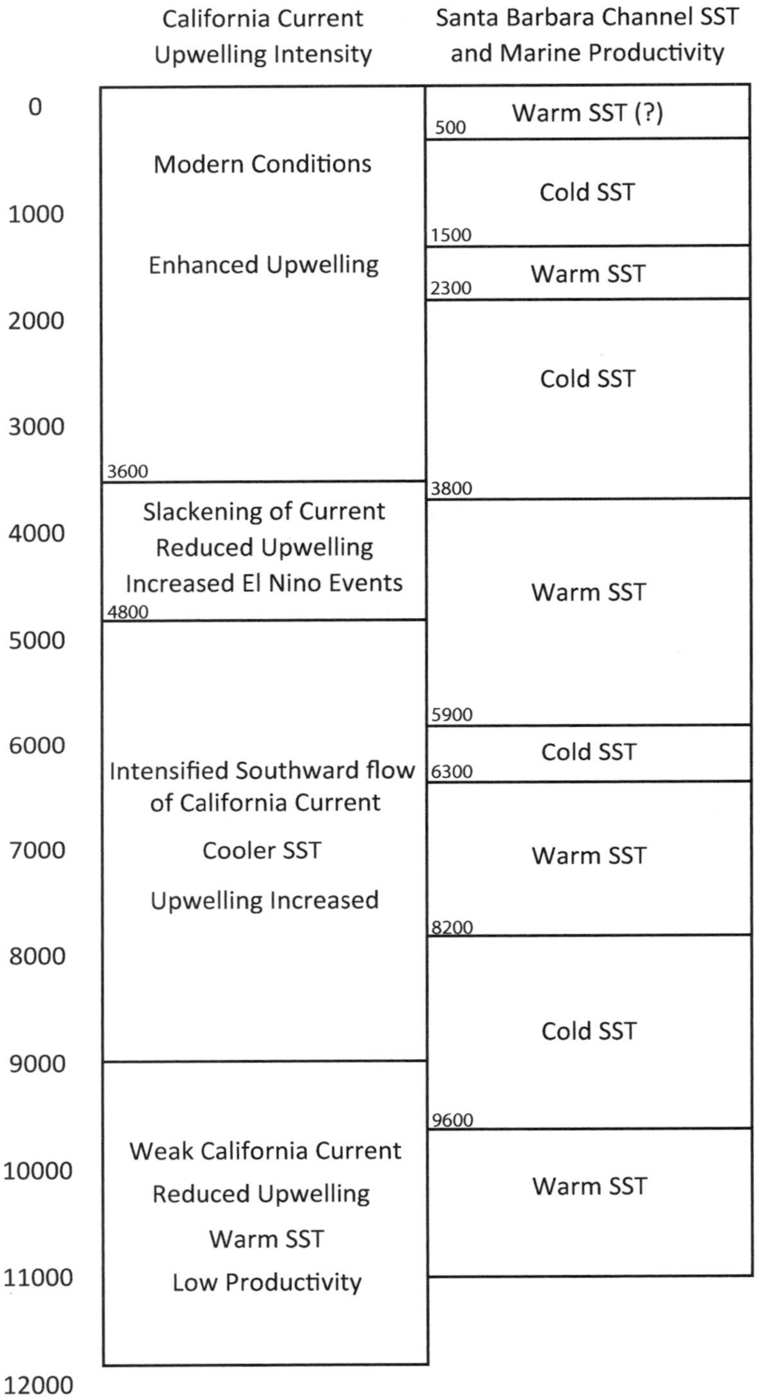

FIGURE 2.1. Comparison of diachronic marine productivity trends for the California Current (Baron and Bukry 2007) and the Santa Barbara Channel (Kennett 2005).

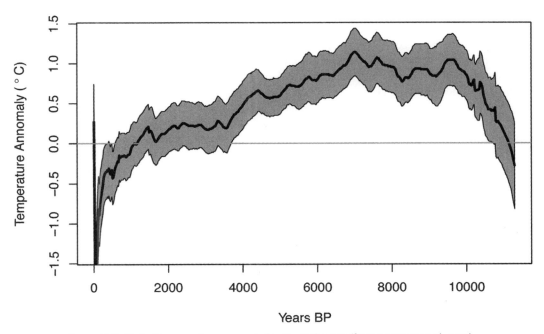

FIGURE 2.2. Global temperature anomaly for the Holocene (from Marcott et al. 2013).

nature of past climatic intervals. That western North America was warmer and/or drier during mid-Holocene has been recognized since at least 1948 (Antevs 1948, 1953, 1955), but the exact chronology and magnitude of this variation are characterized differently from region to region.

While general global patterns have been recognized for some time, of more relevance to the current project are regional and local sequences that speak directly to the conditions experienced by hunter-gatherers on the central California coast in the past. Until recently, the closest important studies of terrestrial vegetation relevant to the Pecho Coast were from the Santa Barbara Channel Basin (e.g., Heusser 1978, 1995, 1998; Kennett and Ingram 1995). The earliest of these by Heusser (1978) established the basic trends in Holocene vegetation and climate change, showing general correlations with worldwide patterns—again with caveats about exact dating and the magnitude of changes. The earliest Holocene before ca. 7800 BP was marked by a continuation of Pleistocene–Holocene transition warming and drying, but climate was still cooler and wetter than present, and pine pollen occurred in its highest frequencies of the Holo-

cene. After 7,800 years ago oaks and sagebrush became more dominant. This warming trend peaked at mid-Holocene ca. 5,600–4,200 years ago, marked by the highest frequency of sunflower pollen. After peak warming ca. 4,200 years ago, there was a trend toward cooler, wetter climate with essentially modern conditions established after ca. 3,200 years ago. The late Holocene cooling and wetting was still modest relative to the Pleistocene with oaks continuing to dominate over pines by a considerable margin. The transition from Pleistocene to Holocene was essentially a replacement of pines with oaks, sagebrush and poison oak (representing the coastal scrub and chaparral communities present historically). Other pollen records from the Santa Barbara area also indicate warm dry conditions during early to mid-Holocene, including findings from Santa Rosa Island which show a peak between 5200 and 3250 BP (Cole and Liu 1994) and a study from Point Conception which suggested peak warm conditions between 7600 and 4380 BP (Morgan et al. 1991).

An important study by Davis (1999) from Tulare Lake in the San Joaquin Valley east of San Luis Obispo County further suggests that maximum temperatures occurred there between 7,000 and 4,000 years ago and were preceded by a cold and wet early Holocene. Cool, moist climate dominated from 4,000 to 2,000 years ago followed by aridity and high temperatures 1,000 years ago (West et al. 2007:25).

Most of the paleoecological studies from the California coast including those from the Santa Barbara Channel have been relatively coarse-grained, covering long periods of time and documenting broad patterns. Archaeologists, however, have been interested in finer-grained climatic chronologies in order to pinpoint possible causes of cultural shifts. This approach is highlighted by Kennett's (2005) reconstruction of terrestrial climate, precipitation, and ocean temperatures for the last 3,000 years in the Santa Barbara Channel which was based on a pollen core from north of Point Conception (Morgan et al. 1991) and tree rings from Bristlecone pines in eastern California.

Here we compare Kennett's (2005) synthesis with findings from the limited number of core studies from the central coast north of Point Conception. These include a marine sediment pollen core collected offshore from Morro Bay (Heusser 1998), recently reported pollen and charcoal cores from the San Antonio Creek area in Vandenberg Air Force Base (Anderson et al. 2015), and two other short-duration cores from northern Santa Barbara County (Mensing 1998). The San Antonio Creek cores include one from Mod Pond that provides a high-resolution record for the period between 2800 and 50 cal BP.

Heusser's coarse-grained core which covers the last 20,000 years shows a general trend of increasing oaks and chaparral after ca. 8,500 years ago coincident with decreasing pine through the Holocene, although a noticeable spike in pine pollen is apparent ca. 2,000 years ago. Oaks and alder show a dramatic decline ca. 13,000 years ago which appears to signal the Younger-Dryas cool/dry event. Oaks show a modest peak between ca. 8500 and 6000 BP while pines are low between ca. 8500 and 3000 BP; together the patterning in these two pollen groups seems consistent with the mid-Holocene warm/dry interval. The increase in pine ca. 2,000 years ago seems consistent with post–mid-Holocene climatic amelioration sometimes referred to as the Medithermal or Neopluvial. Chaparral pollen, however, is not wholly in alignment with these other patterns, showing a steady increase after ca. 8,500 years ago.

The San Antonio Creek cores have inadequate pollen preservation for the early and middle Holocene, but pollen samples are abundant and informative from 2800 to 50 years BP. The record for these three millennia shows very little change with continuity of coastal sage scrub until the onset of the historic period. There is only a very modest signal for the Medieval Climatic Anomaly between AD 1200 and 1500 when aquatic spores reached minimal amounts. After AD 1500 during the Little Ice Age, numbers of these increase, but the overall record from this natural pond shows only muted response to the MCA. There is no evidence to suggest that it dried up entirely during the MCA.

Mensing (1998) reported a pollen sequence from Zaca Lake in northern Santa Barbara County which shows findings dating back to ca. 2,600 radiocarbon years ago. The sequence is inadequately dated, but a sudden decline in oaks coincident with a peak in Asteraceae at 175 cm below surface could represent the Medieval Climatic Anomaly. A core from the Santa Barbara Basin also reported by Mensing (1998) shows no significant changes through the Little Ice Age until historic times.

The Medieval Climatic Anomaly (MCA) and Little Ice Age are thus poorly represented in the local paleoecological record; their occurrence and the relative intensity of changes associated with them continues to be based on findings from elsewhere including the Sierra Nevada (Graumlich 1993), Mono Lake (Stine 1994), and tree rings in southern California (MacDonald 2007). As Anderson and colleagues (2015) note, the occurrence of extreme droughts during the MCA is so widely recognized in southern California and western North America in general (MacDonald 2007) that it is unlikely that similar conditions were not present on the central coast. But, the ambiguity of local studies cannot be wholly ignored either. It is unclear whether the local record simply lacks the fine-grained chronostratigraphic resolution of the varved Santa Barbara Basin sediments (that produced Kennett's SST reconstruction) and the tree rings of eastern and southern California (that provided the evidence for extremely low precipitation during medieval times) or if northern and central California experienced more muted variability during the late Holocene.

Marine/Terrestrial Correlation

The issue of the relationship between ocean temperatures, upwelling intensity, and terrestrial climate is not insignificant, and has been addressed most explicitly by Heusser (1998) and Kennett (2005). Heusser (1998) shows that across the last 20,000 years, broad patterns of SST and land are correlative, with cold conditions during the last glacial interval (24,000–14,000 years), oscillations during the Pleistocene–Holocene transition (14,000–10,000 years), and rapid warming during the Holocene after 10,000 years. Correlations with precipitation showed high rainfall in central California between 24,000 and 14,000, a rapid decrease 14,000 years ago punctuated by two wet intervals, and the onset of modern conditions after 10,000 years (Heusser 1998:259). The Younger-Dryas event at 13,000 years, marked by cool, dry climate and sudden decreases in oak and alder pollen, was associated with a period of decreased upwelling and warmer SST. Terrestrial climate in south-central California inferred from pollen suggests peak warm and dry conditions between 9,000 and 4,000 years ago (Heusser and Sirocko 1997), but contrasts with sea surface temperatures which appear to decline after 9,000 years ago (Heusser 1998:259).

For the late Holocene, Kennett (2005) and Kennett and Kennett (2000) examine smaller-scale climatic intervals for the Santa Barbara Channel and argue for correlations between low SST and low precipitation akin to the Younger-Dryas event. Cold SST between 3800 and 2300 cal BP correlate with reduced marine productivity and lower precipitation (based on Bristlecone records from the eastern Sierra Nevada); between 2300 and 1500 seas were warm and less

productive with greater rainfall; between 1500 and 500 seas were cool and productive and rainfall was low. After 500 years ago seas are argued to have warmed again with increased rainfall, however, this last generalization is probably accurate only for the last two centuries since historic records and archaeological evidence suggest that seas were 2°C colder at the beginning of the twentieth century along the central coast (Jones and Kennett 1999). Recent findings from Morro Bay (Jones et al. 2017) do suggest that seas were exceptionally productive in the general area between 950 and 700 cal BP which supports Kennett's (2005) sequence.

Codding and Jones (2016) show a general correlation between Kennett's (2005) sea surface temperatures and Cook and colleagues' (2004) inferred local Palmer Drought Severity Index (PDSI) over the ca. 2,000-year period during which the two records overlap, suggesting linkages between SST and terrestrial PDSI (Figure 2.3). While there is general correlation in trends, the match is not perfect.

Sea Level Rise

Since the rate of postglacial sea level rise is relatively well established (see Masters and Aiello 2007), bathymetric contours offshore from the Pecho Coast provide a reasonable approximation for the location of the shoreline at various points in the past, with the caveat that Holocene sediments in some cases obscure the actual depth of potential living surfaces. The continental shelf off the Pecho Coast is relatively flat and slopes westward fairly gradually. At the height of the Last Glacial Maximum (ca. 18,000–20,000 years ago) when sea level was 120 m below present, the shoreline was at most 5 km farther west from where it is today. At 12,000 years ago sea levels were ca. 55 m below present and the shoreline was 1–2 km westward of its present location. By 5,000 years ago the shoreline was essentially congruent with its current location. The key point is that between 12,000 and 5,000 years ago coastal settlers would have had access to a reasonably flat shoreline terrace that has since been covered by the sea. The likelihood that shoreline sites still exist on this terrace in some

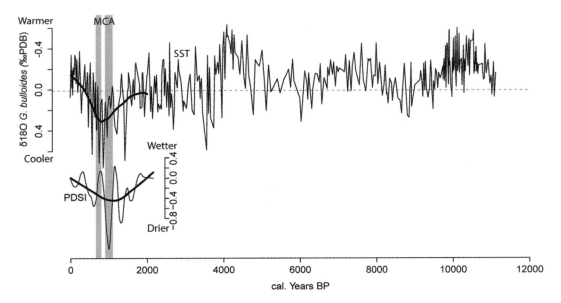

FIGURE 2.3. Sea surface temperature (from Kennett and Kennett 2000) and Palmer Drought Severity Index (from Cook et al. 2013).

kind of intact form is extremely low given the destructive nature of nearshore processes and wave action now and in the past. However, it is not impossible that isolated artifacts could exist.

Food Resources

Local populations interacted dynamically with this environment for thousands of years. As hunter-gatherers, individuals lived and died by the food resources they acquired. Here we discuss the available resources (shellfish and fish, marine mammals, birds, and terrestrial mammals) and examine their relative profitability across marine and terrestrial patches.

Shellfish

The maritime resources include four classes: shellfish, fish, marine mammals, and birds. Shellfish species are dominated by those native to exposed rocky coastlines. Taxa in the littoral zone include mussel (*Mytilus californianus*), barnacle (*Balanus* sp.), black turban snail (*Tegula funebralis*), limpet (*Lottia* sp.), black and red abalone (*Haliotis cracherodii* and *H. rufescens*), and chiton (*Cryptochiton stelleri* and *Mopalia muscosa*). The rock outcroppings and tidal pools host a variety of other intertidal invertebrates,

including sea anemone (*Anthopleura xanthogrammica*), sea urchin (*Strongylocentrotus purpuratus*), ochre starfish (*Pisaster ochraceus*), hermit crab (*Pagurus hirsutiusculus*), and sand crab (*Emerita analoga*). However, previous research along the central coast has shown that four tend to be most prominent in middens: California sea mussels, red abalone, black abalone, and turban snails.

Fish

Marine fish are diverse and vary in availability according to season. Schooling species such as mackerel (Scombridae), anchovy (Engraulidae), and sardine (*Sardinops* sp.) may all be procured year-round, but are most abundant from September to December. Nearshore and kelp-bed-habitat fish, such as the cabezon (*Scorpaenichtys marmoratus*), surfperch (Embiotocid), rockfish (*Sebastes* sp.), and lingcod (*Ophiodon elongatus*) are year-round residents.

Marine Mammals

California Fish and Game records noted sightings of four marine mammal species in this area in 1974: California sea lion (*Zalophus californicus*), harbor seals (*Phoca vitalina*), Stellers sea lion (*Eumetopia jubata*), and the sea otter (*Enhydra lutris*) (Gerdes and Browning 1974). The latter was absent from the area for much of the late nineteenth and twentieth century owing to the near decimation of the species at the hands of historic hunters. It returned to the Pecho Coast in the 1970s. California sea lions and the Steller sea lion make seasonal migrations. The former are absent in the summer while the latter were probably most common offshore in the fall. California sea lions congregate in rookeries in May, and pups are usually born in June to mid-July. The archaeological record indicates that elephant seals (*Mirounga angustirostris*) (Rick et al. 2012) and fur seals (Rick et al. 2009) were at least occasionally present nearshore prior to historic times although the former were nowhere near as numerous as they have become in recent historic times.

Birds

North of Pecho, Morro Bay is an integral part of the Pacific flyway and is visited by a myriad of migratory birds particularly in the winter. Gerdes and Browning (1974) identified no fewer than 75 species that visit or reside year-round at Morro Bay. The Pecho Coast, however, lacks the marshland habitat preferred by aquatic birds and is home to a more reduced subset of marine birds. Those that currently breed on the Pecho Coast include western gull (*Larus occidentalis*), pelagic cormorant (*Phalacrocorax pelagicus*), Brandt's cormorant (*Phalacrocorax penicillatus*), pigeon guillemot (*Cepphus columba*), and black oystercatcher (*Haematopus bachmani*).

Terrestrial Mammals

Twenty-five species of native terrestrial mammals were documented in the area of the Pecho Coast in 1974. These include several small burrowing taxa, the California ground squirrel (*Otospermophilus beecheyi*), and pocket gopher (*Thomomys bottae*) which are major agents of bioturbation within the Pecho Coast archaeological sites. The largest herbivore currently present is the black-tailed deer (*Odocoileus hemionus*), although tule elk remains have been recovered from local archaeological sites in very small numbers (e.g., Mikkelsen et al. 2000). Cottontail

and brush rabbits (*Sylvilagus* sp.) were common inhabitants of the coastal scrub along with jackrabbits (*Lepus californicaus*). Historically, local carnivores included brown bears (*Ursus horribilis*), mountain lions (*Felis concolor*), bobcats (*Lynx rufus*), gray foxes (*Urocyon cinereoargenteus*), coyote (*Canis latrans*), and long-tailed weasels (*Mustela frenata*). Most previous archaeological studies have shown that deer, cottontail rabbits, and jackrabbits were generally the most heavily pursued terrestrial game in the prehistoric past locally (e.g., Codding et al. 2010), albeit in varied proportions.

Resource Profitability

These resources vary in their economic profitability, which, based on ecological and evolutionary theory, should at least partially structure prehistoric resource choice (see Bird and O'Connell 2006; Codding and Bird 2015). Using the logic from the prey choice or diet breadth model (see MacArthur and Pianka 1966; Charnov et al. 1976), a forager should only take resources that maximize their overall returns. To accomplish this, resource selectivity should depend not on resource abundance alone, but on the abundance of highly profitable resources. The first step in implementing this approach is to rank resources based on their postencounter profitability, or the amount of calories acquired per unit of time spent handling that resource, which includes pursuit and processing time. Importantly, the time required to find a resource (search time) is not included in this calculation but is factored in as a function of the foragers' encounter rate with that resource. The second step requires understanding how abundant each resource is within a patch, thereby providing an estimate of a forager's encounter rate. Combined, these data can be used to calculate whether or not taking a resource on encounter should increase a forager's overall harvesting efficiency; if not, the model predicts that the forager should pass over the item in search of more profitable resources. Foragers commonly pass over resources: for example, while most plants are edible and ubiquitous, yet foragers are constantly making the decision to pass over these low-profitability resources in search of more profitable ones.

TABLE 2.1. Postencounter Return Rates for Resource Sets within Marine Patches.

Resource Type	Inclusive Taxa	Inclusive Species	Method of Capture	Postencounter Return Rates (kcal/hr)			Source
				Low	Midpoint	High	
Marine mammal	Ringed seal, Bearded seal	*Phoca hispida, Erignathus barbatus*	Encounter	10,550	18,115	25,680	Smith 1991
Fish	Small saltwater fish	Mixed	Cast/Drag Net	3,806	4,936	6,065	Bliege Bird and Bird 1997; Raven 1990
Waterfowl	Canadian goose	*Branta canadensis*	Canoe		4,930		Smith 1991
Fish	Medium saltwater fish	Mixed	Spear/harpoon	3,206	3,646	4,086	Thomas 2008
Waterfowl	Canadian goose	*Branta canadensis*	Blind	3,460	3,460	3,460	Smith 1991
Waterfowl	Canadian goose, Elder duck	*Branta canadensis*	Encounter	1,720	3,440	5,160	Smith 1991
Waterfowl	Ducks	*Anas sp.*	Encounter	1,975	2,342	2,709	Simms 1987
Shellfish	Gumboot chiton, Katy chiton	*Cryptochiton stelleri, Katharina tunicata*	Encounter	447	1,337	2,228	Kennedy 2005
Shellfish	Red abalone	*Haliotis rufescens*	Encounter	135	1,174	2,213	Kennedy 2005
Fish	Small saltwater fish	Mixed	Spear/harpoon	600	1,100	1,600	Bliege Bird and Bird 1997; Thomas 2008
Fish	Small to large saltwater fish	Mixed	Handline	400	650	900	Bliege Bird and Bird 1997
Shellfish	California mussel	*Mytilus californianus*	Stripping/Plucking	214	404	788	Cook 2016; Jones and Richman 1995
Shellfish	Washington clam	*Saxidomus sp.*	Digging		364		Kennedy 2005
Shellfish	Turban snail	*Tegula funebralis*	Picking	73	113	153	Jones and Ferneau 2002; Kennedy 2005
Shellfish	Sea urchin	*Strongylocentrotus purpuratus*	Encounter	64	95	126	Kennedy 2005
Shellfish	Crab	Mixed	Encounter	21	49	77	Kennedy 2005

Implementing this framework on the Pecho Coast, as anywhere, requires defining patches in which search time is shared between all resources, gathering postencounter return-rate data for each resource, and estimating encounter rates for each resource. Patches can be fairly easily defined in this context as belonging either to the marine or terrestrial environment. But within each of these patches, data on postencounter profitability and encounter rates are lacking. Nonetheless, quantitative data from analogous resources and regions are available and can be used to generate predictions about which resources individuals should take preferentially over others. Optimal diet calculations would be possible from these data if reliable encounter rates were available; however, encounter data vary considerably from species for which return rates have been determined experimentally (Ferneau 1998; Jones and Richman 1995; Kennedy 2005; Simms 1987) to those for which values are based on ethnographic observations made elsewhere. Regardless, these data do provide relative utility rankings upon which we can evaluate the empirical record to assess changes in foraging efficiency and diet breadth through time and across space.

Marine Resources and Resource Patches

As discussed above, foragers would encounter a variety of mammals, birds, fish, and shellfish within marine patches. Available postencounter return-rate data derived from experimental and ethnographic work allows us to make some observations about the subsistence efficiency represented in certain patches and for specific resources (Table 2.1). Previous research shows that some of these resources are more prominent in the regional midden record and have been the subject of extensive research and, in some cases, debate. With regard to patches, distinctions can be made between (1) the intertidal zone that could be exploited without watercraft or any form of specialized marine technology; (2) nearshore patches such as kelp forests that could have potentially been accessed from shore without boats (shore-based line fishing) but in

all likelihood would have been exploited more effectively with some modest form of watercraft; and (3) offshore and deep-water habitats that would have unequivocally required reliable sea vessels of some type.

The Shoreline/Intertidal Patch

As mentioned above, previous work shows that four shellfish dominate middens on the open, rocky coast of central California: mussels, red and black abalones, and turban snails. The energetics associated with exploitation of all of these and the potential impacts of human harvest have been discussed at length.

California Sea Mussels

This abundant, high-intertidal bivalve has been the subject of discussion and debate for decades. Jones and Richman (1995) conducted experiments collecting mussels from beds at Big Sur and Santa Cruz to determine potential return rates. They used two alternate collecting strategies proposed hypothetically by White (1989): stripping and plucking. The former approach involves removing an entire section from a mussel bed indiscriminately, while the latter involves selective harvest of only the largest individuals. They found that plucking was the most efficient method of harvest, potentially yielding 574 Kcal/hour. Stripping was less efficient but could provide a greater quantity of food, albeit with investment of more processing labor. The plucking method is considered more sustainable because mussels can have difficulty recolonizing bare patches. Modern mussel-harvesting operations further confirm that the selective harvest approach represents ecological sustainability (Yamada and Peters 1988). Jones (1996) subsequently compared archaeological mussel-size profiles over time from sites at Big Sur and argued for a shift from plucking to stripping ca. 5,500 years ago which he attributed to increased human population and resource intensification. Only one pre-5500 cal BP component showed selective harvest, and the size profiles from the vast majority of components dating 5500–200 cal BP showed stripping. Subsequent studies from elsewhere on the central

TABLE 2.2. Results of Mussel Collection Experiments.

Location	Month	Collection strategy	Collection time (min.)	Total load Weight (g)	Meat Weight	N Mussels	Processing time (min.)	Meat/Hr.	Kcal¹/Hour
Big Sur	April 1994	Plucking	20	5,954.3	470.7	424	40.0	470.7	543.2
Big Sur	April 1994	Stripping	20	5,506.0	343.5	1,298	90.9	185.6	214.2
Davenport	1994	Plucking	20	4,863.0	564.0	746	48.0	497.6	574.2
Davenport	1994	Stripping	20	10,277.2	750.2	1,478	116.6	116.6	445.9
Diablo	February 2016	Stripping	10	4,996.5	950.0	147	104.5	497.4	574.9
Diablo	February 2016	Plucking	10	3,677.1	629.5	53	61.3	533.5	616.6
Diablo	March 2016	Stripping	5	2,504.4	457.2	76	35.0	682.1	788.3
Diablo	March 2016	Plucking	5	2,021.2	372.5	27	30.1	642.2	742.2

Source: Cook (2016); Jones and Richman (1995).
¹ Based on energy values reported by Gilliland (1985:62)

coast (e.g., Jones and Ferneau 2002) including Pecho (Codding et al. 2009) have repeatedly revealed size profiles suggestive of stripping. In northern California Whitaker (2008) also reported a stripping size profile, but argued *contra* Jones and Richman (1995) and Yamada and Peters (1988) that this represented incipient aquaculture. However, all of the size-based conclusions were reliant on use of a mussel shell template developed by White (1989) that allowed for estimates of complete mussel size to be made from incomplete shells. The latter typically constitute 99.9% of the mussel shells found in central coast middens (Jones, personal observation). Subsequent evaluation of the accuracy of the template (Bell 2009), however, showed that it is unreliable. While this does not negate the experimentally derived return rates for the two mussel collection strategies, it does call into serious question conclusions about archaeologically derived size profiles of harvested mussels from central and northern California. Notably, in the Northern Channel Islands, shell preservation is considerably better than on the central coast mainland and researchers have been able to evaluate size patterns of whole shells without templates. Debate there now centers on whether or not apparent diminution in mussel shells over time represents the effects of human predation (Braje et al. 2017; Flores 2017; Thakar et al. 2017), although the argument in favor of human predation by Braje et al. (2017) seems most reasonable.

Also of note, recent experimental work involving collection and processing of mussels with a pitted stone anvil yielded higher return rates than earlier experiments (Table 2.2; Cook et al. 2017). The likely explanation for this variation is the time of year when the collections took place. Mussels were harvested from the Pecho Coast in February and March which most biologists associate with mussels' seasonal spawning peak (Jones and Richman 1995:38) when the reproductive organs of the shellfish are swollen. This experimental work also suggests that the main function of pitted stones on the central coast was to process mussels (Cook et al. 2017).

Abalones

Black and especially red abalones have been a focus of archaeological discussion and inquiry for decades. On the Northern Channel Islands, conspicuous concentrations of large red abalone concentrations (known as red abalone "middens") have been recognized as distinctive features since at least the 1960s (Hubbs 1967). Red abalones are exclusively subtidal on the islands today so the reason for their archaeological presence has been exhaustively debated (e.g., Braje 2007; Braje and Erlandson 2016; Glassow 1993b, 2015, 2016; Glassow et al. 2012). For the most part, they seem to reflect cool sea surface temperatures which would have allowed abalones to migrate into the low intertidal zone. Red abalone middens mostly coincide with a period between 6300 and 5300 cal BP when sea surface temperatures were indeed colder (Glassow et al. 2012), but recent findings have pushed the dating of the middens middens back to 8200 cal BP (Glassow 2015), which muddles the correlation with sea temperatures.

Some authors have compared red abalone features on the central coast with those of the Channel Islands (e.g., Braje and Erlandson 2016; Joslin 2010), but the value of this comparison remains uncertain. Today, due to ravages of human commercial exploitation, withering syndrome, and sea otters in the last two centuries, red abalones are sparse if not wholly absent from most of the central coast where they were once abundant (Ricketts et al. 1985:102). Because central coast waters are colder than those off the Channel Islands, however, red abalones are found in the low intertidal zone and were collected historically from low-tide rocks and reefs (Ricketts et al. 1985:100). In northern California where sea otters have not re-established themselves following historic decimation, red abalone are today captured by "rock-picking"—standing on shoreline rocks and reaching below the water's surface to find them (Colligan et al. 2015:36). Archaeologically, they are not uncommon along the central coast, but typically they do not dominate deposits south of the Monterey Peninsula. In the absence of modern populations and little or no ethnographic information on how they

were exploited, abalone return rates have been estimated based on experimentation (Kennedy 2005) which suggests they are potentially more highly ranked than mussels, providing perhaps twice as many Kcals per hour (Table 2.1). Further attempts to evaluate their caloric value in the absence of ethnographic specifics include a proposal by Whitaker and Byrd (2012) that increased red abalone exploitation after ca. 950 cal BP on the Monterey Peninsula reflects the onset of diving from watercraft for the shellfish. However, the fact that seas off the Monterey Peninsula are dangerously cold year-round and that there are no historical witnesses to such behavior cast this proposal in serious doubt as do practical realities about the efficacy of diving from boats into relatively shallow water. But this idea does highlight questions about the costs and benefits of watercraft as a marine resource acquisition technology which are critical to interpretations of shoreline foraging, and for which we have no substantive ethnographic or experimental data. Whitaker and Byrd's argument notwithstanding, neither boats nor diving were needed to exploit red abalones in the intertidal patch in central California. Black abalones, however, typically occur higher in the tidal zone, and may have been more readily available. On the Channel Islands nineteenth-century Chinese abalone fishermen targeted only black abalone for this reason (Braje 2016). However, the actual ranking and return rates associated with these two species remain very uncertain due to the highly altered nearshore ecological situation within which they currently exist.

Turban Snails

These small gastropods were evaluated experimentally by Ferneau (1998) who found, not surprisingly, that they are labor-intensive—yielding a maximum of only 153 kcal/hour (Table 2.1). They are common throughout the intertidal zone. However, their densities vary according to the availability of food, predators, and habitat. Archaeological studies show that turban snails were abundant in the Cambria/San Simeon area, where they consistently represent higher proportions in midden residues than elsewhere (see Joslin 2010). Strudwick (1995) proposed that they were processed with pitted stones, and further experimental work is needed to evaluate this possibility (Cook et al. 2017) and also to determine if higher caloric yields might be obtained through this method of processing. Diachronic increases in this low-ranked, labor-intensive resource have consistently been attributed to economic intensification (Ferneau 1998; Jones, Porcasi, Gaeta, et al. 2008; Joslin 2010).

Shorebirds

Potential resources that are sometimes overlooked in discussions of coastal foraging (although see Whitaker 2010) are marine birds. On the Pecho Coast today, six species have been documented: California gull (*Larus californicus*), western gull (*Larus occidentalis*), pelagic cormorant (*Phalacrocorax pelagicus*), Brandt's cormorant (*Phalacrocorax penicillatus*), pigeon guillemot (*Cepphus columba*), and black oystercatcher (*Haematopus bachmani*). Both of the cormorants have nesting colonies on the Diablo property (Kelly Kephart, personal communication 2017). The pelagic cormorant is known as one of the least gregarious or social of the cormorants, and the remoteness of the Pecho Coast is consistent with its social preferences. It nests on steep cliffs along rocky and exposed shorelines, either in loose colonies or far from its nearest neighbors (All about Birds 2017). Brandt's cormorants prefer shores with kelp forests and nest on steep cliffs and offshore rocks. While both are marine species, they and their eggs would have been accessible to shoreline foragers without watercraft. This would presumably make them attractive resources vulnerable to overexploitation (Whitaker 2010) although nesting colonies on offshore rocks would be part of the offshore patch, accessed by boat. Both are year-round residents.

The Offshore Patch

The primary issue related to exploitation of offshore marine habitats is the use of watercraft and related maritime technologies such as nets and harpoons, all of which were used ethnographically to the south by the Channel Islands Chumash (see Hudson and Blackburn 1979, 1983, 1985, 1986, 1987). While watercraft are now known to have significant time depth in southern California based on human occupation of the offshore islands ca. 12,000 years ago (see discussions by Erlandson 2001; Erlandson et al. 2011), the subsistence energetics associated with boats and the exploitation of offshore resources remain topics of discussion and debate. Recognizing watercraft use based on midden residues is not straightforward. Furthermore, maritime technologies, especially nets (see Lindstrom 1996), require significant investments of time and labor to manufacture and maintain. While we have gross estimates for the potential return rates associated with the Pecho offshore resources (Table 2.1), rates associated with pursuit of schooling fish, marine birds, and mammals could potentially vary with or without using watercraft or the specialized labor-intensive technologies.

Perhaps the most cogent thinking on the pursuit of resources in offshore contexts was by Hildebrandt and Jones (1992) who proposed a simple economic intensification model for marine mammals, suggesting that over the course of the Holocene, California foragers invested more and more in boats and harpoons in order to pursue lower-ranked, aquatic-breeding harbor seals and sea otters in offshore contexts. According to this scenario, larger, terrestrially breeding marine mammals (California sea lions, fur seals, and northern elephant seals) were highly ranked when congregated in rookeries, and that overhunting of onshore breeding colonies depressed populations, eventually forcing foragers to develop specialized marine weaponry to pursue the more elusive otters and harbor seals offshore. Faunal and artifact evidence from northern California supported this model, but decades of research in central California have not (Gifford-Gonzalez et al. 2005). Indeed, faunal evidence from the central coast shows the opposite pattern—that sea otters were exploited earlier than terrestrial breeders (Jones

TABLE 2.3. Capture Technologies associated with Pecho Coast Fishes.

By hand	Hook and line (including gorge hooks) nearshore	Hook and line (w/watercraft) offshore	Spear	Nearshore net (mostly small schooling fishes)	Offshore net (w/watercraft) (mostly small schooling fishes)
Pricklebacks	Bat ray	Herrings	Bat ray	Plainfin midshipman	Herrings
Plainfin midshipman	Plainfin midshipman	Pacific hake	Triakid sharks	New World silversides	Northern anchovy
Cabezon	Kelp greenling	Rockfishes	Plainfin midshipman	True smelts	
Pile perch	Lingcod	Lingcod	Lingcod		
Monkeyface prickleback	Pacific staghorn sculpin		Pacific angel shark		
	Cabezon				
	Surfperches				
	Monkeyface prickleback				
	Pricklebacks				
	Flounders and soles				
	Rockfishes				

Source: Boon (2012), Fitch (1972), Gause (2002), Jones et al. (2016), Love (2011), Langenwalter and Huddleston (1991), Salls (1988).

et al. 2011). Nonetheless, the model correctly recognized the costs associated with exploiting offshore patches and the varied ranking of different marine mammals.

Fish have also been used as potential indices of watercraft use and intensified maritime economies. Indeed, Fitch (1972) in the initial assessment of archaeological fish remains on the central coast suggested that while the earliest inhabitants of the Diablo Canyon site mostly pursued shore-based fishing, they must also have had some ability to float offshore in crude rafts or floats in order to capture species that prefer such settings. For the current project we recognize that herrings and northern anchovies are species that almost certainly required watercraft to capture (Table 2.3). This would be especially true if we could be certain that representatives of the herring family found in local archaeological sites are sardines—which is a distinction that often cannot be made with accuracy (see discussion by Gobalet 2001). Furthermore, Plainfin midshipmen, New World silversides,

smelts, herrings, and northern anchovies are species that most likely were caught with nets. Variation in these species over time may signal economic intensification—with the caveat that biologists have documented diachronic fluctuations between sardines and anchovies that can be attributed to oscillations in sea temperature regimes (Chavez et al. 2003).

Deep Water
In the Santa Barbara Channel much has been made about ethnographic and archaeological evidence for pursuit of pelagic species, particularly swordfish, albacore, and other tuna. The exploitation of these species via the sewn-plank canoe (*tomolo*) is considered a hallmark of the much-heralded, intensive maritime adaptation in the Santa Barbara Channel (Arnold 2001, 2004; Davenport et al. 1993; Gamble 2008). Bernard (2001) documented an increase in remains of these species ca. AD 700–800 that she attributed to initial appearance of the *tomolo* although the remains from these pelagic species

TABLE 2.4. Postencounter Return Rates for Resource Sets within Terrestrial Patches.

Resource Type	Inclusive Taxa	Inclusive Species	Method of Capture	Postencounter Return Rates (kcal/hr)			Source
				Low	Midpoint	High	
Terrestrial Mammal	Deer	*Odocoileus hemionus*	Encounter Hunting	12,096	21,773	31,450	Simms 1987
Terrestrial Mammal	Jackrabbit	*Lepus californicus*	Encounter Hunting	13,475	14,438	15,400	Simms 1987
Terrestrial Mammal	Cottontail rabbit	*Sylvilagus* sp.	Encounter Hunting	8983	9392	9800	Simms 1987
Terrestrial Mammal	Black-tailed jackrabbit	*Lepus californicus*	Trapping	1,495	2076	2656	Ugan 2005
Root	Cattail, Bulrush, Bitterroot	mixed	Digging	128	1217	2305	Simms 1987
Nut	Acorn	*Quercus*	Collecting	793	1035	1276	Barlow and Heck 2002; Gremillion 2002; McCarthy 1993
Grass Seed	Misc.	mixed	Collecting	433	836	1238	Gremillion 2004

were found in extremely low frequencies (2–3 NISP [Number of Identifiable Specimens] per component). The presence or absence of such species in the Pecho middens could provide evidence for whether or not the northern Chumash or their local predecessors ventured very far offshore. Interestingly, a recent study from South America documents a dedicated fishery for pelagic billfish on the coast of Chile as early as 7400 cal BP (Béarez et al. 2016). This shows significantly greater use of pelagic species at a considerably deeper time depth than anything in California.

Terrestrial Patches

Terrestrial patches include (1) coastal sagebrush and (2) oak-dominated habitats. Both would contain mammals, roots, and seeds, with the latter also containing abundant tree nuts. In both patches, the available data on postencounter return rates (Table 2.4) suggest that foragers should have preferentially taken deer on encounter, passing over other resources until deer declined in abundance so that it became optimal to take rabbits, then roots, then nuts, and finally grass seeds. As has been noted elsewhere (e.g., Basgall 1987), these values suggest that intensive plant processing should only begin following de-

clines in terrestrial vertebrates. Indeed, if terrestrial vertebrates are more abundant in coastal sagebrush habitats, then prehistoric foragers may have preferred coastal settings over inland oak-dominated habitats, until encounter rates with vertebrate resources declined in coastal sagebrush habitats. There is some supporting evidence for this (e.g., see Codding and Jones 2016; Codding et al. 2012).

However, in reality, high-return items across both patches may have been rare enough (especially seasonally) to encourage foragers to take lower-utility items even from the earliest occupational periods. Furthermore, lower-utility items may be within the optimal diet of foragers with different constraints, such as lower walking speeds (i.e., children; Bird and Bird 2000) and risk-sensitivity (e.g., mothers; Codding et al. 2011; Jochim 1988). More than anything else, these return-rate data provide a context for evaluation of trends in faunal data through time and across space.

Ethnohistory

Any consideration of the past along the Pecho Coast must, of course, take into consideration historic observations of the region's indigenous inhabitants, commonly referred to as the northern Chumash. Direct observations of these people along the Pecho Coast proper are very few because this out-of-the-way stretch of shoreline was not traversed by the early Spanish explorers. In the absence of direct, early observations, we describe accounts and other sources from the broader province of what is today southern San Luis Obispo County. It is important to recognize at the outset, however, that primary sources are extremely limited and provide for only a very incomplete portrait. This contrasts with the Santa Barbara Channel, where Native populations were higher at the time of contact, a greater number of individuals survived the contact period, and more ethnohistoric documentation was completed. The recent publication by Gamble (2008) which provides detailed accounts of many aspects of Chumash culture is a direct reflection of the richer ethnographic and historical record available for that portion of the Chumashan language territory, as does the five-volume compilation on Chumash material culture by Hudson and Blackburn (1979, 1983, 1985, 1986, 1987).

Primary sources of information for the northern Chumash are limited to Spanish documents from the late eighteenth century including diaries of the 1769–1770 Portolá (Brown 2001) and 1775–1776 Font (Bolton 1930) expeditions (Table 2.5), mission records (Milliken and Johnson 2005), and responses to the 1814 Spanish Interrogatorio (Rivers 1994). Early anthropologists who consulted those sources and supplemented them with salvage ethnography include Henshaw in 1884 (Heizer 1955) and John P. Harrington. Henshaw, like many who came after him (e.g., Brown 1967), limited his list of Chumash place-names to those between Point Conception and Malibu, well south of the study area (Heizer 1975). John Peabody Harrington was an exception to this trend, and he conducted salvage ethnography with the last known speaker of northern Chumash, Rosario Cooper, early in the twentieth century (Klar 1991). Even Harrington, however, provides much more information for the Channel area than for San Luis Obispo County. His notes figure prominently in the first attempts to describe and plot

Chumash place-names by Applegate (1974, 1975), Greenwood (1972), King (1969, 1971, 1975), and Klar (1975, 1977a). Following these have been a number of important syntheses of northern Chumash ethnohistory by Farris (1994), Greenwood (1972, 1978b), Krieger (1990:14–21), Rivers (1994, 2000), and Milliken and Johnson (2005). Of these, most important is the work of Milliken and Johnson who summarized the previous research and developed a detailed characterization of northern Chumash ethnogeography based on records from the Spanish missions. Additionally, Rivers's (1994 and 2000) summaries of the primary evidence, especially her work with the Harrington notes, should not be overlooked.

In the absence of a more detailed record for northern Chumash, some scholars (e.g., Gibson 1991; Miller 1988) have tended to project cultural patterns identified in the Santa Barbara Channel area onto the northern mainland Chumash speakers under the implicit pretense that there was a single Chumash prehistoric cultural identity, although Miller (1988:10) does acknowledge that Chumash is a convenient but inaccurate sociopolitical label for all of the people who spoke Chumashan languages. The term *Chumash* was coined by John Wesley Powell (1891) who used it to refer to seven clearly related, but distinctive, languages spoken between Morro Bay and Malibu. Since then, it has been used as shorthand by some scholars (e.g., Grant 1978:505), incorrectly referring to Chumash as a large and important "tribe." The very earliest descriptions of the northernmost speakers of a Chumashan language, however, established that there were significant differences between the inhabitants of the Santa Barbara area and those of what is now San Luis Obispo County. In 1595 Sebastian Rodriguez Cermeño recorded the following description in what is commonly thought to be San Luis Obispo Bay just east of the southern Pecho Coast:

> [Monday, December 11, 1595] There were observed on the shore of the seas many people on top of some bluffs, where they had many settlements. As it was late, I anchored in front of these settlements and I saw how

TABLE 2.5. Summary of Spanish Encounters with Northern Chumash Indians in the San Luis Obispo area.

Date	Location	Population	Notes	Page(s)
Northward to San Francisco Bay, July 14 to November 11, 1769.				
9/2/1769	Oso Flaco Lake	6	Told of two villages near by, soldiers killed a bear, burnt vegetation.	467–471
9/4/1769	Price Canyon/ Harris (Cuevitas) Creek	40–50	1st Buchón encounter, burnt vegetation, "heathens" had no houses, how to cook mush. Compare with entry on May 11th, 1770 (p. 715)	471–479
9/5/1769	See Canyon (corrected latitude 35° 14' see p. 789)	0	Saw tracks and trails made by "the heathens."	479–481
9/7/1769	See Canyon to Los Osos	0	No "heathens" due to bear population, soldiers went bear hunting.	482–489
9/7/1769	Los Osos	8+	Spotted eight "heathen" men and some women looking for seeds.	487
9/8/1769	Morro Bay	"good sized village"	A single underground house (Brown references Clemmer)	489–490
Southward Return to San Diego, November 11, 1769, to January 24, 1770, and to February 11, 1770.				
12/23/1769	Little Pico Creek; Cambria; Cayucos: Old Creek	"a village"	Spanish camped close to a village previously noted on the march north.	641
12/24/1769	Little Pico Creek; Cambria; Cayucos: Old Creek	"some heathens"	Spanish were visited after they set up camp (near *El Osito*).	641
12/25/1769	Little Pico Creek; Cambria; Cayucos: Old Creek	"small sized village"	Visited by "heathens" from a "village belonging to *ensenada del Morro.*"	641
12/26/1769	Los Osos; San Luis Obispo: South Higuera Street	abandoned village	Found a village empty that previously had "a great deal of heathen folk."	643
12/27/1769	Los Osos; San Luis Obispo: South Higuera Street	"some heathens"	While attempting to get to the village of *El Buchón*, the Spanish are caught in a rain storm. While waiting it out, they see several "heathens" from the local area returning from the coast, they are given fish.	643
12/29/1769	Price Canyon/Harris (Cuevitas) Creek	"a large village"	2nd encounter with Buchon. *El Loco* alerted Buchon of their coming.	645
Return Northward to Monterey, 16 April to 3 June 1770, and to 9 November 1770.				
5/8/1770	Vandenberg AFB: MOD (Bass) Lake; Oso Flaco Lake	See Note	Encountered no "heathens" where they had expected to find a "good sized village" they encountered the previous journey north. Crespi notes that he later discovered this spot was abandoned due to fear of El Buchón.	713
5/9/1770	Vandenberg AFB: MOD (Bass) Lake; Oso Flaco Lake	12 houses + 17 people	Upon marching through the dunes, they pass 12 houses around a lake, later they are approached by 3 of Buchon's men who invite them to his village. Later 14 "heathens" bring the Spanish 17 fresh fish.	713–715

TABLE 2.5. (cont'd.) Summary of Spanish Encounters with Northern Chumash Indians in the San Luis Obispo area.

Date	Location	Population	Notes	Page(s)
5/10/1770	Price Canyon/Harris (Cuevitas) Creek	> 60	3rd Buchon encounter: the Spanish were greeted by Buchon and his village in the morning. They then went to the Village of Buchon (San Ladislao).	715–717
5/12/1770	San Luis Obispo: Laguna Lake (The Laguna); Moro Bay	24+children	Left Buchon's village, scouts saw 40–50 bears and killed three, the met up with a group of 12 women and children gathering seeds, the men heard that the Spanish were hunting bears and they "rejoiced" at the speed at which they could kill them with their guns, then they helped skin them.	717–719
5/13/1770	Morro Bay; Cambria	See Note	Saw 3–4 empty houses where there had previously been people, the Spanish presumed that they were out gathering seeds.	719–721

Source: Crespí, Juan in Brown, Alan K., 2001. A Description of Distant Roads: Original Journals of the First Expedition into California, 1769-1770. San Diego State University Press.

the Indians had on shore many balsas made of tule, which are like reeds, or as otherwise called, tule. The balsas were made like canoes, and with these they go fishing. Calling to some of them from the launch, we gave them to understand that we were Christians, and some of the Indians responded with shouts, giving us to understand that they understood, saying "Christians, Christians." And shortly he came down from the bluff, and taking a balsa, got into it and came on board the launch, where we made much of him and gave him some pieces of cotton and taffeta. Soon others came in the same kind of boats and we gave them to understand by signs that they should bring us something to eat, as we had no food. Understanding our necessity, they went ashore and brought some bitter acorns and mush [*atole*] made of these acorns in some dishes [*cestos* or hand baskets] made of straw like large chocolate bowls [*jicaras*]; and during some talk which we had with them they said, "Mexico, Mexico." They are people well set up, of medium height, of a brown color, and like the rest, go naked, not only the men, but women, although the women wear some skirts made of

grass and bird feathers. They use the bow and arrow, and their food consists of bitter acorns and fish. They seemed to be about three hundred in number, counting men, women, and children, some of them with long beards and with the hair cut round, and some were painted with stripes on the faces and arms. The land seemed to be good, as it was covered with trees and verdure. The people seemed to be somewhat covetous as on being given pieces of taffeta and cotton cloth, they asked for more. (Sebastian Rodriguez Cermeño as translated by Wagner 1924:15–16)

This account clearly establishes that people in the vicinity of what is now Avila Beach did not have the sewn-plank boat (*tomol* or *tomolo*), but instead used the tule balsa which was the primary form of watercraft elsewhere in central California (e.g., San Francisco Bay). The *tomol* was the technological centerpiece of the intensive maritime adaptation that was associated with large, dense, sedentary populations on the mainland and especially on the islands of the Santa Barbara Channel. Passage between the islands and the mainland was dangerous, and there would have been ample incentive to develop and employ sturdy watercraft. Some

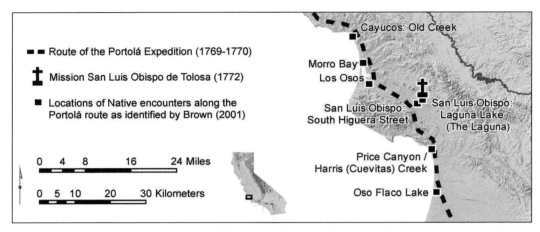

FIGURE 2.4. Approximate route of the Portolá 1769 expedition and locations of Native encounters as identified by Brown (2001).

have suggested that the specific design of the sewn-plank canoe is the result of transoceanic contact from Polynesia (Jones and Klar 2005, 2012; Klar and Jones 2005; Jones et al. 2011), but regardless of its ultimate origin, the *tomolo* facilitated island-mainland commerce in the Santa Barbara Channel. Absent islands, such a craft was probably unnecessary for the type of longshore transport and nearshore fishing that was pursued north of Point Conception. Likewise, in the San Simeon area in 1770, Juan Crespi of the Portolá expedition described a tule float (Brown 2001:723), not a wooden canoe. In contrast, in 1793 the Vancouver expedition noted a wooden canoe in use near what is today San Simeon. However, Wagner (1924:7) attributed that account to missionaries bringing canoes north during the early historic era (Farris 1994:12). Despite this, some scholars have mistakenly assumed that sewn-plank canoes were used at contact in the San Luis Obispo area.

The Cermeño account also hints at a less-maritime subsistence focus among the northern Chumashan-speakers, and it also establishes the presence of the bow and arrow. The number of people attributed to the Avila settlement (300) is large and in this regard appears similar to descriptions from the Channel. Still, many villages in the Santa Barbara area and on the islands were larger with up to 500 people (Gamble 2008).

Diaries from the Portolá Expedition

Following the brief encounters by sea, the Portolá overland expedition of 1769–1770 provides the earliest accounts of the Native inhabitants of San Luis Obispo County. However, the entourage, which was on its way from San Diego in search of Monterey Bay did not pass through the Pecho Coast as defined here, rather it took an inland route from Arroyo Grande Creek to the Laguna Lake Area (Figure 2.4). On August 30, 1769, the group crossed the Santa Maria River into what would become San Luis Obispo County. By September 4 they had made their way to what they proclaimed as Oso Flaco Lake, named after a skinny bear that was shot and eaten. On the morning of September 4 they departed Oso Flaco Lake, initially heading west until they reached the shore where they once again continued north. At one point, Crespi noted that they "came into a range that was not very high nor steep either, having very good soil and good dry grass, burnt off in spots by the heathen" (Brown 2001:473). They traveled four hours and an estimated distance of three leagues (nine miles) where they eventually

> found a good-sized village of very good, well-behaved heathens, who must have amounted to some forty or more souls, encamped under the lush sycamores. All very well pleased and

happy, they greeted us with a row of rush mats laid out on the ground, and as we came up, eight or ten women who had been seated stood up, each one holding a big basket full of their seeds, and one behind another went along pouring them out upon the mats. They went on casting seeds down until a sign was made to them; no telling what the meaning of this ceremony may have been. Our Governor made the chiefs and their wives a present of beads, and they remained with their mats and seeds while we went a bit of a way off to make camp at the tableland I spoke of. And, as we learned, the head chief had not been there, but as I shall tell, he came up later, and he is a great man, a kind of petty king of all this country and much renowned and feared in all the surrounding parts.... A grand spot for a good-sized mission, which I called after Saint Ladislaus at The Goitre's, El Buchón's village. Going about a quarter-league beyond the aforesaid running stream and The Goitre's Village through the north-northeastern hollow here, one comes upon a middling-sized, very swelling knoll some two hundred yards long that consists entirely of tar springs issuing molten out of the ground.

In the afternoon, the head chief, who at our arrival had not been at the village, came over with them all, bringing us large servings of a great many big bowls full of good gruels, a great many others full of very good mush, fresh deer meat, a few fresh fish, and a bowl of a sort of white pies that they said were very good and looked as though made from rice. The head heathen chief or petty king of this country is a tall heathen man of very majestic and grand appearance, with very good features and easily distinguished by a very large tumor that hangs from one side of his neck, large as a swollen ox gall, because of which everyone called him The Goitre, *El Buchón*, and by this name he has become known to everyone. Like the other heathens, this man The Goitre wears a very fine cape that they make from otter skin, covering him from neck to ankles. He always goes around

closely accompanied by many heavily armed heathens, and, as we understood it, because many villages give him tribute, whatever seeds they harvest or gather from the fields, [or] whether they slaughter any meat or catch fish, they take it all—or so we understood—to his village, where he receives it and then they take back whatever he tells them to. In their own fashion, he employs considerable pomp, and they bring a hide and lay it on the ground for him to sit down on. He has two brothers and two or three sons who are almost always with him, and no one sits down in front of him or his family unless ordered to. Great is the fear and awe in which he is held in all the surrounding parts. This Goitre's fame reaches as far as the Channel and the Santa Lucia Mountains; they designate him by making signs for his tumor. It is all a very fine, well-behaved heathen folk here, and this man Goitre bore himself toward us with such consideration and such friendliness as though he had always dealt with us, and I know not how to tell his goodness toward us. Were this heathen to become a Christian, much would be gained on God's account. Our officers made him and all his family many presents.

Among the many items that this man The Goitre brought and presented us with, were a great many bowls of very good mush, just like very good, thick very well flavored blancmange. How can they cook such mush, when these heathens possess neither crockery nor copper pots? Yet cook it they do, and in a very surprising and unusual way that was not devised by any dunce. This is how they cook their mush: they have the dough all made ready from which they mean to make the mush, dissolved in water inside large rushwork-wickerweave baskets made of very close-woven rushes, which they have set out for the purpose. At the same time they have a good amount of clean hard stones set out, made glowing hot; some of these red-hot stones they cast into the baskets of the dissolved dough, which begins immediately to boil, and thus they keep feeding hot stones

into it until the mush is cooked to the point that they wish, without any danger of destroying any of the aforesaid kinds of vessels.
(Juan Crespi translated by Brown 2001:473–479)

On September 5, the expedition left Buchón's village and proceeded in a northwesterly direction. Noting no more villages, they arrived in what is now referred to as the Los Osos Valley on September 7, 1769. Their next encounter with Indians was in the vicinity of Morro Rock on September 8, 1769, where Crespi noted "a good-sized village of very poor heathens who possess no more than a single underground house" (Brown 2001:489). One of the other diarists in the group, Miguel Costansó, noted that this settlement contained about 60 souls and no structures (Milliken and Johnson 2005:8).

The accounts from September 4–8, 1769, are remarkable in that they establish a variety of facts: (1) the use of controlled fire among the northern Chumash; (2) the existence of at least a single fairly small village (population 40) somewhere between Arroyo Grande Creek and the Irish Hills and an equally small community (population 60) at Morro Bay; (3) the existence of a very strong chief, El Buchón (referred to as the head chief or petty king) who seemed to have authority over multiple communities (Fages mentions other chiefs whom he distinguished from the "head chief") in a classic chiefdom form of political organization; and (4) a description of stone boiling that also makes note of the absence of pottery.

The Portolá expedition retraced its steps southward to San Diego after they discovered San Francisco Bay. On December 26, 1769, they reached Morro Bay where no note was made of the settlement that had been seen on the way north. On December 29 they set out from the Los Osos Valley and arrived later in the day once again at Buchón's village:

We continued on our way and ongoing three leagues came to the two streams of running water of the hollow of San Ladislao, or of The

Goitre, the man so renowned and feared in all this vicinity, whom we conceived to be a sort of petty king of these good and far flung heathen folk. In the afternoon after we had been resting at this spot, we saw the whole large village belonging to this great man The Goitre coming over, and himself as leader, and with them our good heathen man from the Channel who, it was obvious, had gone to notify this Goitre, and all of them came laden with vast numbers of bowls of very good gruel and mush, some very good white-colored pies, some fish, and some fresh deer meat. It was all received from them, and of everything there was enough and more than enough to relieve all of our men from their want, coming as it did in very good time. The officers gave generous presents to this man The Goitre, as he is indeed a well-deserving person, seeing the friendship he has treated us with, both in our coming and our returning; may gracious God grant him enlightenment and whatever he needs in order to go to heaven. A three leagues' march this day, from the end of the Bear Level belonging to this San Ladislao village…at which spot we had found a good-sized heathen village upon the way coming, and now also found it here. Since it was on our way, we came to the village, where the heathens as soon as they espied us close by came out of their houses all unarmed as if to greet us. On our reaching them they commenced to give us handfuls of feathers and brought out some small baskets of gruel; plainly they were very short on food. The officers gave them beads; we stopped a while, and then went on.
(Juan Crespi translated by Brown 2001:645–647)

In sum, the Cermeño account and the Portolá diarists provide nothing specific to the Pecho Coast as defined here although the former provides an important description of a very large Chumash settlement possibly in the vicinity of Avila Beach. All other settlements were smaller (40–60 inhabitants). One village was attributed to the powerful leader known as *El Buchón* or

The Goitre that seems to have been somewhere in the vicinity of Pismo Beach, Price Canyon, or Edna Valley. Another small community of 25–30 was encountered northeast of Buchón's village. A settlement of perhaps 60 people was noted at Morro Bay. Importantly, the latter seems to have been unoccupied when the Spanish came back through the area three months later. This suggests that the northern Chumash did not occupy the same villages year-round but moved their settlements at least once per year if not on some kind of seasonal schedule. While not directly referring to the Pecho Coast, the wide-ranging influence of Buchón from Pismo to Morro Bay suggests that he may have had jurisdiction over the Pecho region as well.

The Establishment of Mission San Luis Obispo and the Mission Records

Mission San Luis Obispo was established in 1772. Information available from the mission includes three types: (1) a history of the mission by Engelhardt (1963) which includes anecdotal accounts of activities of local Native people—mostly within and around the mission compound (also Geiger and Meighan 1976); (2) records of births, marriages, and deaths kept by the missionaries, which include names of individual Native people, their village of origin, and some descriptive information on the village's location (these have been analyzed and summarized by Milliken and Johnson [2005]); and (3) responses to a questionnaire sent from Spain to the mission (see below).

The Pedro Fages Report

Pedro Fages, a lieutenant on the Portolá expedition, drafted the first synthetic account of California Native societies as a report in 1775 to the Spanish viceroy. His account was compiled after four years of travel and observation in southern and central California. It includes descriptions specific to the area surrounding Mission San Luis Obispo as well as generalized accounts about aboriginal life in central California:

At the mission of San Luis Obispo and for a radius of about twelve leagues [approxi-mately 40 miles] around it, I have observed the following: The natives are well appearing, of good disposition, affable, and friendly toward the Spaniard. As to their government, it is by captaincies over villages, as in others; the captains here also have wives, with the rights of putting them away and taking maidens only; here also the other Indian men do not have the privilege, for they have only one wife, and do not marry a second time, until they are widowed. They have cemeteries set apart for the burial of their dead. The god whom they adore, and to whom they offer their seeds, fruits, and all that they possess, is the sun....

Their houses, shaped like half globes, are neatly built; each one is capable of sheltering four or five families which, being kin, are accustomed to live together. The houses have one door on the east, and one on the west, with a skylight in the roof, halfway between. Their beds are built up high on bedsteads, which are here called tapextles, of heavy sticks; a reed mat serves as a mattress, and four others as curtains, forming a bedroom.... The men do not often sleep in their houses at night; but, carrying with them their arms, bow and quiver, they are accustomed to congregate in numbers in great subterranean caves.... [T]hey are a warlike people, always roaming from village to village at odds with everyone....

The women wear toupes [bangs] made by burning, and their coiffure is of shells, as I said in a previous chapter. On their cloaks or skirts, stained a handsome red, they put as trimming or decoration various fabrications made from tips of shells and small snail shell, leaving numerous pendants hanging from the margins, after the style of the trinkets of our children. For an ornament and as a protection from the sun, they cover their heads with little woven trays or baskets, decorated with handsome patterns and shapes like the crown of a hat. Both the men and women like to go painted with various colors, the former especially when they go on a campaign, and the latter when they are having a festal occasion, to give a dance.

It is not to be denied that this land exceeds all the preceding territory in fertility and abundance of things necessary for sustenance. All the seeds and the fruits which these natives use, and which have been previously mentioned, grow here and in the vicinity of native profusion. There is a great deal of century plant of the species which the Mexicans call mescali. The mode of using it is as follows: they make a hole in the ground, fill it in compactly with large firewood which they set on fire and then throw on top a number of stones until the entire fire is covered but smothered. When the stones are red hot, they place among them the bud of the plant; this they protect with grass or moistened hay, throwing on top a large quantity of earth, leaving it so for the space of twenty-four hours. The next day they take out their century plant roasted, or tlatemado as they say. It is juicy, sweet, and of a certain vinous flavor; indeed a very good wine can be made of it.

They use the root of a kind of reed of which they have a great abundance [tule; cf. King 1990a:9]; cleansing the earth from it, and crushing it in their mortars, they then spread it in the sun to dry; when it is dry they again moisten it, removing all the fibrous part until only the flour is left. From this they make a gruel and a very sweet, nourishing flour. At the beginning of the rainy season, which, as Spain, occurs in the months of November and December, they gather a quantity of cresses, celery, and amaranth. They also eat a kind of sweet flower similar to the wild rose although smaller, which of the bears are also very fond it grows in swampy humid places in canyons. The cubs of this kind of bear, which the Indians hunt, stealing them from their mothers, are raised and fattened for eating when they are ready, as is done with pigs [see the Portolá expedition above]....

Among the sea fish there are many sea bream, crabs, whitefish, curbina [white seabass], sardines of three kinds, cochinillo [possibly croaker], and tunny; in the streams and rivers there are trout, spinebacks, machuros (an Indian name), and turtles. The fishing canoes [tule balsas]. The tridents they use are of bone; the barb is well shaped and well adapted to its use. The fishhooks are made of pieces of shell fashioned with great skill and art. For catching sardines, they use large baskets, into which they throw the bait which these fish like, which is the ground-up leaves of cactus, so that they come in great numbers; Indians then make their cast and catch great numbers of the sardines. (Fages 1972 [1775]:47–52)

These descriptions again allude to ongoing intergroup conflict, but also add a description of circular houses, the use of tule, and an earthen oven for cooking buds of the century plant. The important description of fishing mentions shell hooks, tridents, and the use of bait and baskets to catch sardines.

The Mission Responses of Fray Luis Antonio Martinez

In 1814, the Spanish Department of Overseas Colonies issued a questionnaire (*interrogatorio*) to the California missions. Fray Luis Martinez provided the response for Mission San Luis Obispo (Geiger and Meighan 1976). The document contained thirty-six questions on native populations, but Father Martinez did not answer them all. Those answers that provide some insights into pre-Mission culture are as follows:

Question 3) The languages spoken at this mission are fifteen different kinds according to the region in which the villages are located whence the converts originated, for every village possessed a distinct idiom. However, when gathered together at this new mission, the natives use only one language although their parents preserve their native idioms in which they have been raised. However, all understand one another in their respective languages (Geiger and Meighan 1976:19–20).

Question 10) Some of the new Christians who are but beginning to hear the name of

God are still found possessed of superstitions especially those who became Christians at an advanced age.... They perform their adorations on a small land which is neat and clean out in the country. There come together all the medicine men offering seeds, plumes, and beads for this service the Indians pay them in accordance with the need they have of rain or seeds (Geiger and Meighan 1976:49).

Question 16)...their pagan religion needs no calendar. They have only knowledge of the various seasons of the year for when it rains they say the water falls (this they call winter). When there are flowers they say that they have seeds, (which time they call spring). When there is much heat they say that winter is about to come.... (Geiger and Meighan 1976:82).

Question 18) The Indians here do not have any kind of fermented drink. They use only a mixture of tobacco and lime. With this they become intoxicated and sometimes they die from it if they drink to excess (Geiger and Meighan 1976:89).

Question 19) I have not observed that they adore the sun and the moon. What I did learn is that the pagans have a sort of oratory but I have not been able to verify the report nor to whom they direct their supplications (Geiger and Meighan 1976:92).

Question 21) In every village or Rancheria the Indians have cemeteries marked with tablets or stones. They also have their songs and ceremonies for the burial of their dead. They distribute beads to all who come to assist in bearing the dead to the grave and there is one who carries the corpse on his shoulders who in virtue of his office has the obligation to open the grave (Geiger and Meighan 1976:98).

Question 25) The Indians readily lend not money but their wild seeds which are to be returned in the same kind. For this it is not necessary to be a relative or an acquaintance. To everyone who enters the cabin of an Indian food is offered without obligation. Such is the mutual understanding which I have

observed practiced among them (Geiger and Meighan 1976:107).

Question 26) Notwithstanding that the Indians in their pagan state hold land by families they have no need for agreements to plant for they live on the products bestowed by nature; yet it is a weighty matter that produces not a few wars if anyone has the effrontery to go gather fruits without previously paying and notifying the legitimate owner.... (Geiger and Meighan 1976:110).

Question 30) Among the Indians are all kinds of classes, poor and rich. Among the rich however, there is one in each village whom all recognize and whose voice is respected by all who live with him. To him, I do not know by what standards, all pay tribute of fruits, goods and breads. These headmen summon to the pagan feasts all that assemble who happen to be his friends. If perchance anyone of them should refuse the invitation, he distributes arms and after notifying the people, he sets out to avenge the injury done to him by the refusal of invitation. He takes the life of not only the chief but of as many as are together with him. For all these services they have no other recompense than the privilege of admiring as a public person him who had the good fortune of killing someone else (Geiger and Meighan 1976:122).

Question 33)...they have among themselves a variety of songs and I have seen among them some wind instruments made of sticks of elder trees (Geiger and Meighan 1976:134).

These answers illuminate (1) the multilinguistic nature of the missions and the Native communities from which they were derived; (2) the presence of formal cemeteries at villages and the conduct of burial ceremonies that included distribution of beads; (3) that the rights to use individual resources were owned and that unauthorized exploitation could precipitate violent retribution; (4) that rich and poor classes existed; and (5) that there was one wealthy headman per village to whom tributes were paid and who had the authority to initiate wars.

Early Channel-Focused Salvage Ethnography and Linguistics

Following the end of the Spanish and Mexican eras, the Chumash-speaking territory was the focus of a number of early attempts at salvage ethnography focused primarily on the Santa Barbara Channel. These included the work of Pinart (Heizer 1952), Henshaw (Heizer 1955), Powell (1891), Leon de Cessac (a French anthropologist/archaeologist), Schumacher (1875), and Taylor (1860–1863). Powell's work was important largely for assigning the term *Chumash* to the related languages spoken between Malibu and Morro Bay. Schumacher's report includes a map that depicts supposed village sites, but its usefulness and accuracy have been questioned by modern scholars (e.g., Greenwood 1978a:521).

Much more significant and enduring was salvage work by C. Hart Merriam and John Peabody Harrington early in the twentieth century. Both were primarily interested in linguistics and neither formally published all of their research in their lifetimes, but instead their works were partially summarized by others later. Merriam was among the first to transcribe and publish lists of village names from Mission San Luis Obispo records (Merriam 1955); however, the lists give virtually no information on where the villages were situated. One publication identifies the San Luis Obispo area as *Tso-yin–ne ah-koo* (Merriam et al. 1974:12).

Before Merriam's posthumous reports, Kroeber (1925) published the first major anthropological summary of Chumash culture which continued the tradition of heavy focus on the Santa Barbara Channel. Kroeber (1925:552) guessed that the boundary between the northern Chumash and Salinan was in the area of present-day Cayucos, but his maps depict no villages north of Point Sal. He stated that the Chumash name for San Luis Obispo was *Tishlini* and that *Pismo* and *Huasna* were Chumash place-names that have carried forward to the present.

Following Kroeber, Landberg (1965) compiled a volume on Chumash culture that for the first time attempted to summarize some of the ecological aspects of their adaptation. As with so many of the works before him, this too was focused almost exclusively on the Santa Barbara Channel. Brown (1967) completed a very detailed analysis of mission records to define the location of 29 villages in the Santa Barbara Channel and reassess the total contact-era population of all Chumash-speaking peoples at no more than 15,000.

King (1971) subsequently completed an equally detailed analysis of Chumash place-name locations, based initially on Mission records, including those of Mission San Luis Obispo. This source for the first time depicts settlements on the Pecho Coast: a village of 60–100 people near Avila and a village of 15–40 people on the outer Pecho Coast.

Harrington's Work with Rosario Cooper

Harrington worked with Rosario Cooper between 1914 and 1916. He was primarily interested in recording all he could of the northern Chumash language (Klar 1991), but he also took down some information on material culture and spiritual beliefs. Although he did quantify certain cultural elements in a 1942 publication, Harrington did not publish most of his northern Chumash ethnography himself, but instead parts of his notes were later summarized by others including Applegate (1974), Greenwood (1972:83–84), King (1975), Klar (1977a, 1977b; 1991), and Rivers (1994, 2000). The Harrington notes provided the first substantive information on the Chumash ethnogeography of central San Luis Obispo County.

Applegate (1974) combined the Harrington notes with Henshaw's earlier word lists and Brown's (1967) findings from the Channel to identify Chumash place-names, mostly south of San Luis Obispo. Lacking a map, this place-name list reflects some of the difficulties involved in working with the Harrington notes. Importantly, this is the first place that an ethnic identifier for people in the vicinity of San Luis Obispo is revealed: these people referred to themselves as *titʸu titʸu*. This term was recognized by Kathryn Klar in the Harrington notes on the Obispeño language, who conveyed it to Applegate (1974:191). Applegate identified the name of the village near Mission San Luis Obispo as *Tilhini* which is similar to Kroeber's *Tishlini*. There was also vague reference to *Lisamu*, "a place by the coast by San Luis Obispo... that is a sacred place." Nothing in this publication, however, identifies any settlement on the Pecho Coast.

King (1975) followed Applegate with a revised map of historic Chumash villages based on the Harrington notes that built upon an earlier publication (King 1971). Collaborating with linguists who were also working with the notes, King defined the southern boundary for the area in which the Obispeño language was spoken (in the vicinity of Grover Beach) and mapped four village locations:

sepaxto
pismu
seleqini
temesati

Sepaxto was the northernmost of these and was depicted in the vicinity of Avila Beach; no villages were recognized for the outer Pecho Coast.

As part of her report on the Diablo Canyon sites, Greenwood (1972) also worked with the Harrington notes, specifically the testament provided by Rosario Cooper. Rosario Cooper mentioned three place names on the Pecho coast:

Tstyiwi = Rancho del Pecho
Tsvhanu = Arroyo between Avila and the
   J. M. Soto Ranch
Tshitqala = Rancho San Miguelito

There is no clear indication that these were necessarily the locations of villages, however.

In her 1978 summary of Obispeño, Greenwood did not depict any village sites at Avila Beach, the outer Pecho Coast, or Morro Bay, but she did place the northern Chumash boundary ca. 2 km north of the mouth of Morro Bay and placed the southern limit of the Obispeño language territory ca. 2 km south of modern-day Pismo Beach. She also pointed out that CA-SLO-2 was not a historic village site.

Recent Mission Record Studies

For the most part, the ethnographic publications of the 1970s demonstrated the potential value of mission record studies and Harrington notes, but were unable to complete enough systematic analyses to produce substantive results. This shortcoming was rectified in the ensuing decades by the systematic studies of Gibson (1983), McLendon and Johnson (1999), and Milliken and Johnson (2005).

Gibson (1983) placed two northern Chumash villages on the Pecho Coast: *Chano*, on the northern Pecho Coast, and *Tsquieu*, to the south near Pecho Creek. Gibson also identified a village of *Chotcagua* on the southern shore of Morro Bay, *Sepjayo* in the vicinity of Avila Beach, and *Pismu* near Price Canyon. The latter two names were recognized in previous studies and placed in the same general vicinities. Gibson's research was somewhat marred by his attempt to use the mission record findings to push the northern boundary of Obispeño language territory much farther north than most readings of the historical records suggest.

In 1999 McLendon and Johnson completed an even more exhaustive reanalysis of Chumash village locations based on a combined database from six missions. They identified two village sites on the outer Pecho Coast: *Chanu* (Gibson's *Chano*) on the northern coast and *Tsikiw* (Gibson's and Greenwood's *Tstyiwi*) near Pecho Creek. They also assigned the name *Tsipxatu* to a village near Avila Beach (King's *Sepaxto*). For the first time they also depict a village, *Petpatsu*, within the Montaña de Oro stretch of the Pecho Coast. They renamed Gibson's *Chotcaqua* to *Chitqawi* and relocated it to the northern edge of Morro Bay rather than the southern edge.

In 2005 Milliken and Johnson completed the most comprehensive report on northern Chumash and Salinan ethnogeography to date, incorporating all previous studies with a continued emphasis on mission records. They also employed social modeling methods to try to refine village locations. The results of this study are as important for their substantive findings as they are in illuminating the uncertainties that seem to

TABLE 2.6. Individuals Associated with the Village of Tstyiwi in Mission San Luis Obispo Records.

| Native Name | Spanish Name | | | Year of | | | Age at | |
	Given	Surname	Sex	Birth	Baptism	Death	Baptism	Death
—	Clara Maria	—	F	1764	1773	1822	9	58
—	Margarita	—	F	1767	1773	1793	6	26
—	Juana Maria	—	F	1766	1773	1792	7	26
Tecum/Stejumu-N	Pablo	Noriega	M	1733	1773	1801	40	68
—	Petra Maria	—	F	1761	1773	1774	12	13
Sonia	Julian	Fages	M	1762	1778	1833	16	71
Tsenasteme	Telmo	Sales	M	1745	1778	1798	33	53
Chihuou	Bernabe	Canizares	M	1755	1775	1787	20	32
Supo	Cristoval	Lasuen	M	1747	1777	1825	30	78
Sulmalanit	Yldefonso	Botiller	M	1757	1777	1820	20	63
Sahuanami, Chuculo, Lgcina	Ladislao	Palacios	M	1766	1778	1806	12	40
—	Silvestre	Anguera	M	1769	1778	1790	9	21
Chichi	Abdon	—	M	1779	1786	1821	7	42
Luiti	Micaela	—	F	1773	1779	1806	6	33
—	Pasquala	—	F	1775	1779	1806	4	31
—	Luis	Palomares	M	1779	1780	1833	1	54
—	Ysabela	—	F	1779	1780	1802	1	23
—	Maximiana	—	F	1772	1780	1791	8	19
Scuicu	Elias	Sombrano	M	1764	1780	1818	16	54
Teese	Samuel	—	M	1766	1780	1801	14	35
—	Flavia	—	F	1754	1780	1782	26	28
—	Germana	—	F	1771	1780	1804	9	33
—	Lucrecia	—	F	1775	1780	1794	5	19
—	Eulalia	—	F	1764	1780	1805	16	41
—	Flora	—	F	1775	1781	1802	6	27
—	Priscila	—	F	1756	1781	1785	25	29
—	Marcos	—	M	1752	1782	1782	30	30
Lhuamasuit	Cayetano	Flores	M	1773	1782	1806	9	33
Tsucay	Lucas	—	M	1781	1783	1809	2	28
—	Policarpa	—	F	1756	1788	1794	32	38
—	Maria Isabela	—	F	1731	1791	1803	60	72
—	Egidia	—	F	1731	1791	1800	60	69
—	Cecilia	—	F	1752	1792	1792	40	40
—	Alodia	—	F	1692	1792	1792	100	100
Extajuagua	Francisco	—	M	1772	1794	1796	22	24
—	Juana	—	F	1758	1800	1808	42	50
—	Narcisa Maria	—	F	1770	1800	1807	30	37
—	Maria Brigida	—	F	1720	1800	1800	80	80
Ljeye	Jose Maria	—	M	1760	1800	1813	40	53
—	Petra	—	F	1800	1801	1801	1	1
Estjase	Martin	—	M	1769	1801	1801	32	32
Asumumahuiti (Lasunumauit)	Pablo	—	M	1767	1802	1825	35	58

TABLE 2.6. (cont'd.) Individuals Associated with the Village of Tstyiwi in Mission San Luis Obispo Records.

Native Name	Given	Surname	Sex	Birth	Baptism	Death	Baptism	Death
	Spanish Name			**Year of**			**Age at**	
Palashuiguiti	Primo	Baquero	M	1776	1802	1806	26	30
Sumuya	Feliciano	—	M	1782	1802	1805	20	23
Mamuija	Feliciana Maria	—	F	1799	1802	1803	3	4
—	Satura	—	F	1772	1802	1826	30	54
Lgualagema	Fermina	—	F	1757	1803	1818	46	61
—	Maria Francisca	—	F	1753	1803	1803	50	50
—	Sergia	—	F	1733	1803	1813	70	80
Elquiluluiat	Samuel	—	M	1763	1803	1825	40	62
Sigui	Justo	—	M	1774	1803	1820	29	46
Chololotpono	Susana	—	F	1781	1803	1815	22	34
Chololotpono	Petra	—	F	1784	1803	1829	19	45
Ltalio	Urbana	—	F	1771	1803	1834	32	63
Ssepese	Samuel	—	M	1746	1803	1809	57	63
Ssohoy	Salvadora	—	F	1740	1803	1810	63	70
Silhuatumit	Patricio	—	M	1766	1803	1831	37	65

be inherent in identifying village locations from mission records. Primary data from this project (utilized below to examine population structure) are available from Far Western Anthropological Research Group. On the final maps for this project, Milliken and Johnson recognize only two village names on the outer Pecho Coast: *Tsquieu* midway between Point Buchon and Point San Luis, and *Petpatsu* in Montaña de Oro State Park. The village of *Chano*, depicted on the northern Pecho Coast by Gibson (1983), was moved inland indicating that the actual location of this village is unclear. The village of *Chotcagua* is again associated with Morro Bay, *Setjala* is shown at Avila Beach, and *Pismu* is in Price Canyon.

The net result of all of these studies is that only one village mentioned in the San Luis Obispo mission records can be confidently assigned to the outer Pecho Coast: *Tsquieu* or *Tstyiwi*. Denardo and Texier (2007) associated the place-name of *Tstyiwi* with archaeological site CA-SLO-51/H which was investigated by Greenwood (1972) (see below). This was indeed one of the only Diablo sites to produce a glass bead (a marker of the mission period), and it also had a higher number of small triangular projectile points. Greenwood herself did not make this association, but felt that the site con-

tained Millingstone, Hunting, and Chumash cultural components. Unfortunately, she was unable to obtain any radiocarbon determinations from CA-SLO-51/H. The void between the ethnography and archaeology in the northern Chumash region represents a major challenge for ongoing research.

Population Structure

Milliken and Johnson (2005) report that 38 adults and 19 children living at *Tstyiwi* were baptized from 1781 to 1803; of them, 32 were female and 25 were male (Table 2.6). If the probability of baptism was not biased by sex, this indicates a female-biased population was living at *Tstyiwi* during the mission period. Mission records estimate that these individuals were born from 1692 to 1800. The average age at death was 44 years old, with men living slightly longer on average (46 years old) than women (42 years old). Of these individuals, 35 were alive in 1769 when the Portolá expedition first traveled through the region. This group consisted of 18 women and 17 men ranging in age from only months old to 77 years old. While there were certainly more individuals present at this location, these data provide a view into the structure of the population (Table 2.7, Figure 2.5).

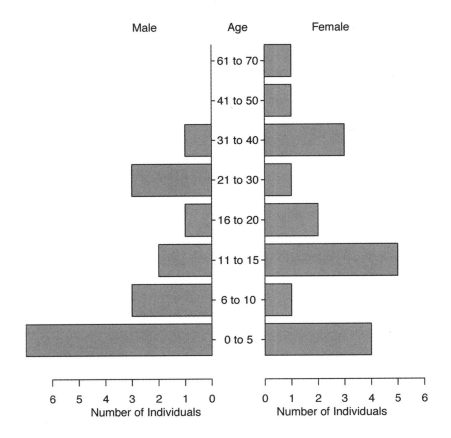

FIGURE 2.5. *Tstyiwi* 1769 age pyramid.

TABLE 2.7. Population structure at *Tstyiwi* in 1769 of individuals who were later baptized.

	0 to 5	6 to 10	11 to 15	16 to 20	21 to 30	31 to 40	41 to 50	61 to 70
F	4	1	5	2	1	3	1	1
M	7	3	2	1	3	1	0	0

Contact Population Size Estimates

Milliken and Johnson (2005) estimate that the pre-Mission population would have been about 80 individuals inhabiting an area of about 105 square kilometers. At 1.31 persons per square kilometer, this makes the Pecho Coast the highest density coastal occupation area between Monterey and Point Conception. This is on par with what Codding and Jones (2013) calculate for the average across the entire Chumash region (1.43 persons per square kilometer). This is also on par with the modeled fit between NPP and population density (Codding and Jones 2013: Figure 3), which suggests a population density between about 1.3 and 1.6 persons per square kilometer for a location with this level of environmental productivity (1.21 grams of carbon sequestered per square meter per day).

CHAPTER 3

Previous Archaeology

Archaeological inquiry began on the Pecho Coast as early as the 1870s when Paul Schumacher (1875) of the Smithsonian Institution conducted preliminary surface investigations. Beginning a trend that would continue for much of the next century, Schumacher preferred to focus on the archaeologically rich Avila Beach area, noting only that the outer coast to the north also harbored many prehistoric middens (Holson 1986). The first systematic subsurface investigation was conducted on the outer coast in 1929 when a team from the Los Angeles County Museum (LACM), who were primarily interested in CA-SLO-56 at Avila Beach (King 1970), excavated a trench at CA-SLO-50. As noted below, the findings from this investigation were never formally reported. Many years later Tom King (1970) published a report on the LACM excavation at CA-SLO-56, noting briefly the work done at CA-SLO-50.

Serious professional research was initiated in the late 1940s when Arnold Pilling, a San Luis Obispo resident who was attending college at U. C. Berkeley, began a systematic survey along the coast (Pilling 1951). Starting in what is now Montaña de Oro State Park (then a private ranch), Pilling completed site records and maps and assigned trinomials. He recorded the enormous midden at Spooner's Cove as CA-SLO-1, and the equally large deposit near the present-day nuclear power plant as CA-SLO-2. The low trinomials of most of the sites discussed below

are the result of their discovery during the very earliest survey by Pilling who published the results of his surface observations in 1951.

In 1966 Hoover undertook a pedestrian survey of a portion of the Pecho Coast, publishing his findings several years later (Hoover 1975). In the meantime Riddell (1966) completed a survey in anticipation of construction of the Diablo Canyon Nuclear Power Plant that would ultimately lead to Greenwood's extensive excavations at six sites including CA-SLO-2. The importance of Greenwood's work cannot be overstated and will be discussed in more detail below site by site.

More recently, extensive overviews, surveys, and resurveys have been completed for PG&E by, among others, Carpenter and colleagues (2010), Davis-King (1991), Davis-King and Williams (1992), Denardo and Texier (2007), Price (2008), Price and colleagues (2006), and Price and Trumbly (2009) that collectively represent a thorough inventory of cultural properties on the coastal lands held by PG&E, although the rugged interior has not yet been systematically surveyed. The work by Price and colleagues (2006) and Price (2008) included recovery of radiocarbon dates from exposed coastal profiles at CA-SLO-1366/H, -1370/H, and -1451/H.

Here we summarize findings from the previous excavations on the Pecho Coast with particular emphasis on the work completed by Greenwood (1972), which still stands as the

Table 3.1. Previous Subsurface Investigations on the Pecho Coast.

Site	Property	Excavation Volume (m³)	Radiocarbon Dates	Overall Span of Occupation	Temporal Components	Reference
CA-SLO-2	Diablo PG&E	109.0	34	10,250–200 cal BP	Millingstone, Middle, Late	Greenwood (1972, 2004), Fitch (1972), Jones et al. (2008a, 2008b), Jones and Codding (2010, 2011), Farquhar (2003), Codding et al. (2010)
CA-SLO-7	Diablo PG&E	5.6	10	3200–300 cal BP	Middle, Late	Breschini and Haversat (1988)
CA-SLO-8	Diablo PG&E	1.3	2	700–320 cal BP	Late	Breschini and Haversat (1988)
CA-SLO-10	Montaña de Oro SP	3.8	6	7200–1000 cal BP	Millingstone, Middle	Dallas (1994)
		0.7	0			Breschini and Haversat (1985)
CA-SLO-50	Diablo PG&E	Trench	0			King (1970)
CA-SLO-51/H	Diablo PG&E	38.0	0			Greenwood (1972)
CA-SLO-52	Diablo PG&E	11.2	0			Greenwood (1972)
CA-SLO-61	Diablo PG&E	15.0	0	4600–1000 cal BP	Early	Greenwood (1972)
	Diablo PG&E	0.1	6			Price et al. (2012)
CA-SLO-497	Montaña de Oro SP	0	2		Early	Barter (1988)
CA-SLO-584	Diablo PG&E	9.9	0			Greenwood (1972)
CA-SLO-585	Diablo PG&E	39.4	10	8980–330 cal BP	Millingstone, Middle, Late	Greenwood 1972, Jones et al. (2011)
CA-SLO-1453	Diablo PG&E	1.4	1		Late	Price (2008)
Totals		235.4	70			

single most important contribution to local archaeology and the starting point for all subsequent research—including our own. A total of 12 sites have been excavated previously (Table 3.1). Ten of these are on the Diablo Canyon Power Plant property and two are within Montaña de Oro State Park. Salient findings from these sites are summarized below.

CA-SLO-2 (Diablo Canyon)

Commonly referred to as "the Diablo Canyon Site," CA-SLO-2 is the most well-known and most heavily studied site on the Pecho Coast. It is marked by an extremely large (ca. 400 × 320 m) midden, situated on a narrow coastal terrace on the north bank of Diablo Creek. Of the six sites investigated by Roberta Greenwood in 1972, CA-SLO-2 was the deepest and most complex (Figure 3.1). It was within the direct impact area of a road that was planned as access to the power plant, and Greenwood's investigations were undertaken to mitigate the impacts of road construction. In the area of her investigations, the site extended to a depth of 3.4 m. A total of 30 units, each measuring 1 × 2 m, was excavated in arbitrary 10 cm levels and processed through 6 mm mesh screens. Two column samples were recovered for microanalysis: a 0.5 × 0.5 column excavated to the base of the deposit (0.725 m³) that was water-processed with 1 mm mesh to recover fish bones, and a 1 m × 1 m unit, processed with nested 6 mm (¼ in) and 3 mm (⅛ in) mesh to recover shell remains. Greenwood (1972:5) reported a total recovery volume of 109 m³. In 2008 Jones, Porcasi, Gaeta, and Codding reanalyzed the site's vertebrate remains but data representing only 98.9 m³ were available at that time. Some findings from the fish-bone column (Fitch 1972) and shell column were reported in detail in the 1972 monograph, as was the site's artifact collection (Greenwood 1972, 2004).

Greenwood (1972) found that the deep midden at CA-SLO-2 was relatively homogeneous with little evidence of discrete layering. In the absence of such physical stratigraphy, she relied on three radiocarbon dates and a robust assemblage of formal artifacts to define three cultural components: a variant of the California Milling-

FIGURE 3.1. Excavations under way in the deep shell midden at CA-SLO-2 (photograph courtesy of Roberta Greenwood).

stone Culture, dating ca. 9,400–5,000 radiocarbon years ago from 240–340 cm; a Hunting Culture component in the middle levels of the deposit (240–120 cm), dating ca. 5,000–1,000 radiocarbon years ago; and a Late Period or Chumash component, postdating 1,000 radiocarbon years ago, above 120 cm (Figure 3.2).

As part of their study of the site's fauna, Jones and colleagues (2008) obtained 28 additional radiocarbon dates from CA-SLO-2, supplementing three dates reported by Farquhar (2003) to bring the site total to 34 (Appendix C). Farquhar (2003) also obtained 16 obsidian hydration readings and source analyses. The enhanced chronometric database generally corroborates Greenwood's cultural-stratigraphic assessment of the site's occupational history, although Jones and colleagues used a more contemporary cultural historical structure that breaks local prehistory into six periods that are also recognized in adjoining regions (Figure 3.3). Radiocarbon results also indicate some vertical, intercomponent mixing due to rodent activity and the presence of

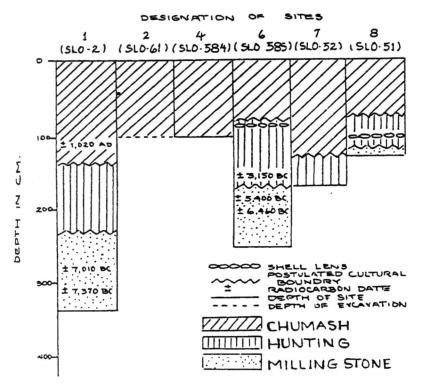

FIGURE 3.2. Greenwood's (1972) chronostratigraphic summary of the Diablo Canyon sites.

66 human burials. Jones and colleagues (2008) broke the deposit into four temporal components, but here we retain Greenwood's original chronostratigraphic divisions. The human remains were repatriated by the San Luis Obispo County Archaeological Society (SLOCAS) in the 1990s. To facilitate a more fine-grained analysis of terrestrial mammal-hunting patterns on the Pecho Coast, Codding and colleagues (2010) further subdivided the remains from SLO-2 into 1,000-year intervals assigned using age-depth analysis: dating to 9000–8000, 8000–7000, 6000–5000, 3000–2000, 2000–1000, and 1000–0 cal BP, respectively.

The Diablo tool assemblages showed consistent diversity which Greenwood (1972) attributed to continuity in the basic adaptation through time. Artifacts associated with the site's basal occupation were relatively sparse, but all of the temporal components yielded diverse arrays of ground stone (handstones, milling slabs, mortars, pestles, and/or pitted stones), bone awls,

projectile points, bifaces, scrapers, and debitage that reflect a wide range of domestic and subsistence activities. CA-SLO-2 functioned as a residential base during all habitation periods, an assessment further supported by the association of human interments with each temporal component. The only significant change in the tool inventory over time was the addition of fishing implements (circular shell hooks, notched and grooved stones) during the late Holocene.

Jones and colleagues (2008) identified a total of 2,789 mammal, bird, and reptile bones to the genus level or better representing 29 species of birds, 15 terrestrial mammals, 7 marine mammals, and one reptile (the western pond turtle [*Clemmys marmorata*]). Overall, the collection was dominated by the remains of black-tailed (mule) deer (NISP=1201; 43%), sea otters (*Enhydra lutris*; NISP=431; 15.5%), cottontail rabbits (*Sylvilagus* sp.; NISP=365; 13.1%), and cormorants (*Phalacrocorax* sp.; NISP=278; 9.9%). The site's basal component (NISP=44) showed a

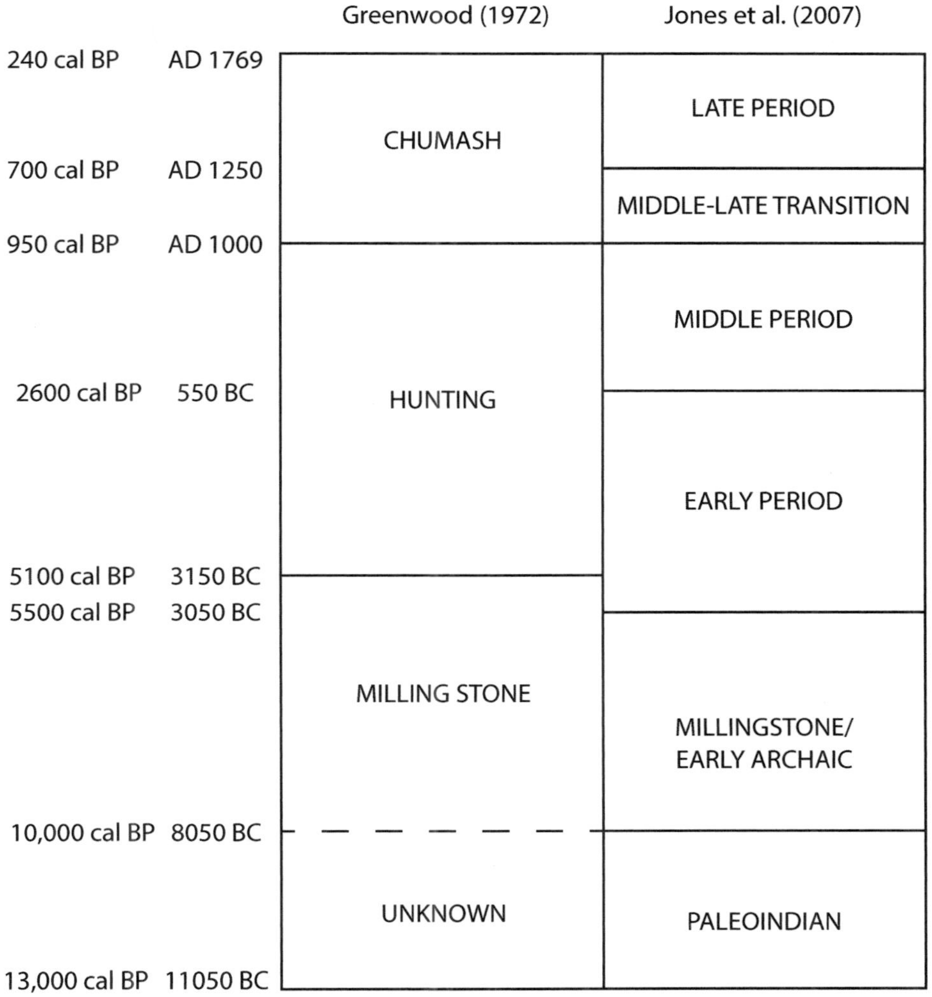

FIGURE 3.3. Greenwood's cultural chronology and more recent scheme by Jones et al. (2007).

preponderance of mule deer (NISP=18; 40.1%), cottontail rabbit (NISP=8; 18.2%), and the extinct flightless duck (*Chendytes lawi*; NISP=8; 18.2%). Aquatic birds overall, including the sooty shearwater (*Puffinus griseus*) and the flightless duck, account for 38.6% of the NISP. Component II (Late Millingstone/Lower Archaic) was dominated by mule deer (NISP=187; 44.6%), cottontail rabbit (NISP=66; 15.8%), and the flightless duck (NISP=50; 11.9%). Component III (Middle Period) also showed mule deer (NISP=673; 41.1%) as the dominant taxon, followed by sea otter (NISP=278; 16.9%) and cottontail rabbit

(NISP=221; 13.5%). Component IV (Late Period) was dominated by mule deer (NISP=323; 46.9%), sea otters (NISP=136; 19.8%), and cottontail rabbit (NISP=70; 10.2%). Jones and colleagues (2011) discussed the otter bones from CA-SLO-2 showing that otters and red abalone had been harvested together throughout the site's occupation.

Hildebrandt and colleagues (2010) subsequently challenged the observation of mule deer preponderance in the earliest Diablo component, suggesting that the apparent pattern was a product of inaccurate component definition and vertical mixing. They contend that early Holocene hunting in most of California was dominated by rabbits. Jones and Codding (2010) countered that there was no legitimate reason to question the components or faunal patterns from CA-SLO-2, but Hildebrandt and colleagues' characterization of early Holocene hunting does seem to hold true for most of central and southern California, including other components from the Pecho Coast (Codding et al. 2010; Jones and Codding 2010).

Most recently Stevens (2012; also see Stevens and McElreath 2015) examined the bowl mortars from CA-SLO-2 and -585 under the pretense that rim thickness also serves as a useful index of specialization. He found a general trend for thicknesses to decrease over time which he interpreted as later, more gracile forms being used for increasingly restricted sets of tasks while earlier, thicker mortars were overdesigned, perhaps with a goal of multifunctionality.

CA-SLO-7

Tested by Breschini and Haversat in 1987 and reported a year later (Breschini and Haversat 1988), CA-SLO-7 is a large (214 × 116 m) shell midden situated on the northern side of a small unnamed creek, 850 m north of Diablo Canyon. They completed five units (two 1 × 1 m, one 1 × 2 m, and two 0.75 × 1.25 m) and a 0.2 × 0.2 m column sample for a total recovery volume of 5.6 m³. They also obtained ten radiocarbon dates. The radiocarbon dates are difficult to interpret accurately due to the changes in procedure and advances in calibration that have taken place in the intervening decades. Also, the dates were obtained from composite samples of multiple shell fragments. Breschini and others realized since then that such samples potentially mix shells from different time periods and cannot be relied upon for precise age estimates. It is also unclear if the dates obtained from the Washington State University (WSU) laboratory were corrected for isotopic fractionation. Assuming that they were not, we add 410 years to the uncalibrated date and calibrate following the procedures outlined in chapter 5. Overlooking one inverted date (WSU-3789) in the depth-age sequence, the re-

sults (Appendix C) show that the upper portion (0–90 cm) of the midden dates between approximately 1000 and 300 cal BP, while the lower level (below 100 cm) harbored a Middle Period component dating ca. 3200–2300 cal BP, with a level of mixing in between (90–100 cm). Breschini and Haversat (1988) recognized the presence of the Middle Period dates from the deeper portion of the CA-SLO-7 midden, but treated the site as essentially a single Late Period component.

Despite the relatively small recovery volume, the site produced a respectable array of artifacts including 97 beads representing the A1 spire-lopped Olivella (N=13), K1 cupped Olivella (N=29), Class G saucers (N=5), Haliotis epidermis disks (N=1), clam shell disk (N=1), Mytilus disk (N=1), volcano limpet beads (N=38), and stone (steatite or talc schist?) disks (N=19), 2 bone awls, 2 indeterminate bone tools, 13 bifaces, 1 contracting-stemmed projectile point, 1 small leaf-shaped point, 9 battered stones, 7 pitted stones, and 1 tarring pebble. The bead assemblage was typologically consistent with the Late Period dating suggested by most of the radiocarbon dates, although Olivella saucer beads (wall disks) also were used during the Middle Period and seem to have been more common during that time. All of the beads except one saucer were recovered from the upper 100 cm of the deposit.

The site also yielded 9,943 vertebrate faunal remains, of which 7,917 were fish, 46 were reptiles, 29 were birds, and 1,951 were mammals. Most of the specimens in all categories were unidentifiable and there was also a healthy representation of remains of small burrowing animals that were probably intrusive. Eliminating the unidentifiable fish remains (N=6,688), the remaining sample of 1,229 NISP was dominated heavily by rockfish (NISP=700; 56.9%) followed by sardines (Sardinops sajax) (NISP=160; 13%), and surfperches (NISP=54; 4.4%). The high frequency of sardine bones varies from CA-SLO-2 where Fitch (1972) concluded that anchovy and sardine bones were introduced into the site as the stomach contents of other, larger fish. Langenwalter and colleagues (1988), who analyzed the remains from CA-SLO-7, argued against that conclusion suggesting instead that these diminutive taxa represented the use of nets for fishing. Langenwalter and colleagues (1988) also sectioned nine rockfish otoliths to determine season of capture and concluded that fishing was pursued at CA-SLO-7 during the spring only. Unfortunately, the reliability of seasonality determinations based on otolith sectioning has been questioned (Andrews et al. 2003). The sample of nonintrusive bones from nonpiscine taxa that could be identified to the genus level or better was extremely small (NISP=31) and was dominated by rabbits (NISP=15; 48.4%) and deer (NISP=7; 22.6%). Shellfish remains recovered from the column sample were dominated by mussels (76.9%) and turban snails (8%) by weight. The shell weights were derived from processing of the column sample through 1.5 mm (1/16 inch) mesh.

CA-SLO-8

In 1988 Breschini and Haversat also reported the results of modest testing at CA-SLO-8, situated on the southern side of the unnamed drainage adjacent to CA-SLO-7. Three 1 × 1 m units were excavated to a maximum depth of 50 cm. Total recovery volume was 1.3 m³. They also obtained two radiocarbon dates both of which suggested that the site dated to the Late Period, ca. 700–300 cal BP.

A small collection of beads (N=8) represented four of the types recovered from CA-SLO-7: 4 spire-lopped, 3 cupped, 1 saucer, and 1 stone disk. With the exception of the saucer, the beads are temporally consistent with the radiocarbon dates. Two indeterminate fragments of bone tools were also recovered, rounding out the entire formal artifact collection.

A total of 1,298 vertebrate remains was reported including 713 fish bones, 11 reptile bones, 119 mammal bones, and 455 unidentifiable vertebrates. The majority of fish bones (N=609) could not be identified to family. Among the 104 identifiable specimens, the dominant species was rockfish (NISP=46; 44%) followed by monkeyface prickleback (NISP=36; 35%). Only 15 nonpiscine, nonintrusive mammal specimens could be identified to the genus level; these were

dominated by badger (NISP=11), and rabbits (NISP=2). Shellfish was dominated by remains of California mussel (76.9%), and turban snail (8.1%). The shell analysis in this instance was completed with remains recovered from 3 mm (1/8 in) mesh so that the shell weight values are not directly comparable to the findings from CA-SLO-7 which were processed with 1.5 mm (1/16 in) mesh.

CA-SLO-10 (Spooner Ranch House)

CA-SLO-10 is situated under and around the Spooner Ranch House at Spooner's Cove in Montaña de Oro State Park. The site is marked by a moderate-sized midden deposit on the south bank of Islay Creek across from the more expansive CA-SLO-1. Breschini and Haversat (1985) excavated a single 1 × 1 m test unit on the edge of CA-SLO-10 in anticipation of installation of a power pole. The unit extended to a depth of only 70 cm, and cultural materials were fairly limited. The site was tested more extensively by State Parks archaeologist Herb Dallas in 1986 who reported his findings in 1994. His investigation was done to facilitate stabilization of the historic ranch house, and he excavated one 0.5 × 1.5 m unit and one 1 × 2 m test unit in areas proposed for new foundations. The midden was recognized to extend to a maximum depth of 1.0 m and his total recovery volume was 3.8 m³. He obtained three radiocarbon dates from the upper 70 cm of the deposit. One from the first 10 cm level dates to the historic period and is undoubtedly derived from the historic-era occupation of the Spooner Ranch. The other two range from about 1300 to 1200 and 800 to 600 cal BP, representing the Middle and Middle–Late Transition Periods, respectively. The associated artifact assemblage included seven nondiagnostic bifaces, seven cores, and debitage. The lithics were dominated by locally occurring Monterey chert. Six obsidian flakes were also recovered.

The vertebrate faunal remains from CA-SLO-10 were reported in a specialist appendix by Langenwalter. A total of 211 fish bones was recovered of which 114 could be identified to the family level or better. The identifiable fish remains were dominated by rockfish (*Sebastes* sp.) (NISP=52;

45.6%) and surfperch (NISP=11; 9.6%). A total of 346 nonfish bones was reported, of which 297 could not be identified to the family level. Among the 49 NISP, the dominant species were rabbit (NISP=14; 28.6%) and mule deer (NISP=7; 14.3%).

The Dallas investigation also uncovered remains from a single human burial in the form of a partial mandible and five teeth. The sex of the individual was indeterminate, but the teeth indicated that it was an adult.

The site was reinvestigated in 2006 to mitigate construction impacts undertaken by the California Department of Parks and Recreation. These more recent investigations are discussed in chapter 5.

CA-SLO-50

Information on the excavation of CA-SLO-50 by the Los Angeles County Museum is extremely sparse. The site is located on the west bank of Pecho Creek at its mouth, opposite CA-SLO-51 which was investigated by Greenwood (1972). King (1970) reports that a trench was excavated at this location in 1929 under the direction of Alex Keleman:

> The Pecho Site…was sampled with a single trench some 32 feet long. A suggestion of this trench appears to still be visible in an aerial photo taken by Charles Dills in 1969. The midden at SLO-50 was about 24 inches deep for most of the length of the trench; it deepened to over three feet toward the NW end, but this change in depth was not explored. About 35 pitted hammerstones, 3 plain hammerstones, a number of chert flakes, and cores, and a few "crude" chert points were found, as well as one *Tivela* blank and two *Olivella* spire-lopped beads. The midden was very hard, and excavation was not continued. (King 1970: Appendix I)

The findings from CA-SLO-50 were never reported other than this brief note by King who was attempting to salvage some information from this early, crude work. King reported that the collections generated by the Los Angeles County Museum were not cataloged nor were

the trenches back-filled. The landowners who had allowed access to the team in 1929 were still angry about the project in the 1950s when Pilling was completing his survey work. It is assumed that the materials recovered from this investigation are stored at the Los Angeles County Museum.

CA-SLO-51/H (Pecho)

CA-SLO-51/H was one of the six sites investigated by Greenwood (1972) in anticipation of construction of the Diablo Canyon nuclear power plant. She designated it "Site 8" and excavated a total of 19 units, 1 × 2 m each, to an average depth of 1 m for a total recovery of 38 m³. One 1 × 1 m unit was excavated with 3 mm (⅛ in) mesh and was designated a control unit for shell. One human burial was also recovered.

Like nearly all of Greenwood's investigations, this site yielded a large, diverse set of artifacts representing multiple temporal components. The assemblage included 88 projectile points, 39 "blades," 39 knives, 12 choppers, 23 hammerstones, 2 chisels, 107 scrapers, 10 drills, 5 handstones (no milling slabs), 4 portable mortars (2 of which were miniature), 12 pestles, 133 pitted stones, 3 grooved stones, 4 notched stones, 3 sandstone reamers, 141 shell beads, 1 stone (serpentinite?) bead, 1 charmstone, 4 bone awls, 3 tarring pebbles, and 6 shell fishhooks. Importantly, the site also yielded one glass bead and one ceramic sherd. Greenwood (1972:81) likened the sherd to specimens associated with Yokut ceramic production, but it is unclear why she ruled out neophyte production at Mission San Luis Obispo. The vertebrate faunal remains from this site were not analyzed, and they could not be relocated at SLOCAS.

Greenwood was unable to obtain radiocarbon dates from this deposit but felt, based on artifact type frequencies, that it represented her entire cultural sequence, with a very modest Millingstone component at the base of the midden (ca. 100–110 cm), a more substantial Hunting Culture component in the middle levels (ca. 70–100 cm), and a Late Period or Chumash component in the upper 70 cm. The relatively high frequency of small concave base projectile points suggests this was one of the more sub-stantial Late Period components investigated by Greenwood. The site also showed evidence for use in postcontact times. A layer of red abalone shells was present at a depth of approximately 100 cm running through the entire deposit. Cal-cium carbonate (caliche) was abundant below 80 cm. The occurrence of multiple, probably mixed components within a relatively shallow deposit is somewhat problematic in terms of degree of confidence in allocating individual items to temporal periods. This situation, how-ever, was common for the Pecho Coast middens investigated by Greenwood.

This site was investigated more recently by Cal Poly who found clear evidence in the form of glass trade beads and an abundance of Late Pe-riod markers that this was the village of *Tstyiwi*. Results of the investigation are discussed in de-tail in chapter 5.

CA-SLO-52

Designated Site 7, CA-SLO-52 was subjected to only a relatively modest test by Greenwood who excavated six 1 × 2 m units for a total recovery volume of 11.2 m³. The site is situated on the northern bank of Vineyard Creek about 200 m inland. The maximum depth of the deposit was 160 cm. Recovery included 20 projectile points, 6 drills, 2 "flake knives," 3 choppers, 2 hammer-stones, 2 cobble mortar fragments, 4 grooved stones, a shell fishhook blank, and a J-shaped mussel shell fishhook. Human remains were noted in the deposit but were not removed as they were outside of the area of proposed im-pact. Greenwood (1972:4) felt that the site ma-terials represented two temporal components: a Hunting Culture occupation (ca. 120–160 cm), and an upper Late Period or Chumash com-ponent (0–120 cm). She was unable to obtain radiocarbon dates from this site.

CA-SLO-61

CA-SLO-61, situated on the south bank of Diablo Creek across from CA-SLO-2, was des-ignated "Site 2" by Greenwood (1972) who con-ducted only a modest salvage because most of the deposit had already been destroyed by con-struction activities. She excavated approximately 15 m³ of deposit and recovered 38 artifacts rep-resenting a range of temporal and functional types including 5 projectile points, 2 blades, 21 scrapers, 1 drill, 1 core, 1 pestle, and 7 pitted stones. She did not obtain radiocarbon dates but assigned the site tentatively to the Late or Chu-mash Period (Greenwood 1972:4).

The site was investigated more recently by Applied Earthworks who excavated four 20 × 20 cm column samples for a total recovery vol-ume of ca. 0.1 m³. Six radiocarbon dates suggest the deposit dates between 4700 and 3000 cal BP. The tool assemblage included a bowl mortar and pestle, pitted stones, and large corner-notched and side-notched projectile points which are consistent with the Hunting Culture (Price et al. 2012).

CA-SLO-497
(Little Morro Rock)

Situated on the top of a 12 m tall, offshore sea stack in Spooner's Cove, CA-SLO-497 is one of the more unusual middens investigated along the Pecho Coast. In 1988 when it was resurveyed and augered by a team of California State Parks archaeologists led by Eloise Barter, the deposit covered an area of approximately 12 × 16 m. At that time, the midden was suffering from un-authorized surface collection and erosion, and Barter elected to complete six auger borings, map, and collect surface artifacts. She also com-pleted a profile of deposit exposed in a large looter pit. She found the midden to extend to a depth of ca. 100 cm with extensive evidence of deflation. She also described two distinct strata: an upper homogeneous sandy midden with shell (0–60 cm), and a lower dark sand (60–100) with many rodent burrows. Two shell samples were obtained for radiocarbon dating: one from near the top of the deposit (25–30 cm), and another from the base (90–105 cm). The upper sample returned a date of ca. 2700–2400 cal BP, while the lower sample yielded a date of 3200–2900 cal BP. The two dates suggest that the deposit contains a single-component occupation from the Early Period. A total of 96 fish bones was re-covered from the augers. Of these, only 16 could

FIGURE 3.4. Layer of red abalone shells (photograph courtesy of Roberta Greenwood).

be identified to species. Dominant species were Pacific sardine (NISP=4), rockfish (NISP=3), and surfperch (NISP=3). A total of 845 nonfish bones was recovered of which six were identified to species. The dominant species (NISP=4) was ground squirrel (*Otospermophilus beecheyi*).

This site was investigated again by California State Parks in 2008 with assistance from Cal Poly. Results are described in chapter 5 herein.

CA-SLO-584

Greenwood's Site 4, or CA-SLO-584, was the only inland deposit she investigated. The site is situated 1.1 km upstream from the mouth of Diablo Creek at an elevation of about 230 feet. Greenwood's investigation was limited to testing rather than the more extensive work she completed at several other locations. She excavated seven 1 × 2 m units ranging in depth from 50 to 100 cm. Total recovery was 9.9 m³. A cupule rock was associated with the deposit.

The site was different from the others investigated by Greenwood in that it produced only a scanty yield of artifacts. Ten projectile points

were recovered but only three were complete enough to classify: two were large side-notched, one was contracting-stemmed. Other flaked-stone implements included three blades, eight scrapers, one knife, and two cores. Ground stone included three bowl mortar fragments, one hopper mortar, two pitted stones, two pestles, and two handstones. Two aboriginal potsherds and five glass trade beads were also recovered. Shell remains were dominated by mussel (70.7%) and turban snail (18%). Greenwood (1972:55) interpreted the site as marking a single Late Period component that included postcontact occupation. She was unable to obtain radiocarbon dates for this deposit.

CA-SLO-585

Designated Site 6 by Greenwood, CA-SLO-585 is situated 400 m inland at an elevation of 52 m (170 ft.). Excavation showed that the cultural deposit at CA-SLO-585 extended to a maximum depth of 250 cm and was semistratified. The upper levels of the units (0–80 cm) consisted of dark midden with a high clay content and modest quantities of fragmented marine shell. Between 80 and 100 cm below surface was a dense, compacted layer of largely whole red abalone shells (Figure 3.4). This layer was highly indurated and could only be excavated with a pick and crow bar. Beneath the red abalone layer was a markedly different soil that extended from 110–250 cm and was much more friable than the levels above it. It was also lighter in color and showed deposits of calcium carbonate. At the base of this lower midden, the natural substratum was a black clay dispersed with pockets of calcium carbonate precipitate.

As at CA-SLO-2, Greenwood employed a mixed recovery strategy designed to sample artifacts, and micro-, and macro-faunal remains effectively. A total of 11 units were excavated at Locus 6A, including ten 1 × 2 m units processed dry with 6 mm (¼ in) mesh and one 1 × 1 m control column used to sample shell and small fish remains. A total of 39.4 m³ was excavated by hand. In addition, Greenwood employed a backhoe to excavate the site mechanically in order to recover more formal artifacts (particularly milling slabs and handstones which were abundant in the site's lower depths). An additional 30.0 m³ of deposit was excavated mechanically for a total recovery volume of 69.4 m³. One human burial was found near the base of the lower midden deposit at 180–200 cm. The low frequency of burials contrasts significantly with CA-SLO-2 where a large number of interments caused intercomponent mixing of deposits (Jones, Porcasi, Gaeta, et al. 2008:294).

For the 1 × 1 m control column, Greenwood dry-screened the deposit through 6 mm mesh and collected all of the shell retained in the 6 mm screen. All of the residues that passed through the 6 mm mesh were also collected, bagged, and sent to the fish bone analyst, John Fitch. Greenwood reported the weight of all of the shell recovered from the control column and analyzed two levels to species. There is nothing in her report to suggest, however, that John Fitch completed analysis of the fish remains from the column sample, and it is reasonable to assume that he exhausted all of his time and labor in the analysis of the column sample from CA-SLO-2 which took him over 900 hours (Fitch 1972:102).

Greenwood (1972:4) obtained four radiocarbon dates from the lower levels (160–200 cm) of CA-SLO-585. Calibrated, these dates range from ca. 9500–5400 cal BP (Appendix C). Based on these findings and the vertical distribution of diagnostic artifacts, she further divided the occupation into three cultural components: a Millingstone occupation in the basal levels of the deposit (ca. 170–250 cm) dating ca. 9500–7700, a Hunting Culture occupation in the middle levels beneath the red abalone layer (80–170 cm) dating post 7700 cal BP, and a Late Period ("Chumash") component above the abalone layer (0–80 cm) dating approximately (without radiocarbon) to post 500 cal BP. Six additional radiocarbon dates were acquired by Jones, Garza, and colleagues (2009) who undertook a reanalysis of the site's faunal collection. The enlarged sample of dates generally supports Greenwood's assessment of the distribution and age of cultural components with some refinements. Dating of the middle-upper levels showed that the red abalone layer was indeed a reliable stratigraphic marker; all dates from below 79 cm range between 9500 and 5300 cal BP, while three from above the layer ranged from 3000 to 300 cal BP. The earlier occupations are represented exclusively from beneath the red abalone layer, and their combined dating correlates exceptionally well with the span of time associated with the Millingstone culture on the central coast (9950–5450 cal BP). The break at 5300 cal BP is particularly important in this region because it marks a strong transition from Millingstone to the Hunting Culture, marked by increased frequencies of bifaces and projectile points after ca. 5500 cal BP (Fitzgerald and Jones 1999; Greenwood 1972:4, 90; Jones 1993; Jones et al. 2002, 2007). At CA-SLO-585, this transition corresponds with an abandonment of the site after deposition of the red abalone layer which is consistent with patterning at nearby CA-SLO-2 where there is also a dearth of evidence for occupation between 5000 and 3000 cal BP (Jones, Porcasi, Gaeta, et al. 2008:296). For this reason, Jones, Garza, et al. (2009) consider the lower levels of the deposit (80–250 cm) to represent a single, undifferentiated Millingstone/Lower Archaic component, dating ca. 9000–5400 cal BP (referred to as Early–Middle Holocene), while the upper site levels (0–80 cm) marked the Late Holocene or Middle and Late periods (later than 3000 cal BP). The recovery volume associated with the Early–Middle Holocene component from the hand excavation sample was 23.4 m³, while the Late Holocene component was represented by 16 m³. As with SLO-2, Codding and colleagues (2010) produce a slightly more fine-grained chronology for SLO-585 based on these dates, subdividing the site into five temporal components ranging from 10,000–8000, 8000–6000, 6000–4000, 4000–2000, and 2000–0 cal BP, respectively.

CA-SLO-1453

Applied Earthworks excavated a 2 × 2 m unit at this site to depths of 40 cm in one half and 30 cm in the other, for a total volume of 1.4 m³. Materials were dry-screened in the field with 3 mm

TABLE 3.2. Excavation Samples from Previous Excavations on the Pecho Coast by Temporal Component.

Period	Components with Adequate Samples			Shellfish	Human Burials
	Artifacts	Mammal and Birds	Fish		
Late	SLO-2	SLO-2	SLO-2	SLO-2	SLO-2*
			SLO-7	SLO-7	
			SLO-8	SLO-8	
Middle–Late	—	—	—	—	—
Middle	SLO-2	SLO-2	SLO-2	SLO-2	SLO-2*
			SLO-7	SLO-7	
	SLO-10**	SLO-10**	SLO-10**		
Early Millingstone	—	—	—	—	—
	SLO-2	SLO-2	SLO-2	SLO-2	SLO-2*
	SLO-585**	SLO-10	SLO-10	SLO-10	SLO-585*
		SLO-585**	SLO-585**	SLO-585**	

* Dating unclear, unavailable for further study
** Questionable component integrity

(⅛ in) mesh. Materials recovered from this investigation are presently stored in the Applied Earthworks laboratory at Lompoc pending availability of funds for analysis. A single shell sample returned a date of 139–0 cal BP (Appendix C), indicating a very late prehistoric or historic occupation.

Additional Radiocarbon Dates

Supplementing the radiocarbon dates obtained during the subsurface investigations discussed above are additional dates obtained from surface contexts and naturally exposed profiles such as cut-banks and cliff faces. Most of these were obtained by Applied Earthworks performing compliance work on behalf of PG&E. From CA-SLO-1451/H, two shell samples from the midden yielded dates ranging between 2000 and 1800 cal BP, suggesting a Middle Period component. Likewise, two dates from CA-SLO-5 also suggest Middle Period occupation ranging from 1300 to 1100 cal BP. A series of seven samples from CA-SLO-1452/H, -1453, -1455, -1458, -1459, -1460, and -1461 suggests very late prehistoric occupation or possibly the modern/historic era (Appendix C). One additional sample from CA-SLO-1466 produced a calibrated date of ca. 700–600 cal BP, likely representing the early Late Period.

Summary

Greenwood's (1972) investigations established the basic cultural/historical structure for the Pecho Coast, if not the entire central California mainland. Using substantial artifact assemblages from six sites and six radiocarbon dates from CA-SLO-2 and -585, she delineated thirteen temporal components that defined a three-part sequence consisting of: Millingstone (9370–5150 RCYBP), Hunting (5150–1000 RCYBP), and Chumash (post-100 RCYBP). Excavations subsequent to Greenwood's (and prior to those discussed in chapter 5) have added an additional 73 radiocarbon dates that illuminate at least seven additional temporal components. However, there is great variation in the type and quantity of data associated with components identified by Greenwood and by subsequent investigators. Components well dated by radiocarbon and for which there are robust samples of artifacts, micro- and macro-fauna are fairly few (Table 3.2). Of the six sites investigated by Greenwood, only two, CA-SLO-2 and -585, were originally dated with radiocarbon; both of these have now been redated. Radiocarbon dates are now available from another of Greenwood's sites, CA-SLO-61, indicating that the portion of it investigated by Applied Earthworks dates to the Early Period.

CHAPTER 4

Field and Laboratory Methods

As discussed in chapter 1, archaeological investigations by California Polytechnic State University, San Luis Obispo began on the Pecho Coast at CA-SLO-9 (Coon Creek) within Montaña de Oro State Park in 2004 and continued at seven more sites between 2006 and 2017. Laboratory analyses were completed by classes that were held following completion of field work. In nearly all cases, excavations were intended to salvage materials from the western edges of middens that were eroding into the Pacific Ocean. In this chapter we describe the field-sampling strategies and basic laboratory methods used during these projects.

Field Methods

In 1972 Greenwood employed a mixed recovery strategy to investigate the Pecho Coast shell middens. Her approach included sampling techniques designed to recover adequate samples of both macro- and micro-constituents. Her work was conducted within a very early cultural resource management (CRM) framework that involved data recovery from large impact areas in rich, deep deposits. Her program combined hand excavation of 1 × 2 m units processed in the field with 6 mm (¼ in) mesh with 1 × 1 m control units that were water-screened and sorted in the laboratory using 3 mm and smaller mesh. She did not collect shell remains from the 1 × 2 m units, but rather from the control units only. She also used a backhoe to mechanically excavate

large areas of at least one site, CA-SLO-585. Her methods resulted in robust samples of artifacts, features, and faunal remains of all sizes although she was unable to fully identify all of the remains from all of the sites—a problem that remains common in California midden studies today.

Greenwood's investigation is still the single most important contribution to San Luis Obispo archaeology to date, and the effectiveness of her mixed recovery sampling strategy cannot be overlooked. However, in the intervening years it has generally become standard in California to employ 3 mm (⅛ in) mesh for unit excavation due to concerns that too many tiny objects like fish, small mammal bones, and beads are lost through larger mesh apertures (Casteel 1972; Gordon 1993; James 1997; Schaffer and Sanchez 1994; Stahl 1996; Thomas 1969; Zohar and Belmaker 2005). In some parts of California, especially on the Channel Islands, recovery strategies have switched to a near-exclusive focus on micro-constituents and methods (water screening) designed to capture abundant small constituents, particularly fish bones which are found in enormous quantities in many island deposits.

The sampling strategy used in the Cal Poly investigations was essentially an updated version of the mixed approach employed by Greenwood and was based on a similar goal of recovering meaningfully sized samples of all the types of artifacts and ecofacts that occur in these deposits. A variety of excavation techniques was

FIGURE 4.1. Excavation of 1 × 2 m unit beginning on the eroding edge of CA-SLO-1366/H in 2011 (photograph by Kacey Hadick).

employed in order to obtain adequate samples of both macro- and micro-constituents. The majority of the excavation volume targeted macro-constituents using relatively large units (1 × 2 m) dry-screened through 3 mm (⅛ in) mesh in the field. Exceptions to this were two instances where larger 6 mm (¼ in) mesh was used due to dense soils and/or a shortage of field time. In addition to the 1 × 2 m units, at least one 1 × 1 m control unit was also excavated at each site. Soils from control units were first reduced in the field through 3 mm (⅛ in) mesh dry screens with remaining residues collected in labeled buckets and transferred to the Cal Poly Archaeological Laboratory for water (wet-screen) processing through 3 mm (⅛ in) mesh and sorting by laboratory students. To sample shellfish, one or two 20 × 20 cm column samples was also excavated from each field site and trans-

ferred to the Cal Poly Archaeological Laboratory for wet-screening through nested 3 mm (⅛ in) and 1.5 mm (¹⁄₁₆ in) mesh screens. Further details on the rationale and objectives for each of these techniques are provided below.

Macro-samples

The 1 × 2 m units were intended to recover formal artifacts and larger bone fragments from mammals and birds. Soil was removed from the individual units (Figure 4.1) in 10 cm levels with a variety of hand tools (shovel, pick-maddox, trowel, etc.) and placed either directly into screens or into buckets that were then transferred to screens (Figure 4.2). All formal artifacts, debitage, and bone were collected from each level and placed in separate bags for each analytical category for later laboratory processing and analysis. Fire-affected rock (FAR) was collected, weighed, and then discarded from the macro-sampling units. Because all of the deposits were relatively shell-rich middens, it was deemed impractical to attempt to recover 100% of the invertebrate remains from the macro-units since it would require inordinate amounts of time. For invertebrate remains, all whole and nearly whole shells (especially abalone and mussel) and all large fragments were collected from the macro-sample units, but small fragments were not. An exception to this was *Olivella* shell fragments (possible bead production residues) which were collected. Shell was only collected in order to (1) develop a complete list of invertebrate taxa represented in the deposit (as column samples often do not yield examples of species that occur in low frequencies), and (2) provide samples for oxygen isotope analysis and radiocarbon dating. Other information on the shell constituents within the deposits was obtained with micro-sampling techniques.

Micro-samples

Micro-samples included 1 × 1 m control units that were wet-screened through 3 mm (⅛ in) mesh and 20 × 20 cm column samples. Control units were excavated with the specific goal of obtaining representative samples of fire-affected rock, fish bone, and obsidian pressure flakes. Soil

FIGURE 4.2. Students dry-screening midden residue at CA-SLO-1370/H in 2009.

from control units was excavated with hand tools in 10 cm levels. Soil was then reduced through 3 mm (⅛ in) mesh screens and placed in labeled plastic bags within buckets. The buckets were then transferred to the archaeological laboratory at Cal Poly where the soil was processed with water through 3 mm (⅛ in) mesh screens. Student laboratory technicians then sorted the materials, recovering, tabulating, and weighing all cultural constituents except shell fragments.

The 20 × 20 cm column samples were excavated primarily to recover a controlled sample of shell. Columns were excavated with hand tools in 10 cm levels. Soil from each level was double-bagged in labeled plastic and paper bags without field screening, placed in archive boxes or buckets, and transferred to the Cal Poly Archaeological Laboratory where the samples were processed with water through nested 6 mm (¼ in), 3 mm (⅛ in), and 1 mm (¹⁄₁₆ in) mesh. Student laboratory technicians then sorted all of the cultural materials including shell.

Summary

The total recovery volume from the seven investigations with which Cal Poly was involved was 97.996 m³ (Table 4.1). The largest investigation

was at CA-SLO-9 where excavations were completed by field classes in 2004, 2005, and 2007 for a total of 34.84 m³. The smallest excavation was at CA-SLO-497 where a small salvage project was undertaken by California State Parks (assisted by Cal Poly) in 2008 with a total recovery of 2.328 m³.

Laboratory Processing

All materials recovered from the field were transferred at the end of each field class to the Cal Poly Archaeological Laboratory for storage until the following fall or winter when students in Archaeological Laboratory Methods classes completed processing and preliminary analyses.

Materials recovered from the 1 × 2 m macro-sampling units were delivered to the laboratory in archive boxes containing individual unit bags. Materials within the bags were segregated into gross analytical categories (e.g., debitage, formal artifacts, obsidian, fish and nonfish bone, shell samples). At the laboratory, materials from the bags were washed and set aside to dry in labeled artifact drying screens. Once dry, materials were placed into 4 ml archival-quality curation bags. Formal and diagnostic artifacts were placed within their own bags, while debitage and shell

TABLE 4.1. Summary of Field Recovery, California Polytechnic State University–San Luis Obispo Investigations on the Pecho Coast.

Site	6 mm (¼ inch) dry Volume (m³)	3 mm (⅛ inch) dry Volume (m³)	3 mm (⅛ inch) wet Volume (m³)	6 mm (¼ inch) wet Volume (m³)	Columns (0.2 × 0.2 m) N	Volume (m³)	Total (m³)
CA-SLO-5	0.0	8.46	1.8	0.0	2	0.048	10.308
CA-SLO-9	1.8	30.40	2.0	0.0	2	0.064	34.264
CA-SLO-10	0.0	4.40	4.2	4.3	1	0.056	12.956
CA-SLO-51/H	0.0	4.70	0.5	0.0	1	0.020	5.220
CA-SLO-58	0.0	10.60	1.0	0.0	1	0.040	11.640
CA-SLO-497	0.0	2.30	0.0	0.0	1	0.028	2.328
CA-SLO-1366/H	0.0	9.00	1.2	0.0	2	0.080	10.28
CA-SLO-1370	2.2	7.80	1.0	0.0	0	0.000	11.00
Total	4.0	77.66	11.7	4.3	10	0.336	97.996

* Shell sample recovered from 1 × 1 m control unit

(with the exception of whole *Mytilus* and shells from specific proveniences) were placed in lot bags. Fish bone was distinguished from nonfish bone (bird and mammal bone) and both were placed in separate lots.

Micro-samples (wet-screened control units and column samples) required further processing at the Cal Poly Laboratory. Soil from control units was reduced in the field, without water, through 3 mm (⅛ in) mesh screens. Soil retained in the 3 mm screens was placed in labeled plastic buckets. At the laboratory, each bucket was poured into labeled 3 mm mesh screens, and the material was carefully rinsed with water to remove any remaining soil. Materials were then set aside to dry. After the residues dried, Cal Poly archaeology students, under the supervision of the instructor, carefully sorted through all of the material, segregating formal artifacts, debitage, FAR, and bone. Column samples were delivered to lab in archive boxes which contained labeled plastic bags within labeled paper bags. The soil from each bag was individually poured into nested 3 mm and 1.5 mm mesh screens. Hoses were used to gently wash soil through the screens, leaving clean residue which was set aside to dry in screens labeled with provenience information and mesh size. After the material was dry, it was placed into labeled plastic bags. Later, Cal Poly archaeology students, also under the supervision of the instructor, sorted the 3 mm sample, separating all formal artifacts,

shell, bone (both fish and nonfish), and debitage. The 1.5 mm samples were collected and stored for possible future analysis. All materials were then cataloged, using the accession number from one of two institutions to whom the collections would be sent for permanent curation. Collections recovered from Montaña de Oro State Park were curated at the California State Parks Facility in Sacramento. Accession numbers were as follows:

CA-SLO-9: P1387
CA-SLO-10: P1028
CA-SLO-497: P1759

The remaining sites on PG&E property were curated at the San Luis Obispo County Archaeological Society (SLOCAS) curation facility at Cuesta College. Accession numbers were:

CA-SLO-5: SLO-5-1-
CA-SLO-51/H: SLO-51-2-
CA-SLO-1366/H: SLO-1366/H-1-
CA-SLO-1370/H: SLO-1370-1-

Processing of materials from SLO-58 is still underway, but it will be curated at SLOCAS under number SLO-58-1. All artifacts and lots that received numbers were given a designation beginning with the accession number, followed by a unit number, and specimen number. For example, the first specimen from Unit 1 from CA-SLO-9 was designated:

P1387-1-1-1

The first specimen Unit 1 from CA-SLO-5 was designated:

SLO-5-1-1-1

For column samples, the designation CS was added to the unit designation as follows:

P1387-CS1-1

All cataloged materials were entered into an Excel® workbook. Diagnostic and formal artifacts were given individual numbers, while debitage was cataloged in lots. After identification, individual lots of fish bone retained single numbers, while all nonfish bone elements (except for unidentifiable fragments) were assigned a separate sub-letter within the catalog. Lots of shellfish received one number with the exception of whole shells and shell fragments from specific proveniences that were retained for ^{14}C dating. These were assigned their own numbers. Cataloged materials were segregated into analytical categories which were distributed to appropriate analysts. Methods employed in the analyses of these materials are described further in chapter 5.

Analytical Methods

Here we detail the methods employed in post-field identification and analyses of materials recovered from the field investigations in which Cal Poly, San Luis Obispo was involved.

Chronology and Component Identification

We define components as discernible chrono-stratigraphic units (e.g., Phillips and Willey 1953). These constituted the main unit of analysis used to examine variation through time. The age of individual site components was established primarily on the basis of radiocarbon dating results that were in almost all cases obtained from single-shell samples. Time-sensitive beads were also evaluated. Hydration readings were also obtained from obsidian specimens, but these were not weighed seriously in making chronological evaluations because source-specific conversion formulae do not provide accurate dating estimates (i.e., consistent with radiocarbon dates) on the coast (King 2000), probably due to the more complex climatic/humidity regimes as opposed to the arid interior of California where such rates seem to have at least some validity. Combined, these methods allowed us to divide the archaeological sites into horizontally and/or vertically delineated temporal components.

Radiocarbon Analysis

For the current investigations, shells were selected from a range of vertical and horizontal proveniences in order to attempt to define the full span of occupation represented in each cul-tural deposit. Samples were submitted to Beta Analytic Inc. who provided conventional age estimations (corrected for isotopic fractionation) that were then calibrated in OxCal v4.2.4 (Bronk Ramsey 2013). All dates from current investigations and most dates from previous work were on marine shell and were calibrated based on the Marine 13 calibration curve (Reimer et al. 2013) with a local correction of 290±35 (Ingram and Southon 1996). Some dates reported from previous investigations derived from terrestrial mammals, these were calibrated based on the IntCal 13 curve (Stuiver et al. 2016). Four previously reported dates were analyzed at a lab (WSU) that did not account for fractionation; to account for this, we added 410 years to each date prior to calibration. Dates for each site component are discussed in chapter 6. Complete probability distributions for all dates from all investigated sites are also shown in chapter 7. Appendix C reports 1-Sigma (68%) and 2-Sigma (95%) ranges and midpoints for all calibrated dates.

Obsidian Hydration and Source Determinations

Obsidian flakes were sent to the Northwest Obsidian Laboratory for source (XRF) and hydration analysis but, as mentioned above, the hydration readings were considered to be of only minimal chronological value. Readings were not converted into calendric dates, but were evaluated relative to blocks of absolute time based on hydration readings paired with radiocarbon dates from single component sites along the central coast developed by Jones and Ferneau (2002) and Jones and Waugh (1995). In this way, obsidian readings were interpreted as only the crudest markers of a very coarse-grained time scale. Complete readings and results are presented in Appendix D.

Temporally Sensitive Beads
(with Kaya Wiggins)

Shell and stone beads are typically encountered in California sites in large numbers only in direct association with human burials—presumably as offerings or as decoration on clothing or grave-associated perishables such as baskets. Because none of our investigations encountered human burials, beads were limited to loose, unassociated items recovered from midden deposits.

The shell and stone beads were described, classified by type, and measured to capture quantitative data useful for comparative research and cross-dating. Measurements captured the length, maximum diameter (width), diameter of the perforation, and curvature. All shell beads were measured and classified according to the Bennyhoff and Hughes (1987) typology recently updated by Milliken and Schwitalla (2012). King's (1982, 1990) typology which is the defining work for the Santa Barbara Channel was also consulted. Because the San Luis Obispo coast falls between the central and southern California study areas, there is some uncertainty about the applicability of these alternate typologies. More importantly, the different regional typologies suggest alternate dating for some types. Shell beads have been recognized as temporally sensitive in California since the 1930s, but for most of this period their ordering was in relative rather than absolute time. This situation has been improved in the last decade or so with increased direct accelerator mass spectrometry (AMS) dating of types (Gibson and Koerper 2000; Groza 2002; Groza et al. 2011). Below we summarize the radiocarbon date–based age spans developed by Groza and colleagues (2011) for key types that occur in the San Luis Obispo area and also reference comparable data from Orange County reported by Gibson and Koerper (2000).

Most bead types in the region were made from the purple olive shell, formerly designated *Olivella biplicata* but recently reclassified as *Callianax biplicata*. Because of the long tradition in use of the name *Olivella*, we continue to employ it here. The temporal significance of the represented types is discussed below. Examples of the most common bead types are shown in Figure 5.1.

Class A Spire-Lopped *Olivella*
A1 Simple Spire-Lopped

A1 beads are simply whole *Olivella* shells without a spire. These beads did not necessarily require any actual modification on the part of Native people because shells without spires can be readily found on central coast beaches. Regardless, these are the earliest beads used in California; examples from the Mojave Desert have been dated ca. 10,000–9000 cal BP (Fitzgerald et al. 2005). However, they were also used in all subsequent time periods and have no value as time markers (Bennyhoff and Hughes 1987).

A4 Punched Spire-Lopped

A4 beads are spire-lopped *Olivella* with a perforation in the body of the shell that was not drilled, but punched. Bennyhoff and Hughes (1987:119) considered them uncertain time markers at best.

A5 Applique Spire-Lopped

Applique spire-lopped beads have no spire and the side of the body is ground flat, diagonal to the shell axis (Bennyhoff and Hughes 1987:119). The dating of this type varies regionally, but it appears to be a marker of the Protohistoric–Historic periods in the San Joaquin Valley (Milliken and Schwitalla 2012:17) and likely dates to this time in San Luis Obispo County.

Class B End-Ground *Olivella*
B3 Barrel

Barrel beads lack a spire and parts of the aperture have been removed. Class B beads have the same size categories as Class A. B3 types are characterized by excessive grinding at the base of the shell, giving the bead its maximum

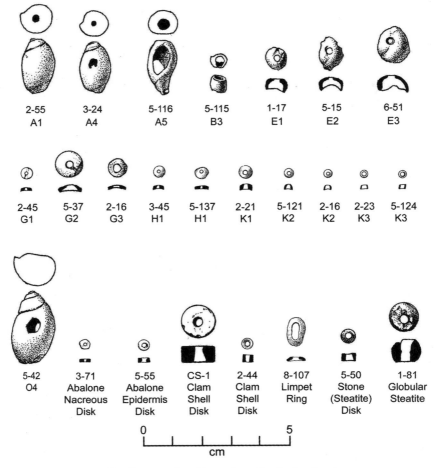

FIGURE 5.1. Common bead types from the Pecho Coast.

diameter towards the middle. These beads are
not good temporal indicators (Bennyhoff and
Hughes 1987:122).

Class C Split *Olivella*
C2 Split Drilled
These are half-shell beads, sometimes with a
shelf, and all of the edges are ground. Class C
beads are generally considered markers of the
Middle Period and adjacent transitions (Bennyhoff and Hughes 1987:122). However, direct dating by Groza and colleagues (2011:146) shows
that C2/C3 seem to be restricted to early Middle
(ca. 2100–1550 cal BP) and Middle–Late Transition (850–700 cal BP) contexts in the San Francisco Bay area.

Class E Lipped *Olivella*
Class E lipped beads are oval to round beads
produced from the upper callus of the *Olivella*
shell and portions of the body whorl. The upper
callus is also referred to as the inner lip, hence
the name of the class. Class E beads developed
later from cupped beads, Class K. Lipped *Olivella*
beads have long been recognized as markers of
the Late Period. Bennyhoff and Hughes (1987)
ascribe them to post 450 cal BP times and King
(1982) dates them similarly. Direct dating by
Groza and colleagues (2011) shows that one example dated as early as 680 cal BP, indicating that
the range of time associated with the type is actually longer than originally thought: 680–180
cal BP. Whether subtypes can be ascribed to

briefer spans of time within the Late Period remains to be determined. Three subdivisions of Class E beads were identified by Bennyhoff and Hughes (1987) that were thought to have temporal meaning. However, AMS dating by Groza and colleagues (2011:150) raises doubts about the temporal significance of these subtypes.

E1 Thin-Lipped

Class E1 beads are thin lipped and can be round or oval in shape. They are considered markers of Phase 2 of the Late Period (450–180 cal BP) in central California by Bennyhoff and Hughes (1987:127). Three directly dated specimens from central California confirm that age estimate, with calibrated midpoints between 300 and 220 cal BP (Groza et al. 2011:141).

E2 Thick-Lipped

The thick-lipped subtype is distinguished from E1 by a curvature measurement greater than or equal to 5.0 mm. Bennyhoff and Hughes (1987:128) suggest it is a marker of late Phase 2 of the Late Period (ca. 300–180 cal BP). Two examples directly dated by Groza and colleagues (2011:141) support that age estimate.

E3 Large-Lipped

E3 beads are lipped and oval in shape, and generally larger than E1 and E2. Bennyhoff and Hughes (1987:129) suggested that this is the youngest of the Class E subtypes, dating to the Historic Period. However, direct dating shows this to, in fact, be the oldest E subtype with a midpoint range 380–250 cal BP (Groza et al. 2011:141).

Class G *Olivella* Saucers

G1 Tiny Saucers

The G1 subtype is one of three saucer variants recovered from the Pecho Coast. G1s are the smallest saucers with maximum diameters no greater than 5.0 mm (Bennyhoff and Hughes 1987:132). Bennyhoff and Hughes (1987:132) stated fairly strongly that this saucer variant has no temporal significance, and that it can be found during any period. Milliken and Schwitalla (2012) ascribe it to all phases within the Middle and Late periods

in southern California and conclude that it is a poor time marker. More recently, Haversat and Breschini (2014) reported the results of six AMS dates on G1 beads that all fell between 1250 and 500 cal BP. Based on those results the authors suggested that the G1 type might be a useful marker of the late Middle, Middle-Late Transition, and early Late (Phase 1; 700–450 cal BP) periods. However, a historic period date (ca. 200 cal BP) reported by Groza and colleagues (2011:141) from a G1 specimen from CA-YOL-69 renders some doubt about that conclusion.

G2 Normal Saucers

Larger G2 saucers have long been considered solid markers of the Middle Period although Bennyhoff and Hughes (1987:132) emphasized their occurrence during the earlier portion of the Middle Period in central California, but throughout the Middle Period in southern California. Direct dating of an extensive suite of G2 beads by Groza and colleagues (2011) showed a limited temporal range between 2150 and 1365 cal BP. This finding suggests strongly that G2 saucers should now be recognized as markers only of the early Middle Period.

G3 Rings

Rings are large saucers distinguished from G2 by a larger perforation. These G3 beads are now ascribed to the same time span as G2 (Milliken and Schwitalla 2012).

Class H *Olivella* Disks

Disks are shallow, circular beads made from the shell wall that have distinctly small perforations as a result of the holes being made with metal needle drills as opposed to stone (Bennyhoff and Hughes 1987:135). This trait makes all subtypes reliable markers of the postcontact era.

H1 Ground Disks

H1 subtypes have either ground or semiground edges.

H2 Rough Disks

These small disk beads are distinguished by rough edges that have been chipped.

K1 Cupped *Olivella*

For central California, Groza and colleagues (2011) documented a brief chronology for Class K Callus beads between ca. 600 and 500 cal BP. King (1982) ascribes them to the full Late Period, between 750 cal BP and contact in the Santa Barbara area. Gibson and Koerper (2000) reported a date of 1040±685 radiocarbon years BP (ca. 900–750 cal BP) from a K1 bead from Orange County. Collectively, these data suggest that callus beads can be considered markers of the Middle–Late Transition and Late Periods, ca. 800–200 cal BP.

Class O Whole *Olivella* Shells

O4 Double-Punched Whole Shell

This is a whole *Olivella* shell with holes punched on opposing sides of the wall. Bennyhoff and Hughes (1987:143) note that examples were recovered from Early Period contexts on Santa Cruz Island, but they did not suggest that these beads are necessarily limited to that time interval. As such, we did not consider them to be reliable time markers for the Pecho Coast.

Abalone Shell Beads

Beads were made from two different parts of the abalone shell: the inner nacreous part and the outer epidermis of the red abalone. Both portions of the shell were made into small, disk-shaped beads. Abalone epidermis beads are associated with the Protohistoric and Historic periods (King 1978:59) although they seem to be most commonly postcontact. Nacreous disks are associated with the earlier portion of the Middle Period in the Santa Barbara area ca. 2200–1300 cal BP (King 1990:28).

Clam Shell Disks

Clam shell disks are common markers of Phase 2 of the Late Period in central California (ca. 450–180 cal BP), but in southern California they were also used much earlier—during the Early Period (King 1990). Examples from Early Period context are known from CA-SLO-877 north of the Pecho Coast (Gibson 1988:69), but Protohistoric examples were recovered from CA-SLO-214 near Morro Bay (Hoover and Sawyer 1977). Owing to

this dichotomous temporal pattern, these beads were viewed cautiously as time markers.

Mussel Shell Disks

These are small, disk-shaped beads produced from shell of California sea mussel. The type dates between the Middle–Late Transition and postcontact times in southern California, but has been recovered almost exclusively from Late Period contexts on the central coast (Jones 1993:43).

Limpet Rings

These beads were made expediently from the apex of cone-shaped volcano or keyhole limpet shells by taking advantage of the natural, oval-shaped hole that occurs there. These beads are especially common on the open coast of central California, but their dating is unclear; they seem to occur in any time period (Jones 1993).

Dentalium

Dentalium shells were used as currency during historic times from northwest California to Alaska. *D. pretiosum* shells are rarer farther south and were infrequently used as beads in the Santa Barbara Channel. King (1982) associates them with the Late and Historic periods. *Dentalium* beads were recovered from early Middle Period context at CA-SLO-56 near Avila Beach (D. Jones 2012), so their local chronological significance is unclear.

Stone Disks (Talc Schist or Steatite)

While the exact stone used to produce these beads has not been firmly established (and more than one type might have been used), these beads are morphologically distinct. Because they cannot be directly dated, they are more challenging to place in time. The most common stone beads are small steatite disks that are unquestionably associated with the Late Period in Monterey County (Jones 2003), and in the Morro Bay area just north of the Pecho Coast (Far Western Anthropological Research Group 2016). However, King (1990) assigns them a considerably longer chronology in the Santa Barbara area extending back into the Middle Period. Larger, globular stone beads are also known, sometimes referred to as ornaments. Their chronological significance is uncertain.

Glass Beads (Thad Van Bueren)

Glass beads were recovered from only one site, CA-SLO-51/H. The glass beads were described, classified by type, and measured to capture quantitative data useful for comparative research and cross-dating. Recorded measurements included maximum diameter, maximum length, and maximum diameter of the perforation (Appendix A). Descriptive observations were made regarding bead manufacture methods, shape, glass color and diaphaneity, and the condition of the specimens (e.g., burnt, patinated, fragmentary, etc.).

The glass beads were classified using types originally established by Kidd and Kidd (1970), later supplemented by Karklins (2012). That typology was used because it is the most widely employed system across North America, a matter crucial for understanding the spatial and temporal distribution of these extremely diverse artifacts. Bead shapes were also described using standard terminology following Meighan (1979) to supplement the typological assignments. Because many of the glass beads were covered with a patina, they were wetted to ensure accurate assessment of clarity and color. Clarity is described as either opaque, translucent, or transparent when viewed against a strong light source. Color is described in this analysis using numbers assigned in the Pantone and Munsell color systems.

Prior regional analyses of glass beads have employed diverse typologies, hindering meaningful comparisons. To overcome that obstacle, matches to glass beads in other collections were predicated on similarities in manufacturing method, color, shape, clarity, size, and condition, all of which may have specific implications for the timing of bead use and their sources of supply and distribution. Matches to other collections were generally made using color photographs and figures or, on a more provisional

basis, with published descriptions. The most secure comparisons to other glass bead assemblages were made with reference to color photographs and published color figures in Clement Meighan's (1979) type collection at the Phoebe Hearst Museum at the University of California in Berkeley, and color figures of collections from other places such as the Hudson's Bay Company settlement at Fort Vancouver, Washington (Ross 1990).

Matches were also sought among collections known only through written descriptions and black-and-white images. These latter comparisons were given less weight in this analysis because minor variations in color are often significant and cannot be discerned in the absence of accurate color definitions. Many typologies do not employ verifiable systems for describing minor variations in color. Collections from Hispanic settlements were given particular scrutiny for the entire period prior to American seizure of California in 1846. However, other work for the period after the Treaty of Guadalupe Hidalgo was also examined to assess distributions of glass beads in Native American sites (e.g., Van Bueren 1983) and locations associated with later settlers (e.g., Motz and Schulz 1979).

Flaked Stone

Formal flaked-stone artifacts and debitage were the most abundant cultural constituents recovered from the Pecho sites. These items were classified according to morphological/functional categories discussed below. Like virtually all sites on the central California coast, these materials consisted overwhelmingly of two types of local stone named for the geological formations from which they are derived: Monterey chert and Franciscan chert.

Monterey Chert

Monterey chert is one of a series of fine-grained, metamorphosed sedimentary rocks found in the Miocene-age Monterey Formation which occurs along much of the central and southern California coast south of Fort Bragg. On the Pecho Coast the San Luis Range is dominated by this formation which is of marine origin and includes sandstone, mudstone, clay shale, phosphatic shale, and fine-grained, thin-bedded, cream-colored siliceous shales (Chipping 1987) that grade into black, gray, and brown banded cherts. Of the two cherts found in the region, Monterey generally has superior flaking qualities and tends to dominate tool and debitage assemblages in areas where both stones were available.

Because the Monterey Formation forms the geologic substrate of the Pecho Coast, streams that drain the San Luis Range or Irish Hills tend to contain cobbles of Monterey chert which also are found along the shoreline and on beaches. At least one outcrop with evidence of quarrying has reportedly been identified several kilometers inland from the shoreline (Elise Wheeler, personal communication 2016), but such point sources or outcrops do not seem to have been important as sources of this stone for prehistoric people along the Pecho Coast. Virtually all of the creeks and beaches have cobbles of black- or gray-banded dull-colored chert as well as siliceous shale. Although these cobbles are not overwhelmingly abundant, they are not uncommon either.

In some cases a distinction was made between Monterey chert and shale, but the two often grade into one another so that the differences between them are at times somewhat arbitrary. Shale ranges from coarse-grained chalky material to finer-grained siliceous material with flaking qualities comparable to chert with the latter distinguished by a duller, grainier texture. However, our ability to distinguish one from the other confidently without additional geological analysis was limited.

Franciscan Chert

Northwest of Morro Bay is the Santa Lucia Range which is predominantly Mesozoic Age granites and some Cretaceous sedimentary rocks with overlying Miocene marine and other more recent sedimentary complexes. The local portion of the Santa Lucias is considered part of the Franciscan melange which includes a wide range of rock types including distinctive red and green cherts which are not banded and are duller in color and less lustrous than Monterey cherts.

Analytical Definitions and Procedures

Definitions of the eight morphological categories into which the flaked-stone specimens were segregated are listed below.

Cores

According to Andrefsky (1998:12), a core is "a mass of homogeneous lithic material that has had flakes removed from its surface. The primary purpose of a core is to supply flakes that can be used for the production of various tools." For the present analysis, we considered a core to be a cobble or block of tool stone from which flakes were detached for use or further modification. Cores exhibit flake-scar removal, albeit in some instances very weak, which indicate the production of usable flakes. One or more complete flake scars must be present in order for the stone to be classified as a core. This is consistent with definitions employed in other recent local studies. Included as cores were assayed cobbles, large flake blanks, and large pieces of shatter. Cores were considered to be waste (debitage or nontools) unless they showed evidence of intentional shaping or edge modification, suggesting use as core tools (e.g., a "chopper").

Core Tools

Core tools are defined as cores (mostly cobbles) that exhibited patterned flake removal suggestive of intentional shaping. These implements seem to have been used for some type of pounding/chopping tasks. Distinguishing between core tools and simple cores was difficult particularly with shale which does not lend itself to discerning edge battering.

Flake Tools

Flake tools were defined as those flakes that showed patterned macroscopic edge modification (i.e., the edge modification was continuous along a portion of the flake edge). In some instances, flake tools reflected a simple core/flake technology; flake tools could be generated at any stage in either core or biface reduction, however. Flake tools were considered to be either formal (showing intentional shaping) or informal (no evidence of shaping). Despite the fact that experimental research has shown that patterned edge modification can result from human trampling (Gifford et al. 1985) as well as any variety of other processes including cattle and cultivation, we keep with regional tradition and classify edge-modified flakes as tools, but have not relied upon them heavily for interpretations.

Bifaces

A biface is an artifact with two sides that meet to form a single edge that circumscribes the entire artifact (Andrefsky 1998:20). Local reduction trajectories for chert bifaces can be seen in Jones and Ferneau (2002:88) and for shale in Codding and colleagues (2009). We classified bifaces into production stages, using the stage definitions developed by Gilreath (1989) and Skinner (1986, 1990), with minor modifications as follows.

Stage 1 bifaces are thick, crude, bifacial cores or flake blanks that show incipient bifacial reduction. These cores are generally lenticular or irregular in cross section, with sinuous margins and rough bifacial edges. Less than 50% of the perimeter edge is shaped, except at the ends, and they are irregular in outline.

Shaped strictly by percussion, Stage 2 bifaces are often semirectangular in outline. They are generally lenticular in cross section, with closely to semiregularly spaced flake scars, and they exhibit a moderate degree of variability in flake scar morphology.

Stage 3 bifaces are percussion-thinned preforms, flattened in cross section, and have relatively regularly spaced flake scars and a low degree of variability in flake scar morphology. They tend to be regular in outline.

Unlike bifaces from earlier stages, Stage 4 bifaces are thin, partially pressure-flaked preforms that reflect intentional shaping that conforms to a predetermined outline (Skinner 1990:220).

Stage 5 bifaces are finished, pressure-flaked tools. Included in this category are large projectile points, drills, and knives, complete with notches, serrations, or basal modifications to accommodate hafting (Skinner 1990:220).

Projectile Points

Stage 5 bifaces were further classified as projectile points based on the presence of a pointed distal end and evidence of complete shaping and/or thinning. Classifications were made following regional projectile-point typologies (Jones 1993, 2003; Jones et al. 2007). Stage 5 bifaces that could not be typed to a specific projectile-point type were still classed as projectile points. While these bifaces could have had many uses (Stevens and Codding 2009), the use of the term projectile point remains consistent with regional reporting traditions (e.g., Greenwood 1972).

Drills and Reamers

The functional designation of drill or reamer was assigned based on the presence of an elongated blade or drill bit. The distinction between reamer and drill was somewhat arbitrary, but the former are generally more robust and thicker with less formalized (nonbifacial or only partially bifacial) bits, whereas drills were thinner, well formed, and bifacial.

Notched Stones

Notched stones are distinguished by V- or U-shaped notches that are either unifacially or bifacially flaked into opposite sides of a stone or cobble. Artifacts in the category have been classified elsewhere as "stone sinkers" (Pohorecky 1976) or "net weights" (Jones 2003), but here we follow Greenwood (1972) and Jones and Ferneau (2002) in adopting the morphological term "notched stone" (Codding and Jones 2006).

Debitage

Debitage includes all flaking debris resulting from the manufacture, use, and repair of stone tools. Flakes were assigned to one of twelve technological categories: (1) *primary decortication*, flakes with more than 70% dorsal cortex; (2) *secondary decortication*, flakes with less than 70% cortex or only a cortical platform; (3) *cortical shatter*, small, chunky pieces of debitage that exhibit cortex; (4) *simple interior percussion*, flakes straight in cross section, with one dorsal arris; (5) *complex interior percussion*, flakes straight in cross section with more than one dorsal arris; (6) *early biface thinning*, flakes curved in longitudinal section with one to two dorsal arrises; (7) *late biface thinning*, flakes curved in longitudinal section, with more than two dorsal arrises; (8) *angular percussion*, cuboidal or chunky pieces of shatter without cortex; (9) *percussion fragments*, sections of percussion flakes lacking other diagnostic attributes; (10) *edge preparation/pressure*, small flakes retaining remnants of tool or core margins with complex dorsal surfaces that cannot be definitively related to pressure-retouch; (11) *pressure*, small flakes with punctate platforms and either linear or round/amorphous outlines and simple dorsal surfaces; (12) *indeterminate percussion*, whole percussion flakes that cannot be typed due to weathering or other hindrance.

These twelve flake types were collapsed into six broader classes reflecting stages of lithic production. The first class, *decortication*, includes flake types 1, 2, and 3. The second class, *interior percussion*, includes flake types 4 and 5. The third class, *biface thinning*, includes flake types 6 and 7. The fourth class, *pressure*, includes flake types 10 and 11. All other flakes were classified as miscellaneous or nondiagnostic: *angular percussion* (type 8), *percussion fragments* (type 9), or *indeterminate* (type 12).

Ground Stone

Ground stone implements were classified based on morphology and wear according to regional categories based primarily on Greenwood's (1972) seminal excavations. These categories include: handstones, pestles, milling slabs, mortars, pitted stones, battered stones, miscellaneous, manuports, and polished stone.

Handstones

Handstones are small, frequently loaf-shaped ground stone artifacts. Sometimes termed manos, handstones were likely used in conjunction with milling slabs to process plant and other subsistence items.

TABLE 5.1. Technological Debitage Types.

Decortication	Biface Thinning
Primary decortication	Early biface thinning
Secondary decortication	Late biface thinning
Cortical shatter	
Interior percussion	Pressure flaking
Simple interior	Edge preparation/
Complex interior	Pressure
	Pressure
Miscellaneous	
Angular percussion	
Percussion fragment	
Indeterminate percussion	

Pestles

Pestles are elongated ground and pecked stone artifacts that were used in conjunction with mortars, typically for processing (i.e., pounding or grinding) food. Some pestles exhibit intentional shaping and design while others appear to take advantage of naturally occurring elongate cobbles.

Milling Slabs

Milling slabs are relatively flat in appearance and retain smooth surfaces upon which material was ground in conjunction with a handstone. Some may show more formal manufacture than others. Although ubiquitous throughout the record, they are frequently associated with the Millingstone Culture (Jones et al. 2007). Evidence suggests that their dominance gradually declines through prehistory as they were replaced by mortars and pestles (Basgall 1987; Codding et al. 2012; Stevens 2012).

Mortars

Mortars are circular or globular cobble implements with pecked or ground impressions in their center. Used in conjunction with pestles, they likely served to process plant and other subsistence remains. Some, particularly those developed in the Late Period (Jones et al. 2007) are very well manufactured, others are more expedient and developed through use.

Pitted Stones

Pitted stones are made of variable material suggesting perhaps expedient manufacture through use. Typically, they will have one shallow pit on one side (single) and may or may not have a symmetrically placed pit on the opposite side (double). Pitting is developed either through intentional pecking or though use. Despite being commonly recovered along the central coast, their use has long been unknown. However, a recent experimental evaluation suggests that while they likely served multiple functions (Strudwick 1995), they were most commonly used to process mussels and occasionally turban snails (Cook et al. 2017).

Battered Stones (General)

Battered stones and cobbles are those that show signs of being used to strike other rocks but lack any definitive morphology or identifiable wear to be assigned to a more specific artifact class. These could include hammerstones, assayed cobbles, pecked stone, etc.

Miscellaneous Ground Stone

Ground-stone artifacts that could not be fit within any of the other categories were labeled as miscellaneous. These could include very fragmentary remains, those with limited diagnostic surfaces, or those that defy classification based on a unique set of traits.

Unmodified Stone (Manuport)

Due to their morphology, size and material, some natural stones amenable to production or use as ground stone are sometimes recovered within cultural deposits. While their intended use (if any) is unknown, they were transported to the site location by human hands (manuport) and may warrant attention.

Polished Stone

Polished stone artifacts could include objects of soft stone (often steatite) that have been intentionally shaped. Elsewhere on the central coast, these could include drilled pebbles or lenticular ornaments (e.g., Jones and Ferneau 2002).

Bone and Shell (Nonbead) Artifacts

Bone artifacts were classified according to the functional categories defined by Gifford (1940) for California with reference also to King's (1982) cultural chronology for the Santa Barbara Channel.

Faunal Remains

Faunal remains were analyzed according to the following broad taxonomic categories: birds and mammals, fish, and invertebrates. Each category required its own specialized analytical procedures.

Bird and Mammal Bones

Identification of nonpiscine faunal specimens was accomplished by Judith Porcasi via direct comparison with reference collections from the Los Angeles County Natural History Museum and the Zooarchaeology Laboratory at the Cotsen Institute of Archaeology at UCLA. Each archaeological specimen was identified to the most discrete taxonomic level possible, using species and/or genus when possible, element, portion of element, side of body, and weight, as well as age/sex and condition (burned, cut, gnawed, or worked) to the extent that these characteristics could be determined. Specimens not identified to the species or genus level were identified more broadly to the family, order, or class level as appropriate. The nomenclature and taxonomy for mammals was based on Jameson and Peeters (1988) and for birds, Peterson (1990) (Table 5.2). In order to evaluate relative diversity of the assemblages, we further calculated Margalef Diversity indices for each temporal component following procedures described by Magurran (1988) in order to minimize the effects of sample size. Margalef provides an index of the relative richness or number of species represented in an assemblage: the higher the value, the greater the number of species exploited.

Fish Bone

All fish bone recovered during investigations was submitted to Dr. Ken Gobalet for taxonomic identification. Using a reference collection housed at the Department of Biology, California

TABLE 5.2. Mammals, Birds, and Reptiles of the Central California Coast. (Terminology follows Jameson and Peeters [1988] and Peterson [1990].)

Scientific Name	Common Name	Scientific Name	Common Name
Amphibians		*Zalophus californianus*	California sea lion
Bufo boreas	Southern toad	*Eumetopias jubatus*	Steller sea lion
		Phoca vitulina	Harbor seal
Reptiles		*Callorhinus ursinus*	Northern fur seal
Clemmys marmorata	Western pond turtle	*Enhydra lutris*	Sea otter
Lacertilia	Lizard	*Taxidea taxus*	Badger
Elgaria multicarinata	Southern alligator lizard	*Mephitis mephitis*	Striped skunk
Serpentes	Unidentified snake	*Procyon lotor*	Raccoon
Colubridae	Colubrid snake	*Odocoileus hemionus*	Black-tailed (mule) deer
Pituophis catenifer	Gopher snake	Cetacea gen. spp.	Whale
Thamnophis sirtalis	Garter snake	*Delphinidae*	Dolphin
Lampropeltis getulus	King snake		
Crotalus viridis	Rattlesnake	**Birds**	
		Anas sp.	Duck
Mammals		*Anas acuta*	Northern pintail
Otospermophilus beecheyi	California ground squirrel	*Anser albifrons, cf.*	White fronted goose
Dipodomys sp.	Kangaroo rat	*Melanitta* sp.	Scoter
Perognathus californicus	California pocket mouse	*Callipepla californica*	California quail
		Phasanidae	Pheasant family
Peromyscus maniculatus	California deer mouse	*Gavia* sp.	Loons
Thomomys bottae	Botta's pocket gopher	*Phalacrocorax* sp./ *auritus*	Cormorants
Microtus californicus	California vole	*Diomedea immutabilis*	Laysan albatross
Neotoma sp.	Woodrat	*Laridae*	Gull
Onychomys torridus	Southern grasshopper mouse	*Fratercula cirrhata*	Tufted puffin
		Ptychoramphus aleuticus	Cassin's auklet
Reithrodontomys megalotis	Western harvest mouse	*Uria aalge*	Common murre
Lepus californicus	Jack rabbit	*Puffinus griseus*	Puffin
Sylvilagus audubonii	Cottontail rabbit	*Oceanodroma* sp.	Storm petrel
Sylvilagus bachmani	Brush rabbit	*Scolopacidae* sp.	Sandpiper/phalarope
Scapanus latimanus	Broad-footed mole	*Tyto alba*	Barn owl
Vulpes vulpes	Fox	*Aphelocoma californica*	Scrub Jay
Lynx rufus	Bobcat	*Mimus polyglottos*	Northern mockingbird
Canis sp.	Dog/coyote	*Turdus migratorius*	American robin

State University–Bakersfield, Gobalet identified all elements to the most specific taxonomic level possible. In some cases where species identifications are not reliable (e.g., distinguishing among the 59 ecologically and morphologically similar species of *Sebastes* sp., or Rockfish), more general identifications were made. Specimens and a specimen catalog were sent back to the Cal Poly Archaeological Lab where they were weighed and subsequently aggregated into analytical categories based on the sampling method from which they were derived. Results are reported in chapter 6 by sampling method. The minimum number of individuals (MNI) was calculated per unit/level. To examine variability across time periods and sampling strategies, the richness

TABLE 5.3. Fishes of the Pecho Coast. (Terminology and order follow Page et al. [2013].)

Scientific Name	Common Name	Scientific Name	Common Name
Lamna ditropis	Salmon shark	*Paralabrax* sp.	Kelp bass
Triakidae	Smoothhound shark	*Scomber japonicus*	Chub mackerel
Charcharhinidae	Requim shark	Embiotocidae	Surfperch
Triakis semifasciata	Leopard shark	*Ophiodon elongatus*	Pile perch
Rhinobatos productus	Shovelnosed guitarfish	*Embiotoca* sp.	Black surfperch or striped seaperch
Myliobatos californica	California bat ray		
Raja sp.	Skates or ray	*E. lateralis*	Striped seaperch
Myliobatis californica	Bat ray	*Hypsurus caryi*	Rainbow seaperch
Engraulis mordax	Northern anchovy	*Rhacochicul toxotes*	Rubberlip seaperch
Clupeidae	Herring	Pomacentridae	Damselfish
Sardinops sagax	Pacific sardine	*Semicossyphus pulcher*	California sheephead
Spirinchus starksi	Night smelt	*Oxyjulis californica*	Señorita
Merluccius productus	Pacific hake	Stichaeidae	Prickleback
Porichthys notatus	Plainfin midshipman	*Anoplarchus* sp.	Cockscomb
Porichthys myriaster	Specklefin midshipman	*Anoplarchus purpurescens* (?)	High cockscomb
Atherinopsidae	New World silversides		
Atherinopsis californiensis	Jacksmelt	*Cebidichthys violaceus*	Monkeyface prickleback
		Xiphister sp.	Black or rock prickleback
Sebastes sp.	Rockfish	Clinidae	Blennies
Hexagrammos sp.	Greenling	*Gibbsonia* sp.	Kelpfish
Ophiodon elongatus	Lingcod	*Heterostichus rostratus*	Giant kelpfish
Cottidae	Sculpin	*Gobiesox meandricus*	Northern clingfish
Artedius sp.	Sculpin	*Gillichthys mirabilis*	Longjaw mudsucker
Clinocottus sp.	Sculpin	*Scomber japonicus*	Pacific chub mackerel
Leptocottus armatus	Pacific staghorn sculpin	*Citharichthys* sp.	Sanddab
Scorpaenichthys marmoratus	Cabezon	Pleuronectidae	Right-eye flounder
		Platichthys stellatus	Starry flounder
Trachurus symmetricus	Jack mackerel		
Sciaenidae	Drums and croaker		
Genyonemus lineatus	White croaker		
Seriphus politus	Queenfish		

and evenness components of diversity were calculated (see Magurran 1988). Richness (S) was determined as the sum number of identifiable (i.e., excluding Actinopterygii) taxa represented. Evenness (D) was calculated as one over the Berger-Parker Dominance index, measured as the number of individuals (NISP) in the dominant taxa divided by the sum total number of individuals across all taxa. For information on the biology and ecology of key fish species, see Jones and Ferneau (2002), Love (2011), and Salls (1988).

Invertebrate Remains

Using reference collections housed at the Cal Poly Archaeological Laboratory, San Luis Obispo, identification of invertebrate remains was completed by Terry Jones, Brian Codding, Kacey Hadick, and David Knight. First, all whole shells collected from all units were identified to species in order to develop a general species list (Table 5.4). Remains from a subsample of the column samples were then identified to the most specific taxonomic level possible. For this analysis, 100% of the shell materials retained in 6 mm (¼ in)

TABLE 5.4. Shellfish Represented in Pecho Coast Middens.

Group	Scientific (Previous)	Common Name
Abalones	*Haliotis cracherodii*	Black abalone
	Haliotis rufescens	Red abalone
Mussels	*Mytilus californianus*	California mussel
	Sepitfer bifurcatus	Platform mussel
Clams	*Leukoma (Protothaca) Staminea*	Pacific littleneck clam
	Saxidomus nuttalli	California butter clam
	Tidacna croea	Borning clam
	Tivela stultorum	Pismo clam
Turban snails	*Paumalax (Astraea) gibberosa*	Red turban snail
	Megasraea (Astraea) undosa	Wavy turban snail
	Tegula brunnea	Brown turban snail
	Tegula funebralis	Black turban snail
Limpets	*Collisella asmi*	Black limpet
	Collisella limatula	File limpet
	Collisella pelta	Shield limpet
	Collisella scabra	Rough limpet
	Lottia gigantia	Owl limpet
	Lottia scutum	Plate limpet
	Lottia instabilis	Unstable limpet
	Lottia digitalis	Finger limpet
	Notoacmea insessa	Seaweed limpet
	Notoacmea persona	Mask limpet
Chiton	*Ischnochiton conspicuus*	Conspicuous chiton
	Ischnochiton heathiana	Heath's chiton
	Mospalia muscosa	Mossy chiton
	Katharina tunicata	Black Katy Chiton
	Cryptochiton stelleri	Gumboot chiton
Misc. snails	*Cerithidea californica*	California horn shell
	Crepidula adunca	Hooked slipper shell
	Serpulorbis squamigerus	Scaly worm snail
	Ademete couthouyi	Couthouy's nutmeg
	Littorina sitkana	Winkle
	Nucella canaliculata	Channeled dogwinkle
Barnacles	*Pollicipes polymerus*	Leaf barnacle
	Pollicipes polymerus	Gooseneck barnacle
Urchins	*Stongylocentrotus purpuratus*	Purple urchin
	Cancer antennarius	Red-spotted rock crab
Crabs	*Cancer* sp.	Crab (indeterminate)
Olivella	*Callinanax (Olivella) biplicata*	Purple Olive
Oyster	*Ostera lurida*	Olympia Oyster
Scallop	*Crassadoma gigantea*	Giant Rock Scallop

mesh were identified and a 25% sample was analyzed from the 3 mm (⅛ in) residues. No shell from the 1 mm (¹⁄₁₆ in) samples was identified.

In order to estimate the life-history distributions of exploited invertebrates, whole or nearly whole abalone (*Haliotis*) were measured. Complete specimens were measured directly; templates were used to approximate measurements of incomplete specimens. If any specimen could potentially fit within more than one template size-class, it was deemed too fragmentary to obtain measurement. The abalone template was developed during initial work at CA-SLO-9 based on modern, complete abalone (Codding and Jones 2006, 2007; Codding et al. 2009). Incomplete abalone shells that were subjected to size evaluation with the template had to be at least one-third or more complete.

CHAPTER 6

Site Investigations

Here we present the results of investigations completed at seven sites on the Pecho Coast by Cal Poly or with Cal Poly support between 2004 and 2015: Crowbar Canyon (CA-SLO-5), Coon Creek (-9), Spooner's Ranch House (-10), Pecho (-51/H), Little Morro Rock (-497), Tom's Pond (-1366/H), and Point Buchon (-1370) (see Figure 1.1). In addition, we describe preliminary findings from CA-SLO-58 which was investigated by Cal Poly in 2017, and from which materials are still being processed and analyzed.

Crowbar Canyon (CA-SLO-5)

Description

The Crowbar Canyon Site (CA-SLO-5) is located on PG&E's Diablo Canyon Lands. It is a relatively small shell midden situated among low bedrock outcrops, two of which contain mortar cups. The midden encompasses an area of only 2200 m². Its western site boundary is marked by a precipitous cliff about 20–30 m above the Pacific Ocean (Figure 6.1). It was investigated by a Cal Poly field class in the spring of 2013. Excavation revealed a dark, rich, high-density shell midden that extended to a maximum depth of 90 cm, averaging 40–50 cm in most areas. Most excavation units encountered bedrock within 20–30 cm of the surface, but excavation continued into subsequent levels until bedrock covered the entire unit floor, causing the volume of soil recovered from each unit to vary (Figure 6.2).

The total recovery from the investigation was 10.25 m³, including 8.56 m³ from ten 1 × 2 m dry-screened test excavation units, 1.8 m³ from the wet-screened control unit, and 0.088 m³ from the micro-sampled column samples (Table 4.1). The primary research findings from the site were described by Jones and colleagues (2015).

Chronology

Eight radiocarbon determinations from a full suite of depths (0–90 cm) reveal a combined one-sigma range from 1270 to 910 cal BP and a two-sigma range from 1300 to 880 cal BP (Appendix C). These dates provide clear evidence that CA-SLO-5 was occupied for only a very brief period of time during the late Middle Period and the beginning of the Middle–Late Transition. The two-sigma probabilities suggest that the occupation could have been less than 100 years (1120–1060 cal BP) or as long as 430 years (1300–870 cal BP). For simplicity's sake we rely on the one-sigma midpoints which indicate an age of 1200–950 cal BP, which represents the last two centuries of the Middle Period.

Seven chronologically diagnostic shell beads were recovered from CA-SLO-5 along with one possible bead blank (Appendix E). The beads include four tiny saucers (G1) and three normal saucers (G2a). Tiny saucers (G1) are fairly common for the region from Middle and Late Period contexts (Far Western Anthropological Research

FIGURE 6.1. Northern edge of CA-SLO-5 looking north (photograph by Kacey Hadick).

FIGURE 6.2. Sidewall with column, CA-SLO-5 (photograph by Brian Codding).

Group 2016; Milliken and Schwitalla 2012). Tiny saucers have been recovered from Middle and Middle–Late Transition contexts elsewhere on the Pecho Coast (Codding and Jones 2007). Normal saucers are also common in central California, and though they have generally been considered markers of the Early–Middle Transition through the Middle Period (Milliken and Schwitalla 2012), recent direct dating (Groza et al. 2011) suggests they may have been most common during the early Middle Period. The bead blank is a square fragment of mussel shell with a central perforation. It is too incomplete to be chronologically significant but suggests that some minimal bead production took place at the site. The G1 tiny saucer beads are compatible with the dating suggested by the radiocarbon results. New dating of G2 normal saucers suggests occupation several centuries earlier than the radiocarbon results. In the absence of radiocarbon support for the latter, we tentatively conclude that the site was occupied 1270–900 cal BP.

Technology

The late Middle Period occupants of Crowbar relied on flaked stone, ground stone, and bone technologies.

Flaked Stone

The flaked-stone assemblage consists of 3,066 specimens: 21 cores, 6 core tools, 6 flake tools (4 formal; 2 informal), 13 bifaces, 8 projectile points, and 3,012 pieces of debitage. The vast majority of these specimens consisted of Monterey chert or shale, including all of the cores. Eight of the cores were cobbles that likely originated from one of the nearby creeks or the beach. The 13 bifaces included 12 of Monterey chert and one of Franciscan chert (Stage 1). The 12 Monterey chert bifaces showed an emphasis on the earlier stages with eight Stage 1 and four Stage 2. All eight formal projectile points were of Monterey chert and were fragmentary, but two were complete enough to be identified as contracting-stemmed and one as a lanceolate (Appendix F) (Figure 6.3). One unidentifiable tip fragment was small and thin enough to represent an arrow point but was too incomplete

TABLE 6.1 Summary of Debitage Sample from Crowbar Canyon (CA-SLO-5).

Flake Type	N	%
Primary decortication	41	7.72
Secondary decortication	3	0.56
Cortical Shatter	47	8.85
Subtotals	91	17.13
Simple interior	184	34.65
Complex interior	75	28.95
Subtotals	259	63.60
Early biface thinning	22	4.14
Late biface thinning	53	9.98
Edge preparation/pressure	87	16.38
Pressure	19	10.49
Subtotal	181	40.99
Total	531	100

for positive identification. However, the dating of CA-SLO-5 is consistent with most estimates for the time when the bow and arrow arrived on the central coast (ca. 1050–950 cal BP). The majority of the finds suggests that the occupants of the site relied on multifunctional bifacial technological systems, mostly associated with spearthrower and dart-projectile technology (Stevens and Codding 2009).

Flaked-stone debitage included 3,006 pieces of Monterey chert, four pieces of Franciscan chert, one obsidian pressure flake, and one flake of indeterminate stone. Debitage was dominated by indeterminate types. Among the diagnostic flakes (n=531), simple interior specimens were the most prevalent, making up 34.7% (Table 6.1), followed by edge preparation/pressure (16.4%). Simple interior and complex interior flakes together account for 63.6% of the diagnostic debitage. These flake types generally reflect the middle stages of lithic reduction. The relatively low frequency of decortication flakes (8.9%) suggests that some primary reduction of raw stone took place off site, though the 21 cores indicate at least some primary reduction. The relatively high frequency of biface thinning and pressure flakes suggests that these later stages of reduction were commonly undertaken on site as well. Based on the controlled recovery from

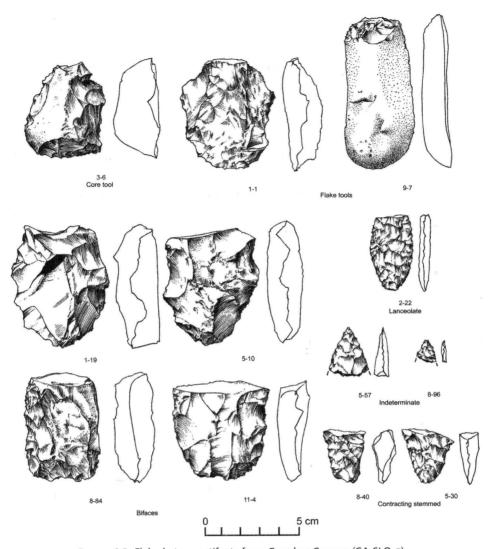

FIGURE 6.3. Flaked-stone artifacts from Crowbar Canyon (CA-SLO-5).

Unit 8, the density of Monterey chert debitage was 768 flakes per m³ of deposit. The relatively low density of flakes is consistent with the transport of partially finished bifacial blanks. This supposition is further supported by flake:biface ratios. While complete reduction sequences result in about 1,215 flakes for each biface (Jones and Haney 1997), the flake:biface ratio at CA-SLO-5 of 143:1 falls far short. These findings are similar to the flake:biface ratio of 97:1 at nearby CA-SLO-9 (Codding and Jones 2006) and 129:1 at CA-SLO-1366/H (Codding et al. 2013).

Ground Stone

Portable ground-stone technology was limited to 15 artifacts, including eight pitted stones, six battered cobbles, and one ornamental drilled pebble. While no pestles were recovered, the site does have two bedrock mortar outcrops each with three individual cups.

Bone and Shell

Only a single fragmentary bone artifact was recovered. Though incomplete, it was likely a bone awl tip.

TABLE 6.2. Amphibian, Reptile, Bird, and Mammal Remains from Crowbar Canyon (CA-SLO-5).

Taxon	Common Name	NISP	%NISP	Wt.(g)	Wt.%
Vertebrata	Unidentifiable vertebrate	1,191	36.4	31.44	3.93
Amphibians					
Bufo boreas	Southern toad	1	0.03	0.04	0.005
Reptiles					
Lacertilia	Lizard	6	0.18	0.05	0.006
Elgaria multicarinata	Western alligator lizard	4	0.12	0.16	0.02
Colubridae	Colubrid snake	3	0.09	0.22	0.028
Crotalus Viridis	Rattlesnake	3	0.09	0.33	0.041
Lampropeltis getulus	King snake	2	0.06	0.16	0.02
Pituophis catenifer	Gopher snake	1	0.03	0.02	0.003
Serpentes	Unidentified snake	32	0.98	0.93	0.12
Thamnophis sirtalis	Garter snake	1	0.03	0.11	0.0138
Mammals					
Mammalia	Unidentified mammal	1,146	35.07	195.56	24.45
Rodentia	Unidentified rodent	174	5.3	3.63	0.454
Spermophilus beecheyi	California ground squirrel	13	0.4	2.4	0.3
Dipodomys sp.	Kangaroo rat	3	0.09	0.09	0.01
Perognathus californicus	California pocket mouse	4	0.12	0.08	0.01
Microtus californicus	California vole	22	0.67	0.51	0.064
Thomomys bottae	Botta's pocket gopher	418	12.8	35.29	4.41
Neotoma sp.	Wood rat	8	0.24	0.3	0.038
Onychomys torridus	Grasshopper mouse	3	0.09	0.05	0.006
Peromyscus maniculatus	Deermouse	9	0.28	0.16	0.02
Sylvilagus sp.	Rabbit	60	1.84	4.72	0.59
Canis sp.	dog/coyote	5	0.15	1.96	0.26
Taxidea taxus	Badger	2	0.06	0.41	0.05
Pinniped	Seal/sea lion	12	0.37	16.33	2
Otariidae	Eared seal	8	0.24	27.94	3.49
Phoca vitulina	Harbor seal	12	0.37	102.2	12.78
Zalophus californianus	California sea lion	11	0.38	194.19	242.8
Callorhinus ursinus	Northern fur seal	2	0.06	14.19	1.77
Enhydra lutris	Sea otter	54	1.65	120.43	15.06
Artiodactyla	Even-toed ungulate	5	0.15	1.2	0.15
Odocoileus hemionus	Mule deer	2	0.06	24.87	3.11
Birds					
Aves	Unidentified bird	28	0.86	6.49	0.81
Uria aalge	Common murre	1	0.03	0.51	0.063
Phalacrocorax sp./*auritus*	Cormorant	22	0.67	12.83	1.6
Grand Total		3,268	99.2	799.8	99.97

TABLE 6.3. Economically Significant Mammal and Bird Remains from Crowbar Canyon (CA-SLO-5).

Taxon	Common Name	NISP	%NISP	Wt.(g)	Wt.%
Terrestrial mammals					
Neotoma sp.	Wood rat	8	4.47	0.30	0.06
Sylvilagus sp.	Rabbit	60	33.52	4.72	0.99
Canis sp.	Dog/coyote	5	2.79	1.96	0.41
Taxidea taxus	Badger	2	1.12	0.41	0.08
Odocoileus hemionus	Mule deer	2	1.12	24.87	5.22
Subtotal		77	43.01	32.26	6.76
Marine mammals					
Zalophus californianus	California sea lion	11	6.14	194.19	40.74
Callorhinus ursinus	Northern fur seal	2	1.12	14.19	2.96
Phoca vitulina	Harbor seal	12	6.70	102.20	21.44
Enhydra lutris	Sea otter	54	30.17	120.43	25.27
Subtotal		79	44.13	431.01	90.43
Birds					
Phalacrocorax/auritus	Cormorant	22	12.29	12.83	2.69
Uria aalge	Common murre	1	0.56	0.51	0.10
Subtotal		23	12.85	13.34	2.79
Grand Total		179	99.99	476.61	99.98

Subsistence Remains

Mammals, Birds, and Reptiles

A total of 3,268 nonpiscine vertebrate specimens weighing 799.80 grams was recovered from the eleven excavation units and two column samples (Table 6.2). About 12% of the specimens (379) had been burned. Although rodents are abundant in the archaeofauna, only one specimen was rodent-gnawed. One specimen had cut marks, and one had been worked into some form of artifact. Excluding likely intrusive elements from burrowing rodents, reptiles, and those remains not identifiable to the genus level, results in a net assemblage of 179 economically significant elements (Table 6.3). The proportional number of identifiable specimens suggests that occupants of the site exploited marine (44%) and terrestrial (43%) mammals equally, focused on rabbits (NISP=60, 34%) and sea otters (NISP=54, 30%). However, the proportional weight of these identifiable specimens suggests a heavy focus on marine mammals (90.42%), including sea lions (41%), sea otters (25%), and harbor seals (21%). The Margalef Diversity score for the bird and mammal remains is 1.927.

Fish

A total of 908 fish remains was recovered including 250 specimens that could only be identified as Actinopterygii (4 from the 3 mm dry sample, 244 from the 3 mm wet sample, and 2 from the column sample). Of the 658 specimens that were identified to at least the family level, 636 bones were recovered from the controlled, wet-screened samples (603 from the control unit [1.8 m³] and 33 from the column sample [0.032 m³]) and 22 bones from the dry-screened sample (8.46 m³) (Table 6.4). Focusing on the combined control unit and column (combined volume=1.832 m³), this sample is dominated by herring (NISP=68; 27.5%) followed by rockfish (NISP=139; 23.1%) and rock or black prickleback (NISP=79; 13.2%). While there are multiple species within the herring family, many of them are schooling species most amenable to capture with nets. Pricklebacks, on the other hand, can be collected by hand from beneath rocks in the intertidal pools. The volumetric density of identifiable remains from the control unit was 347.2 NISP/m³. The density from the dry-screened units was considerably lower: 2.1 NISP/m³.

TABLE 6.4. Fish Remains from Crowbar Canyon (CA-SLO-5, 1200–950 cal BP).

Taxon	Common Name	3mm Dry		3mm Wet		Column Sample		Total	
		NISP	Weight (g)	NISP	Weight (g)	NISP	Weight (g)	NISP	Weight (g)
Elasmobranchi omorphi	Sharks, skates, and rays								
Triakidae	Hound sharks	0	0.00	1	0.02	0	0.00	1	0.02
Subtotal		0	0.00	1	0.02	0	0.00	1	0.02
Actinopterygii	Ray-Finned Fishes								
Clupeidae	Herrings	0	0.00	168	1.13	7	0.02	175	1.15
Sardinops sagax	Pacific sardine	0	0.00	19	0.16	1	0.01	20	0.17
Atherinopsidae	Silversides	0	0.00	22	0.12	3	0.01	25	0.13
Sebastes sp.	Rockfishes	2	0.13	139	2.96	8	0.05	149	3.14
Ophiodon elongatus	Lingcod	2	0.13	4	0.46	0	0.00	6	0.59
Clinocottus sp.	Sculpin	0	0.00	2	0.01	0	0.00	2	0.01
Scorpaenichthys marmoratus	Cabezon	11	3.02	20	3.56	0	0.00	31	6.58
Embiotocidae	Surfperches	1	0.50	80	1.18	8	0.09	89	1.77
Damalichthys vacca	Pile perch	0	0.00	1	0.01	0	0.00	1	0.01
Oxyjulis californica	Señorita	1	0.01	38	0.31	1	0.01	40	0.33
Stichaeidae	Pricklebacks	0	0.00	21	0.72	4	0.07	25	0.79
Cebidichthys violaceus	Monkeyface prickleback	0	0.00	7	1.08	0	0.00	7	1.08
Xiphister sp.	Rock or black prickleback	5	0.43	79	3.87	1	0.02	85	4.32
Clinidae	Kelp blennies	0	0.00	1	0.01	0	0.00	1	0.01
Gobiesox meandricus	Northern clingfish	0	0.00	1	0.01	0	0.00	1	0.01
Subtotal		22	4.22	602	15.59	33	0.28	657	20.09
Grand total		22	4.22	603	15.61	33	0.28	658	20.11

Shellfish

Shellfish remains were identified from a single 20 × 20 cm column that was excavated to 80 cm for an analytical volume of 0.032 m³. In addition, measurements (maximum diameters) were obtained from all whole and nearly whole abalone shells that were collected from units. The relative abundance of shellfish from the column sample reveals 4,030.9 g of shell dominated by the remains of California mussel (79.5%), followed by turban snails (11.19%) and abalone (4.94%) (Table 6.5). The volumetric density of shell in the column sample was 125.9 kg/m³.

A total of 355 abalone shells was complete enough to determine length. Two hundred of these were red abalone (*Haliotis rufescens*) and

155 were black abalone (*H. cracherodii*). The mean size of the red abalones was 100 mm while the mean for the black abalones was 86 mm.

Coon Creek (CA-SLO-9)
Description

The Coon Creek site is a shell-rich midden located adjacent to the Pacific Ocean on the north bank of Coon Creek in the southwestern corner of Montaña de Oro State Park (Figure 6.4). Covering an area of roughly 4,000 m², the deposit lies on a coastal terrace about 40 feet above sea level. Cultural materials occur from the surface down to between 70 and 120 cm below within alluvial and colluvial sediments derived from low hills about a half km to the east. These Still

TABLE 6.5. Summary of Shellfish Remains (by Weight) from Crowbar Canyon (CA-SLO-5, 1200–950 cal BP).

Group	Taxon	Common Name	Total (g)	%
Abalones	*Haliotis cracherodii*	Black abalone	33.7	0.8
	Haliotis rufescens	Red abalone	102.97	2.55
	Haliotis sp.	Abalone (indeterminate)	64.29	1.59
Mussels	*Mytilus californianus*	California mussel	3,204.58	79.5
	Sepitfer bifurcatus	Bifurcate mussel	0.19	<0.01
Turban snails	*Tegula* sp.	Turban snail (indeterminate)	450.89	11.19
	Astraea gibberosa	Red turban snail	0.16	<0.01
Limpets	*Collisella pelta*	Shield limpet	0.64	0.02
	Collisella scabra	Rough limpet	0.15	<0.01
	Lottia gigantia	Owl limpet	0.6	0.01
	Lottia scutum	Plate limpet	0.17	<0.01
	Lottia instabilis	Unstable limpet	1.24	0.03
	Lottia digitalis	Finger limpet	0.14	<0.01
	Notoacmea persona	Mask limpet	0.45	0.01
Chiton	*Cryptochiton stelleri*	Giant gumboot chiton	8.98	0.22
	Mosalia muscosa	Mossy chiton	17.15	0.43
	Katharina tunicata	Black katy chiton	2.13	0.05
Misc. snails	*Crepidula adunca*	Hooked slipper snail	2.07	0.05
	Serpulorbis squamigerus	Scaly worm snail	1.41	0.03
	Ademete couthouyi	Couthouy's nutmeg	1.03	0.03
Barnacles	*Balanus* sp.	Barnacle (indeterminate)	55.87	1.39
	Pollicipes polymerus	Gooseneck barnacle	49.04	1.22
Urchins	*Stongylocentrotus purpuratus*	Purple urchin	26.72	0.66
Crabs	*Cancer* sp.	Crab (indeterminate)	1.24	0.03
Subtotal			4,025.81	99.87
Unidentified		Unidentified	5.10	0.13
Grand total			4,030.91	100.00

Series soils are characterized by gravelly sandy clay loams (A horizon) underlain by grayish-brown gravelly loam (IIC horizon) weathered from sedimentary rocks (United States Soil Conservation Service 1977:92, 148). A total of 34.84 m³ of the relatively homogenous deposit was excavated over field seasons in 2004, 2005, and 2007. Archaeological constituents were dominated by rocky intertidal invertebrate shells, primarily California mussel, and black and red abalone, and include fire-affected rock, stone debitage, cores, various bifacial and unifa-cial flaked-stone implements, obsidian debitage, shell beads and fishhooks, and bird, mammal, fish, and reptile remains. Detailed findings from these investigations were reported by Codding and Jones (2006, 2007) and Codding and colleagues (2009).

Chronology

In previous reporting of CA-SLO-9, we concluded repeatedly that the site was marked by a single temporal component dating to the Middle–Late Transition, ca. 980–720 cal BP.

FIGURE 6.4. Coon Creek site view toward the south with eroding midden (photograph by Terry Jones).

This conclusion was based on seven radiocarbon dates (Appendix C) that show a time range of less than 100 years (880–860 cal BP) at one-sigma or as long as 470 years between 1110 and 640 cal BP at two-sigma. The one-sigma midpoints suggested occupation between 980 and 720 cal BP which is consistent with a single Middle–Late Transition Period (950–700 cal BP) component.

Originally, 28 chronologically diagnostic beads from a total of 86 (Appendix E) were thought to support Middle–Late Transition dating. Twenty-four specimens represented saucers (Class G): two single tiny saucers (G1) and 22 normal saucers (G2). The remaining beads include one *Olivella* ring (G3), three cupped *Olivella* (K1), and a single steatite disk. Cupped *Olivella* are generally considered Late Period markers, but Gibson and Koerper (2000) reported a date of ca. 900–770 cal BP from a K1 bead from Orange County. The original interpretation of the beads (Codding and Jones 2007, 2009; Codding et al. 2009) was that they were thought to represent a combination of elements from the Middle and Late periods and therefore made sense with respect to a Middle–Late Transition. Recent AMS direct dating of central California beads by Groza and colleagues (2011), however, throws these interpretations into doubt. G2 saucer beads now seem to be restricted to pre-1600 cal BP (early Middle Period)

contexts. This suggests that while CA-SLO-9 is dominated by a Middle–Late Transition component, it also contains materials from a less substantial early Middle Period occupation that is unrepresented in the radiocarbon results. Unfortunately, nothing in the vertical or horizontal distribution of the G2 normal saucer beads provides a basis for delineating this apparent component. For this reason we continue to regard CA-SLO-9 as consisting primarily of a Middle–Late Transition component, but we also acknowledge that the site contains evidence for earlier occupation as well.

While we generally eschewed obsidian hydration readings in interpretations of site chronology, the obsidian sample from CA-SLO-9 was the largest of the project, and seems to contribute to the idea that the site was also witness to pre-M-LT occupation. Of 56 obsidian flakes sent for analysis, 53 returned measurable hydration rims. The majority of these (n=27, 48%) came from the Coso source, with hydration rims that cluster between 3.7 and 4.4 microns (Appendix D). Twenty-three specimens (41%) came from the Casa Diablo source with hydration readings clustering between 3.7 and 4.1 microns. A final specimen (n=1, 4%) came from the Napa source and a hydration reading of 1.7 microns. Most interpretations of Casa Diablo and Coso hydration rates ascribe readings in those ranges to pre-1000 cal BP time (Jones and Waugh 1995).

Technology

The individuals who lived at Coon Creek relied on a variety of technologies derived from flaked stone, ground stone, shell, and bone. Fiber technologies were not represented, likely the result of poor preservation.

Flaked Stone

The flaked-stone collection consists of 9,915 specimens including 21 cores, 13 core tools, 11 unifaces, 7 flake tools, 40 bifaces, 44 projectile points, 1 drill, 2 reamers, 20 notched stones, and 9,756 pieces of debitage.

A total of 21 specimens was classified as cores including 17 of shale and 4 of Monterey chert. The cores generally reflected working of locally occurring cobbles, as 17 of the specimens were flat, fist-sized cobbles typical of those found in the immediate vicinity of the site. Two specimens were interior chunks and two were tabular chunks. Seven of the cobbles appeared to have been opened using the bipolar technique. Two of the bipolar specimens were neatly split longitudinally along one of the natural cleavage planes in the shale to produce a split cobble with a single, flat ventral face. The unifacial artifacts described below were produced from cores of this type. One of the specimens (P1387-4-41) was heavily crazed as a result of contact with fire.

Thirteen artifacts were classified as core/cobble tools (Figure 6.5). Nine were shale, two were of Monterey chert, one was siltstone, and one was sandstone. Eleven of these were cobbles, one was an interior chunk, and one was a bifacially modified chunk. All showed evidence of patterned flake removal and/or edge battering. Three were split or halved cobbles with modified edges that conform to the general definition of scraper planes. One was a split cobble with a faceted area of battering on the remaining cortical face. The remaining specimens were halved or split cobbles that exhibited bifacial edges and/or battering. Two specimens (P1387-2-15 and -4-67) resemble choppers, while another (P1387-4-34d) was a split cobble with heavy evidence of battering on one face. While not conforming with the classic definition of a scraper plane, this specimen may have functioned as one.

Eleven unifaces were recovered, most of which seem to represent a unique local industry that took advantage of the cleavage planes in shale cobbles. Two of the implements (P1387-4-18b and -6-72c) were large, broken interior flakes that may represent unfinished bifaces. The remaining nine were all manufactured from cobbles: seven of shale and two of Monterey chert. Specimen P1387-5-18 is a symmetrical, round, split cobble that shows modification and/or battering on all of its edges. It was almost certainly used for some type of scraping function. Specimen P1387-6-17 was a large cortical flake derived from a cobble that appeared to be an unfinished notched stone. Specimen P1387-7-30 is a longitudinally split shale cobble that may also have been intended to be a notched stone but was unfinished. Specimen P1387-8-32 is a small cortical flake of Monterey chert derived from a pebble that appears to have functioned as a scraping tool. Specimen P1382-10-14 is a minimally modified split cobble. Specimen P1387-13-31 is a finely made oval-shaped uniface made from a split cobble. It could be described as a unifacial biface in that care was taken to thoroughly reduce the cortical face of the split cobble in a manner more commonly associated with bifaces. This formal artifact was probably used for some type of scraping function. Specimen P1387-4-34f is a split cobble with minor unidirectional edge modification on one end. At least two specimens resemble notched stones in their morphology and dimensions, but they exhibit no actual notches.

The remainder of the flaked-stone residues reflect the production and use of bifacial tools made from local chert. The assemblage was dominated by projectile points and notched stones (Figure 6.6). The most common projectile point was the contracting stemmed type (n=16) which was used throughout the local sequence and has no value as a time-marker. Small leaf-shaped points were the second most common projectile type. These are thought to have appeared first during the Middle–Late Transition or slightly earlier and may represent a technological shift toward specialized projectile technology (Stevens and Codding

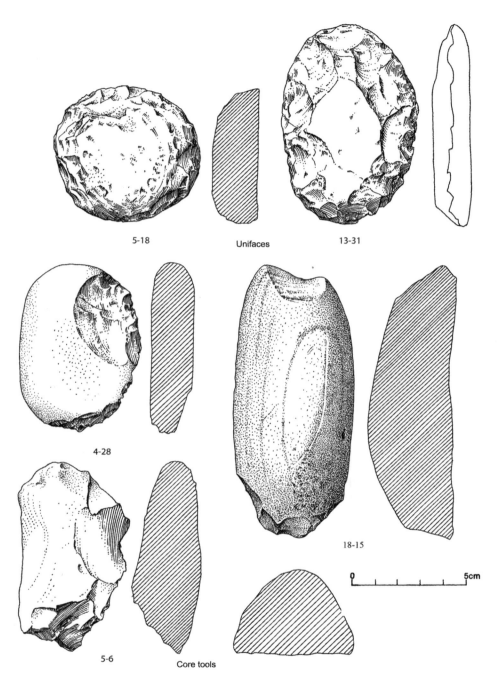

5-18   Unifaces   13-31

4-28

18-15

5-6   Core tools

0   5cm

FIGURE 6.5. Unifaces and core tools from Coon Creek (CA-SLO-9).

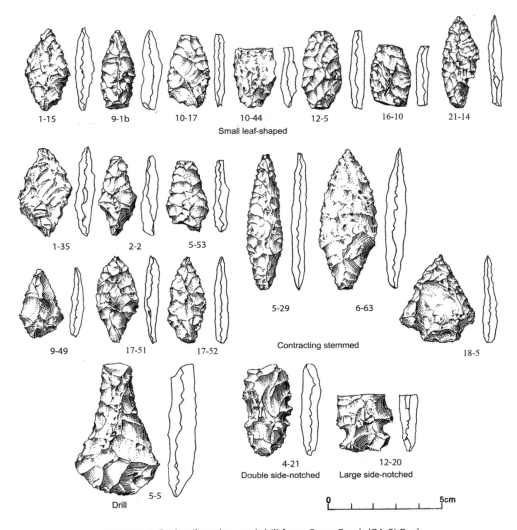

1-15   9-1b   10-17   10-44   12-5   16-10   21-14

Small leaf-shaped

1-35   2-2   5-53

5-29   6-63

Contracting stemmed

9-49   17-51   17-52

18-5

5-5

Drill

4-21
Double side-notched

12-20
Large side-notched

0   5cm

FIGURE 6.6. Projectile points and drill from Coon Creek (CA-SLO-9).

2009), likely the bow and arrow (Codding and Jones 2007). The other two types recovered are represented by single examples: a double–side-notched point and a large side-notched point. The recovery of the former helps to confirm that this type was a marker of the Middle–Late Transition (see Jones and Ferneau 2002), while the latter is thought to mark the early Holocene (as established at Diablo Canyon and Cross Creek), although several were also recovered from a Middle–Late Transition component to the north in Monterey County (CA-MNT-1233; Jones 2003).

The second most abundant flake-stone arti-

facts were notched stones (Figure 6.7). All 20 were made from shale cobbles. Fourteen were bifacial and six were unifacial. Two specimens are distinguished by the presence of asphaltum staining, indicating their use as a composite tool likely tied to cordage. Most were expediently manufactured, minimally modified cobbles but more deliberate, highly formalized versions were also recovered. Chronologically, high frequencies of notched cobbles as opposed to grooved cobbles seem to distinguish the Middle–Late Transition from the Middle Period. The pattern was first noticed in the stratigraphically distinct Middle and Middle–Late components at

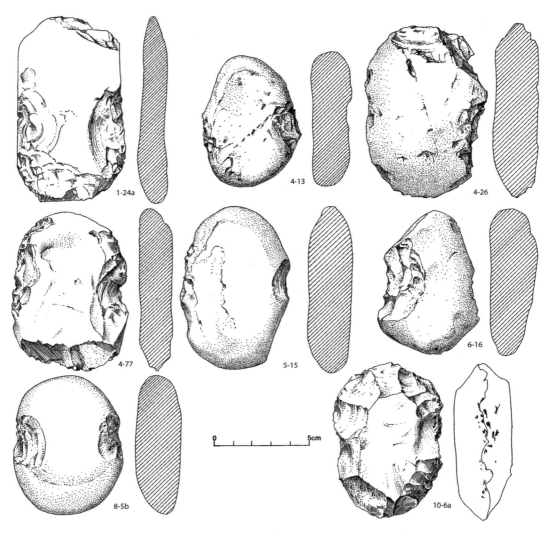

FIGURE 6.7. Notched stones from Coon Creek (CA-SLO-9).

Willow Creek in Monterey County (Pohorecky 1976). Functionally, these artifacts may have been used in conjunction with fishhooks as indicated by their co-occurrence at Coon Creek and the absence of both artifacts from nearby Middle Period sites (e.g., CA-SLO-5, above; CA-SLO-267, Jones and Ferneau 2002). The fishing assemblage also supports this (below, also Codding and Jones 2007).

Other formal flaked-stone tools include two reamers and one drill. Other examples of informal flaked-stone technology include 21 cores, 13 core tools, 11 unifaces, 7 flake tools, and 40 bifaces. Of the bifaces, all five stages were represented, although the production sequence was biased toward early production (17 Stage 1, 16 Stage 2, five Stage 3, five Stage 4, one Stage 5, and three indeterminate). This is supported by a representative sample of flake classes recovered from the site which indicates early manufacture (Table 6.6) and a total flake:biface (9,685:66) ratio of 147:1, an order of magnitude below the expected ratio of 1,659:1 (Jones and Haney 1997) if the full production sequence was represented. The volumetric debitage density was 282.4 flakes/m^3.

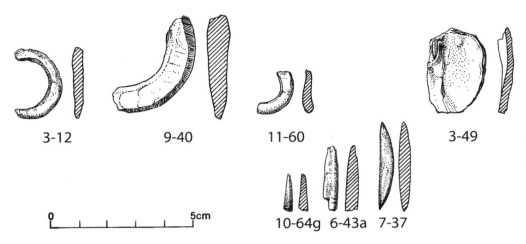

3-12 9-40 11-60 3-49

0 |___|___|___|___|___| 5cm

10-64g 6-43a 7-37

FIGURE 6.8. Shell and bone tools from Coon Creek (CA-SLO-9).

TABLE 6.6. Summary of Debitage sample from Coon Creek (CA-SLO-9, 1000–700 cal BP*).

Flake Class	MNT	FCT	Total	%
Decortication	125	1	126	10.60
Interior Percussion	129	2	131	11.00
Biface thinning	32	1	33	2.80
Pressure	9	0	9	0.80
Percussion fragments	873	16	889	74.80
Total	1,168	20	1,188	100.00

* Early Middle Period materials also mixed in with Middle–Late Transition component.

Ground Stone

Ground-stone technology was limited to 15 battered cobbles, four pitted stones, and one pestle fragment. The former were probably associated with the production of flaked-stone tools. The latter two were likely associated with plant processing. The limited number of ground stone may indicate minimal reliance on plants.

Shell and Bone

Shell artifacts include nine fishhooks, one fishhook blank, and a nearly complete red abalone shell that was coated with asphaltum (Figure 6.8). Five of the hooks were manufactured from mussel shell, the other four from abalone. All represent the "C-shaped" or circular variety. While the single-piece circular shell fishhooks are older in other regions of California (see Rick

et al. 2002), they are not common in Middle Period deposits in San Luis Obispo County (see Jones and Ferneau 2002).

Bone tools include two awls, a bipointed object, and two indeterminate forms. The awls were probably used in the manufacture of baskets or clothing. The bipointed bone may have served a number of purposes ranging from the functional (e.g., fishing equipment) to the ornamental (e.g., nose sticks). It may have been a compound bone fishhook or bone harpoon barb (King 1982) but lacks the definitive distinguishing characteristics to be positively classified as either.

Subsistence Remains

Subsistence remains represent dietary contributions from birds and mammals, fish, and invertebrates.

Mammals, Birds, and Reptiles

The mammal and bird bone assemblage includes 2,755 bones of which 754 could be identified to the family level or more specific (Table 6.7). Unfortunately, 67% of these were burrowing animals that may have been intrusive. Including only those that were not intrusive, 160 bones could be assigned to economically significant taxa (Table 6.8). The economically significant assemblage was dominated by rabbits (*Sylvilagus* sp.; NISP=52; 33%), cormorants (NISP=31; 19.7%), sea otter (NISP=20; 12.5%),

TABLE 6.7. Reptile, Bird and Mammal Remains from Coon Creek (CA-SLO-9).

Taxon	Common Name	NISP	% NISP	Weight (g)	% Weight (g)
Vertebrata	Unidentifiable vertebrate	750	27.00	22.47	3.00
Reptiles					
Lacertilia	Lizard	1	0.04	0.03	0.00
Elgaria multicarinata	Southern alligator lizard	1	0.04	0.03	0.00
Sceloporus sp.	Fence lizard	1	0.04	0.02	0.00
Serpentes	Snake	3	0.10	0.07	0.00
Mammals					
Mammalia	Unidentified mammal	1,139	41.04	284.83	37.80
Rodentia	Unidentified rodent	95	4.00	5.36	0.70
Otospermophilus beecheyi	California ground squirrel	11	0.40	0.70	0.01
Tamias sp.	Chipmunk	1	0.04	0.09	0.01
Dipodomys sp.	Kangaroo rat	1	0.04	0.01	0.01
Perognathus sp.	Pocket mouse	2	0.07	0.03	0.01
Chaetodipus sp.	Pocket mouse	1	0.04	0.02	0.01
Thomomys bottae	Botta's pocket gopher	358	13.00	41.86	6.00
Microtus californicus	California vole	53	2.00	1.89	0.30
Neotoma sp.	Woodrat	13	0.50	1.01	0.10
Onychomys sp.	Grasshopper mouse	1	0.04	0.01	0.01
Onychomys torridus	Southern grasshopper mouse	6	0.20	0.16	0.01
Peromyscus sp.	Deermouse	5	0.20	0.11	0.01
Lepus californicus	Black-tailed jackrabbit	1	0.04	0.20	0.01
Sylvilagus sp.	Rabbit	35	1.00	2.89	0.40
Sylvilagus audubonii	Desert cottontail	14	0.50	2.38	0.30
Sylvilagus bachmani	Brush rabbit	3	0.10	0.61	0.01
Scapanus latimanus	Broad-footed mole	2	0.07	0.31	0.01
Carnivora	Unidentified carnivore	13	0.50	0.07	0.01
Lynx rufus	Bobcat	1	0.04	0.49	0.01
Canis sp.	Dog/Coyote	13	0.50	6.92	0.90
Pinniped	Seal/sea lion	11	0.40	12.40	2.00
Phoca vitulina	Harbor seal	2	0.07	3.19	0.40
Otariidae	Fur seals and sea lions	11	0.40	37.26	5.00
Zalophus californianus	California sea lion	2	0.07	39.44	5.00
Arctocephalinae	Fur seals	3	0.10	5.38	0.70
Callorhinus ursinus	Northern Fur Seal	1	0.04	1.24	0.20
Enhydra lutris	Sea Otter	20	0.70	22.21	3.00
Mephitis mephitis	Striped skunk	1	0.04	0.30	0.01
Procyon lotor	Raccoon	3	0.10	0.41	0.00
Artiodactyla	Artiodactyl	10	0.40	19.43	3.00
Odocoileus hemionus	Mule deer	7	0.30	4.30	0.50
Cetacea	Dolphin/porpoise/whale	1	0.04	0.64	0.01
Bos taurus	Cow	1	0.04	170.46	23.00
Birds					
Aves	Unidentified bird	113	4.00	26.93	4.00
Anatidae	Swans/Ducks/Geese	1	0.04	1.27	0.20
Anser albifrons	White-fronted goose	1	0.04	0.91	0.10
Gavia sp.	Loons	1	0.04	0.33	0.00
Phalacrocorax sp.	Cormorants	31	1.00	19.73	3.00
Phoebastria immutabilis	Laysan albatross	1	0.04	6.35	0.90
Uria aalge	Common murre	6	0.20	1.24	0.20
Fratercula cirrhata	Tufted puffin	1	0.04	0.27	0.00
Ptychoramphus aleuticus	Cassin's auklet	2	0.07	0.37	0.01
Mimus polyglottos	Northern mockingbird	1	0.04	0.07	0.00
Grand Total		2,755	100.00	746.70	100.00

TABLE 6.8. Economically Significant Bird and Mammal Remains from Coon Creek (CA-SLO-9).

Taxon	Common Name	NISP	% NISP	Weight (g)	% Weight (g)
Terrestrial mammals					
Neotoma sp.	Woodrat	13	8.0	1.01	0.9
Lepus californicus	Jack rabbit	1	0.6	0.20	0.2
Sylvilagus sp.	Rabbit	35	22.0	2.89	3.0
Sylvilagus audubonii	Cottontail rabbit	14	9.0	2.38	2.0
Sylvilagus bachmani	Brush rabbit	3	2.0	0.61	0.5
Lynx rufus	Bobcat	1	0.6	0.49	0.4
Canis sp.	Dog/Coyote	13	8.0	6.92	6.0
Mephitis mephitis	Striped skunk	1	0.6	0.30	0.3
Procyon lotor	Raccoon	3	2.0	0.41	0.4
Odocoileus hemionus	Mule deer	7	4.0	4.30	4.0
Subtotal		91	57.0	19.51	17.0
Marine mammals					
Phoca vitulina	California harbor seal	2	1.0	3.19	3.0
Zalophus californianus	California sea lion	2	1.0	39.44	34.0
Callorhinus ursinus	Northern fur seal	1	0.6	1.24	1.0
Enhydra lutris	Sea otter	20	13.0	22.21	19.0
Subtotal		25	16.1	66.08	58.0
Birds					
Anser albifrons	White fronted goose	1	0.6	0.91	0.8
Gavia sp.	Loons	1	0.6	0.33	0.3
Phalacrocorax sp.	Cormorants	31	19.0	19.73	17.0
Phoebastria immutabilis	Laysan albatross	1	0.6	6.35	6.0
Uria aalge	Common murre	6	4.0	1.24	1.0
Fratercula cirrhata	Tufted puffin	1	0.6	0.27	0.2
Ptychoramphus aleuticus	Cassin's auklet	2	1.0	0.37	0.3
Mimus polyglottos	Northern mockingbird	1	0.6	0.07	0.0
Subtotal		44	27.0	29.27	25.0
Grand Total		160	100.0	114.86	100.0

and dog/coyote (NISP=13; 8.1%) (Table 6.8). These same taxa dominate the control sample.

Fish

A total of 2,320 fish elements weighing 41.4 g was recovered including 754 specimens identifiable to the family level or more specific. Of the latter, 34 specimens were recovered from a test unit in which 6 mm (¼ in) mesh was employed, and thus are methodologically incompatible with the rest of the sample. Of the 720 elements recovered from 3 mm mesh (Table 6.9), a total of 515 was from dry-screened units (recovery volume=30.4 m³), while 205 were from the wet-screened control unit and column sample combined (recovery volume=2.164 m³). Both samples were dominated by rockfish; the wet-screened sample yielded a NISP of 66 rockfish (32.1%), while the dry-screened sample showed 246 rockfish elements (47.7%). The controlled wet-screened sample showed a volumetric density of 94.7 identifiable elements per cubic meter. The volumetric density from the dry-screened sample was only 16.9/m³. Following rockfish, the wet-screened sample showed cabezon (NISP=34; 16.6%), followed by señorita

TABLE 6.9. Fish Remains* from Coon Creek (CA-SLO-9, 1000–700 cal BP**).

Taxon	Common Name	3 mm dry-screen		3 mm wet-screen	
		NISP	Weight (g)	NISP	Weight (g)
Elasmobranchiomorphi	Sharks, skates, and rays				
Triakidae	Hound shark	1	0.89	0	0.00
Subtotal		1	0.89	0	0.00
Actinopterygii	Ray-finned fishes				
Clupeidae	Herring	2	0.02	17	0.13
Sardinops sagax	Pacific sardine	3	0.04	3	0.03
Merluccius productus	Pacific hake	2	0.08	0	0.00
Porichthys notatus	Plainfin midshipman	2	0.02	0	0.00
Atherinopsidae	Silverside	6	0.09	18	0.16
Sebastes sp.	Rockfish	246	31.30	66	4.03
Hexagrammos sp.	Kelp greenling	3	0.16	2	0.09
Ophiodon elongatus	Lingcod	1	1.37	0	0.38
Cottidae	Sculpin	0	0.00	1	0.01
Scorpaenichthys marmoratus	Cabezon	166	32.50	34	5.13
Sciaenidae	Drums and croakers	0	0.00	1	0.01
Embiotocidae	Surfperch	26	1.00	18	0.45
Oxyjulis californica	Señorita	25	0.26	27	0.28
Stichaeidae	Prickleback	24	1.72	12	0.43
Cebidichthys violaceus	Monkeyface prickleback	1	0.03	2	0.05
Xiphister sp.	Black prickleback	4	0.36	1	0.04
Clinidae	Kelp blennies	0	0.00	2	0.02
Gibbonsia sp	Crevice kelpfish	3	0.06	0	0.00
Gillichthys mirabilis	Longjaw mudsucker	0	0.00	1	0.01
Subtotal		514	69.01	205	11.25
Grand total		515	69.90	205	11.25

* 3 mm mesh sample only; additional 34 elements recovered with 6 mm mesh.
**Early Middle Period materials also mixed in with Middle–Late Transition component.

(NISP=27; 13.2%). The dry-screened sample had cabezon (NISP=166; 32.2%) and surfperches (NISP=26; 5.0%).

Shellfish

Shellfish remains were identified from two column samples (Units 1 [0–60 cm] and 3 [0–100 cm]) (Table 6.10). In addition, measurements (maximum diameters) were obtained from whole and nearly whole abalone shells collected from units. Combined analytical volume from the two columns was 0.064 m³. Total shell weight from the two columns combined was 2,474.4 g (Table 6.10) so the volumetric density of shell for the component was 38.7 kg/m³. By shell weight, shellfish remains were dominated by mussel (61%), followed by turban snails (15%) and abalone (13%) (Table 6.10).

A total of 319 abalone shells was complete enough to determine length. Of these, 221 were red abalone (*Haliotis rufescens*) and 98 were black abalone (*H. cracherodii*). The mean size of the red abalones was 95 mm while the mean for the black abalones was 85 mm.

Spooner's Ranch House (CA-SLO-10)

Description

The Spooner's Ranch House site is a prehistoric shell midden located on a knoll above the southern bank of Islay Creek and east of Spooner's (Islay) Cove. The site is named after the historic Spooner family ranch house—now the

TABLE 6.10. Shellfish Remains from Column Samples, Coon Creek (CA-SLO-9, 1000–700 cal BP*).

Group	Taxon	Common Name	Shell Wt (g)	%
Abalones	*Haliotis cracherodii*	Black abalone	44.86	2.1
	Haliotis rufescens	Red abalone	119.46	5.5
	Haliotis sp.	Abalone (indeterminate)	115.29	5.3
Mussels	*Mytilus californianus*	California mussel	1,307.47	60.6
	Sepitfer bifurcatus	Platform mussel	1.60	0.1
Clams	*Protothaca Staminea*	Pacific littleneck clam	2.04	0.1
	Protothaca sp.	Clam (indeterminate)	1.46	0.1
Turban snails	*Astraea gibberosa*	Red turban snail	7.86	0.4
	Astraea undosa	Wavy turban snail*	2.51	0.1
	Astraea sp.	Astraea (indeterminate)	34.13	1.6
	Tegula brunnea	Brown turban snail	37.76	1.7
	Tegula funebralis	Black turban snail	112.84	5.2
	Tegula sp.	Turban snail (indeterminate)	131.55	6.1
Limpets	*Collisella asmi*	Black limpet	0.00	0.0
	Collisella limatula	File limpet	0.00	0.0
	Collisella pelta	Shield limpet	1.51	0.1
	Collisella scabra	Rough limpet	0.05	0.0
	Lottia gigantia	Owl limpet	3.53	0.2
	Notoacmea insessa	Seaweed limpet	0.01	0.0
	Notoacmea persona	Mask limpet	11.47	0.0
	Limpet sp.	Limpet (indeterminate)	1.26	0.6
Chiton	*Ischnochiton conspicuus*	Conspicuous chiton*	0.00	0.0
	Ischnochiton heathiana	Heath's chiton	0.0	0.0
	Mospalia muscosa	Mossy chiton	11.87	0.0
	Cryptochiton stelleri	Gumboot chiton	32.04	0.5
	Chiton sp.	Chiton (indeterminate)	0.18	1.5
Misc. snails	*Cerithidea californica*	California horn shell	0.34	0.0
	Crepidula adunca	Hooked slipper shell	0.26	0.0
	Nucella canaliculata	Channeled dogwinkle	72.1	0.0
Barnacles	*Balanus* sp.	Barnacle (indeterminate)	33.81	3.3
	Pollicipes polymerus	Leaf barnacle		1.6
Urchins	*Stongylocentrotus purpuratus*	Purple urchin	21.28	2.3
Crabs	*Cancer antennarius*	Red-spotted rock crab	0.00	0.0
	Cancer sp.	Crab (indeterminate)		1.0
Subtotal			2,158.52	100.0
Unidentified	—	Unidentified	315.9	
Total			2,474.42	

* Early Middle Period materials also mixed in with Middle–Late Transition component.

headquarters of Montaña de Oro State Park—which was built on top of the site. Recent disturbances to the site include grading 15 m east of the ranch house and foundational repairs (immediately west of the current study area) that prompted the earlier investigation of the site by Dallas (1994) described in chapter 3. Historic disturbances associated with the ranch house impacted the site to an unknown degree and historic materials were abundant in the first ten centimeters of the deposit, decreasing in abundance with depth, but present in almost every level. These historic materials were collected but not analyzed for this project. Investigations reported here were undertaken in 2006 by a Cal Poly field class under the direction of Elise Wheeler and Nathan Stevens on behalf of California State Parks. The excavation was undertaken to mitigate disturbance associated with the installation of a new septic tank. A 3×3 m² exposure made up of four 1×2 m and one 1×1 m contiguous test units was excavated in 2006 to between 140 and 150 cm below the surface. A total of 12.9 m³ of the midden was excavated including 4.4 m³ processed dry with 3 mm (⅛ in) mesh, 4.2 m³ water-processed through 3 mm mesh, and 4.3 m³ water-processed through 6 mm (¼ in) mesh. One 20×20 cm column sample also recovered (0.056 m³).

Chronology

Six radiocarbon determinations suggest that the Spooner's site represents two prehistoric occupational periods (Appendix C). One date from the top ten centimeters ranges from 106 to modern and is clearly of recent origin. Four other dates recovered between 50 and 130 cm range from 2674–823 cal BP, and suggest that the bulk of the deposit represents a Middle Period occupation that extends into the Middle–Late Transition Period. The final date obtained from a red abalone sample from the 120–130 cm level returned a date between 7430–7240 cal BP, indicating a Millingstone/Lower Archaic Period occupation in the bottom site levels. As detailed in the discussion of the site's shellfish below, this date was obtained from a cluster of red abalone shells (Figure 6.12, Feature 1).

Four temporally diagnostic beads were recovered from 10–70 cm. These include two complete normal large saucers (G2b) and one incomplete normal saucer (G2), all known from Middle Period contexts. One cupped (K1) bead, known from Middle–Late Transition or Late Period contexts, was also recovered. Two split *Olivella* shells, without perforations, likely represent bead blanks and possible production of beads in the C series. Beads without temporally diagnostic characteristics include ten simple spire-lopped (A1) beads, and 7 limpet beads. All of the beads were from the upper 120 cm of the deposit.

Seventeen of the 23 obsidian specimens recovered from the site were submitted for geochemical and hydration analysis. All of these were recovered from between 0 and 90 cm. Eleven (65%) came from the Casa Diablo (Lookout Mountain) source and returned hydration rims between 2.7 to 4.3, with the majority (N=8) falling between 4.1–4.3, suggesting occupation during the Middle Period. The remaining six were from the Coso Volcanic Field (one from West Sugarloaf subsource), all of which returned hydration rims between 4.1–4.9, also suggesting Middle or possibly Early Period occupation for the site above 120 cm.

Combined, the chronological indicators suggest that the Spooner's Ranch House site is dominated by a Middle Period component that runs through to the Middle–Late Transition Period in the upper 120 cm of the deposit. The site also contains an important Millingstone/Lower Archaic Period component below 120 cm although there is evidence of some vertical mixing. Total recovery volume associated with the Millingstone/Lower Archaic component was 2.5 m³ (1.6 m³ 3 mm wet screen; 0.9 m³ 6 mm wet screen); total from the Middle Period component was 10.4 m³ (4.4 m³ 3 mm dry screen; 2.6 m³ 3 mm wet screen; 3.4 m³ 6 mm wet screen). These totals do not include the column sample.

Technology

Artifacts included flaked-stone materials, ground stone, and artifacts made of bone and shell.

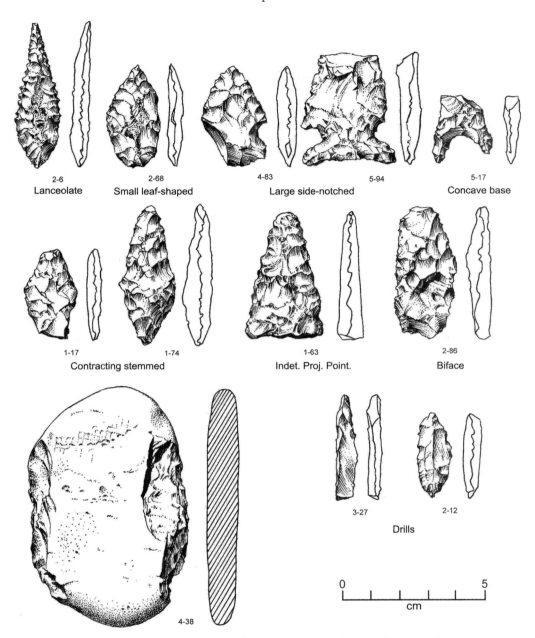

2-6
Lanceolate

2-68
Small leaf-shaped

4-83

5-94
Large side-notched

5-17
Concave base

1-17   1-74
Contracting stemmed

1-63
Indet. Proj. Point.

2-86
Biface

3-27   2-12
Drills

4-38

0   cm   5

FIGURE 6.9. Flaked-stone tools from Spooner's Ranch House (CA-SLO-10).

Flaked Stone

The flaked-stone assemblage consisted of 14 projectile points, 13 bifaces, five cores, three core tools, two drills, two notched stones, and 2,117 pieces of debitage.

Formal artifacts associated with the Millingstone/Lower Archaic Period component were technically limited to a single large side-notched projectile point (Figure 6.9) which is a type commonly associated with Millingstone occupations. However, a second large side-notched point, recovered from the 50–60 cm level, was also assigned on typological grounds to the Millingstone component.

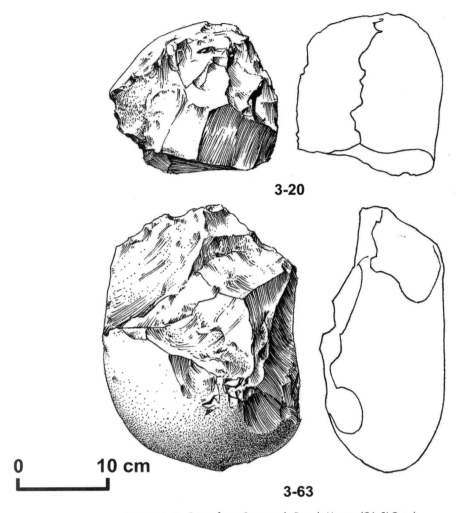

3-20

0   **10 cm**

3-63

FIGURE 6.10. Cores from Spooner's Ranch House (CA-SLO-10).

The majority of the flaked-stone implements was associated with the Middle/Middle–Late Transition occupation. The assemblage included 12 projectile points, 13 bifaces, two drills, and two notched stones. Of the 12 projectile points recovered from the top 120 cm, nine were diagnostic: four contracting-stemmed, two concave base, one large side-notched, one lanceolate, and one small leaf-shaped. The two concave points were made of obsidian while one contracting-stemmed (Specimen 1-8) and one indeterminate point (1-68a) were made of Franciscan chert. The remainder were Monterey chert.

The bifaces include two specimens of Francis-

can chert with the rest made of Monterey. One Franciscan specimen (3-54b) represented stage 3 while the other (1-18) was stage 1. The Monterey chert specimens represent a range of stages: one Stage 1, two Stage 2, three Stage 3, four Stage 4, and one indeterminate.

The cores included four of Monterey chert/ shale and one of Franciscan chert (1-43). Two were bifacial, one was an interior chunk, and two were modified cobbles. The latter two specimens, both Monterey chert, provide clear evidence that non-outcrop sources of stone were exploited by local inhabitants of the Pecho Coast (Figure 6.10). The core tools include one informal edge-modified core of Franciscan chert, one shale/Monterey chert chopper, and one Monterey chert core hammer.

A total of 1,995 pieces of debitage was associated with the Middle/Middle–Late Transition component while 122 pieces were associated with the Millingstone/Lower Archaic component. A sample of 662 pieces of Monterey chert debitage from Unit 3 was selected for analysis. Of these, nine flakes were from the Franciscan Formation and were not analyzed, leaving a net analytical sample of 653. Eliminating the nondiagnostic flake types, the resulting sample consists of 397 pieces of debitage (Table 6.11), the majority of which (385 flakes) represents the upper Middle Period temporal component. This sample shows a slight emphasis on biface reduction which represents 41.8% of the diagnostic debitage (Table 6.12). Of course, decortication of chert cobbles is also represented among the diagnostic flake sample (28.3%) which is consistent with the recovery of cobble cores of the same material.

Ground Stone

Ground stone technology included 10 pitted stones, two pestles, and four battered cobbles. Other ground-stone finds included a drilled steatite pebble fragment along with one complete and two fragmented tarring pebbles. All of these artifacts were associated with the Middle/Middle–Late Transition component.

Bone and Shell Artifacts

A circular piece of worked abalone was also recovered from the Millingstone levels, but it appears to represent a circular shell fishhook blank, a technology that was not known locally until ca. 3000 years BP (Breschini and Haversat 2000; Codding and Jones 2007; also Rick et al. 2002). Its recovery from below 120 cm at CA-SLO-10 can be attributed to downward mixing, and we assign it to the Middle Period component. Other nonstone artifacts included two circular shell fishhook fragments (both mussel), a second shell hook blank, two bone awls, two bone gorges (Figure 6.11), and two indeterminate fragments of worked bone—all ascribed to the Middle Period.

Subsistence Remains

Mammals, Birds, and Reptiles

A total of 1,681 bird, mammal, and reptile bones was recovered from the site as a whole (Table 6.13). Of the 94 mammal and bird bone specimens recovered from the Millingstone/Lower Archaic component, only 19 derived from economically significant fauna identifiable to the genus level or more specific (Table 6.14). These were also dominated by rabbits (63%, n=12) followed by deer (21%, n=4) and sea otters (16%, n=3).

Mammal and bird remains recovered from Middle/Middle–Late Transition component suggest that the occupants of the site relied on a mix of marine and terrestrial mammals similar to that of the earlier inhabitants. Of the 388 specimens belonging to economically significant species identifiable to the genus level or more specific, the assemblage is dominated by cottontail rabbits (42%, n=161), followed by deer (29%, n=112) and sea otter (14%, n=52).

Fish

A total of 5,631 fish bones was recovered. Of these, however, 405 were recovered from the Millingstone/Lower Archaic Period component, of which 103 could be identified to genus or more specific (Table 6.15). The number of identifiable specimens is dominated by rockfish, with the 3 mm wet-screened sample indicating a majority of rockfish (NISP=53; 51.4%), followed by surfperches (NISP=18; 17.4%), and cabezon (NISP=12; 11.7%). The volumetric density of fish bone (excluding specimens only identified as remains of ray-finned fishes) was 64.3 NISP/m^3 for the 3 mm wet-screened Millingstone/Lower Archaic sample.

A total of 5,226 fish bones was associated with the Middle/Middle–Late Transition Period component. Of these, a total of 1,114 could be identified to at least the family level. A total of 362 of these was recovered via 6 mm (¼ in) mesh and thus are not methodologically compatible with the other samples. Examining the 3 mm wet-screened sample of 752 identifiable specimens (combined unit and wet-screened volume of 2.648 m^3), rockfish contribute 43.5%

TABLE 6.11. Diagnostic Monterey Chert Debitage Unit 3, Spooner's Ranch House (CA-SLO-10) by Temporal Component.

Flake Type	Middle Period (2700–800 cal BP)														Millingstone/ Lower Archaic (7400–7200 cal BP)		Grand Total
	0–10	10–20	20–30	30–40	40–50	50–60	60–70	70–80	80–90	90–100	100–110	110–120	Total	%	130–140	%	
Primary decortication	2	3	2	2	2	7	5	6	3	6	4	3	45	11.69	0	0.00	90
Secondary decortication	1	0	2	1	2	4	2	0	3	2	0	1	18	4.68	1	8.33	37
Cortical shatter	5	2	3	1	6	4	6	6	6	1	3	3	46	11.94	1	8.33	93
Subtotal													109	28.31			
Simple interior	9	4	3	3	1	10	9	8	8	7	5	4	71	18.44	3	25.00	145
Complex interior	5	1	3	8	2	3	6	2	3	4	3	4	44	11.43	3	25.00	91
Subtotal													115	29.87			
Early biface thinning	0	1	1	4	2	3	1	1	2	3	1	0	19	4.94	0	0.00	38
Late biface thinning	3	3	5	10	4	15	9	4	6	5	0	2	66	17.14	2	16.67	134
Edge preparation/pressure	1	4	4	6	4	1	5	3	6	10	6	4	54	14.03	1	8.33	109
Pressure	3	0	0	5	4	1	3	1	1	2	2	0	22	5.71	1	8.33	45
Subtotal													161	41.82			
Total	29	18	23	40	27	48	46	31	38	40	24	21	385	100.00	12	100.00	397

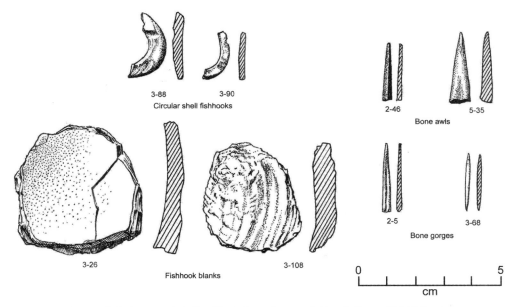

FIGURE 6.11. Bone and shell artifacts from Spooner's Ranch House (CA-SLO-10).

TABLE 6.12. Debitage Summary, Spooner's Ranch House (CA-SLO-10), Middle Period Component (2700–800 cal BP).

Category	Total	%
Decortication	109	28.31
Interior percussion	115	29.87
Biface reduction	161	41.82
Total	385	100.0

TABLE 6.13. Summary of Reptile, Mammal, and Bird Remains from Spooner's Ranch House (CA-SLO-10).

Taxon	Common Name	Middle/MLT			Milling	
		3mm Dry	3mm Wet	6mm Wet	3mm Wet	6mm Wet
Vertebrate	Unidentifiable Vertebate	20	18	10	6	1
Reptiles						
Lacertilia	Lizard	0	1	0	0	0
Elgaria multicarinata	Western alligator lizard	0	3	1	0	0
Serpentes	Snake	4	9	1	1	1
Crotalis sp.	Snake	1	8	10	3	2
Lampropeltis sp.	Kingsnake	0	1	0	0	0
Pituophis sp.	Gopher snake	1	2	2	0	0
Thamnophis sp.	Garter snake	1	3	0	0	0
Mammals						
Mammalia	Unidentified mammal	209	153	183	24	13
Rodentia	Unidentified rodent	22	32	9	6	0
Otospermophilus beecheyi	C. ground squirrel	0	4	6	2	0
Dipodomys sp.	Kangaroo rat	0	2	0	0	0
Reithrodontomys megalotis	Western harvest mouse	1	1	0	0	0
Chaetopidus californicus	California pocket mouse	0	11	0	0	0
Microtus californicus	California vole	10	17	3	2	0

TABLE 6.13. (cont'd.) Summary of Mammal, Reptile and Bird Remains from Spooner's Ranch House (CA-SLO-10).

Taxon	Common Name	Middle/MLT			Milling	
		3mm Dry	3mm Wet	6mm Wet	3mm Wet	6mm Wet
Thomomys bottae	Botta's pocket gopher	66	81	58	5	3
Neotoma sp.	Woodrat	5	1	1	0	0
Onychomys sp.	Grasshopper mouse	0	2	0	0	0
Peromyscus sp.	Deermouse	2	1	0	0	0
Scapanus latimanus	Broad-footed mole	0	1	1	0	0
Leporidae	Hare	2	3	2	0	0
Lepus californicus	Jackrabbit	2	6	2	0	0
Sylvilagus sp.	Rabbit	52	75	34	9	3
Felis catus	Cat	1	0	0	0	0
Canis sp.	Dog/Coyote	5	2	3	0	0
Pinniped	Seal/sea lion	5	1	0	0	0
Otariidae	Eared seal	3	1	3	0	0
Phoca vitulina	Harbor seal	0	1	2	0	0
Zalophus californianus	California sea lion	2	0	0	0	0
Eumetopias jubatus	Steller sea lion	0	0	1	0	0
Arctocephalinae	Fur seal	0	0	1	0	0
Callorhinus ursinus	Northern fur seal	0	2	0	0	0
Enhydra lutris	Sea otter	16	24	12	2	1
Taxidea taxus	American badger	2	1	1	0	0
Mephitis mephitis	Skunk	1	1	0	0	0
Procyon lotor	Raccoon	0	0	1	0	0
Artiodactyla	Even-toed ungulate	29	12	21	1	2
Cervidae	Deer family	0	0	1	0	0
Odocoileus hemionus	Mule deer	42	29	41	0	4
Ovis Aries	Sheep	0	0	1	0	0
Cetacean	Dolphin/porpoise/whale	0	0	2	0	0
Delphinidae	Dolphin	1	0	0	0	0
Bovid	Cow	5	1	2	0	0
Sus scrofa	Wild boar	3	0	1	0	0
Birds						
Aves	Unidentified bird	48	28	34	2	1
Anas sp.	Anserforms	2	0	2	0	0
Anas acuta	Northern pintail	1	0	0	0	0
Melanitta sp.	Scoter	0	1	0	0	0
Phasianidae sp.	Pheasant family	1	0	0	0	0
Callipepla californica	California quail	2	1	0	0	0
Domesticated	Chicken	7	0	1	0	0
Phalacrocorax	Cormorants	9	1	1	0	0
Uria aalgae	Common murre	4	0	0	0	0
Puffinus griseus	Puffin	1	0	0	0	0
Laridae	Gull	1	0	0	0	0
Aphelocoma californica	Scrub jay	0	0	1	0	0
Tyto alba	Barn owl	1	1	0	0	0
Grand Total		590	542	455	63	31

TABLE 6.14. Economically Significant Mammal and Bird Remains from CA-SLO-10, by Component.

Taxon	Common Name	Middle/MLT				Millingstone			
		NISP	%NISP	Weight	%Weight	NISP	%NISP	Weight	%Weight
Terrestrial mammals									
Lepus californicus	Jackrabbit	10	2.6	4.02	0.5	0	0.0	0	0.0
Sylvilagus sp.	Cottontail rabbit	161	41.5	24.58	2.8	12	63.2	1.17	5.7
Canis sp.	Dog/Coyote	10	2.6	12.61	1.4	0	0.0	0	0.0
Mephitis mephitis	Skunk	2	0.5	0.23	0.0	0	0.0	0	0.0
Procyon lotor	Raccoon	1	0.3	0.07	0.0	0	0.0	0	0.0
Taxidea taxus	American badger	4	1.0	7.45	0.8	0	0.0	0	0.0
Odocoileus hemionus	Mule deer	112	28.9	557.95	63.5	4	21.1	6.84	33.4
Subtotal		300	77.4	606.91	69	16	84.3	8.01	39.1
Marine mammals									
Phoca vitulina	Harbor seal	3	0.8	13.85	1.6	0	0.0	0	0.0
Zalophus californianus	California sea lion	2	0.5	4.54	0.5	0	0.0	0	0.0
Eumetopias jubatus	Steller sea lion	1	0.3	101.07	11.5	0	0.0	0	0.0
Callorhinus ursinus	Northern fur seal	2	0.5	2.08	0.2	0	0.0	0	0.0
Enhydra lutris	Sea otter	52	13.4	137.24	15.6	3	15.8	12.46	60.9
Subtotal		60	15.5	258.78	29.4	3	15.8	12.46	60.9
Birds									
Anas sp.	Ducks	4	1.0	0.95	0.1	0	0.0	0	0.0
Anas acuta	Northern pintail	1	0.3	0.29	0.0	0	0.0	0	0.0
Melanitta sp.	Scoter	1	0.3	0.95	0.1	0	0.0	0	0.0
Callipepla californica	California quail	3	0.8	0.09	0.0	0	0.0	0	0.0
Phalacrocorax sp.	Cormorants	11	2.8	9.18	1.0	0	0.0	0	0.0
Uria aalgae	Common murre	4	1.0	0.72	0.1	0	0.0	0	0.0
Puffinus griseus	Puffin	1	0.3	0.46	0.1	0	0.0	0	0.0
Aphelocoma californica	Scrub jay	1	0.3	0.08	0.0	0	0.0	0	0.0
Tyto alba	Barn owl	2	0.5	0.21	0.0	0	0.0	0	0.0
Subtotal		28	7.3	12.93	1.4	0	0.0	0	0.0
Total		388	100.0	878.62	100.0	19	100.0	20.47	100.0

TABLE 6.15. Summary of Fish Remains from the Spooner's Ranch House Site (CA-SLO-10).

| Taxon | Common Name | Middle (2700–800 cal BP) | | | | | |
| | | 3mm Dry | | | 3mm Wet | | |
		NISP	Wt	%NISP	NISP	Wt	%NISP
Elasmobranchiomorphi	Sharks, skates, and rays						
Charcharhinidae	Requiem shark	2	1.03	0.46	2	0.12	0.30
Triakis semifasciata	Leopard shark	5	0.99	1.15	7	1.17	1.05
Rajiidae	skates and rays	0	0	0.00	1	0.05	0.15
Rhinobatos productus	Shovelnosed guitarfish	13	1.52	3.00	13	2.43	1.95
Myliobatos californica	California bat ray	9	1.15	2.07	25	1.16	3.75
Subtotal		29	4.69	6.68	48	4.93	7.21
Actinopterygii	Ray-finned fish						
Clupeidae	Herrings and sardines	7	0.06	1.61	3	0.03	0.45
Sardinops sagax	Pacific sardine	0	0	0.00	0	0	0.00
Merluccius productus	Pacific hake	4	0.19	0.92	8	0.4	1.20
Porichthys sp.	Plainfin midshipman	0	0	0.00	3	0.03	0.45
Atherinopsidae	New World silversides	0	0	0.00	3	0.05	0.45
Sebastes sp.	Rockfish	213	32.3	49.08	319	34.08	47.90
Hexagrammidae	Greenling	4	0.26	0.92	5	0.53	0.75
Hexagrammos sp.	Greenling	30	1.48	6.91	41	1.78	6.16
Hexagrammos decagrammos	Kelp greenling	0	0	0.00	0	0	0.00
Ophiodon elongatus	Lingcod	3	0.81	0.69	3	0.4	0.45
Scorpaenicthys marmoratus	Cabezon	53	13.2	12.21	107	15.18	16.07
Paralabrax sp.	Kelp bass	0	0	0.00	3	0.06	0.45
Trachurus symmetricus	Jack mackerel	3	0.01	0.69	0	0	0.00
Embiotocidae	Surfperch	59	3.46	13.59	62	3.62	9.31
Rhacochilus vacca	Pile perch	2	0.09	0.46	4	0.2	0.60
Pomacentridae	Damselfish	0	0	0.00	0	0	0.00
Semicossyphus pulcher	California sheephead	0	0	0.00	1	0.03	0.15
Oxyjulis californica	Señorita	2	0.02	0.46	5	0.03	0.75
Clinidae	Kelpfish	3	0.13	0.69	5	0.09	0.75
Gobiidae	Gobies	1	0.01	0.23	0	0	0.00
Scomber japonicus	Chub mackerel	1	0.02	0.23	0	0	0.00
Stichaeidae	Prickleback	48	3.73	11.06	83	4.94	12.46
Cebidichthys violaceus	Monkeyface prickleback	0	0	0.00	0	0	0.00
Xiphister sp.	Rock prickleback	1	0.3	0.23	11	0.73	1.65
Subtotal		434	56.07	100.00	666	62.18	100.00
Total		463	60.76		714	67.11	

TABLE 6.15. (cont'd.) Summary of Fish Remains from the Spooner's Ranch House Site (CA-SLO-10).

| Middle (2700–800 cal BP) | | | Millingstone/Lower Archaic (7400–7200 cal BP) | | | | | | | | |
| 6mm Wet | | | 3mm CS | | | 3mm Wet | | | 6mm Wet | | |
NISP	Wt	%NISP	NISP	Wt	%NISP	NISP	Wt	%NISP	NISP	Wt	%NISP
						1					
10	2.18	2.92	0	0	0.00	1	0.02	1.00	0	0	0.00
2	0.75	0.58	0	0	0.00	2	0.8	2.00	0	0	0.00
0	0	0.00	0	0	0.00	0	0	0.00	0	0	0.00
7	1.07	2.05	0	0	0.00	0	0	0.00	0	0	0.00
1	0.26	0.29	0	0	0.00	0	0	0.00	1	0.03	2.44
20	4.26	5.85	0	0	0.00	3	0.82	3.00	2	0.03	4.88
0	0	0.00	2	0.02	5.26	0	0	0.00	1	0.01	2.44
0	0	0.00	1	0.01	2.63	0	0	0.00	0	0	0.00
4	0.25	1.17	1	0.01	2.63	2	0.16	2.00	0	0	0.00
0	0	0.00	0	0	0.00	0	0	0.00	0	0	0.00
0	0	0.00	5	0.04	13.16	0	0	0.00	1	0.01	2.44
184	26.92	53.80	8	0.56	21.05	53	5.22	53.00	21	2.7	51.22
1	0.07	0.29	0	0	0.00	0	0	0.00	0	0	0.00
7	0.8	2.05	1	0.01	2.63	4	0.35	4.00	2	0.09	4.88
0	0	0.00	0	0	0.00	2	0.1	2.00	0	0	0.00
4	0.98	1.17	0	0	0.00	1	0.2	1.00	0	0	0.00
94	20.08	27.49	2	0.19	5.26	12	1.58	12.00	10	1.93	24.39
0	0	0.00	0	0	0.00	1	0.02	1.00	0	0	0.00
0	0	0.00	0	0	0.00	0	0	0.00	0	0	0.00
28	2.71	8.19	12	0.32	31.58	18	1.05	18.00	4	0.39	9.76
0	0	0.00	1	0.01	2.63	0	0	0.00	0	0	0.00
0	0	0.00	2	0.01	5.26	0	0	0.00	0	0	0.00
0	0	0.00	0	0	0.00	0	0	0.00	0	0	0.00
0	0	0.00	0	0	0.00	0	0	0.00	0	0	0.00
0	0	0.00	0	0	0.00	1	0.01	1.00	0	0	0.00
0	0	0.00	0	0	0.00	0	0	0.00	0	0	0.00
0	0	0.00	0	0	0.00	0	0	0.00	0	0	0.00
20	2.08	5.85	1	0.04	2.63	6	0.29	6.00	2	0.09	4.88
0	0	0.00	1	0.01	2.63	0	0	0.00	0	0	0.00
0	0	0.00	1	0.05	2.63	0	0	0.00	0	0	0.00
342	53.89	100.00	38	1.28	100.00	100	8.98	100.00	41	5.22	100.00
362	58.15		38	1.28		103	9.8		43	5.25	

TABLE 6.16. Shellfish Remains from the Spooner's Ranch House Site (CA-SLO-10).

Group	Genus/species	Common Name	Middle (2700–800 cal BP)		Millingstone/Lower Archaic (7400–7200 cal BP)		Millingstone Feature (7400–7200 cal BP)	
			Weight	%	Weight	%	Weight	%
Abalones	*Haliotis cracherodii*	Black abalone	0.00	0.00	0.00	0.00	—	—
	Haliotis rufescens	Red abalone	0.50	0.01	0.00	0.00	1,548.1	-93.57
	Haliotis sp.	Abalone (indeterminate)	47.05	0.89	0.00	0.00	—	—
Mussels	*Mytilus californianus*	California mussel	4,534.86	86.15	9.08	65.75	34	2.06
Turban snails	*Tegula* sp.	Turban snail (indeterminate)	251.81	4.78	4.03	29.18	47.7	2.88
	Pomaulax gibberosus	Red Turban	1.17	0.02	0.00	0.00	—	—
	Megastraea undosa	Wavy Turban	0.10	0.00	0.00	0.00	—	—
Limpets	*Lottia* sp.	Limpet (indeterminate)	3.18	0.06	0.01	0.07	0.3	0.02
	Lottia gigantia	Owl limpet	3.20	0.06	0.00	0.00	—	—
Chiton	*Cryptochiton stelleri*	Giant Gumboot Chiton	7.32	0.14	0.00	0.00	8.1	0.49
	Chiton sp.	Chiton (indeterminate)	18.38	0.35	0.00	0.00	—	—
Misc. snails	*Crepidula adunca*	Hooked slipper snail	0.54	0.01	0.00	0.00	0	0
	Littorina sitkana	Winkle	1.70	0.03	0.00	0.00	—	—
Olivella	*Callinanax biplicata*	Purple Olive	0.10	0.00	0.00	0.00	0	0
Oyester	*Ostera lurida*	Olympia Oyster	2.54	0.05	0.00	0.00	0	0
Barnacles	*Balanus* sp.	Barnacle (indeterminate)	167.51	3.18	0.06	0.43	0	0
	Pollicipes polymerus	Gooseneck barnacle	15.63	0.30	0.00	0.00	—	—
Urchins	*Stongylocentrotus purpuratus*	Purple urchin	107.62	2.04	0.38	2.75	16.2	0.98
Crabs	*Cancer* sp.	Crab (indeterminate)	4.03	0.08	0.00	0.00	0	0
Clams	*Saxidomus nuttalli*	California butter clam	0.70	0.01	0.00	0.00	0	0
	Leukoma staminea	Pacific littleneck clam	16.40	0.31	0.00	0.00	—	—
	Tidacna croea	Borning clam	0.32	0.01	0.00	0.00	—	—
	Tivela stultorum	Pismo clam	2.27	0.04	0.00	0.00	—	—
	Macoma sp.	Clam (indeterminate)	4.04	0.08	0.00	0.00	—	—
Subtotal								
Unidentified			72.61	1.38	0.25	1.81	—	—
Grand total			5,263.89	100.00	13.81	100.00	1,654.4	100.00

(n=319), followed by cabezon (14.5%, n=107), and pricklebacks (11.2%, n=83). The volumetric density of fish is 283.9 NISP/m³; for the 3 mm wet-screened sample.

Shellfish

Shellfish remains were identified from a single 20 × 20 cm column excavated from 0 to 140 cm (total recovery volume=0.056 m³) and wet-screened through 3 mm mesh (Table 6.16). Measurements (maximum diameters) were also obtained from all whole and nearly whole abalone shells collected from units. Measurements for the Millingstone/Lower Archaic component were also obtained from a concentration of large red abalone shells that made up a feature (Figure 6.12, Feature 1) uncovered between 133 and 140 cm below the surface.

Recovery volume for the Millingstone/Lower Archaic component of the column sample was 0.008 m³. Only 13.8 g of shell was recovered from these levels for a volumetric density of 1.6 kg/m³. The sample was dominated by California sea mussels (66% of shell weight), followed by turban snail (29%).

The Middle/Middle–Late Transition Period component yielded 5,263.9 g of shell for a volumetric density of 109.6 kg/m³. Mussel shell fragments dominate the assemblage by shell weight (86.1%). Abalone shell diameters estimates suggest foragers exploited an average size between 80–100 mm (mode from 100–120) for red abalone and between 60–80 mm (mode from 40–60) for black abalone.

The only feature identified from the 2006 excavation (Feature 1) consisted of a cluster of red abalone shells 15–25 cm thick covering an area of approximately 60 × 50 cm in the southeast corner of Unit 4 between 120 and 140 cm (Figure 6.12). The Millingstone/Lower Archaic Period radiocarbon date came from one of the red abalone shells in this feature. The feature continued into the sidewall of the unit. Shells were all red abalone, fairly large, and extremely fragile. A total of 14 was estimated to be present within the portion of the concentration that was exposed, piled two deep. The specimens were too deteriorated to be removed intact; field sketches were

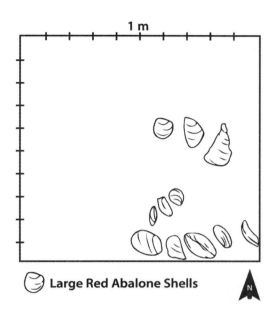

1 m

🦪 **Large Red Abalone Shells** N

FIGURE 6.12. Feature 1, Unit 4, Spooner's Ranch House.

drawn to estimate sizes. These data indicate that the average shell size in the feature was between 125 and 145 mm in diameter with modes at 100–120 and 180–200 (n=14). A bulk soil sample was also pulled from the abalone feature. The results show that it is dominated by abalone (94%).

Pecho (CA-SLO-51/H)
Description

The Pecho Site (CA-SLO-51/H) is located on the west bank of Pecho Creek ca. 400 m inland from its mouth on PG&E's Diablo Canyon South Ranch (Figure 6.13). The site was first recorded in 1948 by Arnold Pilling who described it as an "occupation site" with a two-story adobe on it (Pilling 1948). Following acquisition of the site area by PG&E, the deposit was recorded by archaeologists from U. C.–Santa Barbara in 1978 who described it as a very large (200 × 200 m), dense shell midden. This description is consistent with other recent characterizations that define the site as ca. 300 m × 200 m including historic remains of the adobe (Texier and Denardo 2007). The site was investigated by Greenwood in 1968 who excavated 38 m³ and found it to extend to a depth of ca. 1 m (see discussion

FIGURE 6.13. Pecho site area (CA-SLO-51/H). © 2002–2017 Kenneth & Gabrielle Adelman, California Coastal Records Project, www.californiacoastline.org.

chapter 3). Greenwood was unable to obtain any radiocarbon determinations for CA-SLO-51/H, but she felt that it contained materials representing all three of her local prehistoric cultures: Millingstone, Hunting, and Chumash. Among the items recovered by Greenwood were a single glass bead and a sherd of plain brown ceramic. She also noted the ethnographic northern Chumash name for Rancho del Pecho, *Tstyiwi*, but stopped short of associating the name with the archaeological deposit. The materials recovered by the Cal Poly field class in 2015 show unequivocally that the site represents the village of *Tstyiwi*. The primary documentation on the findings from this site are presented in Jones, Codding, Cook, and colleagues (2017).

The site was investigated by a Cal Poly field class in the spring of 2015 during which six units were opened. Five of these were 1 × 2 m in dimension and were dry-screened with 3 mm (⅛ in) mesh by students in the field. One 1 × 1 m unit was wet screened with residues brought to the Cal Poly Archaeology Laboratory for water

processing and sorting by laboratory students. In addition, one 20 × 20 cm column sample was recovered from the sidewall of Unit 6. The units were placed in two different areas. Units 1–4 were positioned along the eastern site boundary on the edge of the plowed field, just above Pecho Creek. Evidence for plowing-related disturbances in these units was extensive. Units 5 and 6 were located near the northern edge of the midden deposit, southwest of a corrugated metal barn. Importantly, these units were on the northern side of a fence that marks the limits of the agricultural field and they appeared to be less affected by plowing and other historic disturbances. For example, mussel and other shells were considerably less fragmented in the area of Units 5 and 6. None of the units were excavated to sterile, but instead they all were terminated at a maximum depth of 50 cm. This was partially due to the high clay content in the soil which slowed excavation, and to the fact that Greenwood (1972) reported a human burial at 60 cm from her excavation in 1968. Auger borings in

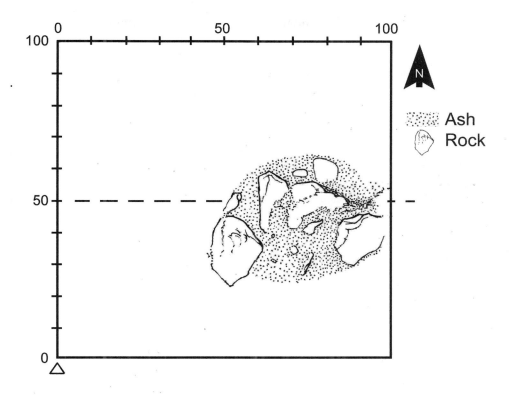

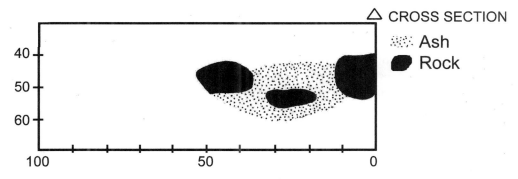

Figure 6.14. Feature 1, Unit 6, Pecho site (CA-SLO-51/H.)

Units 1 and 5 showed that the deposit extended to a maximum depth of ca. 1 m (consistent with Greenwood's findings). The total recovery from the investigation was 5.22 m³, including 4.8 m³ from the five 1 × 2 m dry-screened test excavation units, 0.5 m³ from the wet-screened control unit, and 0.02 m³ from the column sample.

In general, the deposit was extremely homogeneous, owing, in part, to the effects of plowing. No meaningful stratigraphic distinctions were recognized; soils from all units were consistently described as 10YR 2/1 black midden with a high clay content. However, a discrete feature was encountered in Unit 6 between depths of 40 and 60 cm. The feature consisted of a cluster of large (10–20 cm in length) rocks on top of a dense concentration of ash and charcoal (Figure 6.14). Flotation samples were collected and processed from the feature. Results are described in Appendix B.

Chronology

Radiocarbon

Nine radiocarbon determinations were obtained from single-shell samples selected from a range of vertical proveniences in Units 1 and 5. One sample was obtained from a mussel shell from the base of the midden that was recovered via auger. Eight of the nine calibrated radiocarbon determinations show one-sigma midpoints between 1900 and 60 cal BP. One sample from the 20–30 cm level of Unit 5 was of very recent historic age. The oldest date (one-sigma range 2000–1900 cal BP) was returned from the auger mussel shell from a depth of 90–100 cm (Unit 1) which indicates that materials marking the early Middle Period are present in the deposit below the depths reached in the 10 cm levels (50 cm) excavated in 2015. All of the other dates are considerably younger with a combined one-sigma range of 650–0 cal BP and a two-sigma range of 670–0 cal BP. The minimal one-sigma range is 550–130 cal BP, and the two-sigma minimum is 330–130 cal BP. Overall, the dates indicate occupation during the Late Prehistoric Period and early postcontact times.

The radiocarbon determinations also suggest some horizontal separation of temporal residues. Four dates from Unit 5, which was located off of the agricultural field, show one-sigma midpoints between 270 and 0 cal BP. The one-sigma range of these dates is 300–0 cal BP. The two-sigma range is 380–0 cal BP. These dates suggest strongly that the midden materials recovered from Unit 5 and adjacent Unit 6 primarily represent postcontact (post-240 cal BP) occupation between approximately 250 and 120 cal BP, although it should be noted that radiocarbon dates from recent time are not highly precise. Two of the dates from Unit 5, however, show two-sigma ranges that do not extend into precontact time, indicating with 98% probability that they represent postcontact occupation. The dates from Unit 5 do not in general exhibit superposition, however, as one of the youngest dates was recovered from 30–40 cm, and the second-oldest was from 10–20 cm. This is consistent with other evidence for some vertical mixing within the deposit.

The dates from Units 1–4 are generally older than those obtained from Unit 5. Excluding the Middle Period date obtained via auger noted above, the four remaining dates from Units 1 and 4 show a one-sigma maximal range of 650–80 cal BP with a minimal range of 550–250 cal BP. The one-sigma midpoints range from 600 to 170 cal BP. The two-sigma maximal range is 670–0 cal BP and the minimal range is 520–170 cal BP. The two-sigma midpoints range from 600 to 140 cal BP. Three samples from Units 1 and 4 exhibit two-sigma ranges that do not extend into postcontact time, ranging between 670 and 280 cal BP. Only one of the four samples from this area of the site produced a two-sigma range that was predominately within the postcontact era (280–0 cal BP). In summary, three of the four dates obtained from Units 1 and 4 represent the Late Prehistoric Period (700–180 cal BP) while one represents postcontact (after AD 1769). While some mixing is apparent, the radiocarbon determinations suggest that Units 1–4 primarily represent the Late Prehistoric ca. 600–250 cal BP, while Units 5 and 6 are predominately postcontact. Midden soils below the depth reached in 2015 (50 cm) date to the early Middle Period. Dating results do not exhibit strict superposition in any site area, however, and it is likely that some materials dating to the Middle Period have mixed upward and are incorporated into the Late Prehistoric residues in Units 1–4. Further, while Units 1–4 are dominated by prehistoric materials, dating results also indicate some admixture with postcontact materials.

Obsidian Hydration

Seven pieces of obsidian were recovered—all from Units 1, 2, 3, and 4 (Appendix D). Five of the specimens originated from the Coso source, and two were from Casa Diablo. Hydration readings range between 2.4 and 4.5 microns for the Coso specimens and 2.8 and 4.4 for Casa Diablo.

Beads

A total of 275 beads was recovered from the excavation of Units 1–6 (Appendix E). The beads represent 23 major types of shell, stone, and glass. Sixteen types of *Olivella* shell beads were represented (n=205), along with five clam shell disks, ten limpet rings, four *Dentalium* fragments, nine abalone epidermis beads, one abalone nacreous disk, 11 steatite disks, one globular steatite bead, and nine glass beads. Based on the radiocarbon results which suggest some horizontal temporal variation in the deposit, beads were aggregated into two groups: those from Units 1–4, and those from Units 5 and 6 (Table 6.17).

Forty-two beads represent types that have no clear temporal significance: the A1 spire-lopped (n=17), A4 punched spire-lopped (n=4), B3 barrel (n=1), clam disks (n=5), limpet rings (n=10), *Dentalium* (n=4), and globular steatite (n=1). A total of 51 G1 tiny saucers is consistent with the Middle, Middle–Late Transition, and Late periods, but provides no additional insight into component chronology.

The overall dating suggested by the rest of the beads (n=162) is highly compatible with the radiocarbon results. A total of five beads (two G2, one G3, one C2, one nacreous disk) is consistent with occupation during the Middle Period. The low frequency of these beads further suggests that they are intrusive into the upper levels of the deposit from the lower levels (beneath 50 cm) where the Middle Period radiocarbon date originated.

The remaining 157 beads represent types that are Late Period and postcontact markers. These indicate that the majority of residues excavated in 2015 represent the Late and early Historic (ca. AD 1769–early 1800s) periods. With varying degrees of reliability, the 17 subtypes represented in this sample are also commonly assigned to more restricted intervals within that overall period. Most important in this regard are nine glass trade beads (discussed in more detail in Appendix A). The glass beads represent four types in the Kidd and Kidd (1970) typology. Two examples from the Unit 5–6 site area represent type DIIa7 which is generally Mission Period (AD 1769–1821). One example of type DIIa24 from the same site area is thought to predate AD 1800. Two examples of type DIIa35, also from the Unit 5–6 area, represent beads that seem to have arrived in southern California between AD 1800 and 1830. Finally, four examples of type DIIa45 were recovered, two from the area

TABLE 6.17. Beads from Pecho (CA-SLO-51/H).

Type	Units 1–4	Units 5, 6	Total
Olivella			
A1	9	8	17
A4	2	2	4
A5	0	1	1
B3	0	1	1
C2	0	1	1
E1	5	8	13
E2	0	10	10
E3	0	3	3
G1	8	43	51
G2	0	2	2
G3	0	1	1
H1*	2	4	6
H2*	0	1	1
K1	18	23	41
K2	7	32	39
K3	3	10	13
K3i	0	1	1
Subtotal	54	151	205
Other			
Clam disk	4	1	5
Limpet ring	6	4	10
Dentalium	1	3	4
Abalone epidermis	0	9	9
Abalone nacreous	1	0	1
Steatite disk	2	9	11
Steatite globular	1	0	1
Glass	2	7	9
Subtotal	18	39	57
Grand total	71	184	275

of Units 1–4 and two from Unit 6. These represent the period between the 1810s and 1820s. The trade beads are one of several postcontact markers that were recovered in greater numbers from Units 5 and 6; the others include abalone epidermis disks (n=9), E3 *Olivella* (n=3), and H *Olivella* (five from Units 5 and 6; 2 from Units 1–4). Overall, Units 5 and 6 produced 24 postcontact beads representing 20.3% of the bead assemblage from that area, while Units 1–4 yielded only four postcontact beads (10.2%). In this regard the beads support the radiocarbon results which suggest that while both site areas were occupied during

TABLE 6.18. Late-Contact Period Beads from Pecho (CA-SLO-51/H).

Type	Units 1–4	%	Units 5, 6	%	Total
Late Period (700–180 cal BP)					
A5	0	0.00	1	0.85	1
Steatite disk	2	5.12	9	7.62	11
E1	5	12.82	8	6.78	13
Subtotal	7	17.94	18	15.25	25
Late Period Phase 2-Contact (450–180 cal BP)					
E2	0	0.00	10	8.47	10
K1	18	46.15	23	19.49	41
K2	7	17.94	32	27.11	39
K3	3	7.69	10	8.47	13
K3i	0	0.00	1	0.85	1
Subtotal	28	71.78	76	64.39	104
Postcontact (Post 180 cal BP)					
Abalone epidermis	0	0.00	9	7.62	9
E3	0	0.00	3	2.54	3
H1*	2	5.12	4	3.39	6
H2*	0	0.00	1	0.85	1
Glass DIIa7	0	0.00	2	1.69	2
Glass DIIa24	0	0.00	1	0.85	1
Glass DIIa35	0	0.00	2	1.69	2
Glass DIIa45	2	5.12	2	1.69	4
Subtotal	4	10.24	24	20.32	28
Grand total	39	99.96	118	99.96	157

the Late and Historic periods, more of the residues from Units 5 and 6 represent the postcontact era, while most of the material from Units 1–4 is precontact. These results suggest that Units 1–4 can be considered a precontact (Late Period) component while Units 5 and 6 together can be considered primarily postcontact.

In addition to the beads the excavation yielded 12 unmodified whole *Olivella* shells (six per component), and 10 broken *Olivella* shells and/or fragments of shells that resemble bead-making detritus (six from the Late Period [precontact] component and four from postcontact context). These items provide a suggestion that there was some low-level production of beads at the site. More compelling in this regard were three bead blanks that were incompletely drilled (Figure 6.15). These include two abalone epider-

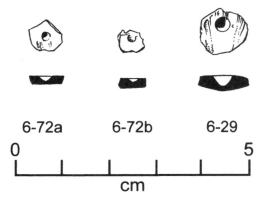

6-72a   6-72b   6-29

0   5

cm

FIGURE 6.15. Incomplete shell bead blanks from Pecho (CA-SLO-51/H).

mis disk bead blanks (specimens 76-72a and 76-72b) recovered from Unit 6 and a mussel-shell disk also from Unit 6 (specimens 6–29). The latter are associated with the Middle–Late Transition, Late, and postcontact periods. Abalone epidermis disk beads, however, are generally considered postcontact artifacts which is consistent with their recovery from Unit 6. They suggest some minor production of this bead type onsite during the Mission era.

Technology

The excavation produced flaked-stone, ground-stone, bone, and shell implements.

Flaked Stone

A total of 7,579 flaked-stone specimens was recovered including 33 cores, 2 core tools, 17 bifaces, 19 projectile points, 30 flake tools, 5 drills, and 7,473 pieces of debitage.

Twenty-three of the cores were recovered from the precontact component while ten were recovered from Units 5 and 6 (postcontact). The cores were predominately Monterey chert (n=28), with two Franciscan chert specimens, two basalt, and one glossy red indeterminate rock. The most common morphology was cobbles (n=16), followed by interior chunks (n=14), and cortical chunks (n=3). Twelve of the Monterey chert specimens were a dark gray color and nonvitreous, and seem to represent a locally occurring variant of this stone. The high frequency of rounded cobbles suggests that chert nodules were frequently collected from creeks along the Pecho Coast (many of which drain through chert-bearing geologic formations). Both core tools are relatively informal Monterey chert specimens made from cobbles that show battering and or use wear on one edge. Both were recovered from the precontact component.

The 17 bifaces are all fragments. Nine are ends, four are margin fragments, three are midsections, and one specimen (3-76) was nearly complete (Figure 6.16). Fourteen are Monterey chert, two are Franciscan chert, and one is basalt. Thirteen were recovered from the Late Period (precontact) component and the remaining four

were from postcontact context. The bifaces show an even distribution of stages: three Stage 1, three Stage 2, two Stage 3, four Stage 4, and five indeterminate.

The three drills were subjected to edge-wear analysis by Nathan Stevens at California State University–Sacramento to determine if they exhibited microscopic wear consistent with drill use. The three specimens (3-56, 6-227, CS6-27) indeed exhibited use-wear consistent with use as drills. Use-wear observed on all three drills included flakes and step fractures along lateral edges. Two (6-227, CS6-27) had light edge-rounding and one (3-56) had heavy edge-rounding. Specimen 6-227 retained the tip end, which also exhibited flaking, step fractures, and rounding. Polish consistent with bone, antler, or shell contact was evident on two of the three specimens (6-227 and CS6-27). Two of the specimens (3-56 and 6-227) exhibit helical fractures. In sum, the three specimens exhibited wear consistent with use as drills. Two had polish consistent with use on bone, antler, or shell, with the shape and size of the drills, as well as their context, suggesting shell is the most likely. Based on these results and their morphologies, specimens 6-227 and CS6-27, both recovered from the postcontact component, are considered bead drills. Specimen 3-56, from the precontact component, did not show definitive evidence for use on shell or bone. Nonetheless, the morphology is similar enough to the other two specimens that it too is considered a bead drill, albeit with less certainty.

Nineteen projectile points were recovered: 12 from the Late Period (precontact) component and seven from postcontact contexts. The points represent five formal types: Desert Side-notched (n=4), Canaliño/Coastal Cottonwood (n=2), small leaf-shaped (n=2), contracting-stemmed (n=1), and concave base (n=1). Four points were indeterminate with respect to type, while one fragment was an indeterminate arrow point. The Desert Side-notched and Canaliño/Coastal Cottonwood are solid markers of the Late Prehistoric and postcontact periods, and are consistent with the dating indicated by the

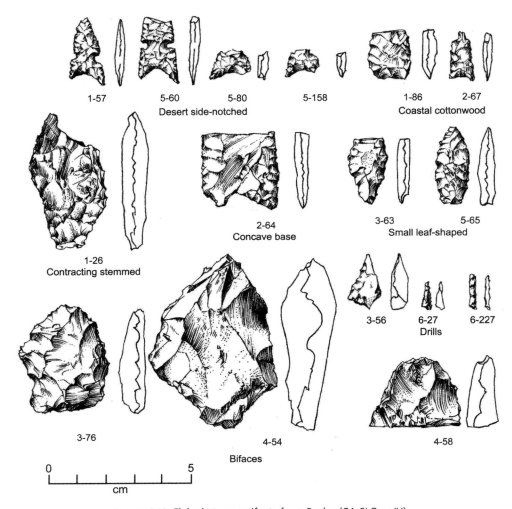

FIGURE 6.16. Flaked-stone artifacts from Pecho (CA-SLO-51/H).

radiocarbon and beads. Contracting-stemmed points are temporally ubiquitous. The concave base is not common in the San Luis Obispo area but seems to occur during the Middle Period. Its presence is consistent with the other evidence (radiocarbon and beads) for a Middle Period component in the basal portion of the deposit. It is considered intrusive within the predominantly later materials identified in the units. Small leaf-shaped types are arrow points that are generally considered markers of the Middle–Late Transition locally, but may have continued in use through the Late Period. Overall, the dominance of Desert Side-notched and Canaliño/

Coastal Cottonwood points in both site areas is consistent with Late Prehistoric and postcontact occupation. The distribution of point types by component is: Late (precontact): Canaliño/ Coastal Cottonwood (n=2), Desert Side-notched (n=1), contracting-stemmed (n=1), concave base (n=1), small leaf-shaped (n=1), indeterminate arrow (n=1), indeterminate (n=5); postcontact: Desert Side-notched (n=3), small leaf-shaped (n=1), indeterminate (n=3).

All 30 flake tools were informal artifacts that showed no intentional shaping. No formal flake tools were identified. Among the 30 informal tools, 21 were Monterey chert, six were basalt, and three were Franciscan chert. Twenty-four were associated with the precontact occupation while the remaining six were postcontact. Seven tools were made from late biface thinning flakes, seven were complex interior, seven were simple interior, four were early biface thinning, three were primary decortication, and one was interior shatter.

Six specimens that morphologically resembled drills were sorted from the debitage; four of these were subjected to microscopic edge-wear analysis to determine if they exhibited modification/damage consistent with use as drills. This analysis was completed by Nathan Stevens from the Archaeological Research Center, California State University–Sacramento. Three of the four specimens (3-56, 6-227, and CS6-27) exhibited wear consistent with use as drills. One did not appear to be used and was merely a fortuitously shaped piece of debitage. Use-wear observed on all three drills included flakes and step fractures along lateral edges. Two (6-227 and CS6-27) had light edge-rounding and one (3-56) had heavy edge-rounding. Specimen 6-227 retained the tip end, which also exhibited flaking, step fractures, and rounding. Polish consistent with bone, antler, or shell contact was evident on two of the three specimens (6-227 and CS6-27). Two of the specimens (3-56 and 6-227) exhibited helical fractures. Bit diameters of the three drills range from a minimum of 1.1 mm to a maximum of 10.4 mm, the latter an incomplete measurement at the proximal end of specimen 3-56. The two specimens with polish consistent with application to shell or bone were recovered from the postcontact component while specimen 3-56, used on an indeterminate material, was recovered from the precontact component. The drills are consistent with the recovery of detritus and blanks from the postcontact component to indicate bead manufacture. Specimen 3-56 is less definitive in this regard but may also represent bead production, although the larger bit could also reflect production of shell fishhooks. Subsequent to completion of the edge-wear study, two additional specimens that resemble drills (6-227 and CS6-27) were sorted from the debitage. These too were associated with the postcontact

occupation although their use as drills was not microscopically confirmed.

Debitage

A total of 7,473 pieces of debitage was recovered including 6,938 pieces of Monterey chert, 505 pieces of Franciscan chert, seven obsidian pressure flakes, three pieces of quartzite, two pieces of basalt, and one quartz flake. Debitage from units representing the two temporal components (Unit 1, precontact occupation [n=1,646]; and Unit 5, postcontact occupation [n=451]) was analyzed (Tables 6.19 and 6.20). Both units were excavated using 3 mm mesh (dry).

As with the site as a whole, the precontact debitage from Unit 1 was dominated by Monterey (n=1,646; 93.7%) over Franciscan chert (n= 108; 6.1%). Among the Monterey chert debitage, nondiagnostic flakes (indeterminate and interior shatter) were by far the most abundant classes (N=1,065) accounting for 64.7% of the analyzed sample. Among the diagnostic Monterey chert flakes from the precontact component (n=581), simple interior specimens were the most prevalent (n=205) accounting for 35.3% (Table 6.20), followed by edge preparation/pressure (18.4%). Decortication flakes (primary, secondary, and cortical shatter) account for 16.5% of the diagnostic Monterey chert debitage from Unit 1. These flakes and the cores show clearly that some primary reduction of locally available chert cobbles took place onsite. Perhaps the most notable trait of the precontact debitage is the near absence of early biface thinning flakes. This seems consistent with the reduced emphasis on large bifacial implements during the Late Period when projectile points were dominated by small types associated with the bow and arrow. These patterns are generally seen in the smaller Franciscan chert sample as well (Table 6.20).

For the most part, the postcontact debitage from Unit 5 exhibits the same pattern as Unit 1. The frequency of cortical debitage is higher (n=45; 22.9%) suggesting local cobbles may have been relied upon more heavily.

The density of debitage in the precontact component is 1,757 flakes per m³ of deposit. Debitage density for the postcontact component

TABLE 6.19. Chert Debitage, Precontact (600–250 cal BP, Unit 1) and Postcontact (250–180 cal BP, Unit 5) Components, Pecho Site (CA-SLO-51/H).

| | Monterey Chert | | | | Franciscan Chert | | | |
| | Unit 1 | | Unit 5 | | Unit 1 | | Unit 5 | |
Type	Total	%	Total	%	Total	%	Total	%
Prim. decort	28	1.70	18	3.99	0	0.00	8	7.77
Sec. decort	7	0.43	0	0.00	0	0.00	1	0.97
Cortical shatter	61	3.71	27	5.98	0	0.00	4	3.88
Simple interior	205	12.45	78	17.29	28	25.92	29	28.16
Complex interior	59	3.58	20	4.43	11	10.18	7	6.79
Interior shatter	351	21.32	87	19.29	19	17.59	12	11.65
Early bif. Thinning	7	0.43	5	1.11	1	0.93	10	9.71
Late bif. thinning	58	3.52	14	3.10	10	9.25	6	5.83
Edge prep/pressure	107	6.50	28	6.21	11	10.18	9	8.74
Pressure	49	2.97	6	1.33	4	3.70	4	3.88
Indeterm. percussion	95	5.77	25	5.54	6	5.56	3	2.91
Microblade	0	0.00	1	0.22	0	0.00	0	0.00
Indeterm.	619	37.6	142	31.48	18	16.67	10	9.71
Total	1,646	99.98	451	99.97	108	99.98	103	100.00

TABLE 6.20. Summary of Diagnostic Chert Debitage from Precontact (600–250 cal BP, Unit 1) and Postcontact (250–180 cal BP, Unit 5) Components, CA-SLO-51/H.

| | Monterey Chert | | | | Franciscan Chert | | | |
| | Unit 1 | | Unit 5 | | Unit 1 | | Unit 5 | |
Flake type	N	%	N	%	N	%	N	%
Primary decortication	28	4.81	18	9.18	0	0.00	8	10.25
Secondary decortication	7	1.20	0	0.00	0	0.00	1	1.28
Cortical Shatter	61	10.49	27	13.77	0	0.00	4	5.12
Subtotals	96	16.50	45	22.96	0	0.00	13	16.66
Simple interior	205	35.28	78	39.79	28	43.07	29	37.17
Complex interior	59	10.15	20	10.20	11	16.92	7	8.97
Subtotals	264	45.43	98	50.00				
Early biface thinning	7	1.20	5	2.55	1	1.53	10	12.82
Late biface thinning	58	9.98	14	7.14	10	15.38	6	7.69
Subtotals	65	11.18	19	9.69	11	16.92		
Edge preparation/pressure	107	18.41	28	14.28	11	16.92	9	11.53
Pressure	49	8.43	6	3.06	4	6.15	4	5.12
Subtotal	156	26.84	34	17.34	15	23.07	13	16.66
Total	581	100.00	196	100.00	65	100.00	78	100.00

is lower at 802 flakes/m³. The precontact value is higher than most of the previously excavated sites on the Pecho Coast and seems to reflect the availability of chert nodules in the adjacent creek and along the shoreline. Still, flake density is lower than the 16,578 flakes/m³ from the quarry-associated site of CA-SLO-267 on the San Simeon coast (Jones and Ferneau 2002:129) and another quarry-associated site at Camp San Luis Obispo (CA-536) with 17,553 flakes/m³ (Farquhar et al. 2014). CA-SLO-51/H did not function as a major quarry, but the local cobbles were probably used to supplement imported biface or flake blanks perhaps due to the relatively poor quality of the raw material found locally.

Ground and Battered Stone

A total of 20 ground- and battered-stone implements was recovered including seven pitted stones (four from precontact, three from postcontact), three hammerstones (two from precontact; one postcontact), two pestle fragments (both postcontact), two grooved stones (one per component), two stone spheres (one per component), one charmstone (postcontact), one stone with an asphaltum smear from the postcontact units, and two miscellaneous pieces from precontact contexts. Two of the pitted stones were also heavily battered on their edges suggesting that they had multiple functions. The grooved stones are generally interpreted as net weights, and these elongated variants seem to be restricted to Late and postcontact times. Although one specimen is fragmentary, both are long, narrow cobbles with deep grooves encircling the long axis of the stone (Figure 6.17). Stone spheres are typically interpreted as gaming pieces.

Bone and Shell

The nonstone artifacts include 13 shell fishhook fragments, two abalone hook blanks, and one bone awl tip (Figure 6.18). The fishhook fragments were more abundant in the postcontact component (n=11) than the precontact component (n=2). None of the hook fragments are large enough to determine whether they were J-shaped or C-shaped. However, shell hooks were used on the central coast during the

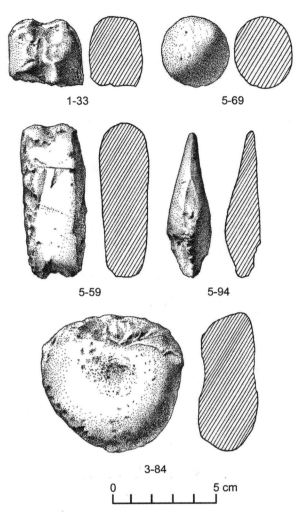

1-33　　　5-69

5-59　　　5-94

3-84

0　　　5 cm

FIGURE 6.17. Ground-stone artifacts from Pecho (CA-SLO-51/H).

Middle, Middle–Late Transition, Late, and postcontact periods. Both of the hook blanks were associated with the postcontact occupation. The bone awl tip is a small fragment recovered from Unit 5.

Subsistence Remains

Mammals, Birds, and Reptiles

A total of 2,162 nonpiscine vertebrate specimens was recovered weighing 631.1 grams (Table 6.21). The majority of these (n=1,864) was associated with the postcontact component represented in

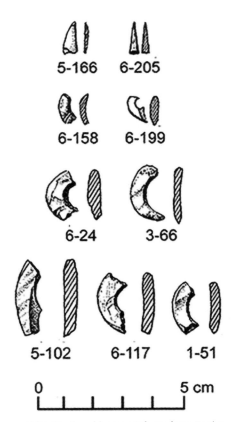

5-166   6-205

6-158   6-199

6-24   3-66

5-102   6-117   1-51

0   5 cm

FIGURE 6.18. Shell and bone artifacts from Pecho (CA-SLO-51/H).

Units 5 and 6. A total of 298 specimens was re-covered from Units 1–4 (precontact). Fifty-one were recovered from Late Period component (Table 6.31). Overall, unidentifiable vertebrates, mammals, pocket gophers, and ground squirrels dominate both components. Excluding likely intrusive elements from burrowing rodents, reptiles, and those remains not identifiable to at least the genus level, the precontact assemblage is limited to 28 specimens dominated by cotton-tail rabbits (NISP=16; 57.1%), and sea otters (NISP=3; 10.7%) (Table 6.22). The postcontact assemblage is larger with 112 specimens domi-nated by sea otter (NISP=29; 25.9%) and cotton-tail rabbits (NISP=25; 22.3%). The postcontact component also yielded three bone fragments from domestic cattle (*Bos taurus*) indicating some modest reliance on introduced animals. No cattle remains were recovered from the pre-contact component. Remains of marine birds

(cormorants [NISP=10] and murre [NISP=1]) were more abundant in the postcontact compo-nent contributing to a slight overall emphasis on marine animals.

Fish

A total of 11,701 fish bones was recovered weighing 731.91 g. Overall, the piscine fauna were dominated by rockfish (NISP=7,958; 68%), rock or black prickleback (NISP=1,157; 9.9%), and cabezon (NISP=664; 5.7%). Fish remains were recovered from Units 1–4 (precontact) via dry-screening through 3 mm (⅛ in) mesh (analytical volume=4.0 m³) while the postcon-tact component is represented by remains from Unit 5 which was dry-screened and Unit 6 and the column sample which were wet-screened (analytical volume=1.22 m³) (Table 6.23). A total of 327 NISP weighing 19.4 g was associated with the precontact component. This sample was dominated by rockfish (NISP=222; 67.9%), cabezon (NISP=46; 14%), and rock or black prickleback (NISP=22; 6.7%). The volumetric density of remains in the Precontact sample is 81.8 NISP/m³. The dry-screened sample asso-ciated with the postcontact occupation (Unit 5) includes 4,348 NISP weighing 299.86 g. This sample is dominated by rockfish (NISP=3,018; 69.4%), rock or black prickleback (NISP=354; 8.1%), and cabezon (NISP=301; 6.9%). The volu-metric density of remains in the dry-screened sample is 6,211.4 NISP/m³. The wet-screened sample from the unit and column sample con-sists of 7,026 NISP weighing 412.6 g. It is domi-nated by rockfish (NISP=4,718; 67.2%), rock or black prickleback (NISP=781; 16.6%), and her-rings (NISP=355; 7.5%). The combined analytical volume for the wet-screened sample is 0.52 m³ for a volumetric density of 13,511 NISP/m³ for the postcontact component. This is the highest value obtained from any of the sites.

Shellfish

Shell was sampled with a single 20 × 20 cm col-umn excavated to 50 cm (0.02 m³ recovery vol-ume) in the sidewall of Unit 6. No sample was recovered from the precontact component. In addition, measurements (maximum diameters) were obtained from all whole and nearly whole

TABLE 6.21. Bird, Mammal, and Reptile Remains from Pecho (CA-SLO-51/H).

Taxon	Common Name	Postcontact			Precontact		
		N	%	Wt (g)	N	%	Wt (g)
Vertebrata	Unidentified Vertebrate	553	29.67	31.19	30	10.07	1.72
Amphibians							
Bufo boreas	Western toad	1	0.05	0.06	0	0	0
Reptiles							
Sceloporus sp.	Lizard	1	0.05	0.01	0	0	0
Clemmys marmorata	Western pond turtle	3	0.16	1.39	0	0	0
Serpentes	Snakes	0	0.00	0.00	2	0.67	0.04
Colubridae	Snakes	3	0.16	0.12	1	0.33	0.01
Pituophis catenifer	Pacific gopher snake	1	0.05	0.03	2	0.67	0.24
Lampropeltis getulus	Kingsnake	0	0.00	0.00	2	0.67	0.24
Crotalus viridis	Western rattlesnake	1	0.05	0.05	2	0.67	0.06
Mammals							
Mammalia	Unidentified mammal	1,496	80.23	367.67	153	51.32	29.99
Rodentia	Rodents	33	1.77	0.97	17	5.70	0.42
Otospermophilus beecheyi	California ground squirrel	41	2.20	4.65	16	5.36	2.23
Dipodomys sp.	Kangaroo rat	2	0.11	0.18	0	0	0.00
Thomomys bottae	Botta's pocket gopher	51	2.74	4.05	46	15.43	4.58
Microtus sp.	Vole	3	0.16	0.08	5	1.68	0.10
Microtus townsendii	California vole	10	0.53	0.33	10	3.35	0.52
Neotoma sp.	Wood rat	2	0.11	0.15	2	0.67	0.07
Peromyscus sp.	Mouse	0	0.00	0.00	2	0.67	0.02
Peromyscus maniculatus	Deer mouse	5	0.26	0.12	3	1.01	0.04
Lagomorpha	Rabbit/hare	0	0	0	0	0	0
Lepus californica	Black-tailed jackrabbit	1	0.05	0.41	0	0	0.00
Sylvilagus sp.	Rabbit	22	1.18	2.90	16	5.36	1.48
Sylvilagus auduboni	Desert cottontail	3	0.16	0.59	0	0	0.00
Scapanus latimanus	Broad-footed mole	0	0.00	0.00	1	0.33	0.03
Canidae	Dog/coyote/fox	1	0.05	1.37	1	0.33	0.10
Vulpes vulpes	Fox	1	0.05	1.19	1	0.33	0.00
Canis sp.	Dog/coyote	8	0.43	6.93	0	0	0.00
Procyon lotor	Racoon	0	0.00	0.00	0	0	5.99
Pinniped	Seal/sea lion	6	0.32	5.31	0	0	0
Otariidae	Eared seal	8	0.43	4.58	2	0.67	0.33
Arctocephalinae	Fur seal	2	0.11	3.75	0	0	0
Phoca vitulina	Harbor seal	13	0.70	25.90	1	0.33	0.38
Enhydra lutris	Sea otter	29	1.56	22.11	3	1.01	1.79
Artiodactyla	Even-toed ungulate	33	1.77	52.13	2	0.67	1.81
Cervidae	Deer/elk	2	0.11	2.16	1	0.33	0.32
Odocoileus hemionus	Mule deer	10	0.53	38.22	0	0	0.00
Birds							
Aves	Unidentified bird	54	2.89	10.47	6	2.01	0.47
Callipepla californica	California quail	2	0.11	0.12	0	0	0
Phalacrocorax sp.	Cormorants	6	0.32	2.85	0	0	0
Phalacrocorax auritus	Double-crested cormorant	4	0.21	2.47	1	0.33	0.24
Uria aalge	Common murre	1	0.05	0.21	0	0	0
Catharus sp.	Thrushes	1	0.05	0.10	0	0	0
Turdus migratorius	American robin	1	0.05	0.04	0	0	0
Total		1,864	99.92	579.61	298	99.90	51.50

TABLE 6.22. Economically Significant Mammal, Bird, and Reptile Remains from Pecho (CA-SLO-51/H).

		Postcontact			Precontact		
Taxon	Common Name	N	%	Wt (g)	N	%	Wt (g)
Terrestrial mammals							
Neotoma sp.	Woodrat	0	0.00	0.00	2	7.14	0.07
Lepus californicus	Jackrabbit	1	0.89	0.41	0	0.00	0.00
Sylvilagus sp.	Desert cottontail	25	22.32	3.49	16	57.14	1.48
Vulpes vulpes	Fox	1	0.89	1.19	0	0.00	0.00
Canis sp.	Dog/coyote	8	7.14	6.93	0	0.00	0.00
Procyon lotor	Raccoon	0	0.00	0.00	1	3.57	5.99
Odocoileus hemionus	Mule deer	10	8.93	38.22	0	0.00	0.00
Bos taurus	Cattle	3	2.68	15.94	0	0.00	0.00
Subtotal		48	42.85	66.18	19	67.85	7.54
Marine mammals							
Phoca vitulina	Harbor seal	13	11.61	25.90	1	3.57	0.38
Enhydra lutris	Sea otter	29	25.89	22.11	3	10.71	1.79
Subtotal		42	37.50	48.01	4	14.28	2.17
Reptiles and amphibians							
Bufo boreas	Western toad	1	0.89	0.06	0	0.00	0.00
Clemmys marmorata	Western pond turtle	3	2.68	1.39	0	0.00	0.00
Sceloporus sp.	Lizard	1	0.89	0.01	0	0.00	0.00
Pituophis catenifer	Pacific gopher snake	1	0.89	0.03	0	0.00	0.00
Lampropeltis getulus	Kingsnake	0	0.00	0.00	2	7.14	0.24
Crotalus viridis	Western rattlesnake	1	0.89	0.05	2	7.14	0.06
Subtotal		7	6.25	1.54	4	14.28	0.30
Birds							
Phalacrocorax sp.	Cormorants	10	8.93	5.32	1	3.57	0.24
Callipepla californica	California quail	2	1.78	0.12	0	0	0
Uria aalge	Common murre	1	0.89	0.21	0	0	0
Catharus sp.	Thrush	1	0.89	0.10	0	0	0
Turdus migratorius	American robin	1	0.89	0.04	0	0	0
Subtotal		15	13.38	5.79	1	3.57	0.24
Grand total		112	99.99	121.52	28	99.98	10.25

abalone shells collected from units. These were limited to finds from Units 5 and 6. The column produced a total of 2,255.2 g of shell (Table 6.24) for a shell density of 112.7 kg/m³. California mussel accounted for 53.6% of the column followed by turban snail (31.5%). Abalone (all species) was insignificant representing less than 2% of the sample. The next most abundant taxa include *Cancer* sp. (3.7% and 3.9%), *Balanus* sp. (3.4% and 1.9%), and Polyplacophora (2% and 0.9%). A total of 24 abalone shells was com-

plete enough to yield measurements (all from the postcontact component). These included 12 red abalones (mean=72.5 mm), and 12 blacks (mean=71.3 mm).

Charred Plant Remains (by Eric Wohlgemuth)
The only intact feature from the entire Pecho project to yield meaningful charred plant remains was Feature 1 Unit 6 at CA-SLO-51/H. Methods and findings described in detail in Appendix B are summarized here. Three samples

collected from the feature produced a total of 1,373 identified specimens including 562 dietary nutshell fragments representing four genera, 786 small seeds (identified to plant family, of which 175 were identified to 19 genera), two *Brodiaea*-type corms, 11 manzanita berry pits, and 12 Eurasian cultigen grains, including four barley and three wheat. The charred plant remains are consistent with those found previously at Morro Bay and Avila Beach, and for the most part are consistent with central California ethnobotanies. Most abundant in the sample were acorn (*Quercus* sp.) and islay (*Prunus ilicifolia*) nutshell, along with seeds of brome, fescue, red maids, goosefoot, and clover, as well as nightshade berries. Nearly all of these can be associated with prehistoric Native Californian subsistence activities. Gray-pine nutshell was present in all three samples, albeit in low frequency, and was probably brought to the site and eaten. The nearest gray pines are some 15–17 km to the northeast (Calflora 2016; Griffin and Critchfield 1976:89) and thus reflect logistical gathering from distant patches, exchange with other social groups living in those patches, or both. Tarweed and maygrass seeds were also found in all samples but at lower frequency, suggesting their regular use as well, if not as intensively as the others.

While only in low numbers, Eurasian cultigens were represented in all three samples. Cultigens have been found in many postcontact Native American archaeological sites in California where they are clearly in context (Wohlgemuth 2004), suggesting the CA-SLO-51/H wheat and barley could have been obtained from Spanish explorers, or from contact with mission agricultural communes. However, CA-SLO-51/H has been used as a wheat and barley field for decades, if not more than a century, which raises the issue of whether the charred cultigens in flotation samples are recent or historic-era farming contaminants, and not actually associated with the postcontact Native community. There are, however, multiple reasons to believe that the cultigens are actually in context. First, no other Eurasian plant seeds were found in the flotation samples. Cultigens in postcontact Native American archaeological sites are invariably found with Eurasian weeds, notably filaree and mallow (Wohlgemuth 2004). Second, all other plant taxa identified in the flotation samples are typical finds in California Native American sites, and most are well-documented foods. It is much more complex to argue that the cultigens are contaminants while all other taxa are not, than to conclude that the cultigens are also in context. Third, at least two flotation samples are from an intact feature that was clearly used by Native Americans.

The charred remains reflect plant taxa which ripen in the full range of seasons that plants can be gathered. Four fall-ripening nut crops were present, along with six genera of small seeds and berry pits that reflect summer gathering, and 11 spring-ripening small seed genera. Focusing only on the key plant foods, the full range of seasonal indicators is also included, with fall nuts (acorn and islay), vernal seeds (brome, red maids, clover, and fescue), and summer seeds (goosefoot) and berries (nightshade). The plant data suggest CA-SLO-51/H was occupied at least from spring through the fall nut harvest. Additionally, the high frequency of nuts and small seeds suggests intensive occupation typical of a year-round village community.

Little Morro Rock (CA-SLO-497)
Description

Little Morro Rock is a prominent sea stack on the edge of the beach at Spooner's Cove in Montaña de Oro State Park. An actively eroding, well-developed but small (12 × 16 m) midden is present on the flat upper surface of the sea stack. Almost certainly this small deposit was originally part of the massive midden situated ca. 50 m to the north at CA-SLO-1. The present-day isolation of the small deposit designated CA-SLO-497 is a product of the erosion of the intervening land mass in the years since the site was occupied. The midden on Little Morro Rock has long been the target of local artifact collectors, and California State Parks completed a series of auger borings in 1988 to offset the impacts of the looting and heavy erosion. The results of that investigation are described in chapter 3 (Barter 1988). In 2008 the California

TABLE 6.23. Fish Remains from Pecho (CA-SLO-51/H).

Taxon	Common Name	Units 1–4 (600–250 cal BP) (Dry)		Unit 5 (250–180 cal BP) (Dry)		Unit 6 (250–180 cal BP) (Wet)		Column NISP	Sample Wt (g)	Total NISP	Total Wt (g)
		NISP	Wt (g)	NISP	Wt (g)	NISP	Wt (g)				
Elasmobranchiomorphi	Sharks, Skates, Rays										
Lamna ditropis	Salmon shark	0	0.00	0	0.00	1	0.05	0	0.00	1	0.05
Triakidae	Hound sharks	0	0.00	1	0.15	1	0.01	0	0.00	2	0.16
Rajidae	Skates or rays	1	0.02	2	0.01	1	0.01	0	0.00	4	0.04
Myliobatis californica	Bat ray	1	0.28	0	0.00	0	0.00	0	0.00	1	0.28
Subtotal		2	0.30	3	0.16	3	0.07	0	0.00	8	0.53
Ray-finned fishes	Actinopterygii										
Engraulis mordax	Northern anchovy	0	0.00	1	0.01	9	0.04	3	0.02	13	0.07
Clupeidae	Herring	7	0.07	151	1.55	334	2.98	21	0.21	513	4.81
Sardinops sagax	Pacific sardine	0	0.00	13	0.14	41	0.54	2	0.03	56	0.71
Spirinchus starksi	Night smelt	0	0.00	0	0.00	1	0.01	1	0.01	2	0.02
Merluccius productus	Pacific hake	0	0.00	0	0.00	2	0.05	0	0.00	2	0.05
Porichthys. notatus	Plainfin midshipman	0	0.00	61	2.26	114	3.79	7	0.52	182	6.57
Atherinopsidae	New World silversides	0	0.00	7	0.12	11	0.17	3	0.05	21	0.34
Atherinopsis californiensis	Jacksmelt	0	0.00	0	0.00	0	0.00	1	0.01	1	0.01
Sebastes sp.	Rockfish	222	11.91	3,018	209.05	4,465	273.52	253	20.18	7,958	514.66
Hexagrammos sp.	Greenling	0	0.00	0	0.00	6	0.27	0	0.00	6	0.27
H. decagrammus	Kelp greenling	4	0.09	77	4.54	81	3.78	11	0.33	173	8.74
Ophiodon elongatus	Lingcod	5	0.69	33	4.34	59	5.73	0	0.00	97	10.76
Cottidae	Sculpin	0	0.00	1	0.01	6	0.2	0	0.00	7	0.21
Artedius sp.	Sculpin	0	0.00	0	0.00	8	0.15	0	0.00	8	0.15
Clinocottus sp.	Sculpin	2	0.03	6	0.08	9	0.14	1	0.02	18	0.27
Leptocottus armatus	Pacific staghorn sculpin	0	0.00	0	0.00	1	0.01	0	0.00	1	0.01
Scorpaenichthys marmoratus	Cabezon	46	4.32	301	42.32	294	43.16	23	2.91	664	92.71
Trachurus symmetricus	Jack mackerel	1	0.01	0	0.00	1	0.04	0	0.00	2	0.05
Sciaenidae	Drums and croakers	0	0.00	4	0.15	0	0.00	0	0.00	4	0.15
Genyonemus lineatus	White croaker	0	0.00	7	0.25	14	0.23	0	0.00	21	0.48
Seriphus politus	Queenfish	2	0.03	2	0.01	0	0.00	0	0.00	4	0.04

Embiotocidae	Surfperch	5	0.5	37	2.28	62	2.65	2	0.09	106	5.52
Damalichthys vacca	Pile perch	3	0.21	8	1.05	16	1.37	0	0.00	27	2.63
Embiotoca sp.	Black surfperch or Striped seaperch	1	0.09	2	0.23	1	0.07	0	0.00	4	0.39
E. lateralis	Striped seaperch	1	0.10	0	0.00	0	0.00	1	0.03	2	0.13
Hypsurus caryi	Rainbow seaperch	0	0.00	0	0.00	2	0.01	0	0.00	2	0.01
Rhacochicul toxotes	Rubberlip Seaperch	0	0.00	0	0.00	1	0.04	0	0.00	1	0.04
Oxyjulis californica	Señorita	2	0.03	31	0.3	49	0.56	1	0.01	83	0.9
Stichaeidae	Prickleback	0	0.00	74	2.29	81	2.71	0	0.00	155	5
Anoplarchus sp.	Cockscomb	0	0.00	0	0.00	1	0.01	0	0.00	1	0.01
Cebidichthys violaceus	Monkeyface prickleback	1	0.05	95	8.6	114	8.94	2	0.1	212	17.69
Xiphister sp.	Black or rock prickleback	22	0.98	354	18.85	736	33.01	45	1.65	1,157	54.49
Clinidae	Blennies	0	0.00	21	0.36	11	0.15	0	0.00	32	0.51
Gibbsonia sp.	Kelpfish	0	0.00	24	0.44	86	1.41	6	0.07	116	1.92
Heterostichus rostratus	Giant kelpfish	0	0.00	1	0.01	3	0.07	0	0.00	4	0.08
Gobiesox meandricus	Northern clingfish	0	0.00	6	0.09	9	0.09	2	0.02	17	0.2
Scomber japonicus	Pacific chub mackerel	1	0.03	10	0.37	5	0.33	2	0.02	18	0.75
Citharichthys sp.	Sanddab	0	0.00	0	0.00	1	0.01	0	0.00	1	0.01
Platichthys stellatus	Starry flounder	0	0.00	0	0.00	2	0.02	0	0.00	2	0.02
Subtotal		325	19.14	4,345	299.7	6,636	386.26	387	26.28	11,693	731.38
Grand total		327	19.44	4,348	299.86	6,639	386.33	387	26.28	11,701	731.91

TABLE 6.24. Shellfish Remains from Pecho (CA-SLO-51/H) Postcontact Component (250–180 cal BP).

Group	Taxon	Common Name	6 mm (¼ in) Mesh		3 mm (⅛ in) Mesh		Total	
			Weight (g)	%	Weight (g)	%	Weight (g)	%
Abalones	*Haliotis cracherodii*	Black abalone	10.50	0.7	1.29	0.2	11.79	0.56
	Haliotis rufescens	Red abalone	8.43	0.5	2.76	0.5	11.19	0.53
	Haliotis sp.	Abalone (indeterminate)	8.71	0.6	1.32	0.2	10.03	0.47
Mussels	*Mytilus californianus*	California mussel	800.26	51.6	336.37	59.0	1,136.63	53.62
	Tegula funebralis	Black turban snail	495.36	32.0	172.15	30.2	667.51	31.49
	Astraea gibberosa	Red turban snail	24.43	1.6	3.79	0.7	28.22	1.33
Clams	*Leukoma (Protothaca) staminea*	Pacific littleneck clam	8.21	0.5	0.79	0.1	9.00	0.42
	Patellogastropoda	Misc. limpet	23.04	1.5	3.23	0.6	26.27	1.24
Chiton	*Cryptochiton stelleri*	Giant Gumboot chiton	18.70	1.2	0.23	0.0	18.93	0.89
	Polyplacophora	Misc. chiton	30.43	2.0	5.10	0.9	35.53	1.68
Misc. snails	*Crepidula adunca*	Hooked slipper snail	1.27	0.1	0.39	0.1	1.66	0.08
	Callianax (Olivella) biplicata	Purple olive	0.00	0.0	0.02	0.0	0.02	0.00
	—	Misc. snail	2.14	0.1	0.11	0.0	2.25	0.11
Barnacles	*Balanus* sp.	Barnacle (indeterminate)	53.20	3.4	10.60	1.9	63.80	3.01
	Pollicipes polymerus	Leaf barnacle	6.62	0.4	4.17	0.7	10.79	0.51
Urchins	*Stongylocentrotus purpuratus*	Purple urchin	0.84	0.1	5.97	1.0	6.81	0.32
Crabs	*Cancer* sp.	Crab (indeterminate)	57.39	3.7	22.02	3.9	79.41	3.75
Subtotal			1,549.53	100.0	570.31	100.0	2,119.84	100.00
Unidentified		Unidentified	34.53	—	100.84	—	135.37	—
Grand total			1,584.06	—	671.15	—	2,255.21	—

Department of Parks and Recreation conducted a second salvage under the direction of Parks archaeologist Elise Wheeler. With assistance from Cal Poly students, three adjacent 1 × 1 m units were excavated in the remaining intact portion of the deposit and dry-screened with 3 mm (⅛ in) mesh. The midden proved to range from 70–80 cm in depth in the area excavated in 2008. A total of 2.3 m³ was excavated from the three units in addition to a single 20 × 20 cm column sample (0.028 m³).

Chronology

Five radiocarbon determinations are available from CA-SLO-497 including two from samples recovered via auger in 1988 and three from the 2008 test excavation. The dates suggest two intervals of occupation. The oldest date was obtained from an abalone shell from the 40–50 cm level of Unit 1. It has a one-sigma range of 5700–5600 cal BP and a one-sigma midpoint of 5700 cal BP. The two-sigma range is 5800–5600 cal BP also with a midpoint of 5700 cal BP. This date suggests some modest occupation of the site around the time of the transition from Millingstone/Lower Archaic to the Early Period. However, this was the only date of that age recovered from the deposit; all others, including those obtained from samples from lower depths range between 3200 and 2300 cal BP with midpoints between 3000 and 2300 cal BP (one sigma). The two-sigma range from these four dates is 3300–2100 cal BP with midpoints between 3000 and 2300. While the single older date indicates some use of the site at the very end of the Millingstone/Lower Archaic Period, the portion of the deposit tested in 2008 is dominated by materials marking the very end of the Early Period ca. 3000–2500 cal BP. While some intermixing from Millingstone/Lower Archaic materials is evident, the sample can be considered a single component representing the terminal Early Period. No other chronological indicators were recovered.

Technology

Owing to a rather small recovery volume, the artifact assemblage from CA-SLO-497 was fairly limited, although both flaked and ground/battered implements were represented.

Flaked Stone

The flaked-stone collection includes one projectile point, one biface, three cores, one flake tool, and 541 pieces of debitage. All but 20 pieces of debitage were Monterey chert. The projectile point is a complete contracting-stemmed variant. The biface is a fragment that represents Stage 1. The cores are all cobbles from the Monterey formation that show multidirectional flaking; one exhibits only a single broken face suggesting that it was assayed and discarded. The flake tool was made from a large simple interior flake; it exhibits modest modification along one edge.

A sample of 279 pieces of Monterey chert debitage from Unit 1 was analyzed. Eliminating the nondiagnostic flake types, the resulting sample consists of 216 pieces of debitage. The analytical sample shows a heavy emphasis on biface reduction which represents 53.2% of the diagnostic debitage (Table 6.25). Of course, decortication of chert cobbles is also represented as it is by the three cores.

Ground Stone

The ground/battered stone category is represented by two pitted stones. One of these is a rectangular shaped, broken shale cobble with two pits on the same face while the other is a split shale cobble with a single pit. The only other cultural materials recovered from the deposit were several small samples of ochre which appears to be present in the natural rock layers exposed adjacent to the site.

Subsistence Remains

Mammals and Birds

A total of 1,085 nonpiscine vertebrate specimens weighing 223.1 grams was recovered (Table 6.26). The most abundant species represented was the pocket gopher (NISP=71; 32.3%). Excluding that and other species thought to be intrusive, the economically significant taxa are rabbits (NISP=103) and deer (NISP=10) (Table 6.27).

Fish

Fish remains were analyzed only from the dry-screened unit samples from CA-SLO-497 which yielded a total of 110 fish elements of which 74

TABLE 6.25. Debitage from Little Morro Rock (CA–SLO–497, 3200–2300 cal BP).

Flake type	0–10	10–20	20–30	30–40	40–50	50–60	60–70	70–80	Total
Primary decortication	5	2	4	5	3	1	0	0	20
Secondary decortication	1	1	1	0	0	0	0	0	3
Cortical shatter	0	1	2	0	5	3	0	4	15
Subtotal	6	4	7	5	8	4	0	4	38
Simple interior	13	4	2	0	7	6	2	1	35
Complex interior	7	5	3	3	5	3	0	2	28
Subtotal	20	9	5	3	12	9	2	3	63
Early biface thinning	1	5	2	1	1	1	0	3	14
Late biface thinning	22	6	4	8	7	2	1	7	57
Edge preparation/pressure	5	2	0	4	3	0	0	7	21
Pressure	5	2	3	2	4	1	4	2	23
Subtotal	33	15	9	15	15	4	5	19	115
Total	59	28	21	23	35	17	7	26	216

TABLE 6.26. Mammal and Reptile Remains from Little Morro Rock (CA-SLO-497).

Taxon	Common Name	NISP	Wt. (g)
Vertebrata	Unidentifiable vertebrate	72	1.33
Reptiles			
Serpentes	Unidentifiable snake	2	0.11
Colubridae	Colubrid snake	1	0.01
Pituophis sp.	Gopher snake	1	0.12
Crotalus sp.	Rattlesnake	1	0.10
Mammals			
Mammalia	Unidentifiable mammal	762	128.59
Rodentia	Unidentifiable rodent	11	0.33
Dipodomys agilis	Agile kangaroo rat	1	0.20
Reithrodontomys sp.	Harvest mouse	1	0.01
Thomomys bottae	Botta's pocket gopher	71	4.77
Microtus sp.	Vole	9	0.21
Neotoma sp.	Wood rat	3	0.09
Onychomys sp.	Grasshopper mouse	1	0.03
Leporidae	Rabbit/hare	5	0.25
Lepus californicus	Jackrabbit	3	1.17
Sylvilagus sp.	Rabbit	64	4.24
Sylvilagus audubonii	Desert cottontail	39	8.95
Canis sp.	Dog/coyote	1	0.76
Pinniped	Seal/sea lion	1	1.25
Otariidae	Eared seal/sea lion	1	0.95
Enhydra lutris	Sea otter	4	2.45
Artiodactyl	Deer/sheep/goat	11	22.09
Odocoileus hemionus	Mule deer	10	42.48
Grand Totals		1,085	1.33

TABLE 6.27. Economically Significant Mammal and
Bird Remains from Little Morro Rock (CA-SLO-497).

Taxon	Common Name	NISP	Wt. (g)
Terrestrial mammals			
Lepus californicus	Jackrabbit	3	1.17
Sylvilagus sp.	Rabbit	64	4.24
Sylvilagus audubonii	Desert cottontail	39	8.95
Canis sp.	Dog/coyote	1	0.76
Odocoileus hemionus	Mule deer	10	42.48
Subtotal		117	57.60
Marine mammals			
Enhydra lutris	Sea otter	4	2.45
Subtotal		4	2.45
Grand Totals		121	60.05

could only be classified as the remains of ray-
finned fishes. The remaining sample (NISP=35)
was dominated by rockfish (NISP=18) and cabezon (NISP=8) (Table 6.28). The volumetric density of fish bones from this dry-screened sample
is 15.2/m³.

Shellfish

Shell was sampled with a single 20 × 20 cm
column excavated to 80 cm (0.032 m³ recovery
volume). In addition, measurements (maximum diameters) were obtained from all whole
and nearly whole abalone shells collected from
units. The column produced a total of 1,207.8 g of
shell (Table 6.29). California mussel accounted
for 83.4% of the column, followed by turban snail

(7.9%) and barnacle (3.1%). Abalone was insignificant representing less than 1% of the sample.
The volumetric density of shell was 37.7 kg/m³.
A total of 14 abalone shells was complete enough
to yield measurements; these included seven red
abalones (mean=94.3 mm) and seven black abalones (mean=89.3 mm).

Tom's Pond (CA-SLO-1366/H)
Description

The Tom's Pond Site (CA-SLO-1366/H) is located
on PG&E's Diablo Canyon lands within a small
coastal valley formed by a rocky outcrop on the
west and a secondary marine terrace on the east.
Covering nearly 53,000 m², the site is bound by
the Pacific Ocean to the west and the base of a
steep ridge that backs the coastal plain to the
north and east (Figure 6.19). In the middle of
the site, a natural spring is partially contained
by a dam, forming the pond for which the site
is named. The site is dominated by its prehistoric component which is an expansive, dark,
rich, high-density, coastal shell midden with
two distinct loci, the first of which is adjacent
to an outcrop of bedrock mortars. The midden
was investigated by a Cal Poly field class in 2011.
Excavation revealed a deposit between 120 and
130 cm in depth at Locus 1, and about 70 cm at
Locus 2. The total recovery from the 2011 investigation was 10.28 m³, including 9 m³ from four
1 × 2 m test excavation units, 1.2 m³ from the 1 ×
1 m control unit (water-screened through 3 mm
mesh), and 0.08 m³ from the column samples.
A dense deposit of bottle and window glass,

TABLE 6.28. Fish Remains from Little Morro Rock (CA-SLO-497, 3200–2300 cal BP).

Taxon	Common Name	NISP	Weight (g)
Elasmobranchiomorphi	Sharks and rays		
Triakidae	Hound sharks	1	0.02
Rhinobatos productus	Shovelnose guitarfish	7	0.90
Subtotal		8	0.92
Actinopterygii	Ray-finned fishes		
Sebastes sp.	Rockfishes	18	2.05
Hexagrammos sp.	Greenling	1	0.03
Scorpaenichthys marmoratus	Cabezon	8	1.79
Subtotal		27	3.87
Grand total		35	4.79

TABLE 6.29. Shellfish Remains from Little Morro Rock (CA-SLO-497, 3200–2300 cal BP).

Group	Taxon	Common Name	Weight (g)	%
Abalones	*Haliotis cracherodii*	Black abalone	2.21	0.18
	Haliotis rufescens	Red abalone	0.00	0.00
	Haliotis sp.	Abalone (indeterminate)	4.10	0.34
Mussels	*Mytilus californianus*	California mussel	1,007.25	83.39
Turban snails	*Chlorostoma* sp.	Turban snail (indeterminate)	96.05	7.95
	Megastraea undosa	Wavy Turban	1.47	0.12
Limpets	*Lottia* sp.	Limpet (indeterminate)	0.87	0.07
Chiton	*Cryptochiton stelleri*	Giant Gumboot chiton	27.59	2.28
	Chiton sp.	Chiton (indeterminate)	3.13	0.26
Misc. snails	*Crepidula adunca*	Hooked slipper snail	0.61	0.05
Scallop	*Crassadoma gigantea*	Giant rock scallop	1.43	0.12
Barnacles	*Balanus* sp.	Barnacle (indeterminate)	37.21	3.08
	Pollicipes polymerus	Gooseneck barnacle	8.08	0.67
Urchins	*Stongylocentrotus purpuratus*	Purple urchin	3.16	0.26
Crabs	*Cancer* sp.	Crab (indeterminate)	0.24	0.02
Clams	*Saxidomus nuttalli*	California butter clam	0.64	0.05
	Leukoma staminea	Pacific littleneck clam	4.90	0.41
Subtotal			1,198.94	99.26
Unidentified		Unidentified	8.91	0.74
Grand total			1,207.85	100.00

FIGURE 6.19. Tom's Pond site (CA-SLO-1366/H) (photograph by Kacey Hadick).

remnants of a collapsed water tank, ceramics, and agricultural debris attest to historic activity. Greater detail on historic portions of the site is available from Price and colleagues (2006). Primary reporting of the prehistoric investigations is available from Codding and colleagues (2013).

Chronology

Seven radiocarbon determinations are available from Tom's Pond, but three were recovered during surface survey and are not associated spatially or vertically with the excavation materials. Four samples were recovered from the 2011 excavation in Locus 1. The maximal one-sigma range represented by these dates is 5900–2330 cal BP; the minimal range is 5840–2480 cal BP. Midpoints range from 5900 to 2400 cal BP. The oldest date with a midpoint of 5900 cal BP was recovered from a depth of 118 cm and predates the generally accepted age for the beginning of the Early Period at ca. 5500 cal BP. It suggests the possibility of a Millingstone Period expression within the deposit which is supported by the date of 7000 cal BP obtained by Applied Earthworks from elsewhere in the site (Price et al. 2006). Unfortunately, a date of 4700–4500 cal BP was recovered from below the 5900 cal BP determination. This more recent date fits squarely within the Early Period. The fourth date was obtained from 10–20 cm and has a one-sigma midpoint of 2400 cal BP. These results are far from perfect, but they suggest that the portion of the site investigated in 2011 consists mostly of a single component centered on the Early Period (5500 to 2500 cal BP), with slight overlap into adjacent periods. The two earliest dates (7000 and 5900 cal BP) may represent ephemeral occupations during the late Millingstone/Lower Archaic Period (Beta-312939). All but the date of 5900 cal BP are superimposed. The mixing indicated by this last date is typical of the central coast and reflects the vertical movement of materials due primarily to rodent activities.

Two additional dates were obtained from surface/near surface contexts at Locus 2. One is clearly of modern/historic origin. The other has a one-sigma range of 3900–3700 cal BP which is consistent with the Early Period dating of Locus 1.

The excavation in Locus 1 yielded six small obsidian flakes (no obsidian was recovered from Locus 2). Four originated from the Coso source (one from Sugarloaf Mountain and three from West Sugarloaf), one was from Casa Diablo (Lookout Mountain) and one could not be sourced. The samples range from 0–10 cm to 30–40 cm with readings from 4.5–5.8 microns. This range is loosely consistent with the Early and Middle periods.

Five *Olivella* shell beads were recovered from Locus 1 at CA-SLO-1366/H (none were recovered from Locus 2). These included a full thick-lipped bead (E2a), a tiny saucer (G1), a symmetrical irregular saucer (G6a), and two cupped (K1) beads. The full thick-lipped bead (E2a), likely of the normal variant (E2a1) (Milliken and Schwitalla 2012), was recovered from the 20–30 cm layer and is a reliable marker of the Late Period (Phase 2b persisting into the Historic Period [Bennyhoff and Hughes 1987]). The tiny saucer (G1) was recovered from 0–10 cm. This specimen is a fairly typical example for the region. These were manufactured during the Middle and Late periods (Milliken and Schwitalla 2012). The other saucer was recovered from 50–60 cm and represents either the small normal (G2a) or the symmetrical irregular (G6a) variant. Both the G2a and G6a types have the same chronological significance, being common in the Monterey Bay area from the Early–Middle Transition through the entire Middle Period (Milliken and Schwitalla 2012). Tiny saucers are known from Middle and Middle–Late Transition contexts from Monterey Bay south to the Pecho Coast (Codding and Jones 2007, Jones 2003). The two cupped beads (K1) were recovered within the top 20 cm of the deposit. Cupped beads are robust Late Period indicators in central and southern California (Bennyhoff and Hughes 1987; King 1990; Milliken and Schwitalla 2012). They are also present in Middle–Late Transition contexts along the Pecho Coast (Codding and Jones 2007).

The combined chronometric indicators suggest that the deposit sampled at Locus 1 represents at least two occupations. The first dates to the Late Period, the second, to the Early Period. While the evidence suggests some mixing

TABLE 6.30. Technologically Diagnostic Monterey Chert Debitage from Tom's Pond (CA-SLO-1366/H).

Flake Type	0–20 (Late, 700–250 cal BP)	%	20–130 (Early, 5800–2500 cal BP)	%	Total	%
Primary decortication	6	2.25	24	4.59	30	3.80
Secondary decortication	4	1.49	10	1.92	14	1.77
Cortical shatter	12	4.49	36	6.89	48	6.08
Subtotal	22	8.24	70	13.41	92	11.66
Simple interior	66	24.72	126	24.14	192	24.33
Complex interior	34	12.73	97	18.59	131	16.60
Subtotal	100	37.45	223	42.72	323	40.93
Early biface thinning	11	4.12	27	5.17	38	4.81
Late biface thinning	40	14.98	62	11.88	102	12.93
Subtotal	51	19.10	89	17.04	140	17.74
Edge preparation/pressure	51	19.10	95	18.19	146	18.50
Pressure	43	16.10	45	8.62	88	11.15
Subtotal	94	35.20	140	26.82	234	29.66
Total	267	99.99	522	99.99	789	99.99

within the top 30 cm of the deposit, overall the chronological findings suggest a break from the Early to Late Period at about 20 cm. This is most clearly indicated by temporally diagnostic artifacts including a type K1 bead. As such, we define a Late Period component in the upper 20 cm of Units 1–3 and 5 from Locus 1 and an Early Period component from 20–130 cm in the same units (excavated as a trench). The recovery volume from the Late Period component was 1.408 m³, which included 1.200 m³ that were dry-screened and 0.208 m³ wet-screened.

Radiometric findings from Locus 2 suggest a more mixed deposit ranging from the modern era to about 5,000 BP. Given the uncertain chronology and limited findings, the material from Unit 4 in Locus 2 is not included in any further discussions of the site.

Technology

The occupants at Tom's Pond relied on flaked-stone, ground-stone, bone, and shell tools.

Flaked Stone

The flaked-stone assemblage consists of 3,240 specimens, including six cores, three cobble/core tools, five flake tools, five bifaces (<Stage 4), 20 projectile points, two drills, and 3,199 pieces

of debitage. One contracting-stemmed projectile point, three core tools, two cores, and one drill were recovered from Unit 4 and could not be assigned to a temporal component. Fifteen projectile points were associated with the Early Period component including four contracting-stemmed, one large side-notched, one concave base, one Rossi Square-stemmed, and eight indeterminate fragments (Figure 6.20). These types are generally consistent with the Early Period (Greenwood's Hunting Culture) (Greenwood 1972; Jones et al. 2007; Rogers 1929). Also associated with the Early occupation were one core, five bifaces, five flake tools, and one drill.

The Late Period component was marked by one core, two core tools, three contracting-stemmed projectile points, one indeterminate arrow point, and one indeterminate point fragment.

A sample of Monterey chert debitage from units 2 and 5 (N=1,306) was analyzed. Nondiagnostic flakes were by far the most abundant class in the analyzed collection (N=517) accounting for 39.6% of the sample. Among the remaining diagnostic flakes (N=789), simple interior flakes were the most prevalent, making up 24.14%, followed by edge preparation/pressure (18.19%) (Table 6.30). Based on the controlled recovery

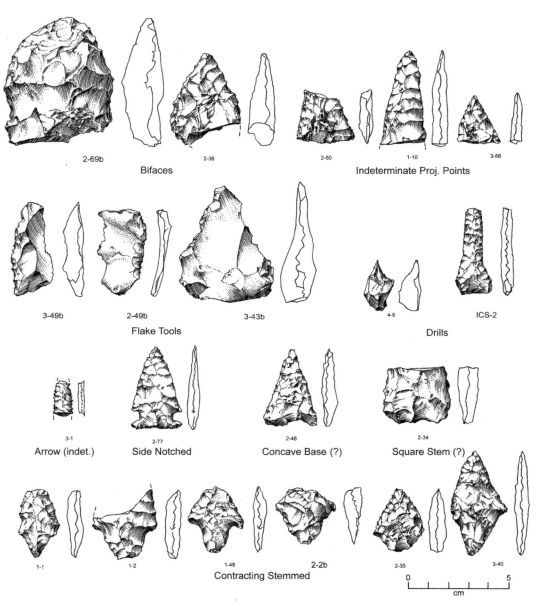

2-69b
Bifaces
2-36
2-50
1-10
3-56
Indeterminate Proj. Points

3-49b
2-49b
3-43b
Flake Tools
4-5
ICS-2
Drills

3-1
Arrow (indet.)
2-77
Side Notched
2-48
Concave Base (?)
2-34
Square Stem (?)

1-1
1-2
1-48
2-2b
Contracting Stemmed
2-35
3-40

0 _____ 5
cm

FIGURE 6.20. Flaked-stone artifacts from Tom's Pond (CA-SLO-1366/H).

from Unit 5, the density of Monterey chert debitage was only 266 per m³ during the Early Period. This, along with flake to biface ratios of 129:1 suggest that individuals were acquiring and reducing stone offsite, then transporting early stage bifaces for further reduction into usable tools.

With a density of 470 flakes per m³ of deposit during the Late Period, this component suggests a similar pattern, but with less decortication debitage and a higher frequency of pressure flakes, shows evidence of later-stage biface transportation and the production of arrow points.

Ground Stone
The Early Period component included two milling slab fragments (probably deriving from the same artifact), one mortar fragment, three

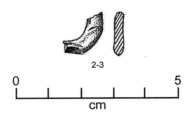

0   5

cm

FIGURE 6.21. Shell fishhook fragment from Tom's Pond (CA-SLO-1366/H).

battered cobbles, and nine pitted stones. The Late Period component included one globular steatite bead/pendant and three pitted stones.

Bone and Shell Artifacts
Three bone artifacts were associated with the Early Period component although only one, a fish gorge (specimen 3-28), could be fully identified (Figure 6.21). The other two were indeterminate fragments. One chipped abalone shell specimen (1-49b) resembles a fishhook blank. It was recovered from levels associated with the Early Period component (100–110 cm) but likely dates to the very end of that occupation represented in that component (ca. 3000–2500 cal BP). The Late Period component yielded a circular fishhook fragment (specimen 2-3).

Subsistence Remains
Mammals, Birds, and Reptiles
The site yielded 656 nonpiscine vertebrate specimens weighing 300.6 grams. The majority of these (n=413) was from the Early Period component at Locus 1. Fifty-one were recovered from Late Period component (Table 6.31). Overall, unidentifiable terrestrial mammals and pocket gophers dominate the Late Period (43.2% NISP and 29.4% NISP, respectively) and Early Period (38.2% NISP and 29.3% NISP, respectively) assemblages. Overall, five specimens were burned, one was gnawed by a rodent, and none of the remains showed evidence of butchering. Excluding likely intrusive elements from burrowing rodents, reptiles, historic specimens, and those remains not identifiable to the genus level, four elements remain from the Late Period, 24 from the Early Period (Table 6.32). The Late Period assemblage consists of two rabbit bones (50%),

a bobcat bone (25%), and one sea otter bone (25%). The Early Period assemblage is dominated by rabbits (NISP=10, 42%), dog/coyote (NISP=5, 21%), sea otter (NISP=4, 17%), and deer (NISP=3, 13%).

Fish
Overall, the piscine fauna were dominated by rockfish, cabezon, and members of the Prickleback family (Table 6.33). Of the identifiable specimens recovered from the Late Period component, 39% were identified as rockfish, 29% as cabezon, and 22% as pricklebacks. Of those from the Early Period component, 46% were rockfish, 26% cabezon, and 10% pricklebacks. For the dry-screened samples the volumetric density of fish bone was $22.5/m^3$ for the Late Period component and only $6.1/m^3$ for the Early Period component. For the wet-screened control sample the volumetric values were $21.1/m^3$ for the Early Period component and $4.8/m^3$ for the Late Period component.

Shellfish
Shell was sampled with a single 20 × 20 cm column excavated to 130 cm. From the column, a total of four 10 cm levels was analyzed, two from each temporal component. For this analysis, 100% of the shell materials retained in 6 mm (¼ in) mesh were identified while a 25% sample was analyzed from the 3 mm (⅛ in) residues. In addition, measurements (maximum diameters) were obtained from all whole and nearly whole abalone shells collected from units. A total of 30 invertebrate species was identified representing 15 groups: abalones, mussels, clams, oysters, cockles, piddocks, scallops, turban snails, limpets, chitons, miscellaneous snails, barnacles, urchins, worms, and crabs. The four analyzed levels produced a total of 4,017.98 g of shell (including extrapolated total values from the 25% 3 mm [⅛ in] subsamples) which were dominated (80.4%) by the remains of California sea mussel followed by turban snails (8.5%) (Table 6.34). As shown in Table 6.34, the two upper levels associated with the Late Period occupation produced a greater amount of shell: 2,448.73 g from an excavation recovery volume of 0.008 m³. This trans-

TABLE 6.31. Mammal, Bird, and Reptile Remains from Units 1–4, Tom's Pond (CA-SLO-1366/H).

| | | Locus 1 | | | | | |
| | | Late Component | | | Early Component | | |
Taxon	Common Name	N	%	Wt (g)	N	%	Wt (g)
Vertebrata	Unidentifiable vertebrates	1	2.0	0.03	48	11.6	1.1
Amphibians							
Bufo boreas	Western toad	0	0.0	0	1	0.2	0.11
Reptiles							
Elgaria multicarinata	Southern alligator lizard	0	0.0	0	1	0.2	0.01
Serpentes	Snake	0	0.0	0	3	0.7	0.1
Thamnophis sirtalis	Common garter snake	0	0.0	0	1	0.2	0.13
Crotalus viridis	Western rattlesnake	0	0.0	0	3	0.7	0.65
Mammals							
Mammalia	Unidentifiable mammals	22	43.2	9.13	162	38.2	61.00
Rodentia	Rodents	6	11.8	0.24	23	5.6	0.88
Otospermophilus beecheyi	California ground squirrel	0	0.0	0	2	0.5	0.36
Thomomys bottae	Botta's pocket gopher	15	29.4	1.35	121	29.3	12.55
Microtus sp.	California vole	0	0.0	0	1	0.2	0.03
Onychomys sp.	Mouse	2	3.9	0.05	1	0.2	0.03
Peromyscus maniculatus	Deermouse	0	0.0	0	6	1.5	0.14
Sylvilagus sp.	Cottontail rabbit	2	3.9	0.08	10	2.4	1.46
Scapanus latimanus	Townsends mole	0	0.0	0	2	0.5	0.33
Lynx rufus	Bobcat	1	2.0	1.43	0	0.0	0
Canis sp.	Dog/coyote	0	0.0	0	5	1.2	3.21
Phoca vitulina	Harbor seal	0	0.0	0	1	0.2	0.73
Otariidae	Eared seal	0	0.0	0	2	0.5	18.38
Enhydra lutris	Sea otter	1	2.0	0.14	4	1.0	5.9
Artiodactyla	Even-toed ungulate	0	0.0	0	4	1.0	6.65
Odocoileus hemionus	Mule deer	0	0.0	0	3	0.7	18.08
Cetacean	Whale/dolphin	0	0.0	0	1	0.2	3.52
Ovis arias	Sheep	1	2.0	0.87	0	0.0	0
Birds							
Aves	Unidentifiable bird	0	0.0	0	8	1.9	0.92
Total		51	100.0	13.32	413	100.0	136.27

lates to 306.1 kg of shell per m³. The dominant taxa were mussel (82.4%) followed by turban snails at 8.5%. All of the other taxa were represented in extremely low frequencies, including abalone, which were barely represented at all in the column residues. The lower levels associated with the earlier occupation of CA-SLO-1366/H show very similar patterns (Table 6.34). A total of 1,569.25 g was recovered from these two levels

combined, representing 196.2 kg of shell per m³. Like the later occupation, the lower component was dominated by California sea mussel (77.2%) followed by turban snails (8.5%).

Forty-five abalone shells were complete enough to determine length. Thirty-two of these were red abalone from the Early Period component at Locus 1 averaging 165 mm in length. Four black abalone from the Early Period component

TABLE 6.32. Economically Significant Mammal, Bird, and Reptile Remains from Units 1–4, Tom's Pond (CA-SLO-1366/H).

| | | Locus 1 | | | | | |
| | | Late | | | Early | | |
Taxon	Common Name	N	%	Wt (g)	N	%	Wt (g)
Amphibians and Reptiles							
Bufo boreas	Western toad	0	0.0	0	1	4.2	0.11
Clemmys marmorata	Western pond turtle	0	0.0	0	0	0.0	0
Subtotal		0	0.0	0	1	4.2	0
Terrestrial Mammals							
Sylvilagus sp.	Desert cottontail	2	50.0	0.08	10	41.7	1.46
Lynx rufus	Bobcat	1	25.0	1.43	0	0.0	0
Canis sp.	Dog/coyote	0	0.0	0	5	20.8	3.21
Odocoileus hemionus	Mule deer	0	0.0	0	3	12.5	18.08
Subtotal		3	75.0	1.51	18	75.0	22.75
Marine mammals							
Phoca vitulina	Harbor seal	0	0.0	0	1	4.2	0.73
Enhydra lutris	Sea otter	1	25.0	0.14	4	16.7	5.9
Subtotal		1	25.0	0.14	5	20.9	6.63
Grand total		4	100	1.65	24	100	29.49

averaged between 120 and 130 mm. Only one individual was complete enough to measure from the Late Period component: a black abalone falling within the 120–130 mm size class.

Point Buchon (CA-SLO-1370/H)

Description

The Point Buchon Site (CA-SLO-1370/H) is a low-density coastal midden situated on the tip of Point Buchon west of the mouth of Coon Creek (Figure 6.22). In 1990 a larger, denser midden to the east originally was recorded as a separate site, CA-SLO-1467/H, but it was combined in 2006 under one trinomial: CA-SLO-1370/1467/H (Price et al. 2006). Here, we refer to the smaller, western midden at Point Buchon as CA-SLO-1370/H. At an elevation of about 34 feet (10.4 m) above sea level, the westernmost midden covers an area of only ca. 400 m² on an eroding Pleistocene terrace. Adjacent areas also contain an early twentieth-century Euroamerican component marked by a trash deposit in a swale on the northern edge of the point. The

site was investigated by a Cal Poly field class in 2009. Excavation showed that the deposit extends from the surface to between 90 and 110 cm below the surface. Two soil strata were apparent: Stratum I (0–80 cm), a friable, dark grayish-brown loam, and Stratum II (80–120 cm), an indurated midden with a high content of calcium carbonate. The latter is similar to caliche and is common in sites over 3,000 years old on the central California coast. The dominant constituents in both of these layers were shells of rocky intertidal invertebrates, primarily California sea mussel and black and red abalone. The deposit yielded fire-affected rock, flaked-stone debitage, cores, various bifacial and unifacial flaked-stone implements, obsidian debitage, a shell bead, and bird, mammal, fish, and reptile remains. Investigations recovered 11.0 m³ of the deposit, with 10.0 m³ processed through 3 mm (⅛ in) mesh dry and sorted in the field and 1.0 m³ processed through 3 mm mesh wet and sorted in the laboratory. Site findings are reported in fuller detail by Hadick et al. (2012).

TABLE 6.33. Fish Remains from Tom's Pond (CA-SLO-1366/H; Late=700–250 cal BP; Early=5800–2500 cal BP).

Taxon	Common Name	3mm Dry-Screened Late NISP	Wt (g)	3mm Dry-Screened Early NISP	Wt (g)	3mm Wet-Screened Late NISP	Wt (g)	3mm Wet-Screened Early NISP	Wt (g)	Total Late NISP	%NISP	Wt (g)	Total Early NISP	%NSIP	Wt (g)
Elasmobranchiomorphi	Sharks, Skates, Rays														
Rajiformes	Rays	1	0.01	0	0	0	0	0	0	1	4	0.01	0	0	0
Subtotal															
Actinopterygii	Ray-finned fishes														
Sebastes sp.	Rockfishes	10	1.04	20	2.31	1	0.05	8	0.54	11	39	1.09	28	46	2.85
Hexagrammidae	Kelp greenling	0	0	3	0.17	0	0	1	0.07	0	0	0	4	7	0.24
Ophiodon elongates	Lingcod	1	0.09	0	0	0	0	2	0.89	1	4	0.09	2	3	0.89
Cottidae	Sculpins	0	0	0	0	0	0	1	0.05	0	0	0	1	2	0.05
Scorpaenichthys marmoratus	Cabezon	8	2.94	12	1.97	0	0	4	0.51	8	29	2.94	16	26	2.48
Paralabrax sp.	Kelp bass	0	0	1	0.1	0	0	0	0	0	0	0	1	2	0.1
Embiotocidae	Surfperches	1	0.09	0	0	0	0	2	0.18	1	4	0.09	2	3	0.18
Stichaeidae	Pricklebacks	4	0.14	2	0.17	0	0	3	0.08	4	14	0.14	5	8	0.25
Xiphister sp.	Black prickleback	1	0.03	0	0	0	0	0	0	1	4	0.03	0	0	0
Cebidichthys violaceus	Monkeyface prickleback	1	0.11	1	0.04	0	0	0	0	1	4	0.11	2	2	0.04
Heterostichus rostratus	Giant kelpfish	0	0	0	0	0	0	1	0.03	0	0	0	1	2	0.03
Subtotal		26	4.44	39	4.76	1	0.05	22	2.35	27	98	4.49	61	101	7.11
Grand total		27	4.45	39	4.76	1	0.05	22	2.35	28	102	4.50	61	101	7.11

TABLE 6.34. Shellfish Remains from Tom's Pond (CA-SLO-1366/H).

Group	Taxa	Common Name	Late (700–250 cal BP)		Early (5800–2500 cal BP)		Total	
			Wt (g)	%	Wt (g)	%	Wt (g)	%
Abalones	*Haliotis cracherodii*	Black abalone	6.64	0.3	7.7	0.5	14.34	0.4
	Haliotis sp.	Abalone	18.27	0.7	11.62	0.7	29.89	0.7
Mussel	*Mytilus californianus*	California mussel	2,017.36	82.4	1,211.88	77.2	3,229.24	80.4
Clams	*Protothaca staminea*	Pacific littleneck clam	1.71	0.1	0.36	0.0	2.07	0.1
		Indet. clam	0	0.0	1.96	0.1	1.96	0.0
Cockles	*Clinocardium nuttallii*	Nuttall's cockle	0	0.0	0.36	0.0	0.36	0.0
Turban Snails	*Chlorostoma* sp.	Indet. turban snail	207.88	8.5	133.27	8.5	341.15	8.5
Limpets	*Lottia scabra*	Rough limpet	0.06	0.0	0	0.0	0.06	0.0
		Indet. limpet	0.04	0.0	0.35	0.0	0.39	0.0
Chiton	*Cryptochiton stelleri*	Gumboot chiton	11.5	0.5	12.45	0.8	23.95	0.6
	Isnochiton sp. *or Mopalia* sp.	Small chiton	17.17	0.7	8.59	0.5	25.76	0.6
Misc. snails	*Crepidula* sp.	Slipper	0.56	0.0	0.08	0.0	0.64	0.0
Barnacles	*Balanus* sp.	Barnacle	35.09	1.4	30.52	1.9	65.61	1.6
	Pollicipes sp.	Leaf barnacle	6.76	0.3	13.04	0.8	19.8	0.5
Urchin	*Stongylocentrotus purpuratus*	Purple urchin	28.8	1.2	43.29	2.8	72.09	1.8
Crab	*Cancer antennarius*	Red-spotted rock crab	2.64	0.1	0.98	0.1	3.62	0.1
Unidentifiable			94.25	3.8	92.8	5.9	187.05	4.7
Total			2,448.73	100.0	1,569.25	100.0	4,017.98	100.0

Chronology

Eight radiocarbon readings provide the main chronological determinations for the westernmost midden. Seven of these cluster together and span the Early Period with a combined one-sigma range between 5600 and 3300 cal BP. The midpoints of these dates range from 5500 and 3400 cal BP. Depth distribution shows that all of the samples that yielded Early Period dates were from below 20 cm although depth information is not available for three of the samples. One date with a one-sigma range of 560–480 cal BP was obtained from a sample in the 10–20 cm level of Unit 2. This is interpreted as an indication that the upper 20 cm of the deposit reflect a more limited occupation during the Late Period, although the upper levels are also heavily mixed with historic material.

One temporally diagnostic shell bead was recovered. Identified as a G2a Normal Saucer,

this bead type was manufactured during the Early–Middle Period Transition and extending into the early Middle Period (Groza et al. 2011). Two nondiagnostic beads, an A1a *Olivella* spire-lopped and a limpet bead, were also recovered.

Three pieces of obsidian were recovered. Two were from Coso source with hydration rims of 4.1 and 2.7 microns. The third was from Casa Diablo with a reading of 5.6 microns, which suggests the Early Period (Mikkelson et al. 2000). In the end, the obsidian readings were considered too ambiguous to aid in the assessment of the site's age.

Combined, the chronological findings suggest that the lower portion of the deposit from 20 to 100 cm represents an occupation during the Early Period. The upper 20 cm represents a mixture of Late Prehistoric and historic materials. A total of 8.8 m³ of recovery volume is associated with the primary Early Period com-

FIGURE 6.22. Point Buchon (CA-SLO-1370/H) (photograph by Kacey Hadick).

ponent while 2.2 m³ from the upper 20 cm of the deposit represent the Late Period (with considerable historic contamination). There was no discernible correlation between the dating results and the two soil strata recorded in the sidewalls; the physical variation in the deposit did not appear to have cultural or chronological significance. This suggests that the accumulation of calcium carbonate in the soil that distinguished Stratum II was a postdepositional phenomenon.

Technology

Foragers at Point Buchon emphasized flaked-stone technology, but also relied on some battered and ground stone. The entire collection includes only nine cores, four core tools, two bifaces, six projectile points, three pitted stones, three battered cobbles, and a single charmstone fragment.

Flaked Stone

The Early Period sample includes nine cores, three core tools, four indeterminate projectile point fragments, and two bifaces (Figure 6.23). The Late/Historic Period sample includes one core tool, one contracting-stemmed point, and one indeterminate arrow-point fragment.

In addition to the nine cores, flaked-stone tool-reduction residues included 6,250 pieces of debitage. Debitage from Unit 6 was taken as a representative sample for analysis (Table 6.35). The two temporal components in this sample exhibited generally similar profiles, but some variation is apparent as well. Of the diagnostic classes, simple interior flakes were most prevalent in each component (45% Early component, 34% Late/Historic component), followed by edge preparation/pressure. Cortical flakes were somewhat more abundant in the Early Period residues (15%) as opposed to the Late (9%) which is consistent with the high frequency of cores in the Early component. More noteworthy is the high frequency of edge preparation/pressure flakes in the Late component (45%) compared with the Early (16%). Overall, these findings suggest that the Late/Historic Period site inhabitants may have pursued a more limited range of flaked-stone production, emphasizing production and/or resharpening of arrow points, and less primary reduction.

Ground Stone

The ground- and battered-stone assemblage was limited to three pitted stones, three battered

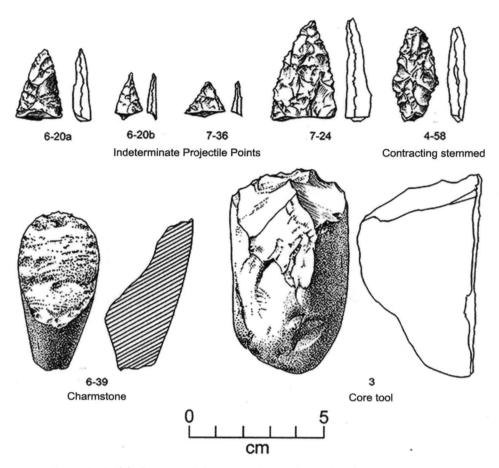

6-20a   6-20b   7-36   7-24   4-58

Indeterminate Projectile Points   Contracting stemmed

6-39   3
Charmstone   Core tool

0 ————————— 5
cm

FIGURE 6.23. Flaked stone and charmstone from Point Buchon (CA-SLO-1370/H).

cobbles, and a charmstone fragment (Figure 6.23). Of the battered stones, one has distinctive battering on one end suggestive of use as a hammerstone. The charmstone was represented only by a medial fragment, leaving it impossible to determine its complete shape or whether it was perforated. All of these implements were associated with the Early Period occupation.

Subsistence Remains

Mammals, Birds, and Reptiles

A total of 1,386 mammal and bird bones was recovered from the Early Period deposit (Table 6.36). Overall, the assemblage is dominated by intrusive pocket gophers and unidentifiable bone fragments. Focusing only on 26 elements belonging to economically significant species identified to the genus level or more specific,

the most common elements represent cottontail rabbits (NISP=8; 31%), cormorants (NISP=7; 27%) and Cassin's auklet (NISP=4; 15%) (Table 6.37). The assemblage associated with the Late/Historic Period component includes 182 bones, with general trends also showing the dominance of unidentifiable bones and pocket gophers and the nonintrusive finds indicating the dominance of cormorants (NISP=5; 50%).

Fish

A total of 411 identifiable fish elements was recovered from this site (Table 6.38). The dry-screened sample produced a total of 108 fish elements from the Early Period component and 181 from the Late/Historic Period component. From the wet-screened control unit, a total of 50 fish elements was recovered from the Early

TABLE 6.35. Debitage from Point Buchon (CA-SLO-1370/H).

Flake Type	0–20 (Late, 600–500 cal BP)	%	>20 (Early, 5500–3400 cal BP)	%	Total	%
Primary decortication	0	0	7	5	7	4
Secondary decortication	2	3	4	3	6	3
Cortical shatter	3	5	9	7	12	6
Subtotal	5	9	20	15	25	13
Simple interior	20	34	59	45	79	42
Complex interior	3	5	14	11	17	9
Subtotal	23	40	73	56	96	51
Early biface thinning	1	2	5	4	6	3
Late biface thinning	3	5	11	8	14	7
Subtotal	4	7	16	12	20	11
Edge preparation/pressure	26	45	21	16	47	25
Pressure	0	0	0	0	0	0
Subtotal	26	45	21	16	47	25
Total	58		130		188	

component and 72 from the Late/Historic component. Across all sampling methods, the overall identifiable sample was dominated by rockfish, Pacific hake, and plainfin midshipman.

The Early Period assemblage was dominated by rockfish in both the dry-screened (40.7%) and wet-screened (38%) samples. The Late/Historic Period assemblage was also dominated by rockfish (43.6%) in the dry-screened sample and 26.4% in wet-screened sample. The recovery volume from the dry-screened sample of the Early Period component was 8.0 m³ which translates to a volumetric density of 13.5 NISP/m³; the wet-screened Early Period volume was 0.8 m³ for a volumetric density of 62.5 NISP/m³. For the Late/Historic Period, the dry-screened volume was 2.0 m³ for 90.5 NISP/m³, and the wet-screened volume was 0.2 m³ for a volumetric density of 360 NISP/m³.

Shellfish

Analyzed shellfish remains include 3,877.95 g of shell from the 1.0 m³ control unit. In addition, measurements (maximum diameters) were obtained from all whole and nearly whole abalone shells collected from units. Thirty-two taxa were

identified to the genus level or more specific from the control unit. A total of 236.18 g of shell was recovered from the Late Period component (recovery volume = 0.08 m³). By shell weight, the Late Period component was dominated by California mussel (160.6 g, 68%), chiton (30.5 g, 12.9%), and turban snails (24.93 g, 10.56%). The Early Period component (3,641.77 g shell) was dominated by mussels (2,793.49 g, 76.71%) and turban snails (523.34 g, 14.37%). The volumetric density of shell for the Late component is 1.3 kg/m³; for the Early component it is 4.6 kg/m³. Length estimates of 34 red abalone shells from the Early Period component averaged between 120 and 140 mm (approximately 125 mm, mode=140) while length estimates from nine black abalone from the same component averaged between 80 and 100 mm (approximately 95 mm).

Rattlesnake Creek (CA-SLO-58)

CA-SLO-58, located on the east bank of Rattlesnake Creek at its mouth, was investigated by Cal Poly–San Luis Obispo field class students in the spring of 2017. Processing of site materials is ongoing, and full information on findings will

TABLE 6.36. Mammal, Bird, and Reptile Remains from Point Buchon (CA-SLO-1370/H).

Taxon	Common Name	Early		Late/Historic	
		NISP	Wt (g)	NISP	Wt (g)
Vertebrata	Unidentified vertebrate	521	16.74	41	1.52
Reptiles					
Squamata	Lizard/snake	1	0.02	0	0
Elgaria multicarinata (cf)	Southern alligator lizard	3	0.06	2	0.09
Colubridae	Colubrid snake	1	0.08	0	0
Crotalus sp.	Rattlesnake	3	0.23	0	0
Mammals					
Mammalia	Unidentified mammal	108	44.64	18	7.79
Rodentia	Unidentified rodent	105	2.27	10	0.34
Otospermophilus beecheyi	California ground squirrel	3	0.12	15	2.83
Thomomys bottae	Botta's pocket gopher	455	42.26	54	5.15
Microtus californicus	California vole	92	0.75	11	0.45
Microtus sp.	Vole	10	2.13	2	0.02
Peromyscus maniculatus	California deermouse	1	0.01	1	0.02
Peromyscus sp.	Deermouse	15	0.31	2	0.05
Sylvilagus sp.	Rabbit	8	0.66	0	0
Scapanus latimanus	Mole	2	0.06	0	0
Pinniped	Unidentified pinniped	0	0	4	6.52
Otariidae	Eared seal	4	11.08	1	0.87
Zalophus californianus	California sea lion	1	62.8	0	0
Callorhinus ursinus	Northern fur seal	1	7.07	0	0
Enhydra lutris	Sea otter	0	0	1	1.15
Procyon lotor	Raccoon	2	0.62	0	0
Artiodactyl	Even-toed ungulate	2	0.98	0	0
Birds					
Aves	Unidentified bird	34	8.89	11	2.19
Anas sp.	Duck	2	1.43	0	0
Phalacrocorax sp.	Cormorant	7	18.10	5	7.87
Oceanodroma sp.	Storm petrel	0	0	1	0.09
Ptychoramphus aleuticus	Cassin's auklet	4	0.44	0	0
Scolopacidae sp.	Sandpiper/phalarope	0	0	1	0.03
Mimus polyglottos	Northern mockingbird	1	0.03	0	0
Aphelocoma coerulescens	Scrub jay	0	0	1	0.04
Turdus migratorius	American robin	0	0	1	0.04
Total		1,386	221.78	182	37.06

not be available in time for inclusion here. The site is a modest-sized shell midden, ca. 120 × 40 m in dimension. It was seriously eroding on its western edge where eight excavation units were established in order to salvage some of the eroding materials. A total of 11.64 m³ was exca- vated including 10.6 m³ processed dry through 3 mm mesh in the field, one 1 × 1 m wet-screened unit (1 m³) and one 20 × 20 cm column sample. The deposit had a maximum depth of only 1 m and there was no visual stratigraphy. Evidence of rodent disturbance was apparent in all units.

TABLE 6.37. Economically Significant Mammal and Bird Remains from Point Buchon (CA-SLO-1370/H).

Taxon	Common Name	NISP	Early		Late/Historic	
			% NISP	Wt (g)	NISP	Wt (g)
Terrestrial mammals						
Sylvilagus sp.	Rabbit	8	30.76	0.66	0	0.00
Procyon lotor	Raccoon	2	7.69	0.62	0	0.00
Subtotal		10	38.46	1.28	0	0.00
Marine mammals						
Zalophus californianus	California sea lion	1	3.85	62.80	0	0
Callorhinus ursinus	Northern fur seal	1	3.85	7.07	0	0
Enhydra lutris	Sea otter	0	0.00	0.00	1	1.15
Subtotal		2	7.69	69.87	1	1.15
Birds						
Anas sp.	Duck	2	7.69	1.43	0	0.00
Phalacrocorax sp.	Cormorant	7	26.92	18.10	5	7.87
Oceanodroma sp.	Storm petrel	0	0.00	0.00	1	0.09
Ptychoramphus aleuticus	Cassin's auklet	4	15.38	0.44	0	0.00
Scolopacidae sp.	Sandpiper/phalarope	0	0.00	0.00	1	0.03
Mimus polyglottos	Northern mockingbird	1	3.85	0.03	0	0.00
Aphelocoma coerulescens	Scrub jay	0	0.00	0.00	1	0.04
Turdus migratorius	American robin	0	0.00	0.00	1	0.04
Subtotal		14	53.84	20.00	9	· 8.07
Grand total		26	99.99	91.15	10	9.22

Qualitative observations from the field also suggested very low frequency of formal artifacts and vertebrate remains. Midden residues consisted primarily of California mussel shell fragments.

Following completion of field work in June 2017, six radiocarbon determinations were obtained from Beta Analytic from four samples of mussel shell and two of red abalone. Samples were from a range of depth proveniences between 10–20 and 90–100 cm. A mussel shell fragment from Unit 1, 10–20 cm, yielded a date of 3570±30 RCYBP (Beta-466817), with a calibrated 2-sigma age range of 3250–2950 cal BP. A sample from the 20–30 cm level of Unit 1 yielded a date of 2040±30 RCYBP (Beta-466817) which calibrates to 1400–1200 cal BP. A sample from the 30–40 cm level of Unit 2 (7 m east of Unit 1) yielded a date of 1780±30 RCYBY (Beta-466818), which calibrates to 1150–950 cal BP.

All in all, three dates from depths between 20 and 60 cm suggested occupation between 1300 and 850 cal BP (late Middle and Middle–Late Transition), while three dates from depths between 10 and 100 cm indicated occupation between 3200 and 2900 cal BP. Unfortunately, the vertical distribution of the dates shows no clear superposition, reflecting the omnipresent bioturbation from ground-burrowing rodents. However, the generally low frequency of formal implements suggests that the site probably had the same function during both periods of occupation. Of note was the recovery of 39 pitted stones from the surface to 90 cm. Projectile points, bifaces, and cores were recovered, but not in large quantities. Beads were limited to two steatite disks with no shell beads except A1 spire-lopped *Olivellas*.

TABLE 6.38. Fish Remains from Point Buchon (CA-SLO-1370/H, Early = 5500–3400 cal BP; Late = 600–500 cal BP).

Taxon	Common Name	3 mm Dry Early NISP	3 mm Dry Early Weight	3 mm Dry Late/Historic NISP	3 mm Dry Late/Historic Weight	3 mm Wet Early NISP	3 mm Wet Early Weight	3 mm Wet Late/Historic NISP	3 mm Wet Late/Historic Weight
Elasmobranchiomorphii									
Rajiformes	Rays	0	0	0	0	1	0.01	0	0.00
Myliobatos californica	California bat ray	2	0.09	1	0.01	0	0.00	0	0.00
Subtotal		2	0.09	1	0.01	1	0.01	0	0.00
Actinopterygii	Ray-finned fish								
Clupeidae	Herrings and sardines	4	0.03	7	0.09	2	0.02	8	0.05
Merluccius productus	Pacific hake	14	0.91	33	1.28	4	0.11	15	0.37
Porichthys sp.	Midshipman	3	0.09	0	0.00	6	0.10	6	0.16
Porichthys myriaster	Specklefin midshipman	1	0.01	0	0	0	0.00	0	0.00
Porichthys notatus	Plainfin midshipman	19	0.74	30	1.32	3	0.04	7	0.27
Atherinopsidae	New World silversides	0	0.00	1	0.01	0	0.00	0	0.00
Sebastes sp.	Rockfishes	44	3.29	79	2.79	19	1.13	19	0.57
Hexagrammos sp.	Greenlings	2	0.09	8	0.14	2	0.02	0	0.00
Ophiodon elongatus	Ling cod	1	0.01	0	0.00	0	0.00	0	0.00
Cottidae	Sculpins	2	0.03	2	0.03	0	0.00	0	0.00
Scorpaenichthys marmoratus	Cabezon	6	1.56	3	0.16	5	0.54	2	0.19
Trachurus symmetricus	Jack mackerel	1	0.02	0	0.00	0	0.00	0	0.00
Sciaenidae	Drums and croakers	0	0.00	2	0.03	0	0.00	0	0.00
Genyonemus lineatus	White croaker	1	0.03	2	0.1	0	0.00	1	0.02
Embiotocidae	Surfperches	3	0.04	4	0.14	1	0.01	1	0.01
Stichaeidae	Pricklebacks	2	0.13	1	0.02	4	0.17	0	0.00
Scomber japonicus	Pacific chub mackerel	1	0.01	4	0.07	0	0.00	2	0.04
Clinidae	Kelp blennies	0	0.00	0	0.00	2	0.03	1	0.01
Pleuronectiformes	Flatfishes	1	0.01	2	0.01	1	0.01	9	0.34
Pleuronectidae	Right-eye flounders	1	0.25	2	0.02	0	0.00	1	0.01
Subtotal		106	7.25	180	6.21	49	2.18	72	2.04
Grand total		108	7.34	181	6.22	50	2.19	72	2.04

TABLE 6.39. Shellfish Remains from Point Buchon (CA-SLO-1370/H).

Group	Taxon	Common name	Early (5500–3400 cal BP)		Late/Historic (600–500 cal BP)		Total	
			Weight (g)	%	Weight (g)	%	Weight (g)	%
Abalones	*Haliotis* sp.	Abalone	107.56	2.95	11.06	4.68	118.62	3.06
Mussel	*Mytilus californianus*	California mussel	2,793.49	76.71	160.55	67.98	2,954.04	76.18
Turban snails	*Chlorostoma* sp.	Indet. Turban snail	523.34	14.37	24.93	10.56	548.27	14.14
Chiton	*Cryptochiton stelleri*	Gumboot chiton	140.21	3.85	30.54	12.93	170.75	4.40
Clams	*Leukoma staminea*	Pacific littleneck	39.98	1.10	9.05	3.83	49.03	1.26
Urchin	*Strongylocentrotus purpuratus*	Purple urchin	20.49	0.56	0.02	0.01	20.51	0.52
Limpets	*Lottia* sp.	Indet. limpet	16.70	0.46	0.03	0.01	16.73	0.43
Total			3,641.77	100.00	236.18	100.00	3,877.95	99.99

CHAPTER 7

Summary

Following an aborted trenching effort in 1929 by the Los Angeles County Museum, the first serious archaeological research on the Pecho Coast was completed by Roberta Greenwood in 1968 when she excavated more than 200 m³ from six sites in anticipation of construction of the Diablo Canyon Nuclear Power Plant. Relying on seven radiocarbon dates, physical stratigraphy, and artifact assemblages, Greenwood defined a tripartite 9,000-year cultural sequence. Since then, subsurface investigations have been completed at an additional eleven locations, further work has been completed at four of Greenwood's original sites (CA-SLO-2, -51/H, -61, and -585), and radiocarbon dates have been recovered from an additional ten sites. Here we integrate the seminal findings from 1968 with the more recent research to develop a refined cultural history and explore variations in foraging efficiency over time, with particular emphasis on the relative importance of marine versus terrestrial resources and interplay between foraging strategies, their impacts, and paleoclimatic variability.

Temporal Components

As of 2017, subsurface investigations have been completed at a total of 17 sites on the Pecho Coast. Findings from six of these (CA-SLO-7, -50, -52, -61, -584, and -1453) are too limited by either chronological controls or sample size to contribute in any meaningful way to enhanced conclusions about the prehistory of this stretch of coast. Based on recovery of 97.996 m³ from the remaining 11 sites which have produced 86 radiocarbon determinations and 205 temporally meaningful shell beads, we've defined 17 temporal components that date between 10,300 and 180 years ago (Table 7.1).

CA-SLO-2

CA-SLO-2 is the most well-known and extensively excavated site on the Pecho Coast. While no additional subsurface work has been completed there since Greenwood, the site's fauna (Jones, Porcasi, Gaeta, et al. 2008), flaked stone (Farquhar 2003), and ground stone (Stevens and McElreath 2015) have been studied more intensely in the intervening years, and a total of 34 radiocarbon dates is now available from the 3.4 m deep midden. While the dates clearly show that occupation spanned between 10,300 and 200 years ago, definition of temporal components has been less than straightforward—if not contentious. Greenwood defined three cultures vertically: Millingstone (ca. 230–340 cm), Hunting (130–230 cm), and Chumash (0–130 cm). More recently, relying on the enhanced radiocarbon sample, Jones, Porcasi, Gaeta, and colleagues (2008) divided the site into four components that reflect the more recent cultural historical scheme for the San Luis Obispo area: Early Millingstone/Lower Archaic (280–340 cm; 10,300–8500 cal BP), Late Millingstone/Lower Archaic (200–280 cm; 7000–5000 cal BP), Middle Period

136

TABLE 7.1. Pecho Coast Temporal Components.

Name	Trinomial	Temporal Period	N Radiocarbon Dates	N Temporally meaningful Beads	Age Span One-Sigma (cal BP)	Depth (cm)	Excavation volume (m³)	Analytical volume bird and mammal remains (m³)	Analytical volume fish remains wet-screen (m³)	Analytical volume fish remains dry-screen (m³)	Analytical volume shell remains (m³)
Pecho	SLO-51/H	Postcontact	4	118	250–180	0–50	1.22	1.22	0.520	0.700	0.020
Diablo Canyon	SLO-2	Late	3	0	550–200	0–70	29.00	29.00	0	—	—
—	SLO-8	Late	2	4	600–400	0–50	1.50	1.500	1.500	—	—
Pecho	SLO-51/H	Late	4	39	600–250	0–50	4.00	4.00	0.000	4.000	0.008
Tom's Pond	SLO-1366/H	Late	0	3	700–250	0–20	1.41	1.41	0.208	1.200	0.008
Point Buchon	SLO-1370/H	Late/Historic	1	0	600–500	0–20	2.20	2.20	0.200	2.000	0.200
Coon Creek	SLO-9	Middle–Late Transition	7	28	1000–700	0–120	34.30	34.30	2.164	30.400	0.064
Diablo Canyon	SLO-2	Middle	11	0	2800–950	70–200	49.50	49.50	2.600		0.028
Crowbar Canyon	SLO-5	Late Middle	8	7	1200–950	0–90	10.30	10.30	1.832	8.460	0.032
Spooner's Ranch House	SLO-10	Middle and Middle–Late Transition	4	4	2700–800	1–120	10.45	10.45	2.648	4.400	0.048
Little Morro Rock	SLO-497	Terminal Early	5	0	3200–2300	0–	2.33	2.33	0	2.300	0.028
Tom's Pond	SLO-1366/H	Early	5	1	5800–2500	20–130	7.44	7.44	1.044	6.400	0.044
Point Buchon	SLO-1370/H	Early	7	1	5500–3400	20–120	8.80	8.80	0.800	8.000	0.800
Diablo Canyon	SLO-2	Initial Early	7	0	5700–5000	200–230	15.00	15.00			
Diablo Canyon	SLO-2	Millingstone/Lower Archaic	13	0	10300–5700	230–340	5.40	5.40			
Spooner's Ranch House	SLO-10	Millingstone/Lower Archaic	1	0	7400–7200	120–150	2.50	2.500	1.600	—	0.008
—	SLO-585	Millingstone/Lower Archaic	4	0	9100–8000	160–220	3.80	3.800	—	—	—
Total			86	205			189.15	189.15			

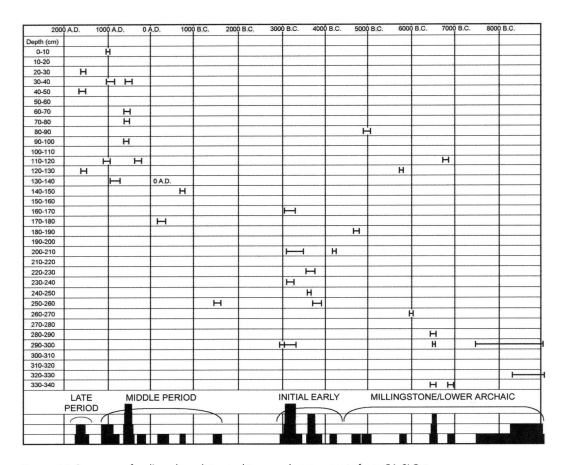

FIGURE 7.1. Summary of radiocarbon dates and temporal components from CA-SLO-2.

(70–200 cm; 3500–1000 cal BP), and Late Period (0–70 cm; 500 cal BP–Contact). Importantly, while the dates show an overall trend of superposition, they also show unequivocal evidence for vertical mixing. With abundant populations of ground-burrowing animals (ground squirrels and pocket gophers), this is one of the unfortunate realities of Pecho Coast archaeology (indeed all of central coastal California). However, the radiocarbon dates do not indicate that site materials were completely overturned or temporally compromised; rather they show a general pattern of superposition with some bioturbation-related anomalies (Figure 7.1).

Impacts of bioturbation aside, the delineation of components was challenged by Hildebrandt

and colleagues (2010) who pointed out that the component definition advanced by Jones and colleagues was not consistent with the generally accepted local cultural-historical sequence that includes a major transition between Millingstone/Lower Archaic and the Early Period (Greenwood's Hunting Culture) at 5500 cal BP. Hildebrandt and colleagues contended that this important transition was improperly dated to 5000 cal BP by Jones and colleagues and that this caused them to misinterpret the site's faunal patterns. Specifically, they felt that the profusion of deer remains in the lower site levels was likely a product of a sharp increase in deer hunting beginning ca. 5500 cal BP and that deer bones dating before that date had intruded into the lower, earlier site levels. Indeed the delineation of components for the lower portion of CA-SLO-2 is problematic. However, recent work on the shore of the Morro Bay estuary just north of the Pecho Coast (Far Western Anthropological Research Group 2016) shows that the period between 5700 and 5000 cal BP stands out as a distinctive cultural interval, and it seems reasonable to recognize it on the Pecho Coast as well. Accordingly, we here revise component definitions at CA-SLO-2: we retain the Middle (70–200 cm) and Late Period (0–70 cm) as originally defined by Jones, Porcasi, Gaeta, and colleagues (2008), but modify the levels ascribed to Millingstone/ Lower Archaic to 260–340 cm, and we recognize what we refer to here as an Initial Early Period component (ca. 5700–5000 cal BP) between 200 and 260 cm. Following this Initial Early occupation, CA-SLO-2 was largely abandoned for most of the rest of the Early Period with occupation commencing again during the Middle Period.

Importantly, the CA-SLO-2 components have been considered here only for their artifacts, bird and mammal remains. The fish-bone sample is methodologically incompatible with samples obtained from the more recent investigation which have employed 3 mm (⅛ in) mesh (see Jones and Codding 2012).

CA-SLO-5

CA-SLO-5 shows evidence for only a single temporal component, dating to the late Middle Period (1200–950 cal BP). The site produced useful samples of artifacts, bird and mammal remains, fish, and shellfish, but the artifact assemblage was limited, possibly an indication of site function.

CA-SLO-8

While the dating of CA-SLO-7, one of the two sites investigated by Breschini and Haversat in 1988, is too inconclusive to use in the current study, two dates from CA-SLO-8 indicate a single-component Late Prehistoric occupation. The vertebrate (birds, mammals, and fish) and invertebrate (shellfish) remains from this component have been considered here.

CA-SLO-9

Seven radiocarbon dates indicate that the Coon Creek Site is dominated by a single Middle–Late Transition component (Codding and Jones 2007; Codding et al. 2009). However, recent reevaluation of shell bead chronologies in central California (Groza et al. 2011) indicates that saucer beads like those found at CA-SLO-9 are restricted to pre-1600 cal BP contexts. This suggests that, although unrepresented in the radiocarbon dates, some early Middle Period materials are present at CA-SLO-9. Lacking dates, there is no clear basis for delineating the early Middle Period component, and as such, we treat the site as a single Middle–Late Transition component.

CA-SLO-10

CA-SLO-10 produced radiocarbon and bead evidence for two superimposed temporal components, a Millingstone/Lower Archaic occupation (120–150 cm), and a more substantial Middle Period and Middle–Late Transition component in the upper levels (0–120 cm). Respectively, these date to 7400–7200 cal BP and 2700–800 cal BP.

CA-SLO-51/H

CA-SLO-51/H, the location of the ethnographic village of *Tstyiwi*, was the only site to produce horizontally segregated temporal components. While the Pecho midden has been impacted by plowing, the site area represented by Units 1–4 harbored materials that were predominantly Late Prehistoric, dating ca. 600–250 cal BP, while the less-disturbed material recovered in Units 5 and 6 dated primarily to the earliest postcontact decades (AD 1769–1830). Records from Mission San Luis Obispo indicate that people from this village joined the mission community beginning in 1781 and continuing into the early 1800s. Most of the residues recovered from the postcontact site area (Units 5 and 6) seem to reflect activities pursued between ca. AD 1769 and 1830.

CA-SLO-497

While CA-SLO-497 produced a single radiocarbon date indicating occupation as early as 5700 cal BP, the remaining four dates testify to site use

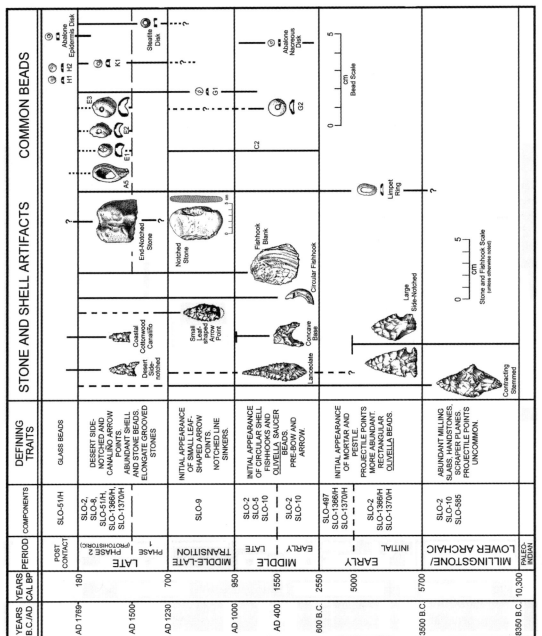

FIGURE 7.2. Cultural chronology for the Pecho Coast.

near the end of the Early Period and extending slightly into the Middle Period, ca. 3200–2300 cal BP. The materials are considered to represent essentially a single component.

CA-SLO-585

Roberta Greenwood completed an extensive investigation of CA-SLO-585 in 1968, excavating 39.4 m³ of deposit. She also obtained four radiocarbon dates from the lower depths of the midden. Based on the dates, artifacts, and physical stratigraphy (a red abalone shell lens at ca. 90 cm), Greenwood (1972:4) delineated three temporal components: Millingstone (160–240 cm), Hunting (80–160), and Chumash (0–80). Jones, Garza, and colleagues (2009) obtained six additional radiocarbon dates but found vertical mixing to be more pervasive than previously recognized. For the current project, we incorporate data only from the Millingstone/Lower Archaic component in the basal levels of the deposit (160–220 cm) dating 9100–5600 cal BP. The total recovery volume associated with this component is 3.8 m³. Owing to methodological incompatibility, the only data from this component used in the current study were the bird and mammal remains.

CA-SLO-1366/H

Combined chronometric indicators suggest that the deposit sampled at Locus 1 at CA-SLO-1366/H represents two periods: a Late Period component in the upper 20 cm, dating ca. 700–250 cal BP, and an Early Period component below that dating 5800–2500 cal BP.

CA-SLO-1370/H

Chronological findings from CA-SLO-1370/H indicate the presence of two temporal components: a modest Late/Historic Period occupation in the upper 20 cm, dating ca. 600–500 cal BP, and a more substantial Early Period component in the lower levels, dating 5500–3400 cal BP.

Cultural Chronology

The combined Pecho findings have been employed to develop a more refined cultural/historical scheme (Figure 7.2) that builds on

previous efforts for the region as a whole (Jones 1993; Jones et al. 2007), including an improved sequence recently developed for the Morro Bay estuary north of the Pecho Coast (Far Western Anthropological Research Group 2016). Developing an accurate, precise cultural history for this area remains a work in progress owing to the preponderance of multicomponent sites and bioturbation caused by prolific populations of ground-burrowing rodents. The sequence described below builds on Greenwood's initial findings and remains reliant on her larger excavation samples for some periods. Nonetheless, the enhanced radiocarbon sample and newly discovered single-component sites allow for a more resolute scheme that includes seven major periods with subdivisions as described below.

Radiocarbon Dates

The combined radiocarbon data set for the Pecho Coast currently includes 128 dates from 22 sites, including 10 dates from nine sites for which no subsurface data are available (Figure 7.3, Appendix C). Recently there has been a revival of the use of radiocarbon "dates as data" (Rick 1987) to infer demographic trends (e.g., Chaput et al. 2016, Kelly et al. 2013, Peros et al. 2010). Typically, such attempts incorporate a formula developed by Surovel and colleagues (2009) to correct for taphonomic bias that likely erases older material and dates. We have incorporated this correction here but examine both observed and "corrected" radiocarbon frequencies in 500-year intervals. We also exclude multiple dates per 500-year interval from the same site to evaluate trends in the number of occupied sites (Figure 7.4). Nonetheless, we are still hampered by the relatively small size of the Pecho date database and the very real possibility that variation in date frequencies could be a reflection only of an inadequate sample.

The available data indicate near continuous occupation of the Pecho Coast with an apparent increase or spike in date frequency ca. 6000–5000 cal BP (Figure 7.4) which we interpret as the long-recognized mid-Holocene transition referred to by Greenwood and others before her (e.g., Harrison and Harrison 1966; Rogers 1929)

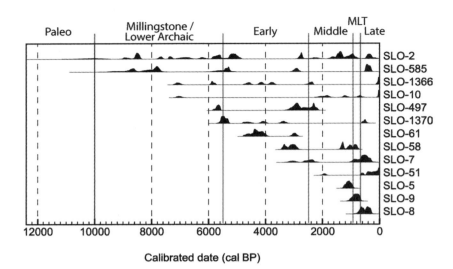

FIGURE 7.3. Summary of radiocarbon date ranges for Pecho Coast components.

as the onset of the Hunting Culture. Based on the distribution of "corrected" dates, this population spike represents the highest prehistoric population levels throughout the sequence. The beginning of this period has been consistently linked to an increase in human population along the central and southern California coasts. It was recognized by Glassow and colleagues (1988:75) for the Santa Barbara coast and it is apparent in tallies of component frequencies by Jones and colleagues (2007:142) and Jones (1992:12) from the broader central coast. More recent studies from Santa Barbara show a similar upturn ca. 5300 cal BP on both the mainland and Channel Islands (Glassow 1997:84), however, no similar peak is evident at Vandenberg Air Force Base in northern Santa Barbara County (see Glassow 1996:101), suggesting that multiple processes are at work structuring populations across the region. Nonetheless, the mid-Holocene increase indicated at Pecho and most locations to the north and south seems to coincide with distinct cultural changes that we recognize here in a newly proposed Initial Phase of the Early Period (5700–5000 cal BP). Such a pattern indicates that demographic shifts covary with changes in subsistence and settlement, though the causal arrow is undetermined.

Perhaps also of some importance is the low frequency of dates during the millennium before the mid-Holocene increase which has also been recognized at the Morro Bay estuary to the north where it has been taken as a possible sign that the coast was abandoned for all or parts of this period. The alternative, however, is that this near-absence of dates only reflects the limitations of the currently available sample.

Finally, the observed component frequencies from Pecho show an all-time high during the Late Period which is consistent with overall regional trends (Jones et al. 2007:142), patterns at Morro Bay (Far Western Anthropological Research Group 2016), and in the Santa Barbara area including the islands, mainland, and Vandenberg Air Force Base (Glassow 1996:101). Whether this patterning in date frequencies accurately reflects population trends through the entire Late Period, however, is a matter of some uncertainty. Our investigations revealed only a single substantive Late Period component at CA-SLO-51/H, with Late Period dates at other sites, like CA-SLO-2, reflecting only light, seasonal occupation.

In addition to elucidating population-linked changes in culture history, these results also generate expectations about foraging competition.

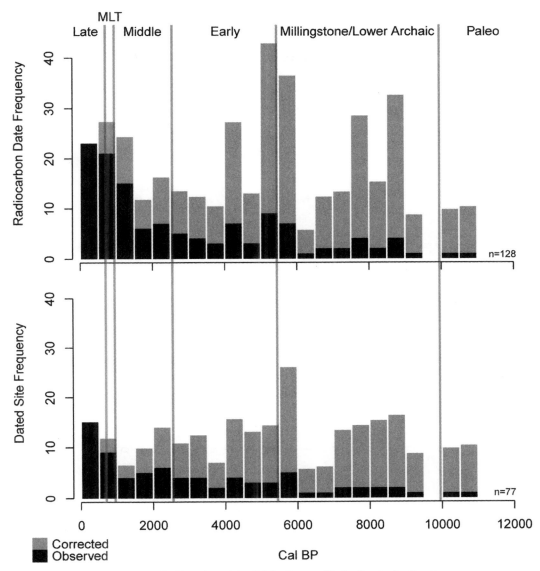

FIGURE 7.4. Radiocarbon date distribution profile for the Pecho Coast.

Higher populations may place greater pressure on local (especially terrestrial) high-profitability resources, encouraging individuals to target alternative, lower-profitability plants and animals. If this is true, then spikes in population density associated with the onset of the Hunting Culture and the Late Period should be coupled with increased reliance on lower-profitability prey, something we evaluate below.

Beads

Because they have long been recognized as temporally sensitive, shell, stone, bone, and glass bead types have been incorporated into the Pecho sequence, but their placement is based on grave-lot seriation studies and direct radiocarbon dating completed in adjacent areas. Neither of these types of data are available for Pecho. Greenwood (1972) recovered a substantial

TABLE 7.2. Summary of Beads and Bead Blanks from Pecho Sites since Cal Poly.

Bead Type	Milling	Early				Middle			Middle–Late	Late				Postcontact	Grand total
	SLO-10	SLO-1366/H	SLO-1370/H	SLO-497	Subtotal	SLO-10	SLO-5	Subtotal	SLO-9	SLO-1370/H	SLO-1366/H	SLO-51/H	Subtotal	SLO-51/H	
A1	0	0	1	0	1	10	0	10	3	0	0	9	9	8	31
A4	0	0	0	0	0	0	0	0	0	0	0	2	2	2	4
A5	0	0	0	0	0	0	0	0	0	0	0	0	0	1	1
B3	0	0	0	0	0	0	0	0	0	0	0	0	0	1	1
C2	0	0	0	0	0	0	0	0	0	0	0	0	0	1	1
E1	0	0	0	0	0	0	0	0	0	0	1	5	6	8	14
E2	0	0	0	0	0	0	0	0	0	0	0	0	0	10	10
E3	0	0	0	0	0	0	0	0	0	0	0	0	0	3	3
G1	0	0	0	0	0	0	4	4	1	0	1	8	9	43	57
G2/G6	0	1	1	0	2	3	3	6	22	0	0	0	0	2	32
G3	0	0	0	0	0	0	0	0	1	0	0	0	0	1	2
H1*	0	0	0	0	0	0	0	0	0	0	0	2	2	4	6
H2*	0	0	0	0	0	0	0	0	0	0	0	0	0	1	1
K1	0	0	0	0	0	1	0	1	3	0	2	18	20	23	47
K2	0	0	0	0	0	0	0	0	0	0	0	7	7	32	39
K3	0	0	0	0	0	0	0	0	0	0	0	3	3	10	13
K3i	0	0	0	0	0	0	0	0	0	0	0	0	0	1	1
Subtotal	0	1	2	0	3	14	7	21	30	0	4	54	58	151	263
Other															
Clam disks	0	0	0	0	0	0	0	0	0	0	0	4	4	1	5
Limpet rings	0	0	1	0	1	7	4	11	55	0	0	6	6	4	77
Dentalium	0	0	0	0	0	0	0	0	0	0	0	1	1	3	4
Abalone epidermis	0	0	0	0	0	0	0	0	0	0	0	0	0	9	9
Abalone nacre	0	0	0	0	0	0	0	0	0	0	0	1	1	0	1
Steatite disk	0	0	0	0	0	0	0	0	1	0	0	2	2	9	12
Steatite globular	0	0	0	0	0	0	0	0	0	0	0	1	1	0	1
Glass	0	0	0	0	0	0	0	0	0	0	0	2	2	7	9
Subtotal	0	0	1	0	1	7	4	11	56	0	0	18	18	39	118
Blanks															
Mussel	0	0	0	0	0	0	1	1	0	0	0	0	0	1	2
Olivella	0	0	0	0	0	2	0	2	0	0	0	0	0	0	2
Abalone	0	0	0	0	0	0	0	0	0	0	0	0	0	2	2
Subtotal	0	0	0	0	0	2	1	3	0	0	0	0	0	3	6
Grand total	0	1	3	0	4	23	12	35	86	0	4	77	79	187	384

number of beads (n=1,607 from CA-SLO-2), but she employed her own typology that does not clearly translate into more recent typological systems, and the beads themselves are no longer available for study because they were reinterred in the 1980s. Only beads recovered from the Cal Poly investigations are considered here. These excavations produced a total of 384 beads representing 25 types and three forms of blanks (Table 7.2). However, the vast majority of beads (n=258) was recovered from the ethnographic village site at CA-SLO-51/H, and as such it is fairly apparent that beads were numerically important only in the more recent periods.

Paleoindian/Paleocoastal
(13,000–10,300 cal BP)

The earliest interval in local prehistory continues to be largely conjectural. There are no radiocarbon determinations or artifacts from the Pecho Coast itself that predate 10,300 cal BP. A fluted projectile point from Nipomo (Mills et al. 2005), 30 km to the south, suggests occupation in the region by Clovis big-game hunters as early as perhaps 13,000 cal BP, while radiocarbon determinations from the northern Channel Islands indicate occupation at least 12,500 years ago by Paleocoastal peoples (Erlandson et al. 2011). Which of these cultural adaptations and their associated entry routes apply to the Pecho Coast is unknown.

Further complicating interpretations of the earliest human entry into the region are recent findings from CA-SBA-1547 (the Sudden Flats Site) on Vandenberg Air Force Base, ca. 75 km to the south of Pecho. Recent findings by Lebow and colleagues (2014, 2015) indicate occupation between ca. 10,900 and 10,500 cal BP in association with large bifaces, burins, and microblades but lacking ground stone. An eccentric crescent was also found in the site vicinity. The assemblage, which also includes obsidian, is inconsistent with characteristics of the Millingstone Culture originally thought to be the earliest post-Clovis culture in the region. Findings from this site cast that conclusion in doubt. For now, the term *Paleoindian/Paleocoastal* is used to refer to the time period predating the 10,300 cal BP associated with the Millingstone assemblage at Cross Creek (CA-SLO-1797 [Fitzgerald 2000; Jones et al. 2002]).

Millingstone/Lower Archaic
(10,300–5700 cal BP)

Greenwood (1972) recognized that the earliest culture represented on the Pecho Coast was a variant of the well-known southern California Millingstone Culture which is marked by high frequencies of handstone and milling slabs, large numbers of core tools (scraper planes), absence of the mortar and pestle, and low frequencies of projectile points. Greenwood further associated large side-notched and contracting-stemmed projectile-point types with Millingstone on the Pecho Coast. Her recognition of the antiquity of the large side-notched type was confirmed by findings from Cross Creek, a buried single-component site (10,300–7600 cal BP) which clearly reflects the Millingstone pattern from southern California with slabs and handstones (n=34) and cobble/core tools (n=20) outnumbering projectile points and other bifaces (n=6). Furthermore, the volumetric densities of tools were 1.1/m³ for milling tools and only 0.2/m³ for combined projectile points and bifaces.

The defining traits of the Millingstone Culture are, in fact, only modestly represented at CA-SLO-2 and -585, the two primary components reported by Greenwood in 1972, and the more recently investigated CA-SLO-10 (Table 7.3). At CA-SLO-2, projectile points are limited to two large side-notched and one contracting-stemmed, equaling the total number of handstones (n=3). The most abundant artifact at CA-SLO-2 was the temporally ubiquitous pitted stone (n=12). Two bowl mortars and one pestle were also recovered from the upper levels of the Millingstone expression at CA-SLO-2, but these are considered intrusive from the upper Hunting Culture levels. Ignoring the mortars and pestle, the ratio of projectile points to milling equipment at CA-SLO-2 is 1:1. If the small assemblage from CA-SLO-10 is folded in, the ratio is 1.7:1. Early Holocene sites on the shoreline seem, in general, to have fewer milling tools or formal artifacts of any kind, reflecting the likelihood that there is intersite functional variability that dampens the Millingstone expression. This

TABLE 7.3. Formal Artifact Assemblage* Summary for Pecho Components.

Artifact	Millingstone/Lower Archaic			Early					Middle				Middle–Late Transition	Late					Post-contact
	SLO-2	SLO-10	Subtotal	SLO-2	SLO-1366/H	SLO-1370/H	SLO-497	Subtotal	SLO-10	SLO-5	SLO-2	Subtotal	SLO-9	SLO-2	SLO-1370/H	SLO-1366/H	SLO-51/H	Subtotal	SLO-51/H
Flaked Stone																			
Desert Side-notched	0	0	0	0	0	0	0	0	0	0	0	0	0	0	0	0	1	1	3
Canaliño/Coastal Cottonwood	0	0	0	0	0	0	0	0	0	0	1	1	0	2	0	0	2	4	0
Small leaf-shaped	0	0	0	0	0	0	0	0	2	0	10	12	8	10	0	0	1	11	1
Double side-notched point	0	0	0	0	0	0	0	0	0	0	0	0	1	0	0	0	0	0	0
Indeterminate arrow point	0	0	0	0	0	0	0	0	0	1	0	1	0	0	1	1	1	3	0
Contracting-stemmed	2	0	2	1	4	0	1	6	4	2	54	60	16	40	1	3	1	45	0
Lanceolate	0	0	0	2	0	0	0	2	1	1	11	13	0	12	0	0	0	12	0
Concave base	0	0	0	0	1	0	0	1	2	0	2	4	0	2	0	0	1	3	0
Rossi square-stemmed	0	0	0	0	1	0	0	1	0	0	6	6	0	0	0	0	0	0	0
Large side-notched	1	2	3	13	1	0	0	14	0	0	12	12	1	3	0	0	0	3	0
Indeterminate point	0	0	0	11	8	4	0	23	3	4	49	56	18	29	0	1	5	35	3
Subtotal	3	2	5	27	15	4	1	47	12	8	145	165	44	98	2	5	12	117	7
Ground stone																			
Milling slabs	0	0	0	0	2	0	0	2	0	0	0	0	0	1	0	0	0	1	0
Handstones	3	0	3	6	0	0	0	6	0	0	2	2	0	1	0	0	0	1	0
Portable mortars	2	0	2	6	1	0	0	7	0	0	22	22	0	19	0	0	0	19	0
Bedrock mortars	0	0	0	0	0	0	0	0	0	4	0	4		0	0	0	0	0	0
Pestles	1	0	1	3	0	0	0	3	2	0	12	14	1	13	0	0	0	13	2

Pitted stones		12	26	8	3	2	39	10	8	354	372	4	213	0	3	4	220	3
Charmstone		0	0	0	1	0	1	0	0	10	10	0	1	0	0	0	1	1
Grooved stones		0	1	0	0	0	1	0	0	10	10	0	6	0	0	0	6	0
Notched stones		0	0	0	0	0	0	2	0	4	6	20	22	0	0	0	22	0
Oblong notched stones (End-notched)		0	0	0	0	0	0	0	0	0	0	0	0	0	0	1	1	1
Tarring pebbles		0	0	0	0	0	0	2	0	0	2	0	0	0	0	0	0	1
Sphere/balls		0	0	0	0	0	0	0	0	0	0	0	1	0	0	1	2	1
Subtotal		18	42	11	4	2	59	16	12	414	442	25	277	0	3	6	286	9
Non-bead Shell and bone																		
Circular/J-shaped fishhooks		0	0	0	0	0	0	2	0	13	15	9	17	0	1	2	20	11
Fishhook blanks		0	0	1	0	0	1	2	0	5	7	1	4	0	0	0	4	2
Bone awls		2	3	0	0	0	3	2	1	17	20	2	10	0	0	0	10	1
Bone gorges		0	0	1	0	0	2	2	0	6	8	1	1	0	0	0	1	0
Subtotal		2	4	2	0	0	6	8	1	41	50	13	32	0	1	2	35	14
Total	23	25	73	28	8	3	112	36	21	600	657	82	407	2	9	20	438	30

*Excludes beads

situation is also evident at Morro Bay where comparably dated early Holocene shoreline components yielded no milling tools whatsoever (Far Western Anthropological Research Group 2016).

Early Period
(5700–2550 cal BP)

Greenwood recognized a major transition somewhere ca. 7,570 and 5,150 radiocarbon years ago when the Millingstone Culture was replaced by the Hunting Culture. This transition was recognized as early as 1929 by David Banks Rogers in the Santa Barbara Channel who noted a significant increase in the number and type of projectile points following the demise of his Oak Grove Culture (now commonly recognized as a regional variant of Millingstone [Moratto 1984: 160; Warren 1968]). At Diablo Canyon, Greenwood described the transition as follows:

> The most obvious developmental stage in the southern California sequence to which the middle and predominant levels of the Diablo Canyon sites must be referred is the Hunting Culture and more precisely, the incipient period defined as the Extraños Phase (Harrison and Harrison 1966:64). Diagnostic characteristics include milling stones and mortars in equal proportion, large side-notched and stemmed points, and blades.... The complex is placed on the Santa Barbara coast by 2900 B.C. (Greenwood 1972:90)

Indeed, mid-Holocene cultural changes are highly recognizable on the central California coast although the exact dating of the transition remains imprecise and somewhat contentious. Pinpointing the date is especially difficult at multicomponent, bioturbated sites like CA-SLO-2. In assigning an age to the onset of what is now referred to as the Early Period, Jones and colleagues (2007) relied instead upon single-component sites with large samples of artifacts and radiocarbon dates. For the San Luis Obispo area, the most important site representing the post–Millingstone cultural pattern is CA-SLO-165 at Morro Bay which was excavated repeatedly in the 1990s (Jones et al. 1994; Mikkelsen

et al. 2000) and from which 38 radiocarbon dates testify to a significant component dating 5700–3000 cal BP (although there is evidence of minor earlier and later occupation). The primary component is marked by 20 projectile points (dominated by eight contracting-stemmed and seven large side-notched), 108 bifaces, six milling slabs, six handstones, six pestles, three mortars, and 30 cobble/core tools. It is assumed that the mortars and pestles in this component represent the initial appearance of these types of implements in the region; the ratio of slab/handstones to mortar/pestles is 1.3:1, very close to Greenwood's description of even proportions. The ratio of projectile points and bifaces to ground stone is 6.1:1 which represents a significant change from Cross Creek where the figure was 0.2:1.

Initial Phase (5700–5000 cal BP)

Greenwood emphasized comparison between the initial Hunting Culture appearance and findings from the Aerophysics site (CA-SBA-54) in Goleta, in particular, ascribing them both to the beginning of the Hunting Culture. Here we build on her assessment and recognize an initial phase of the Early Period in the San Luis Obispo area, dating 5700–5000 cal BP defined primarily by the patterns evident at CA-SLO-165, but also represented at CA-SLO-2. Admittedly, the two millennia prior to 5700 cal BP remain somewhat murky inasmuch as Greenwood detected a gap in her record during that period at Diablo Canyon and the Cross Creek site was also largely abandoned after 7600 cal BP. The radiocarbon records from CA-SLO-2 and Morro Bay both also show hints of a gap between 7600 and 5700 cal BP, but the available sample of dates is also somewhat small. For now, it is assumed that the Millingstone Culture continued from 7600 until 5700 cal BP, but this may not necessarily prove to be accurate.

The Initial Phase of the Early Period as we define it here is marked by the same changes that define the Early Period in general (increased frequency of projectile-point and other bifaces, appearance of mortars and pestles), but findings from Morro Bay show that large side-notched projectile points, holdovers from Millingstone/

Lower Archaic, are the dominate type between 5700 and 5000 cal BP, and that they disappear thereafter. Their co-occurrence with mortars and pestles defines the Initial Phase of the Early Period. Findings from the revised component at CA-SLO-2 (200–260 cm) are consistent with this definition. Large side-notched projectile points are the dominant type, and the ratio of slab/handstone to mortar/pestle is 0.6:1. Rectangular *Olivella* beads (Class L) are also a defining trait of the Initial Phase, as represented at CA-SLO-165, although they are not common. None have been found on the Pecho Coast.

5000–2550 cal BP

The remainder of the Early Period is distinguished primarily by the near absence of large side-notched projectile points, replaced by Contracting-stemmed types, along with mortars and pestles. This pattern is well represented by the Pecho Coast components at CA-SLO-497, -1366/H, and -1370/H which yielded only a single large side-notched and four contracting-stemmed points. Tentatively, plummet-shaped charmstones may also be restricted to the Early Period.

Middle Period
(2550–950 cal BP)

Relying on the larger, more visible artifacts such as projectile points and milling implements, Greenwood (1972) did not define a Middle Period in her original Diablo chronology. She also had no radiocarbon dates suggesting discrete components between 5100 and 930 radiocarbon years BP. The Hunting Culture was seen as continuing until ca. 1,500–1,000 radiocarbon years ago when arrow points marked the beginning of the Chumash or Late Prehistoric Period. The concept of a Middle Period is based on the traditional central California cultural sequence that includes Early, Middle, and Late Periods (or horizons) distinguished by a variety of traits, including shell beads. The Middle Period is distinguished by, among other things, the initial appearance of circular *Olivella* shell beads, specifically Class G saucers, which replaced Class L rectangles. King developed a similar bead-

based, Early–Middle–Late chronology for the Santa Barbara Channel in 1982 (revised in 1990 [King 1990]). Jones (1993) and Jones and colleagues (2007) subsequently attempted to configure San Luis Obispo culture history into this more fine-grained sequence. Subsequent studies have identified discrete components dating ca. 2550–950 cal BP in San Luis Obispo County (e.g., CA-SLO-175, -267) that have helped to flesh out distinctive traits between ca. 2550 and 950 cal BP.

Middle Period components can be recognized in Greenwood's findings and subsequent excavation results. Indeed, Greenwood documented cultural changes that we now ascribe to the Middle Period, but she had no secure basis for distinguishing a major chronological break. Middle Period radiocarbon dates were subsequently obtained for CA-SLO-2 by Jones, Porcasi, Gaeta, and colleagues (2008) who distinguished the component between 70 and 200 cm albeit with some evidence for mixing due to bioturbation. Additional Middle Period occupation is evident at CA-SLO-5 and -10. Recent findings from nearby Morro Bay also show that there is reason to distinguish between earlier and later portions of the Middle Period with a break ca. 1550 cal BP. This division seems to have some meaning on the Pecho Coast as well, with CA-SLO-5 occupied only during the late Middle Period. CA-SLO-10, however, seems to contain evidence for occupation during both the early and late Middle Period as well as the Middle–Late Transition. Owing to bioturbation, it is not possible to segregate distinct subcomponents representing these shorter intervals at CA-SLO-10, however. The same problem exists at CA-SLO-9 where G2 saucer beads suggest the presence of early Middle Period residues that are unrepresented in the site's radiocarbon record.

In general, the Middle Period is distinguished by the initial appearance of *Olivella* saucer beads, circular shell fishhooks, and concave-base projectile points. Contracting-stemmed points continue and are the dominant type. Mortars and pestles become considerably more abundant than milling slabs/handstones. Direct dates of G2 saucer beads suggest they might be restricted to the early Middle Period.

Middle–Late Transition (950–700 cal BP)

This important interval is well represented by a substantial recovery volume from CA-SLO-9 which shows initial appearance of small leaf-shaped projectile points, some of which are clearly arrow sized, indicating the first appearance of the bow. Contracting-stemmed points continue. Notched stones also seem to appear for the first time. As noted above, G2 saucer beads indicate that some early Middle Period materials are present at CA-SLO-9, but here we treat this site as essentially a single Middle–Late Transition component.

Late Period (700–180 cal BP)

Very modest evidence for occupation during the Late Period was recovered from CA-SLO-2, -1366/H, and -1370/H. The only substantive Late Period component that has been identified on the Pecho Coast is at CA-SLO-51/H, the ethnographic village of *Tstyiwi* which produced distinctive Late Period artifacts, including Desert Side-notched and Canaliño/Coastal Cottonwood points, Class E lipped, and K cupped *Olivella* beads, steatite disks, and end-notched stone net weights. Handstones and milling slabs do not seem to have disappeared entirely, but they are significantly outnumbered by mortars and pestles.

There is a longstanding assertion that Desert Side-notched projectile points are restricted to post–AD 1500 contexts in central California (King 1978:68). The post–AD 1500 period is also referred to as the Protohistoric or Phase 2 of the Late Period. While this remains a remote possibility, it is more likely a product of chronology building at a time when radiocarbon dates were rare and central California prehistory was configured in cultural phases that were ambiguously anchored in actual time. Findings from MNT-1223 on the Big Sur Coast (Jones 1993) as well as sites in the Morro Bay area (e.g., CA-SLO-23 [Far Western Anthropological Research Group 2016; CA-SLO-214 [Hoover and Sawyer 1977]) demonstrated that Desert Side-notched points were used on the central coast between AD 1250 and 1700; their recovery from CA-SLO-51/H supports similar dating on the Pecho Coast.

Postcontact (180–130 cal BP or AD 1769–1830)

Postcontact occupation was clearly identified at Units 5 and 6 at CA-SLO-51/H which show continued use of Late Period projectile points and Class E and K beads. Class H *Olivella* beads, *Haliotis* epidermis disk beads, and glass trade beads distinguish this period from prehistoric times.

Variability in Faunal Resource Exploitation

By far the most abundant constituents in the Pecho middens were the dietary remains of mammals, birds, reptiles, fish, and shellfish, and considerable effort was expended over the last thirteen years to sample these materials effectively and efficiently, process them, and complete identifications. Here we describe synchronic and diachronic variation and evaluate hypotheses proposed to explain hunter-gatherer subsistence.

Birds and Mammals

A total of 3,804 elements was identified to the family level or more specific from 17 temporal components (Table 7.4), although 2,712 of these are from the large CA-SLO-2 collection recovered by Greenwood. Diachronic patterns are similar to those reported previously by Jones, Porcasi, Gaeta, and colleagues (2008) and Codding and colleagues (2010, 2012), but the currently available sample provides more complete coverage of the Holocene and shows some different, previously unrecognized (or unemphasized) patterns.

The single most abundant species represented in the overall collection is mule deer (NISP=1,355; 35.6%), followed by desert cottontail (NISP 828; 21.8%) and sea otters (NISP=605; 15.9%). The prevalence of deer remains, however, is governed largely by the materials from CA-SLO-2 which produced a total of 1,201 elements that show deer as the dominant species by considerable margins for all time periods (62–78%). This is the only site in the current sample that exhibits such a trend, and while it certainly cannot be overlooked, its divergence from the other components has to be recognized also. Aquatic and terrestrial birds are represented minimally through the sequence, in contrast with Morro

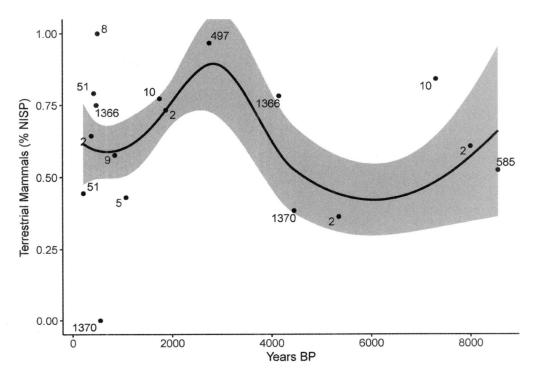

FIGURE 7.5. Terrestrial mammals (% NISP) over time on the Pecho Coast.

Bay, which provides a greater expanse of wetland habitat suitable for waterfowl (Far Western Anthropological Research Group 2016). Terrestrial mammals generally dominate the Pecho sequence throughout the Holocene (Table 7.4, Figure 7.5). Marine mammals were only exploited at minimal levels until Late and postcontact times (Figure 7.6). Marine birds figured much more prominently in the exploited fauna during the early as opposed to later Holocene (Figure 7.7).

To evaluate temporal variation, diachronic trends have been evaluated using locally weighted regression (loess, span = 0.75, unless otherwise noted) with 95% confidence intervals. Fits of nonpiscine indices are weighted by the total NISP to account for variation in component sample size. Figures illustrate each value plotted by the component midpoint. All analysis is performed in the R environment (R Core Team 2016), with plots relying on advanced graphics packages (Slowikowski 2016; Wickham 2009).

The early Holocene represented by the Mill-

ingstone/Lower Archaic components at CA-SLO-2, -10, and -585 shows an emphasis on deer, rabbits, and marine birds. Variation in the proportion of deer relative to rabbits is examined following Bayham (1979), using a more specific version of the artiodactyl index here called the *Odocoileus* or deer:rabbit index, which measures the proportion of deer relative to all lagomorphs plus deer (Figure 7.8). Under the informed assumption that deer provide more food than rabbits per time spent handling (see Broughton et al. 2011; Codding et al. 2012), high *Odocoileus* index values indicate high encounter and hunting success rates with deer which result in relatively high overall foraging efficiency. Millingstone/Lower Archaic components at CA-SLO-10 and -585 are dominated by rabbits while CA-SLO-2 shows the above-noted prevalence of deer. Previous arguments about costly signaling notwithstanding (c.f. Hildebrandt and McGuire 2003; Hildebrandt et al. 2010), we see the prevalence of deer and rabbits as consistent with estimates of postencounter return rates (Tables 2.1

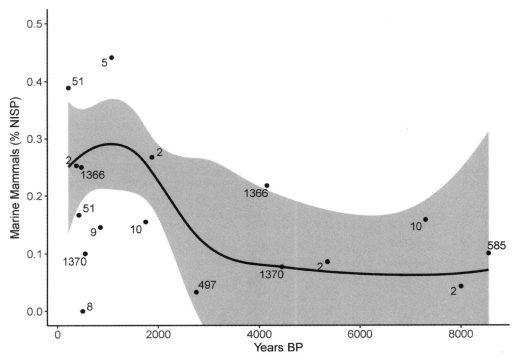

FIGURE 7.6. Marine mammals (% NISP) over time on the Pecho Coast.

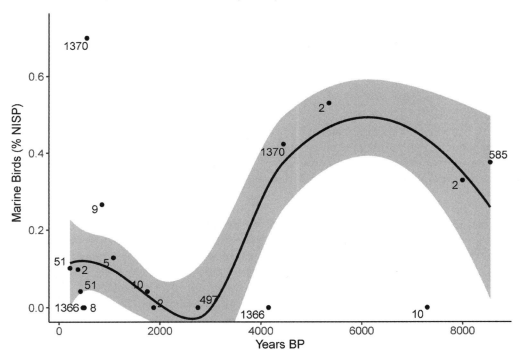

FIGURE 7.7. Marine birds (% NISP) over time on the Pecho Coast.

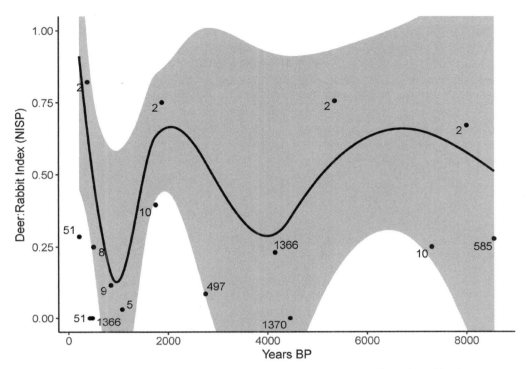

FIGURE 7.8. *Odocoileus* index illustrating the proportion of deer relative to rabbits plotted by the component midpoint and fitted using a loess (span=0.65) with 95% confidence intervals.

and 2.4) and climate and habitat variability. Deer are almost completely absent from the entire Holocene sequence at Morro Bay (Far Western Anthropological Research Group 2016), but they are abundant through time at CA-SLO-2 on the Pecho Coast which seems consistent with variation in habitat (Jones, Porcasi, Gaeta, et al. 2008). Morro Bay is surrounded by coastal scrub, which is better suited for rabbits, while the Pecho Coast lies adjacent to expansive oak woodland habitat (the Irish Hills) that accommodates deer. Furthermore, climatic variation seems to have affected habitat distribution and the deer-rabbit ratio over time. For the early Holocene we equate the high frequency of cottontail rabbits at some sites but the overall low frequency of terrestrial mammals to warmer, drier early Holocene climatic conditions. This is similar to the case made in the Great Basin (Byers and Broughton 2004). Findings from CA-SLO-2, however, show that deer were pursued where they were present, as expected from foraging models (see Codding and Bird 2015).

The high frequency of marine birds in the faunal remains has not been fully appreciated by us in the past, although D. Jones and colleagues (2002, 2004) noted it at CA-SLO-832 on the Halcyon Bay Paleoestuary (south of Pecho near modern Pismo Beach) where it was suggested that early Holocene foragers emphasized trapping of birds and rabbits over hunting of larger game. Certainly the pursuit of waterfowl can in some instances be seen as optimal in that estimated postencounter rates for species like Canadian geese are relatively high, especially when the birds were taken by boat (Table 2.1). While we cannot be certain that such rates apply strictly to the marine species represented at Pecho (cormorants, puffins, and shearwaters), the heavy exploitation of these species seems consistent with optimal diet predictions for people employing watercraft. This would certainly hold true for the extinct flightless duck, which is well represented in the Millingstone/Lower Archaic components at CA-SLO-2 and -585 but is absent from the Late Period. This

TABLE 7.4. Summary of Bird, Reptile, and Mammal Remains from Pecho Components.

Common Name	Scientific Name	Millingstone SLO-2	SLO-585	SLO-10	%
Terrestrial Mammals					
Cattle	*Bos taurus*	0	0	0	0
Canid	*Canis* sp.	5	2	0	3.52
Tule elk	*Cervus elaphus nannodes*	1	0	0	0.5
Bobcat	*Lynx rufus*	0	1	0	0.5
Black-tailed jackrabbit	*Lepus californicus*	0	1	0	0.5
Striped Skunk	*Mephitis mephitis*	0	0	0	0
Dusky-footed woodrat	*Neotoma fuscipes*	0	0	0	0
Woodrat	*Neotoma* sp.	0	0	0	0
Mule deer	*Odocoileus hemionus*	53	5	4	31.2
Raccoon	*Procyon lotor*	0	0	0	0
Cottontail rabbit	*Sylvilagus* sp.	26	12	12	25.1
American Badger	*Taxidea taxus*	0	0	0	0
Long-tailed weasel	*Mustela fenata*	0	0	0	0
Fox	*Vulpes vulpes*	0	0	0	0
Subtotal		85	21	16	61.3
Marine Mammals					
Guadalupe fur seal	*Arctocephalus townsendi*	0	1	0	0.5
Northern fur seal	*Callorhinus ursinus*	1	0	0	0.5
Sea otter	*Enhydra lutris*	4	3	3	5.03
Harbor seal	*Phoca vitulina*	0	0	0	0
Steller sea lion	*Eumetopias jubatus*	0	0	0	0
California sea lion	*Zalophus californianus*	1	0	0	0.5
Subtotal		6	4	3	6.53
Reptile/Amphibian					
Western pond turtle	*Clemmys marmorata*	1	0	0	0.5
Ducks, Geese, and other Aquatic Birds					
Northern pintail	*Anas acuta*	0	0	0	0
Teal	*Anas* sp.	1	0	0	0.5
Goose	*Anser* sp.	1	0	0	0.5
Scoter	*Melanitta* sp.	0	0	0	0
Long-billed curlew	*Numenius americanus*	0	0	0	0
Subtotal		2	0	0	1.01
Marine Birds					
Flightless duck	*Chendytes lawi*	22	10	0	16.1
Albatross	*Dimedea immutablis*	0	0	0	0
Tufted puffin	*Fratercula cirrhata*	0	0	0	0
Northern Fulmar	*Fulmarus glacialis*	1	0	0	0
Loon	*Gavia* sp.		0	0	0
Storm petrel	*Oceanodroma* sp.	0	0	0	0
Pelican	*Pelecanus* sp.	1	0	0	0.5
Double-crested cormorant	*Phalacrocorax auritus*	0	1	0	0.5
Cormorant	*Phalacrocorax* sp.	8	0	0	4.02
Cassin's auklet	*Ptychoramphus aleuticus*	2	0	0	1.01
Pink-footed shearwater	*Puffinus creatopus*	0	4	0	2.01
Puffin	*Puffinus* sp.	10	0	0	5.03
Sandpiper	Scolopacidae	0	0	0	0
Common murre	*Uria aalge*	2	0	0	1.01
Subtotal		46	15	0	30.2
Terrestrial Birds					
Scrub jay	*Aphelocoma californica*	0	0	0	0
California quail	*Callipepla californica*	0	0	0	0
Thrush	*Catharus* sp.	0	0	0	0
Northern mockingbird	*Mimus polyglottos*	0	0	0	0
American robin	*Turdus migratorius*	0	0	0	0
Barn owl	*Tyto alba*	0	0	0	0
Subtotal		0	0	0	0
Total		140	40	19	99.5

*Inadequate sample

	Early				Middle			
SLO-2	SLO-1370/H	CA-SLO-1366/H	SLO-497	%	SLO-2	SLO-10	SLO-5	%
0	0	0	0	0	0	0	0	0
6	0	5	1	1.62	77	10	5	4.78
1	0	0	0	0.13	0	0	0	0
0	0	0	0	0	0	0	0	0
1	0	0	3	0.54	2	10	0	0.62
0	0	0	0	0	0	2	0	0.1
0	0	0	0	0	0	0	0	0
0	0	0	0	0	0	0	8	0.42
152	0	3	10	22.2	673	112	2	40.9
0	2	0	0	0.27	0	1	0	0.05
48	8	10	103	22.8	221	161	60	22.9
0	0	0	0	0	0	4	2	0.31
0	0	0	0	0	0	0	0	0
0	0	0	0	0	0	0	0	0
208	10	18	117	47.6	996	300	77	70.1
0	0	0	0	0	0	0	0	0
2	1	0	0	0.4	0	2	2	0.21
13	0	4	4	2.83	278	52	54	19.9
21	0	1	0	2.96	70	3	12	4.41
0	0	0	0	0	0	1	0	0.05
13	1	0	0	1.89	15	2	11	1.45
49	2	5	4	8.09	363	60	79	26.1
9	0	0	0	1.21	0	0	0	0
0	0	0	0	0	0	1	0	0.05
0	2	0	0	0.27	0	4	0	0.21
3	0	0	0	0.4	0	0	0	0
0	0	0	0	0	0	1	0	0.05
0	0	0	0	0	0	0	0	0
3	2	0	0	0.67	0	6	0	0.31
43	0	0	0	5.8	0	0	0	0
0	0	0	0	0	0	0	0	0
0	0	0	0	0	0	0	0	0
2	0	0	0	0	0	0	0	0
0	0	0	0	0	0	0	0	0
0	0	0	0	0	0	0	0	0
15	0	0	0	2.02	0	0	0	0
0	0	0	0	0	0	0	0	0
214	7	0	0	29.8	0	11	22	1.71
3	4	0	0	0.94	0	0	0	0
0	0	0	0	0	0	0	0	0
13	0	0	0	1.75	0	1	0	0.05
0	0	0	0	0	0	0	0	0
13	0	0	0	1.75	0	4	1	0.26
303	11	0	0	52.97	0	16	23	2.02
0	0	0	0	0	0	1	0	0.05
0	0	0	0	0	0	3	0	0.16
0	0	0	0	0	0	0	0	0
0	1	0	0	0.13	0	0	0	0
0	0	0	0	0	0	0	0	0
0	0	0	0	0	0	2	0	0.1
0	1	0	0	0.13	0	6	0	0.31
572	26	23	121	99.7	1,359	388	179	98.8

TABLE 7.4. (cont'd.) Summary of Bird, Reptile, and Mammal Remains from Pecho Components.

Common Name	Scientific Name	MLT SLO-9	%	Late SLO-2	SLO-8	SLO-51/H
Terrestrial Mammals						
Cattle	*Bos taurus*	0	0	0	0	0
Canid	*Canis* sp.	13	8.23	19	0	0
Tule elk	*Cervus elaphus nannodes*	0	0	0	0	0
Bobcat	*Lynx rufus*	1	0.63	0	0	0
Black-tailed jackrabbit	*Lepus californicus*	1	0.63	0	1	0
Striped Skunk	*Mephitis mephitis*	1	0.63	0	0	0
Dusky-footed woodrat	*Neotoma fuscipes*	0	0	0	0	0
Woodrat	*Neotoma* sp.	13	8.23	0	0	2
Mule deer	*Odocoileus hemionus*	7	4.43	323	1	0
Raccoon	*Procyon lotor*	3	1.9	0	0	1
Cottontail rabbit	*Sylvilagus* sp.	52	32.9	70	2	16
American Badger	*Taxidea taxus*	0	0	0	11	0
Long-tailed weasel	*Mustela fenata*	0	0	0	0	0
Fox	*Vulpes vulpes*	0	0	0	0	0
Subtotal		91	57.6	412	15	19
Marine Mammals						
Guadalupe fur seal	*Arctocephalus townsendi*	0	0	0	0	0
Northern fur seal	*Callorhinus ursinus*	1	0.63	0	0	0
Sea otter	*Enhydra lutris*	20	12.7	136	0	3
Harbor seal	*Phoca vitulina*	2	1.27	26	0	1
Steller sea lion	*Eumetopias jubatus*	0	0	0	0	0
California sea lion	*Zalophus californianus*	0	0	0	0	0
Subtotal		23	14.6	162	0	4
Reptile/Amphibian						
Western pond turtle	*Clemmys marmorata*	0	0	4	0	0
Ducks, Geese, and other Aquatic Birds						
Northern pintail	*Anas acuta*	0	0	0	0	0
Teal	*Anas* sp.	0	0	0	0	0
Goose	*Anser* sp.	1	0.63	0	0	0
Scoter	*Melanitta* sp.	0	0	0	0	0
Long-billed curlew	*Numenius americanus*	0	0	0	0	0
Subtotal		1	0.63	0	0	0
Marine Birds						
Flightless duck	*Chendytes lawi*	0	0	1	0	0
Albatross	*Dimedea immutablis*	1	0.63	0	0	0
Tufted puffin	*Fratercula cirrhata*	1	0.63	0	0	0
Northern Fulmar	*Fulmarus glacialis*	0	0	0	0	0
Loon	*Gavia* sp.	1	0.63	0	0	0
Storm petrel	*Oceanodroma* sp.	0	0	0	0	0
Pelican	*Pelecanus* sp.	0	0	2	0	0
Double-crested cormorant	*Phalacrocorax auritus*	0	0	0	0	0
Cormorant	*Phalacrocorax* sp.	31	19.6	56	0	1
Cassin's auklet	*Ptychoramphus aleuticus*	2	1.27	0	0	0
Pink-footed shearwater	*Puffinus creatopus*	0	0	0	0	0
Puffin	*Puffinus* sp.	0	0	0	0	0
Sandpiper	Scolopacidae	0	0	0	0	0
Common murre	*Uria aalge*	6	3.8	4	0	0
Subtotal		42	26.6	63	0	1
Terrestrial Birds						
Scrub jay	*Aphelocoma californica*	0	0	0	0	0
California quail	*Callipepla californica*	0	0	0	0	0
Thrush	*Catharus* sp.	0	0	0	0	0
Northern mockingbird	*Mimus polyglottos*	1	0.63	0	0	0
American robin	*Turdus migratorius*	0	0	0	0	0
Barn owl	*Tyto alba*	0	0	0	0	0
Subtotal		1	0.63	0	0	0
Total		158	100	641	15	24

*Inadequate sample

Late			Post		
SLO-1366/H	SLO-1370/H	%	SLO-51/H	%	Total
0	0	0	3	2.78	3
0	0	2.74	8	7.41	151
0	0	0	1	0.93	3
1	0	0.14	0	0	3
0	0	0.14	0	0	19
0	0	0	0	0	3
0	0	0	0	0	0
0	0	0.29	0	0	23
0	0	46.7	10	9.26	1,355
0	0	0.14	0	0	7
2	0	13	25	23.1	828
0	0	1.59	0	0	17
0	0	0	0	0	0
0	0	0	1	0.93	1
3	0	64.7	48	44.4	2,413
0	0	0	0	0	1
0	0	0	0	0	9
1	1	20.3	29	26.9	605
0	0	3.89	13	12	149
0	0	0	0	0	1
0	0	0	0	0	43
1	1	24.2	42	38.9	808
0	0	0.58	3	2.78	17
0	0	0	0	0	1
0	0	0	0	0	7
0	0	0	0	0	5
0	0	0	0	0	1
0	0	0	0	0	0
0	0	0	0	0	14
0	0	0.14	0	0	76
0	0	0	0	0	1
0	0	0	0	0	1
0	0	0	0	0	3
0	0	0	0	0	1
0	1	0.14	0	0	1
0	0	0.29	0	0	18
0	0	0	0	0	1
0	5	8.93	10	9.26	365
0	0	0	0	0	11
0	0	0	0	0	4
0	0	0	0	0	24
0	1	0.14	0	0	1
0	0	0.58	1	0.93	31
0	7	10.2	11	10.2	538
0	1	0.14	0	0	2
0	0	0	2	1.85	5
0	0	0	1	0.93	1
0	0	0	0	0	2
0	1	0.14	1	0.93	2
0	0	0	0	0	2
0	2	0.29	4	3.7	14
4	10	100	108	100	3,804

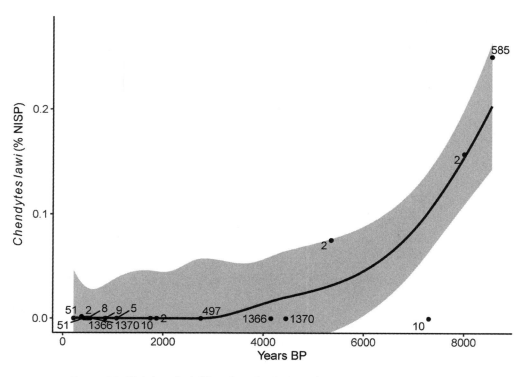

FIGURE 7.9. Flightless duck (*Chendytes lawi*, % NISP) over time on the Pecho Coast.

species is thought to have preferred nearshore rocks as nesting sites and was almost certainly a highly attractive food item. It could have been easily exploited via watercraft, making it both highly profitable and vulnerable, a combination which seems to have brought about its extinction over an 8,000-year period of exploitation (Jones, Porcasi, Gaeta, et al. 2008). This protracted extinction event is clearly illustrated on the Pecho Coast (Figure 7.9). The high frequency of marine birds in early Holocene assemblages also seems consistent with reduced terrestrial productivity and smaller populations of terrestrial animals due to the warmer, drier early Holocene climate.

While the heavy pursuit of sea birds implies some obvious focus on marine foods and habitats, the early Holocene is also marked by a dearth of marine mammals (see Figure 7.6). Remains of large, migratory seals and sea lions are especially uncommon as only one Guadalupe fur seal and one California sea lion bone can be associated with the Millingstone/Lower

Archaic Period. If we assume that these large animals were attractive prey when congregated in onshore breeding colonies (Hildebrandt and Jones 1992), we can further surmise that no such colonies were present on the Pecho Coast. The late Holocene rise in marine mammal hunting seems instead to covary with the demise of the flightless duck, which is replaced by a rise in sea otters (Figure 7.10). The relative differences in escape speed between these taxa (see Codding et al. 2012) suggest that this represents a form of intensification driven by the extinction of the higher-ranking marine taxon. Hildebrandt and McGuire (2012:142–143), however, attribute this change to an increase in costly signaling, related to the high prestige value of otter pelts and larger late Holocene communities that would offer optimal venues for show-off behavior.

A number of authors (e.g., Bertrando 2006; Greenwood 1972; Jones 1996; Jones et al. 2007; Mikkelsen et al. 2000; Warren 1968) have suggested that the key transition point in faunal

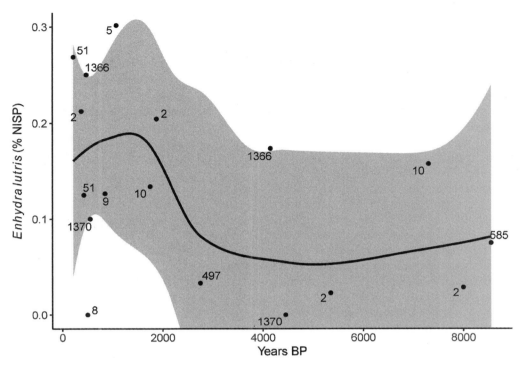

FIGURE 7.10. Sea otters (*Enhydra lutris*, % NISP) over time on the Pecho Coast.

exploitation patterns on the central coast was mid-Holocene ca. 5700–5500 cal BP (the beginning of the Early Period as defined here) when human numbers seem to have increased and settlement strategies are thought to have changed. Diachronic patterns in the Pecho fauna, however, show general continuity from Millingstone/Lower Archaic through Early with major changes coming only at the onset of the Middle Period, ca. 3000–2500 cal years BP. The Early Period shows continued dominance of marine birds, rabbits, and deer, while the Middle Period, on the other hand, is marked by a nearly complete disappearance of marine birds and marked increases in sea otters (Table 7.4). Deer show an increase in the Middle Period, accounting for 41% of the mammal and bird remains as terrestrial mammals, led by deer, and sea otters increased to replace the declining returns from marine birds at the onset of the Middle Period. The increase in terrestrial mammals seems consistent with an amelioration of climate following the mid-Holocene maximum. Comparing general temperature records (see Figures 2.2, 2.3) with the *Odocoileus* index values (see Figure 7.8) affirms earlier hypotheses that deer were a high-ranking taxa, taken whenever encountered, with their abundance in archaeological sites then being driven by their abundance on the landscape (Codding et al. 2010). The illustrative trends include an increase associated with the early Holocene climatic amelioration and the all-time nadir in the deer-rabbit index which coincides with the Middle–Late Transition associated with the droughts of the Medieval Climatic Anomaly. The only major departure from this climate-driven explanation is the decline in deer relative to rabbits about 4,000 years ago. While it may be tempting to explain this decline as a result of human-driven overexploitation attested to by the spike in human populations during the Hunting Culture (Figure 7.4), the decline in deer relative to rabbits over this period is itself not significant as shown by the 95% confidence intervals that incorporate index values ranging from 0.0 to above 0.75. Instead, this decline may not be representative of the general diachronic record, instead illustrating a few anomalous components where hunters acquired rabbits more than deer, perhaps associated with local declines in deer abundance driven by prey avoidance of highly populated areas (Whitaker 2009).

Marine birds decline over the course of the Holocene while sea mammals, largely in the form of sea otters, become much more abundant. The decline in sea birds in general can probably be attributed to the same processes thought responsible for the disappearance of the flightless duck: overexploitation of nesting colonies. Sea otters, however, increase significantly beginning in the Middle Period as represented at CA-SLO-2, -5, and -10.

The postcontact component at CA-SLO-51/H exhibits a very low percentage NISP for terrestrial mammals (44%) and the highest frequency of otter bones of any of the investigated sites (27%). This seems consistent with the reduced foraging radius available to the community as the Spanish presence increased in the area after 1769. With a limited foraging range, individuals would experience lower encounter rates with profitable prey, resulting in lower foraging efficiency driven by competitive exclusion.

Fish

A total of 15,037 fish elements was identified to nearly family level or better from the 17 components we consider here, including 6,065 from 3 mm dry-screened units (Tables 7.5 and 7.6) and 8,972 from wet-screened units (Tables 7.7 and 7.8). Collectively, the remains represent 50 taxonomic categories including 24 definitive genus and species, 12 genera with uncertain species, and 13 definitive families, and one order or subfamily. Also available for comparison are 7,401 fish remains from SLO-2 (Jones, Porcasi, Gaeta, et al. 2008) but these are not wholly compatible methodologically with the more recently recovered samples because some of the remains were obtained with larger (6 mm or ¼ in) mesh (n=

6,070), and some were obtained from smaller mesh (2 mm or ¹⁄₁₆) (n=1,331). The potential hazards associated with comparing fish-bone samples recovered with different methods are discussed by Jones and Codding (2012) and Jones and colleagues (2016). It is also important to recognize that nearly half (n=7,374) of the remains in the current sample came from a single site: the ethnographic village of *Tstyiwi* at CA-SLO-51/H which contained Late Period and postcontact components. No wet-screened sample was obtained from the precontact Late Period component at CA-SLO-51/H, however.

Both the wet-screened and dry-screened samples exhibit the same general patterns, but with some variation. Both show a preponderance of rockfish (n=5,404, 60.2% wet-screened; n=3,872, 63.8% dry-screened) and rock or black pricklebacks (n=874, 9.7% wet-screened; n=387, 6.4% dry-screened), but the wet-screened sample has a higher proportion of herrings (6.3%) than the dry-screened sample (3.5%). The dry-screened remains instead show a high frequency of cabezon (10.2%). In general, nine species account for over 90% of the elements in both samples: rockfish, cabezon, herring, surfperches, pricklebacks (family), rock or black prickleback, plainfin midshipman, señorita, and monkeyface prickleback. It is likely that at most sites and during most times, decisions about fishing were primarily made with a focus on these particular groups of fishes. Of the nine, rockfish, cabezon, herrings, and combined prickleback (black or rock, monkeyface, and the prickleback family) account for almost 90% on their own. The other species, señorita and plainfin midshipman, show intersite variability, being present at some sites and absent from others. Most of these fishes, especially rockfish, cabezon, and pricklebacks, could be taken by hook and line (either curved shell hook or bone gorge) from nearshore contexts. Herrings, however, were more available further from shore, and would have been easiest to procure with watercraft; they could be taken with either hook or net. Taxonomic and quantitative variation over time is apparent as follows.

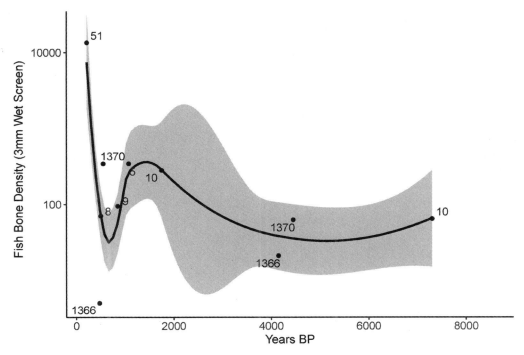

FIGURE 7.11. Fish-bone density for the 3 mm mesh wet-screened sample plotted on a logged y-axis as a function of the component midpoint and fitted using a loess (span=0.5) with 95% confidence intervals.

Millingstone/Lower Archaic Period

Unfortunately, owing to the methodological issues associated with the CA-SLO-2 fish bones, the findings for this time period are limited to the wet-screened sample from the lower component at CA-SLO-10 which shows the typically high proportion of rockfishes (51.5%) and cabezon (11.7%), but also an unusual abundance of surfperches (n=18; 17.5%). Surfperches were also abundant in the micro-sample (1 mm mesh) from the Millingstone/Lower Archaic components at CA-SLO-2 (Fitch 1972; Jones, Porcasi, Gaeta, et al. 2008:304). Surfperches are more common among the fish remains from Morro Bay where they dominate fish assemblages during most time periods (Jones et al. 2016). CA-SLO-10 is the northernmost of the current study sites and it is situated only 4 km south of Morro Bay. It is possible that the higher frequency of surfperches at CA-SLO-10 is a product of the relative proximity of the bay, which might also explain the few requiem shark and

leopard shark remains. Overall, however, the dominance of rockfishes and cabezon marks the exploitation of taxa resident to the exposed rocky coast. The volumetric density of fish bones was relatively low at 64.3 NISP/m³, indicating minimal exploitation of marine fishes.

No artifacts from the current sample indicate how these fishes were caught, but strategies may have included the use of spears, hand catch, or line and gorge. A bipointed bone gorge was recovered from Millingstone/Lower Archaic contexts at Morro Bay (Jones et al. 2004), and this is generally assumed to represent the technology used throughout southern and central California during the early Holocene. No grooved stones or stones ringed with asphaltum (interpreted as net weights, see Glassow [1996:58]) have as yet been recovered from this time depth on the Pecho Coast. None of the species represented in the limited findings from CA-SLO-10 unequivocally indicate the use of watercraft (Table 7.9), but boat use cannot be ruled out either. Watercraft

TABLE 7.5. Fish Remains from Pecho Components (Dry-screened samples).

Taxon	Common Name	Early SLO-497	SLO-1366/H	SLO-1370/H
Elasmobranchiomorphi	Sharks, skates, and rays			
Elasmobranchiomorphi	Sharks, skates, and rays	0	0	0
Triakidae	Hound sharks	1	0	0
Carcharhinidae	Requiem sharks	0	0	0
Triakis semifasciata	Leopard shark	0	0	0
Rhinobatus productus	Shovelnose guitarfish	7	0	0
Rajiidae	Skates and rays	0	0	0
Myliobatis californica	Bat ray	0	0	2
Subtotal		8	0	2
Actinopterygii	Ray-finned fishes			
Engraulis mordax	Northern anchovy	0	0	0
Clupeidae	Herrings	0	0	4
Sardinops sagax	Pacific sardine	0	0	0
Merluccius productus	Pacific hake	0	0	14
Porichthys sp.	Midshipman	0	0	3
P. myriaster	Specklefin midshipman	0	0	1
P. notatus	Plainfin midshipman	0	0	19
Atherinopsidae (Atherinidae)	New World silversides	0	0	0
Gasterosteus aculeatus	Threespine stickleback	0	0	0
Sebastes sp.	Rockfishes	18	20	44
Anoplopoma fimbria	Sablefish	0	0	0
Hexagammidae	Greenlings	0	3	0
Hexagrammos sp.	Greenlings	1	0	2
Hexagrammos decagrammus	Kelp greenling	0	0	0
Ophiodon elongatus	Lingcod	0	0	1
Cottidae	Sculpins	0	0	2
Artedius sp.		0	0	0
Clinocottus sp.		0	0	0
Leptocottus armatus	Pacific staghorn sculpin	0	0	0
Scorpaenichthys marmoratus	Cabezon	8	12	6
Paralabrax sp.	Kelp bass	0	1	0
Trachurus symmetricus	Jack mackerel	0	0	1
Sciaenidae	Drums and croakers	0	0	0
Genonemus lineatus	White croaker	0	0	1
Seriphus politus	Queenfish	0	0	0
Embiotocidae	Surfperches	0	0	3
Amphistichus sp.	Barred surfperch	0	0	0
Cymatogaster aggregata	Shiner perch	0	0	0
Damalichthys vacca (Rhacochilus vacca)	Pile perch	0	0	0
Embiotoca sp.	Black or striped seaperch	0	0	0
E. lateralis	Striped seaperch	0	0	0
Hypsurus caryi	Rainbow seaperch	0	0	0
Rhacochilus toxotes	Rubberlip seaperch	0	0	0
Oxyjulis californica	Señorita	0	0	0

| Middle | | M-L | Late | | | Postcontact | |
SLO-5	SLO-10	SLO-9	SLO-1366/H	SLO-1370/H	SLO- 51/H	SLO- 51/H	Total
0	0	1	0	0	0	0	1
0	0	0	0	0	0	1	2
0	2	0	0	0	0	0	2
0	5	0	0	0	0	0	5
0	13	0	0	0	0	0	20
0	0	0	1	0	1	2	4
0	9	0	0	1	1	0	13
0	29	1	1	1	2	3	47
0	0	0	0	0	0	1	1
0	7	2	0	7	7	151	178
0	0	3	0	0	0	13	16
0	4	2	0	33	0	0	53
0	0	0	0	0	0	0	16
0	0	0	0	0	0	0	1
0	0	2	0	30	0	61	112
0	0	6	0	1	0	7	14
0	0	0	0	0	0	0	0
2	213	246	10	79	222	3,018	3,872
0	0	0	0	0	0	0	0
0	4	0	0	0	0	0	7
0	30	0	0	8	0	0	41
0	0	3	0	0	4	77	84
2	3	1	1	0	5	33	46
0	0	0	0	2	0	1	5
0	0	0	0	0	0	0	0
0	0	0	0	0	2	6	8
0	0	0	0	0	0	0	0
11	53	166	8	3	46	301	614
0	0	0	0	0	0	0	1
0	3	0	0	0	1	0	5
0	0	0	0	2	0	4	6
0	0	0	0	2	0	7	10
0	0	0	0	0	2	2	4
1	59	26	1	4	5	37	136
0	0	0	0	0	0	0	0
0	0	0	0	0	0	0	0
0	2	0	0	0	3	8	13
0	0	0	0	0	1	2	3
0	0	0	0	0	1	0	1
0	0	0	0	0	0	0	0
0	0	0	0	0	0	0	0
1	2	25	0	0	2	31	61

TABLE 7.5. (cont'd.) Fish Remains from Pecho Components (Dry-screened samples).

Taxon	Common Name	SLO-497	Early SLO-1366/H	SLO-1370/H
Stichaeidae	Pricklebacks	0	2	2
Cebidichthys violaceus	Monkeyface prickleback	0	1	0
Xiphister sp.		0	0	0
Clinidae	Kelp blennies	0	0	0
Gibbsonia sp.	Kelpfish	0	0	0
Heterostichus rostratus	Giant kelpfish	0	0	0
Gobiesox meandricus	Northern clingfish	0	0	0
Gobiidae	Gobies	0	0	0
Scomber japonicus	Chub mackeral	0	0	1
Pleuronectiformes	Flounders and Soles	0	0	1
Pleuronectidae	Right-eye flounders	0	0	1
Platichthys stellatus	Starry flounder	0	0	0
Subtotal		27	39	106
Grand total		35	39	108

7.6. SUMMARY of Fish Bone Assemblages (Dry-screened samples).

Trinomial	Temporal Component Period	Exca. volume (m³)	NISP	Dominant Fish Group Name	N	%	NISP/m³	No. species	Margalef Index
SLO-51/H	Postcontact	0.70	4348	Rockfishes	3018	69.4	6,211.43	28	3.223
SLO-51/H	Late	4.00	327	Rockfishes	222	58.1	81.75	18	
SLO-1366/H	Late	1.20	27	Rockfishes	10	37.0	22.50	8	
SLO-1370/H	Late	2.00	181	Rockfishes	79	43.6	90.50	15	
Subtotal		7.20	535				74.30	41	4.299
SLO-9	M-L	30.40	515	Rockfishes	246	47.7	16.90	16	2.402
SLO-5	Middle	10.30	22	Cabezon	11	50.0	2.14	6	
SLO-10	Middle	4.40	463	Rockfishes	213	46.0	105.20	20	
Subtotal		14.70	485				32.90	20	3.072
SLO-497	Early	2.30	35	Rockfishes	18	45.1	15.22	5	
SLO-1366/H	Early	6.40	39	Rockfishes	20	51.1	6.10	6	
SLO-1370/H	Early	8.00	108	Rockfishes	44	40.7	13.50	17	
Subtotal		16.70	182				10.90	23	4.227

of some sort was in use on the Channel Islands 13,000–12,000 years ago 100 km to the south so it remains reasonable to think that it was available on the Pecho Coast, although perhaps not used as regularly or to travel very far offshore.

Early Period

The Early Period is better represented in the current findings by wet-screened samples from CA-SLO-1366/H and -1370/H, and dry-screened materials from CA-SLO-497, -1366/H, and -1370/H which show a relatively low volumetric density of remains (10.9 NISP/m³ dry; 83.6 NISP/m³ wet) (Figure 7.12). Rockfishes and cabezon dominate all sites individually and in the combined Early Period sample. Plainfin midshipmen (10.4%) and Pacific hake (7.7%) show unusually high frequencies in the dry-screened sample from CA-SLO-1370/H. The capture of plainfin midshipman could signal the

| Middle | | M-L | Late | | | Postcontact | |
SLO-5	SLO-10	SLO-9	SLO-1366/H	SLO-1370/H	SLO- 51/H	SLO- 51/H	Total
0	48	24	4	1	0	74	155
0	0	1	1	0	1	95	99
5	1	4	1	0	22	354	387
0	3	0	0	0	0	21	24
0	0	3	0	0	0	24	27
0	0	0	0	0	0	1	1
0	0	0	0	0	0	6	6
0	1	0	0	0	0	0	1
0	1	0	0	4	1	10	17
0	0	0	0	2	0	0	3
0	0	0	0	2	0	0	3
0	0	0	0	0	0	0	0
22	434	514	26	180	325	4,345	6,018
22	463	515	27	181	327	4,348	6,065

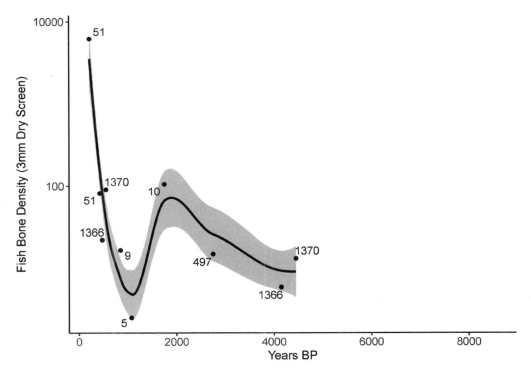

FIGURE 7.12. Fish-bone density for the 3 mm mesh dry-screened sample plotted on a logged y axis as a function of the component midpoint and fitted using a loess (span=0.5) with 95% confidence intervals.

TABLE 7.7. Fish Remains from Pecho Components (Wet-screened samples).

Taxon	Common Name	Milling/Lower Archaic SLO-10		Early SLO-1366/H		Early SLO-1370/H	
		Total	%	Total	%	Total	%
Elasmobranchiomorphi	Sharks, skates, and rays						
Lamna ditropis	Salmon shark	0	0	0	0	0	0
Triakidae	Hound sharks	0	0	0	0	0	0
Galeorhinus galeus	Tope (soupfin shark)	0	0	0	0	0	0
Triakis semifasciata	Leopard shark	2	1.94	0	0	0	0
Carcharhinidae	Requiem sharks	1	0.97	0	1	1	1.39
Rajidae	Skates and rays	0	0	0	0	0	0
Rhinobatus productus	Shovelnose guitarfish	0	0	0	0	0	0
Myliobatis californica	Bat ray	0	0	0	0	0	0
Subtotal		3	2.91	0	1	1	1.39
Actinopterygii	Ray-finned fishes						
Engraulis mordax	Northern anchovy	0	0	0	0	0	0
Clupeidae	Herrings	0	0	0	2	2	2.78
Sardinops sagax	Pacific sardine	0	0	0	0	0	0
Spirinchus starksi	Night smelt	0	0	0	0	0	0
Merluccius productus	Pacific hake	2	1.94	0	4	4	5.56
Porichthys sp.	Midshipman	0	0	0	6	6	8.33
Porichthys notatus	Plainfin midshipman	0	0	0	3	3	4.17
Atherinopsidae	New World silversides	0	0	0	0	0	0
Atherinopsis californiensis	Jacksmelt	0	0	0	0	0	0
Sebastes sp.	Rockfishes	53	51.5	8	19	27	37.5
Hexagrammidae	Greenlings	0	0	1	0	1	1.39
Hexagrammos sp.	Greenlings	4	3.88	0	2	2	2.78
Hexagrammos decagrammus	Kelp greenling	2	1.94	0	0	0	0
Ophiodon elongatus	Lingcod	1	0.97	2	0	2	2.28
Cottidae	Sculpins	0	0	1	0	1	1.39
Artedius sp.		0	0	0	0	0	0
Clinocottus sp.		0	0	0	0	0	0
Leptocottus armatus	Pacific staghorn sculpin	0	0	0	0	0	0
Scorpaenichthys marmoratus	Cabezon	12	11.7	4	5	9	12.5
Paralabrax sp.	Kelp bass	1	0.97	0	0	0	0
Trachurus symmetricus	Jack mackerel	0	0	0	0	0	0
Sciaenidae	Drums and croakers	0	0	0	0	0	0
Genyonemus lineatus	White croaker	0	0	0	0	0	0
Embiotocidae	Surfperches	18	17.5	2	1	3	4.17
Damalichthys vacca (*Rhacochilus vacca*)	Pile perch	0	0	0	0	0	0
Embiotoca sp.	Black or striped seaperch	0	0	0	0	0	0
E. lateralis	Striped seaperch	0	0	0	0	0	0
Hypsurus caryi	Rainbow seaperch	0	0	0	0	0	0
Rhacochilus toxotes	Rubberlip seaperch	0	0	0	0	0	0
Chromis punctipinis	Blacksmith	0	0	0	0	0	0

Middle				M-L				Late				Postcontact		Grand total
SLO-10		SLO-5		SLO-9		SLO-8		SLO-1366/H		SLO-1370/H		SLO-51/H		
Total	%	Total	%	Total	%	Total	%	Total	%	Total	%	Total	%	total
0	0	0	0	0	0	0	0	0	0	0	1	1	0.01	0.01
0	1	1	0.07	0	0	0	0	0	0	0	1	2	0.01	0.02
0	0	0	0	0	0	1	0	0	1	0.56	0	1	0	0.01
7	0	7	0.51	0	0	0	0	0	0	0	0	9	0	0.1
2	0	2	0.15	0	0	0	0	0	0	0	0	4	0	0.04
1	0	1	0.07	0	0	0	0	0	0	0	1	2	0.01	0.02
13	0	13	0.96	0	0	0	0	0	0	0	0	13	0	0.14
25	0	25	1.85	0	0	0	0	0	0	0	0	25	0	0.28
48	1	49	3.61	0	0	1	0	0	1	0.56	3	57	0.04	0.62
0	0	0	0	0	0	0	0	0	0	0	12	12	0.17	0.13
5	175	180	13.2	17	8.29	0	0	8	8	4.49	355	562	5.05	6.26
0	20	20	1.48	3	1.46	3	0	0	3	1.69	43	70	0.61	0.78
1	0	1	0	0	0	0	0	0	0	0	2	2	0.03	0.02
9	0	9	0.59	0	0	0	0	15	15	8.43	2	32	0.03	0.36
3	0	3	0.22	0	0	0	0	6	6	3.37	0	15	0	0.17
0	0	0	0	0	0	0	0	7	7	3.93	121	131	1.72	1.46
8	25	33	2.07	18	8.78	1	0	0	1	0.56	14	66	0.19	0.73
0	0	0	0	0	0	1	0	0	1	0.56	1	2	0.01	0.02
327	147	474	34.5	66	32.2	46	1	19	66	37.1	4,718	5404	67.2	60.2
5	0	5	0.37	0	0	0	0	0	0	0	0	6	0	0.07
42	0	42	3.04	2	0.98	0	0	0	0	0	6	56	0.09	0.62
0	0	0	0	0	0	0	0	0	0	0	92	94	1.31	1.05
3	4	7	0.51	0	0	3	0	0	3	1.69	59	72	0.84	0.8
0	2	2	0.15	1	0.49	0	0	0	0	0	6	11	0.09	0.12
0	0	0	0	0	0	0	0	0	0	0	8	8	0.11	0.09
0	0	0	0	0	0	0	0	0	0	0	10	9	0.14	0.1
0	0	0	0	0	0	0	0	0	0	0	1	1	0.01	0.01
109	20	129	9.41	34	16.6	6	0	2	8	4.49	317	509	4.52	5.67
3	0	3	0.22	0	0	0	0	0	0	0	0	4	0	0.04
0	0	0	0	0	0	0	0	0	0	0	1	1	0.01	0.01
0	0	0	0	1	0.49	0	0	0	0	0	0	1	0	0.01
0	0	0	0	0	0	0	0	1	1	0.56	14	15	0.19	0.17
74	88	162	11.1	18	8.78	4	0	1	5	2.81	64	270	0.91	3.01
5	1	6	0.37	0	0	0	0	0	0	0	16	22	0.23	0.25
0	0	0	0	0	0	0	0	0	0	0	1	1	0.01	0.01
0	0	0	0	0	0	0	0	0	0	0	1	1	0.01	0.01
0	0	0	0	0	0	0	0	0	0	0	2	2	0.03	0.02
0	0	0	0	0	0	0	0	0	0	0	1	1	0.01	0.01
0	0	0	0	0	0	3	0	0	3	1.69	0	3	0	0.03

TABLE 7.7. (cont'd.) Fish Remains from Pecho Components (Wet-screened samples).

| | | Milling/Lower Archaic | | Early | | | |
| | | SLO-10 | | SLO-1366/H | | SLO-1370/H | |
Taxon	Common Name	Total	%	Total	%	Total	%
Pomacentridae	Damselfishes	0	0	0	0	0	0
Semicossyphus pulcher	California sheephead	0	0	0	0	0	0
Oxyjulis californica	Señorita	0	0	0	0	0	0
Stichaeidae	Pricklebacks	6	5.82	3	4	7	9.72
Anoplarchus sp.	Cockscomb	0	0	0	0	0	0
Cebidichthys violaceus	Monkeyface prickleback	0	0	0	0	0	0
Xiphister sp.		0	0	0	0	0	0
Clinidae	Kelp blennies	1	0.97	0	2	2	2.28
Gibbsonia sp.	Kelpfish	0	0	0	0	0	0
Heterostichus rostratus	Giant kelpfish	0	0	1	0	1	1.39
Gobiesox meandricus	Northern clingfish	0	0	0	0	0	0
Gillichthys mirabilis	Longjaw mudsucker	0	0	0	0	0	0
Scomber japonicus	Pacific chub mackeral	0	0	0	0	0	0
Citharichthys sp.	Sandab	0	0	0	0	0	0
Pleuronectiformes	Flounders and Soles	0	0	0	1	1	1.39
Pleuronectidae	Right-eye flounders	0	0	0	0	0	0
Platichthys stellatus	Starry flounder	0	0	0	0	0	0
Subtotal		100	97.1	22	49	71	97.6
Grand total		103	100	22	50	72	99

TABLE 7.8. Summary of Fish-Bone Assemblages, wet-screened samples.

| | Temporal Component | | | Dominant Fish Group | | | | | |
Trinomial	Period	Exca. volume (m³)	NISP	Name	N	%	NISP/m³	No. species	Margalef Index
SLO-51/H	Postcontact	0.520	7,026	Rockfishes	4,718	67.2	13,511.5	28	3.048
SLO-8	Late	1.500	105	Rockfishes	46	43.8	70.0	11	
SLO-1366/H	Late	0.208	1	Rockfishes	1	100.0	4.81	1	
SLO-1370/H	Late	0.200	72	Rockfishes	19	26.4	360.0	12	
Subtotal		1.908	178				93.3	24	4.362
SLO-9	Middle–Late	2.164	205	Rockfishes	66	32.1	94.7	15	2.817
SLO-5	Middle	1.832	636	Herrings	175	27.5	347.2	16	
SLO-10	Middle	2.648	752	Rockfish	327	43.5	283.9	25	
Subtotal		4.48	1,388				309.8	28	3.731
SLO-1366/H	Early	1.044	22	Rockfishes	8	36.4	21.1	8	
SLO-1370/H	Early	0.800	50	Rockfishes	19	38.0	62.5	12	
Subtotal		1.844	72				83.6	16	3.507
SLO-10	Millingstone/ Lower Archaic	1.600	103	Rockfishes	53	51.4	64.3	12	2.373

| Middle | | | | M-L | | | | Late | | | | Postcontact | | Grand total |
| SLO-10 | | SLO-5 | | SLO-9 | | SLO-8 | | SLO-1366/H | | SLO-1370/H | | SLO-51/H | | |
Total	%	Total	%	Total	%	Total	%	Total	%	Total	%	Total	%	
2	0	2	0	0	0	0	0	0	0	0	0	2	0	0.02
1	0	1	0.07	0	0	0	0	0	0	0	0	1	0	0.01
5	39	44	3.25	27	13.2	1	0	0	1	0.56	50	122	0.71	1.36
84	25	109	8	12	5.85	0	0	0	0	0	81	215	1.15	2.39
0	0	0	0	0	0	0	0	0	0	0	1	1	0.01	0.01
1	7	8	0.51	2	0.98	36	0	0	36	20.2	116	162	1.65	1.81
12	80	92	6.74	1	0.49	0	0	0	0	0	781	874	11.1	9.74
5	1	6	0.44	2	0.98	0	0	1	1	0.56	11	23	0.15	0.26
0	0	0	0	0	0	0	0	0	0	0	92	92	1.31	1.02
0	0	0	0	0	0	0	0	0	0	0	3	4	0.04	0.04
0	1	1	0.07	0	0	0	0	0	0	0	11	12	0.15	0.13
0	0	0	0	1	0.49	0	0	0	0	0	0	1	0	0.01
0	0	0	0	0	0	0	0	2	2	1.12	7	9	0.09	0.1
0	0	0	0	0	0	0	0	0	0	0	1	1	0.01	0.01
0	0	0	0	0	0	0	0	9	9	5.06	0	10	0	0.11
0	0	0	0	0	0	0	0	1	1	0.56	0	1	0	0.01
0	0	0	0	0	0	0	0	0	0	0	2	2	0.03	0.02
704	635	1339	96.3	205	100	104	1	72	177	99.4	7,023	8,915	99.9	99.3
752	636	1388	99.9	205	100	105	1	72	178	100	7,026	8,972	99.9	99.9

TABLE 7.9. Capture Technologies associated with Pecho Coast Fishes.

By hand	Hook and line (including gorge hooks) nearshore	Hook and line (w/watercraft) offshore	Spear	Nearshore net (mostly small schooling fishes)	Offshore net (w/watercraft) (mostly small schooling fishes)
Pricklebacks	Bat ray	Herrings	Bat ray	Plainfin midshipman	Herrings
Plainfin midshipman	Plainfin midshipman	Pacific hake	Triakid sharks	New World silversides	Northern anchovy
Cabezon	Kelp greenling	Rockfishes	Plainfin midshipman	True smelts	
Pile perch	Lingcod	Lingcod	Lingcod		
Monkeyface prickleback	Pacific staghorn sculpin		Pacific angel shark		
	Cabezon				
	Surfperches				
	Monkeyface prickleback				
	Pricklebacks				
	Flounders and soles				
	Rockfishes				

Source: Boone (2012), Fitch (1972), Jones et al. (2016), Love (2011), Langenwalter and Huddleston (1991), and Salls (1988).

occasional use of nets for fishing. Net use was evident throughout the 8,100-year sequence at Morro Bay (Far Western Anthropological Research Group 2016), so it is not out of the realm of possibility that nets were employed at Pecho at some point. However, the surf-battered rocky shore and kelp forests are less well-suited to net fishing than the protected waters of the estuary, so it is likely that nets were never the dominant means of capture on the Pecho Coast.

Middle Period

Wet- and dry-screened samples are available for the Middle Period from CA-SLO-5, and -10. The former represents the end of the late Middle Period (ca. 1200–950 cal BP), while the latter represents the inclusive Middle Period and Middle–Late Transition (2700–800 cal BP). Together the two components show continuation of earlier trends but also decided changes, best reflected in the larger wet-screened sample. Rockfish are still the most heavily represented fish in the combined sample from the two sites (34.5%), but CA-SLO-5 shows a dominance of herrings (27.5%), the only component in the study to exhibit such a high frequency of this fish family. Sardines, which are a member of this family, appear for the first time in the record as do New World silversides. In this regard it is perhaps worth noting that the fish remains from CA-SLO-7, although temporally mixed (Middle and Late Periods) also show a high frequency of sardine remains (Breschini and Haversat 1988). Other species present in higher frequencies in the current study in the Middle Period components are sharks, skates, and rays (6.4% at CA-SLO-10), and surfperches which account for 11.1% of the combined Middle Period wet-screened sample. Señoritas and New World silversides appear for the first time. Cabezon (9.4%) and pricklebacks (8.5%) are still important. The volumetric density of remains shows a significant spike upward in the wet-screened sample to 309.8 NISP/m³.

The preponderance of rockfish and cabezon suggests that hook-and-line fishing was still the dominant means of capture although artifacts from CA-SLO-10 show that curved shell fishhooks were used for the first time—along with

bone gorges. It is tempting to suggest that the large number of herrings, including sardines, associated with the Middle Period is an indication that fish were taken via watercraft from offshore contexts. However, the site that yielded the highest frequency of herring remains, CA-SLO-5, is not situated in a boat-friendly setting. Rather, it is perched atop a high cliff that is battered by the open surf. Nonetheless, at CA-SLO-2 grooved stones, which are commonly interpreted as net weights, show a decided increase (n=10) from earlier periods (n=1). These artifacts suggest that at a minimum, some of the herring and perhaps other species were captured with nets. The notched stones recovered from CA-SLO-10 are thought to be line sinkers used in conjunction with shell hooks (see discussion by Codding and Jones 2007) and represent only the Middle–Late Transition portion of the component. McKenzie (2007) suggested that the increase in fishing evident in the Santa Barbara Channel at the same time as the Pecho Coast can be attributed to appearance of the new circular shell hooks. In a study of broader fishing patterns from the entire central California coast, Jones and colleagues (2016) were unable to find support for that idea. However, the onset of the Middle Period on the Pecho Coast does show a decided increase in fishing with shell hooks, nets, and watercraft.

Middle–Late Transition

The Middle–Late Transition is represented only by CA-SLO-9 for which there are reasonable wet-screened (n=205) and dry-screened samples (n=515). These show continuity from the Middle Period with a dominance of rockfish (32.2% wet; 47.8% dry), cabezon (16.6% wet; 32.2% dry), and señorita (13.1% wet; 4.9% dry). Also important are silversides (8.8% wet; 1.1% dry), surfperches (8.8% wet; 5.1% dry), and herrings (including sardines) (9.8% wet; 1.0% dry). Remains of sharks, skates, and rays are absent. The volumetric density of fish bone (94.7 NISP/m³ wet; 16.9 NISP/m³ dry) shows decreases from the high values associated with the Middle Period.

A relative abundance of notched stones (n=20) and shell hook fragments (n=9) from CA-SLO-9 complements the high frequency of rockfish and cabezon to indicate that hook-and-line fishing was still the dominant method of capture. However, the herrings, sardines, and silversides indicate net fishing as well, some in offshore contexts. At the mouth of Coon Creek, CA-SLO-9 is situated adjacent to a cove where watercraft could be easily launched.

Late Period

Late Period samples are available from CA-SLO-8, -51/H, -1366/H, and -1370/H, although SLO-8 is limited to a wet-screened sample and recovery from SLO-51/H was limited to dry-screen. The dry-screened sample is probably more informative because it includes the village site at SLO-51/H. Rockfish (58.1%) and cabezon (10.7%) account for nearly two-thirds of the remains. Also important are Pacific hake (6.2%), plainfin midshipman (5.6%), and combined pricklebacks (5.6%). Herrings (3.2%), surfperches (1.9%), and silversides (0.2%) are present but in lower frequencies than in the Middle and Middle–Late Transition components. Intersite variation is also very apparent as the plainfin midshipmen and Pacific hake all were recovered from SLO-1370/H. The overall volumetric density of remains was lower than the two previous periods with 74.3 NISP/m³ for the dry-screened sample and 93.3 NISP/m³ for the wet-screen. Intersite variation is apparent as well with SLO-1370/H showing a value of 360 NISP/m³ compared to only 4.8 NISP/m³ at SLO-1366/H. Shell hooks, notched, and grooved stones were all recovered from Late Period contexts complementing the faunal evidence for both hook-and-line and net fishing. SLO-51/H produced an end-notched stone which seems to represent a type of net weight restricted to the Late Period. Clearly, a range of fishing activities was pursued, but the intensity of fishing seems reduced from the Middle Period.

Postcontact

The postcontact sample is limited to the wet-screen (n=7,026) and dry-screen (n=4,348) recovery from Units 5 and 6 at CA-SLO-51/H. Despite a relatively small excavation volume (1.2 m³) this was by far the largest set of piscine

remains from any of the investigated sites. Dominant species show continuity from earlier periods. Rockfish account for 67.2% of the wet-screened sample and 69.4% of the dry-screened remains. Also important in the wet-screened sample are pricklebacks (12.3%), herrings (5.1%), and cabezon (4.5%). Silversides (0.2%) and surfperches (0.9%), however, are nearly absent. The dry-screened sample shows very similar amounts of pricklebacks (7.5%), cabezon (6.9%), and herrings (3.5%), along with equally low percentages for silversides (0.2%) and surfperches (0.9%). The volumetric density of fish remains from the wet-screened sample is a staggering 13,511.5 NISP/m³ which is the highest such value in the current study. Further, as best we can tell, this is the second highest density value for any wet-screened site on the central California coast (see Jones et al. 2016: Table 5). A higher density was reported only from one estuarine site in Monterey County (Breschini and Haversat 1995). The dry-screen value of 6,211.4 NISP/m³ is the single highest value for a dry-screened sample that we are aware of from San Luis Obispo, Monterey, or Santa Cruz Counties. It is apparent that during the postcontact era, fishing became extraordinarily important on the Pecho Coast at the village of *Tstyiwi*. However, the low frequency of silversides and surfperches suggests that offshore netting may have been pursued less frequently than it had been previously while pricklebacks, which could potentially be taken by hand along shore, were more important. We are inclined to attribute this extraordinary increase in fishing activities to the changes that must have transpired at the village following contact. Avila Beach, 8 km east of SLO-51/H, was the main port for ships servicing Mission San Luis Obispo, the construction of which began in 1772. Mission records show that inhabitants of the village of *Tstyiwi* began to appear on Mission baptism rolls in 1781, and that 37 adults and 19 children from the village were baptized between 1781 and 1803 (Milliken and Johnson 2005). In the face of the growing, close-by Spanish presence, it is not unreasonable to assume that foraging activities may have been constrained at the village and that people responded by relying more heavily

TABLE 7.10. Summary of Shellfish Findings from Pecho Coast Components.

Trinomial	Period	Excavation volume (m³)	Shell weight (g)	Dominant species	%	Shell weight/m³ (kg)
SLO-51/H	Postcontact	0.020	4,934.3	California sea mussel	53	246.7
SLO-1366/H	Late	0.008	2,448.7	California sea mussel	82	307.3
SLO-1370/H	Late	0.200	236.2	California sea mussel	66	1.3
Subtotal		0.208	2,684.9			12.9
SLO-9	M-L	0.064	2,474.4	California sea mussel	61	38.7
SLO-5	Middle	0.032	4,030.9	California sea mussel	79	125.9
SLO-10	Middle	0.048	5,190.9	California sea mussel	87	108.1
Subtotal		0.08	9,221.8			115.3
SLO-497	Early	0.032	1,207.8	California sea mussel	83	37.7
SLO-1366/H	Early	0.008	1,569.3	California sea mussel	77	196.2
SLO-1370/H	Early	0.800	3,641.8	California sea mussel	75	4.6
Subtotal		0.84	6,418.9			76.4
SLO-10	Millingstone/ Lower Archaic	0.008	13.6	California sea mussel	67	1.6
Subtotal						

on the immediately adjacent marine fisheries. It seems that they may have employed watercraft less frequently and focused more intensely on shoreline species, such as pricklebacks, perhaps to maintain a lower profile in the face of the unprecedented changes occurring around them.

Discussion

Diachronic patterning in the piscine assemblages is fairly clear although different recovery methods show some variation. In general, volumetric densities of fish bones suggest that while fishing was pursued by the Millingstone/Lower Archaic inhabitants, it was not engaged in intensively (see Figures 7.9 and 7.10). The Early Period shows little change, but the Middle Period shows a substantial increase in fish remains that is particularly well represented by the wet-screen recovery from both SLO-5 and -10. Indeed, the wet-screened samples suggest that the Middle Period was the peak time for prehistoric fishing although this trend is not as clear from the dry-screen sample. The Middle–Late Transition component does not stand out as the all-time peak as once thought (cf. Codding and Jones 2007). Instead, the slightly earlier late Middle

Period component at SLO-5 (1200–950 cal BP) distinguishes itself both for a generally high frequency of fish bones (NISP=347.2 NISP/m³) and as the only component dominated by herring, a group of fishes (including sardines) that generally is associated with net-fishing in offshore contexts, suggesting a more intensive fishing economy. Following this apex, the Late Period shows a decrease in fish remains, followed, in turn, by the dramatic spike in fishing during early postcontact time at the ethnographic village of *Tstyiwi* driven by local circumscription limiting the availability of alternative resources.

Shellfish

As is the case along most stretches of rocky coast in central California (e.g., Big Sur [Jones 2003]), shellfish remains throughout the Pecho record are dominated by California sea mussel (*Mytilus californianus*; Table 7.10). Other shellfish that are present in lower frequencies include turban snails (*Tegula* sp.), chiton (*Polyplacophora*), limpets (*Lottia* sp.), and both red and black abalone (*Haliotis rufescens* and *H. cracherodii*, respectively). Using a different sampling strategy than we have employed, Greenwood (1972:51)

TABLE 7.11. Temporal Summary of Abalone Data from the Pecho Coast.

Component	Period	Dating (cal BP)	N Red abalone	Red abalones/m³	Mean size red abalone (mm)	N Black abalone	Mean size black abalone (mm)
SLO-51/H	Postcontact	250–180	12	9.8	72.5	12	71.3
SLO-1366/H	Late	700–250	0	0.0	—	1	125.0
SLO-1370/H	Late	600–500	1	0.5	110.0	1	110.0
SLO-9	M-L-T	1000–700*	221	6.4	95.0	98	85.0
SLO-5	Late Middle	1200–950	200	19.4	100.0	155	86.3
SLO-10	Middle	2700–800	27	2.6	85.2	56	78.8
SLO-497	Terminal Early	3200–2800	7	3.0	94.3	7	89.3
SLO-1366/H	Early	5800–2500	32	4.3	165.0	4	125.0
SLO-1370/H	Early	5500–3400	34	3.9	125.0	9	95.0
SLO-10	Millingstone/ Lower Archaic	7400–7200	14	5.6	135.0	0	—
Total			548			343	

*Early Middle Period materials also mixed in with Middle–Late Transition component.

also found mussels to represent between 73 and 89% of the shell in the 10,000-year sequence at SLO-2.

There is patterned variation in shellfish density across the Pecho components (Figure 7.13). While the 95% confidence intervals suggest that much of this variation is not significant, the overall trend does show a significant increase in shellfish exploitation late in prehistory. This same trend is evident at nearby Morro Bay (Jones, Jones, et al. 2017), but it contrasts with other locations including the Channel Islands (Glassow 1993a), the Santa Barbara mainland (Erlandson 1991), and Big Sur (Jones 2003) where shellfish decreases in importance through the Holocene. Given the relatively low return rates associated with shellfish, the Late Period increase on the Pecho Coast and at Morro Bay may be driven by a process of resource intensification. Because abalone are indeterminate growers with size scaling closely with age, and because larger abalone provide higher yields and should therefore be preferentially targeted, red abalone size measurements can be used as proxy of harvesting intensity (e.g., Klein and Steele 2013). An examination of red abalone size across all available components seems to support this increased attention to intertidal resources later in time (Figure 7.14). These trends reveal

that stable size classes were exploited from the Millingstone Period through the onset of the Hunting Culture period, followed by a gradual decline that culminates in the smallest mean sizes for both black and red abalones during the Postcontact Period (Table 7.11). While not as pronounced as trends observed elsewhere (e.g., Erlandson et al. 2008), these records do seem to indicate sustained harvesting pressure on abalone throughout the sequence resulting in size diminution driven by overexploitation. Notably, the rate of decline seems to accelerate during the period of population growth associated with the onset of the Hunting Culture.

Whole and nearly whole shells recovered from units also show that both red and black abalones were collected during all time periods. Radiocarbon dates from red abalones also show this pattern, albeit with a smaller sample (Figure 7.15). While two periods longer than 500 years occur without a date on red abalone, this may be the result of sampling. Red abalones in fact dominate or are equal to black abalones at nine of the ten temporal components from which quantified data are available. Red abalones are especially abundant in the record during the late Middle and Middle–Late Transition periods (ca. 1200–700 cal BP). The dominance of red over black abalones through time suggests that both

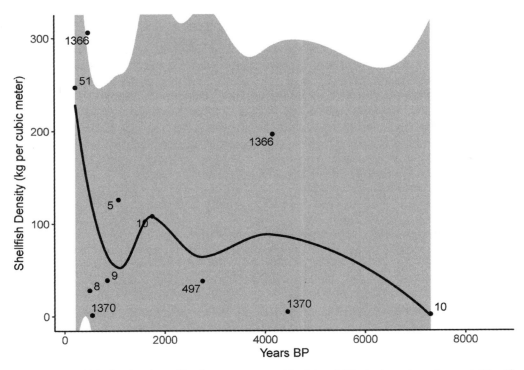

Figure 7.13. Shellfish density plotted by the component midpoint and fitted using a loess (span=0.75) with 95% confidence intervals.

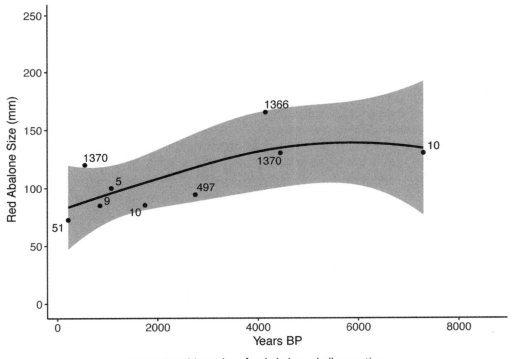

Figure 7.14. Mean size of red abalone shells over time.

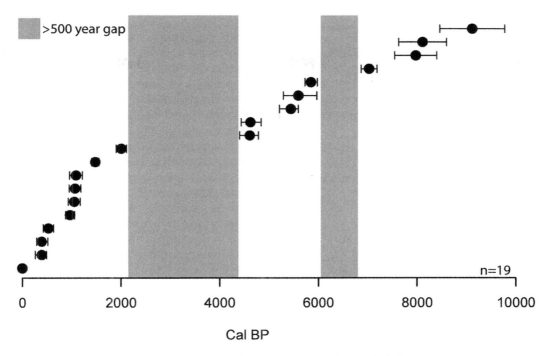

FIGURE 7.15. Summary of radiocarbon dates from red abalones.

were available from the low intertidal, and that neither boats nor diving were needed to procure them. The large red abalone concentration uncovered at SLO-10, dating ca. 7400–7200 cal BP, seems to have some similarity with red abalone middens of the northern Channel Islands in terms of the size of the individual shells and their occurrence in a concentration. Also, Greenwood identified a layer of red abalones at SLO-585 that yielded dates between 8000 and 5600 cal BP (Jones, Garza, et al. 2009:21). The SLO-10 feature and SLO-585 layer seem to conform with the Channel Islands red abalone "middens" in the concentration of the shells, their species, and the large size of individuals in the concentrations. If so, current data further suggest that the phenomenon ceased at the end of the Early Period when red abalone sizes decreased significantly. The range of dates obtained by Greenwood (1972) from the single layer at SLO-585, however, also suggests that postdepositional bioturbation contributed to linear concentrations of shells on the mainland.

Volumetric frequencies show that red abalones were most numerous during the late Middle Period (Table 7.11) and were reasonably abundant during the Middle–Late Transition and postcontact periods, albeit with considerably smaller mean shell sizes. Lack of a meaningful sample for the Late Period prohibits any generalization about that interval. However, red abalones continued to be collected and never disappeared, nor is there any evidence for mass collection during the Late Period as there is in the Monterey Bay Area (Breschini and Haversat 1980; Dietz and Jackson 1981).

Botanical Remains

Botanical remains were limited to the charred materials recovered from Feature 1, Unit 6 at SLO-51/H which are described in detail in Appendix B. Three samples collected from the feature produced a total number of 1,373 identified specimens. Most abundant in the sample were acorn (*Quercus* sp.) and islay (*Prunus ilicifolia*) nutshell, along with seeds of brome, fescue, red maids, goosefoot, and clover, as well as nightshade berries, most of which can be associated with prehistoric Native Californian subsistence. Gray-pine nutshell was present in all three samples in low frequency reflecting exploitation of trees 15–17 km distant. Some Eurasian cultigens were represented in the samples as well and probably reflect acquisition of seeds from Spanish explorers or missionaries and cultivation in the late eighteenth century although contamination from more recent farming operations cannot be ruled out.

Seasonality

A small number of the faunal and floral resources in the Pecho collections are from species that have seasonal restrictions in their availability. These include animals that migrate seasonally to the central coast as well as plants that produce edible nuts and seeds only during certain months. Migratory mammals include California sea lions, which are absent in June and July but present the rest of the year, and northern fur seals, which were present in nearshore waters along the central coast between December and February. Several fish species are also migratory. These include pile perch (present from September–June but absent July and August), Pacific hake (present December–April), and plainfin midshipman that spawn in the intertidal zone between May and August (Love 2011). Thus, only the plainfin midshipman is a summer indicator. Among the more abundant plant remains (limited to those from Feature 1, Unit 6 at SLO-51/H) were fall nuts (acorn and islay), vernal seeds (brome, red maids, clover, and fescue), and summer seeds (goosefoot) and berries (nightshade).

Unfortunately, available samples of seasonal indicators are not robust. The only components that produced substantive numbers of California sea lion remains were the Early, Middle, and Late occupations at SLO-2. Of the other winter markers, Pacific hake was also present in the fish remains from the Middle and Late components at SLO-2 (Jones, Porcasi, Garza, et al. 2008:303), the Middle Period occupation at SLO-10, and both the Early and Late components at SLO-1370/H. Pile perch is only represented in the Middle and Late Period components at SLO-2 and the postcontact component at SLO-51/H. The summer marker, plainfin midshipman, is represented

only in the Middle Period component at SLO-2 and the postcontact occupation at SLO-51/H.

The charred remains from the postcontact feature at SLO-51/H reflect plant taxa which ripen during the full range of seasons that plants can be gathered. Four fall-ripening nut crops were present, along with six genera of small seeds and berry pits that reflect summer gathering, and 11 spring-ripening small seed genera. Focusing only on the key plant foods, the full range of seasonal indicators is also included, with fall nuts (acorn and islay), vernal seeds (brome, red maids, clover, and fescue), and summer seeds (goosefoot) and berries (nightshade). The plant data suggest SLO-51/H was occupied at least from spring through the fall nut harvest.

At a minimum then, two components show evidence for occupation during both winter and summer: SLO-1370/H Late, and SLO-2 Middle Period (Figure 7.16). SLO-2 and SLO-10 Middle Period components show evidence for use in the winter. The only component that shows fairly strong evidence for year-round occupation is the postcontact component at SLO-51/H.

An estimate of seasonality was also obtained for SLO-9 by means of oxygen isotope analysis of mussel shells (Jones, Kennett, et al. 2008). This study suggested that mussels were harvested at SLO-9 from spring through fall, with only one sample (8%) returning a winter signature. This seemed consistent with the dearth of mortars and pestles at this site which implies that acorn processing and consumption (fall and winter activities) were pursued elsewhere or were less important.

Component Function and Settlement Variability

Here we evaluate functional aspects of components in order to determine whether there is evidence for variation in settlement strategies over time. As a starting point, two alternative characterizations of local settlement have been advanced previously: (1) Farquhar (2003) argued that a logistically organized (*sensu* Binford 1980) system featuring residential bases and special-purpose encampments was in place

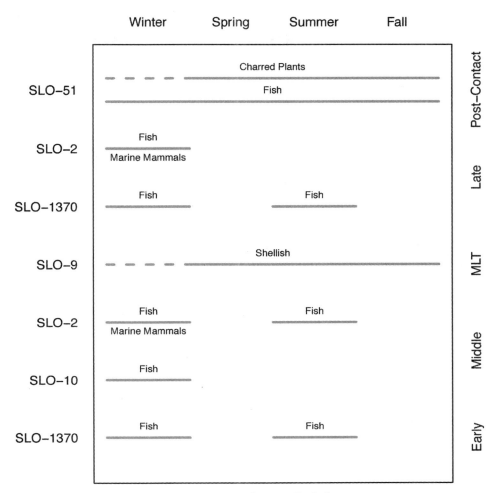

FIGURE 7.16. Summary of seasonality indicators.

from the Millingstone/Lower Archaic Period onward; while (2) Bertrando (2006) argued that a collector-like settlement system did not emerge until the Early Period, marked by primary villages, secondary villages, temporary campsites, and lithic sites. Bertrando's model is consistent with ideas put forward previously by Jones and Waugh (1995) who argued for a major settlement transition ca. 5,500 years ago.

Farquhar's model represents what might be referred to as the "organization of technology" school of hunter-gatherer settlement theory. The approach was largely developed in the interior regions of California and the Great Basin (c.f.

Giambastiani 2004; Kelly 1983, 1988) but has also been employed in south-central California (Bamforth 1991; Hale 2001). Its utility seems greatest in areas where faunal preservation is poor and the archaeological record consists almost entirely of flaked stone. The basic underlying tenet of this approach is that the key insights into site function are found in the range of stone tools present, their uses, degrees of reworking, and amount and type of tool-production detritus. As exemplified especially by the studies of Farquhar (2003) and Hale (2001), flaked stone residues by themselves are seen as the key indices of site function with little if any consideration

TABLE 7.12. Summary of Flaked- Stone Assemblages from Pecho Coast Components.

Artifact	SLO-1366/H M	SLO-1366/H F	SLO-1370/H M	SLO-1370/H F	SLO-497 M	SLO-497 F	SLO-10 M	SLO-10 F	SLO-5 M	SLO-5 F	SLO-9 M	SLO-9 F	SLO-1370/H M	SLO-1370/H F	SLO-1366/H M	SLO-1366/H F	SLO-51/H Precontact M	SLO-51/H Precontact F	SLO-51/H Postcontact M	SLO-51/H Postcontact F
Projectile points	14	2	3	0	1	0	8	2	8	0	38	5	3	0	3	1	12	1	7	0
Early-stage bifaces (1–3)	3	0	0	0	1	0	6	2	12	1	31	0	0	0	0	0	9	0	1	2
Late-stage bifaces (4–5)	1	0	0	0	0	0	4	0	0	0	6	0	0	0	0	0	3	0	1	0
Indet.-stage biface	0	0	1	0	0	0	1	0	0	0	3	0	1	0	1	0	1	0	0	0
Cores Total (N cobble)	4 (3)	0	9 (9)	0	3 (3)	0	5 (5)	0	21 (8)	0	21 (17)	0	0	0	1 (0)	0	17 (8)	4 (2)	12 (7)	0
Core tools	2	0	2	0	0	0	2	1	6	0	13	0	1	0	1	0	1	0	0	0
Drills/reamers	0	1	0	0	0	0	2	0	0	0	3	0	0	0	0	0	1	0	0	0
Bead drills	0	0	0	0	0	0	0	0	0	0	0	0	0	0	0	0	0	0	4	0
Formal flake tools	0	0	0	0	0	0	0	0	1	0	0	0	0	0	0	0	0	0	0	0
Informal flake tools	4	1	0	0	0	0	0	0	5	0	7	0	0	0	0	0	22	1	5	4
Unifaces	0	0	0	0	0	0	0	0	0	0	11	0	0	0	0	0	0	0	0	0
Notched stones	0	0	0	0	0	0	2	0	0	0	20	0	0	0	0	0	0	0	0	0
Flakes	1,608	68	5,293	0	521	0	1,967	0	3,006	4	9,685	57	957	0	1,261	40	5,811	327	1,127	178
Total	1,636	72	5,308	0	526	0	1,997	5	3,059	5	9,838	62	962	0	1,267	41	5,877	333	1,157	184

M=Monterey chert; F=Franciscan chert

of broader tool assemblages, faunal remains, seasonality indicators, or presence/absence of features. In particular, these studies emphasize the number and character of use of flake tools, with the idea that they should reflect the relative intensity of domestic processing and therefore indicate related levels of sedentism. However, we consider informal flake tools to be among the more problematic artifact classes on the central coast owing to uncertainties about the origins of edge-modification that define them. At Vandenberg Air Force Base, analysts have concluded that true, use-derived edge wear can only be recognized microscopically, and they examine every piece of debitage under the microscope in order to identify flake tools (e.g., Lebow et al. 2016). In the absence of such intensive study for the current project, we are hesitant to place great interpretive value in informal flake tools. Instead, while we summarize key aspects of the flaked-stone assemblages, we favor evaluating component function and settlement variability via full tool assemblages including ground stone, bone, and shell implements, presence/absence of features, and faunal residues, along with characteristics of the flaked-stone assemblages. Our inferences from the latter, however, are fairly limited.

Flaked-Stone Tool Production and Use

Evaluation of possible variability in flaked-stone production is hampered by the lack of a meaningful sample from the Millingstone/Lower Archaic Period. The larger mesh used in the 1968 investigations at SLO-2 and SLO-585 (6 mm) is problematic in terms of comparisons with the more recently investigated sites where debitage was recovered using 3 mm mesh. The sample available from the one recently investigated site that might have been useful, SLO-10, is simply too small. A better representation of this important period is SLO-1797, the Cross Creek Site, 17 km inland from Pecho (Fitzgerald 2000; Jones et al. 2002) where the midden was interpreted as the remnant of a residential base. Core hammers, choppers, and domed scrapers were the most abundant tools, outnumbering bifaces by a ratio of approximately 3:1. Almost certainly these

tools reflect a specialized industry related to processing plant foods. Flaked-stone debitage was dominated by Monterey chert (97.1%), and the flake-type profile was characterized by

> an emphasis on late-stage percussion core and biface reduction activities and late-stage pressure flaking, from which it can be inferred that flake blanks were used for production of bifacial tools, and that bifacial tools were sharpened and rejuvenated through pressure flaking. The assemblage is consistent with a location where locally available raw materials, procured from quarries and secondary sources and partially reduced, were used for the production of flake blanks, expedient flake tools, and bifacial tools. (Jones et al. 2002:225)

The ten Pecho components postdating 5700 cal BP constitute a more meaningful sample (Table 7.12). These assemblages feature considerably fewer core tools and more bifaces. All but one of the components produced cores, most of which were rounded cobbles (see Figure 6.10) that seem to have originated from one of the local creeks that drain through the Monterey Formation. All of the assemblages were heavily dominated by black-gray, weakly banded Monterey chert including cores, bifaces, and debitage. The highest frequency of non-Monterey chert was at SLO-51/H, the southernmost of the investigated sites which lies adjacent to an expanse of the Franciscan geologic formation. On some level, the distribution of flaked-stone implements reflects the local geology which provides potentially useful raw material across the landscape albeit in a variety of forms and quality.

Another specialized industry in notched stones and unifaces produced from local cobbles was identified at SLO-9 and may be related to the pursuit of hook-and-line fishing since notched stones seem well suited for use as line weights. Edge-modified or informal flake tools are insignificant in all assemblages except from SLO-51/H, in both the pre- and postcontact components.

The rest of the assemblages generally reflect production of bifaces used predominantly as

TABLE 7.13. Flake-Stone Assemblage Characteristics from Pecho Coast Components.

	Early Period			Middle Period		M-LT	Late Period			Postcontact
	1366/H	1370/H	497	SLO-10	SLO-5	SLO-9	1370/H	1366/H	51/H Pre	SLO-51/H Post
% Monterey chert debitage	95.9	100.0	96.3	98.6	99.9	99.8	100.0	96.9	94.7	85.2
Excavation volume (m³)	7.4	8.8	2.3	10.5	10.3	34.3	2.2	1.4	4.0	1.2
Flakes/m³ dry-screen	163	171	227	190	190	230	683	186	1,539	796
Flakes/m³ wet-screen	470	1,248	—	—	768	1,177	2,090	929	—	1,520
Biface: flake ratio	89:1	1,323:1	260:1	103:1	150:1	124:1	239.3	309:1	232:1	129:1
% Core reduction (Monterey chert)	13.4	15.0	17.6	28.3	17.1	7.6	9.0	8.2	16.5	22.9

weapon tips and cutting tools. Most components showed modest densities of flakes/m³ with dry-screened samples ranging between 100 and 250 flakes/m³ (Table 7.13). Wet-screen residues showed densities over 1100 flakes/m³ at SLO-370/H, SLO-9, and in the postcontact component at SLO-51/H. In the Early Period component at SLO-1370/H the high debitage density correlates with an exceptionally high flake:biface ratio (1,323:1). This suggests strongly that SLO-1370/H functioned at least partially as a quarry reduction locale where cobbles from Coon Creek were reduced. This is supported by a core:biface ratio of 2:1. The increased flake density at SLO-1370/H for the Late Period suggests that this was even more of a functional factor at the site later in time. The high flake density at SLO-9 also suggests some quarrying of local cobbles although the flake:biface ratio is lower. The large number of early-stage bifaces, however, suggests these were produced here for transport elsewhere. Most of the other components show both moderate flake-density values and biface:flake ratios. We interpret these as locations where there was some use of local stone, but bifaces were also commonly imported from other locations.

The high flake densities and lower percentages of Monterey chert set SLO-51/H apart from other sites in the study area. This seems at least partially related to the southern location of the site adjacent to Franciscan chert sources. There is also the possibility that the greater use of Franciscan stone in the postcontact component reflects greater use of locally available material in the face of postcontact restrictions on mobility. The postcontact component shows 10% less Monterey chert than any other component.

Overall
Assemblage Diversity

Here we consider additional factors related to the function of individual components within settlement systems over time. To evaluate variation in settlement activities, we calculate the diversity of formal artifacts per component using Margalef's Index (Magurran 1988). The underlying rationale for this rests on the assumption

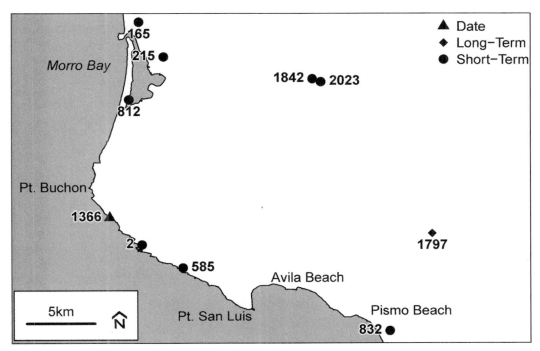

FIGURE 7.17. Millingstone/Lower Archaic components in and around the Pecho Coast.

that shorter-term (specialist) camps will have lower diversity reflecting a narrower range of activities, while longer-term camps will have higher diversity.

Millingstone/Lower Archaic

Currently available radiocarbon dates indicate that at least four sites were occupied on the Pecho Coast during the period between 10,300 and 5700 cal BP: SLO-2, -10, -585, and -1366/H. However, the combined sample from these locations is, for various reasons, problematic. Of the four, the artifact sample from SLO-2 is the most adequate while the samples from SLO-10 and -585 are prohibitively small, and no artifacts whatsoever can be associated with the single radiocarbon date from SLO-1366/H. The SLO-2 assemblage shows a range of implements associated with the pursuit and processing of large and small game, as well as ground-stone implements reflecting the processing of vegetal foods. Bone awls suggest production of textiles, most likely baskets. Notably, there is no obvious fishing gear (hooks, gorges, notched stones) although

fish were certainly caught. Pitted stones, now thought to represent shellfish-processing tools (Cook 2016; Cook et al. 2017), are numerous. The range and diversity of artifacts indicate clearly that SLO-2 functioned as a residential base but the diversity score of 1.443 is low (Table 7.14). We interpret this as an indication that the site functioned as a relatively short-term, nonspecialized residential base (camp).

Very similar residential sites are known from Morro Bay at SLO-165, -215, and -812, dating ca. 8100–7700 cal BP, and SLO-832 at Pismo Beach (Figure 7.17). They share with SLO-2 relatively diverse tool assemblages, evidence for exploitation of fish, shellfish, birds, and mammals, and low numbers of milling tools. These apparent shoreline camps contrast with SLO-1797, the Cross Creek site, which is situated 12 km inland and produced a classic Millingstone tool assemblage dominated by abundant handstones, milling slabs, and core tools (Fitzgerald 2000; Jones et al. 2002). Together, the inland and shoreline sites suggest a Millingstone/Lower Archaic settlement strategy that involved short-term shoreline

TABLE 7.14. Summary of Functional Artifact Classes from Pecho Coast Components.

Artifact	Millingstone/ Lower Archaic		Init. Early		Early		Middle			M-L-T		Late			Post-contact
	SLO-2	SLO-10	SLO-2	SLO-1366/H	SLO-1370/H	SLO-497	SLO-10	SLO-5	SLO-2	SLO-9	SLO-2	SLO-1370/H	SLO-1366/H	SLO-51/H	SLO-51/H
Projectile points and other bifaces	34	2	33	15	4	1	12	8	267	44	242	2	5	12	7
Cores	—	0	—	1	9	3	5	21	—	21	0	1	1	23	10
Core tools	10	0	9	0	3	0	3	6	26	13	15	0	2	2	0
Drills/reamers	0	0	3	1	0	0	2	0	22	3	46	0	1	0	0
Bead drills	0	0	0	0	0	0	0	0	0	0	0	0	0	1	2
Milling slabs	0	0	0	2	0	0	0	0	0	0	1	0	0	0	0
Handstones	3	0	6	0	0	0	0	0	2	0	1	0	0	0	0
Mortars	2	0	6	1	0	0	0	4	22	0	19	0	0	0	0
Pestles	1	0	3	0	0	0	2	0	12	1	13	0	0	0	2
Pitted stones	12	0	26	8	3	2	10	8	354	4	213	0	3	4	3
Charmstone	0	0	0	0	1	0	0	0	10	0	1	0	0	0	1
Grooved or notched stone	0	0	1	0	0	0	2	0	14	20	28	0	0	1	1
Tarring pebbles	0	0	0	0	0	0	2	0	0	0	0	0	0	0	1
Sphere/balls	0	0	0	0	0	0	0	0	0	0	1	0	0	1	1
Fishhooks	0	0	0	0	0	0	2	0	13	9	17	0	1	2	11
Fishhook blanks	0	0	0	1	0	0	2	0	5	1	4	0	0	0	2
Bone awls	2	0	3	0	0	0	2	1	17	2	10	0	0	0	1
Bone gorges	0	0	1	1	0	0	2	0	6	1	1	0	0	0	0
Margalef Diversity Index	1.443	*	2.000	2.058	1.335	*	2.879	1.291	1.929	2.092	2.182	*	1.950	1.828	3.211

— Not reported
* Inadequate sample

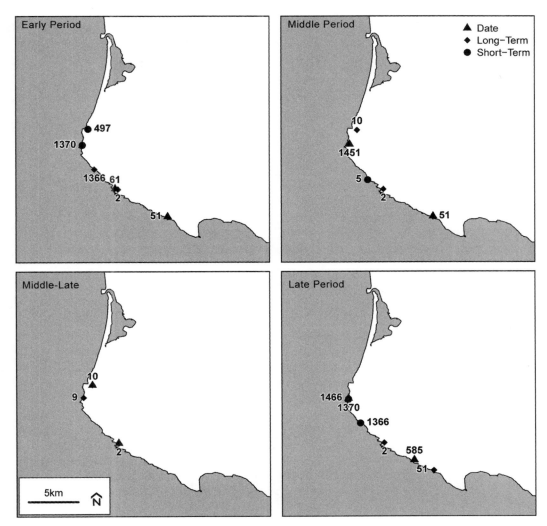

FIGURE 7.18. Early, Middle, Middle–Late, Late, and postcontact components on the Pecho Coast.

camps and more specialized inland residential sites with a focus on vegetal resource collection, processing, and consumption, but with other tasks undertaken as well. A third functional type may be represented by sites like SLO-1842 and -2023, in the interior near Morro Bay (8 km inland), which produced classic Millingstone implements but no shell midden or preserved organic materials (Carpenter et al. 2007). This limited cultural expression suggests briefer occupation, perhaps focused only on plant resource acquisition and consumption.

Early Period

The Early Period is better represented in the excavation sample from Pecho with components at SLO-2, -497, -1366/H, and -1370/H. Radiocarbon dates also indicate a contemporary occupation at SLO-61 (4600–3000 cal BP) (Figure 7.18). SLO-2 represents the Initial Phase of the period (5700–5000 cal BP) which has consistently been associated with an increase in sites and human population on the central coast (Bertrando 2006; Jones et al. 2007; Mikkelsen et al. 2000, among others). As discussed above, this

TABLE 7.15. Volumetric Densities of Key Artifact Classes from Pecho Coast Components.

Site	Component	Recovery Volume (m³)	Projectile Points		Milling Tools[a]		Fishing Equipment[b]		Beads	
			N	Density per m³	N	Density per m³	N	Density per m³	N	Density per m³
SLO-51/H	Postcontact	1.220	7	5.7	2	1.64	14	11.48	186	152.50
SLO-2	Late	29.000	98	3.4	34	1.17	50	1.72	—	—
SLO-51/H	Late	4.000	12	3.0	0	0.00	3	0.75	72	18.00
SLO-1366/H	Late	1.408	5	3.6	0	0.00	1	0.71	4	2.84
SLO-1370/H	Late	2.200	2	0.9	0	0.00	0	0.00	0	0.00
Subtotal		36.608	117	3.2	34	0.92	54	1.48	76	10.00
CA-SLO-9	Middle–Late Transition	34.300	44	1.3	1	0.03	31	0.90	86	2.51
SLO-2	Middle	49.500	145	2.9	36	0.45	38	0.77	—	—
SLO-5	Late Middle	10.300	8	0.8	4	0.39	0	0.00	12	1.17
SLO-10	Middle	10.448	12	1.1	2	0.19	8	0.77	23	2.20
Subtotal		70.248	165	2.3	42	0.59	46	0.65	35	1.69
SLO-497	Terminal Early	2.328	1	0.4	0	0.00	0	0.00	0	0.00
SLO-1366/H	Early	7.444	15	2.0	3	0.40	2	0.27	1*	0.13
SLO-1370/H	Early	8.800	4	0.5	0	0.00	0	0.00	3*	0.34
SLO-2	Initial Early	15.000	27	1.8	15	1.00	2	0.13	—	—
Subtotal		33.572	47	1.4	18	0.50	4	0.12	4	0.21
SLO-10	Millingstone/Lower Archaic	2.500	2	0.8	0	0.00	0	0.00	0	0.00
SLO-2	Millingstone/Lower Archaic	5.400	3	0.6	6	1.1	0	0.00	—	—
Subtotal		7.900	5	0.6	6	0.8	0	0.00	—	—

[a] Includes milling slabs, handstones, mortars, and pestles.
[b] Includes grooved stones, notched stones, end-notched stones, shell fishhooks, fishhook blanks, and bone gorges.
* Not typologically consistent with the Early Period.

increase is represented on the Pecho Coast in the radiocarbon date profile (see Figure 7.4). SLO-2 exhibits a functional artifact profile similar to that of previous occupations with both ground- and flaked-stone implements present. Statistically, the assemblage is slightly more diverse (Margalef Index=2.000). SLO-1366/H shows a nearly identical diversity. SLO-1370/H, however, yielded a decidedly less-diverse tool assemblage with no milling equipment and very low volumetric density of projectile points (Table 7.15). Overall, the period as a whole exhibits the characteristic increase in projectile points, but there is clear variation with a high density of points at SLO-2 and -1366/H, and lower values at SLO-497 and -1370/H. Fishing equipment is evident for the first time, albeit not in large numbers. The variation between these sites in diversity and relative abundance of projectile points and ground stone speaks to the likelihood of two functionally different types of settlements: SLO-2 and -1366/H representing longer-term residential bases, and SLO-497 and -1370/H representing short-term settlements (camps), although sample size from SLO-497 makes conclusions about that site less definitive. Importantly, mortars or pestles were present only at SLO-2 and not SLO-1370/H. If we can be confident that these implements represent use of acorns, this distinction would suggest that SLO-2 was occupied more intensively because it was the location of acorn stores. CA-SLO-1370/H, on the other hand, represents a camp, albeit a nonspecialized one probably occupied by a full complement of societal members. SLO-2 and -1366/H are also associated with reliable water sources while SLO-1370/H is located on a wind-exposed point with no immediately adjacent freshwater. The Initial Early Period seems to be associated with the appearance of this two-pronged approach to settlement (long-term and short-term residential bases), which it distinguishes from the preceding Millingstone/Lower Archaic, and suggests some increased interest in coastal resources. Further, this system seems to characterize settlement approaches from this point onward.

Middle Period

Middle Period components can be recognized at SLO-2, -5, and -10, while radiocarbon dates also show Middle Period occupation at SLO-51/H and SO-1451/H (Price et al. 2006) (Figure 7.18). Diversity scores and projectile-point densities show the same bimodal pattern as the Early Period: high values at SLO-2 and SLO-10 suggesting long-term residential site use, and lower values for SLO-5 suggesting a short-term residential site or camp. Both SLO-2 and SLO-10 produced human burials. Based on depth, a total of 35 burials at SLO-2 represents the Middle Period. Very modest testing at SLO-10 by Dallas (1994) yielded at least three human burials suggesting that many more are present. Large numbers and high density of burials seem to be distinguishing traits of long-term residential sites.

Middle–Late Transition

Unfortunately, only one component, SLO-9, can be clearly assigned to the Middle–Late Transition. Radiocarbon dates also show that SLO-2 and -10 were occupied during the Middle–Late Transition (Figure 7.18), but no discrete components could be isolated at those sites. While the diversity score for SLO-9 is higher than those of the definitive short-term camps, the site also shows a near absence of milling equipment and no human burials despite a fairly large recovery volume. It is perhaps best interpreted as a short-term residential site used in conjunction with longer-term occupation at SLO-10. The relatively low number of sites occupied during this time may be related to the Medieval Climatic Anomaly.

Late and Postcontact Periods

The Late Period is represented by components at SLO-2, -51/H, -1366/H, and -1370/H. Radiocarbon dates further indicate that there was occupation at SLO-585 and -1466 (Figure 7.18). However, the radiocarbon and projectile-point record from SLO-2 is somewhat unclear in regard to the prevalence of Late Period materials. No Desert Side-notched points were reported from SLO-2 but these were the primary marker of Late Period occupation at SLO-51/H and at multiple sites in the Morro Bay area to the north (Far Western Anthropological Research Group 2016; Hoover and Sawyer 1977). SLO-51/H is also associated with an ethnographic village name (*Tstyiwi*) while SLO-2 is not. The small recovery sample from SLO-51/H, however, shows only a modest diversity score. Tentatively, SLO-51/H is still assumed to represent the primary long-term residential base along the coast during the Late Period with shorter-term camps at SLO-2, -585, 1366/H, and -1370/H.

At Morro Bay the Late Period shows a decided terrestrial shift in settlement with the initial appearance of residential sites 1–2 km inland from the present shoreline (Far Western Anthropological Research Group 2016). On the Pecho Coast there is only modest evidence for such a trend: SLO-51/H is situated 200 m inland from the shoreline and stands in contrast to most other sites investigated in this study that are on the current shoreline. A slight inland shift seems consistent with increased reliance on acorns and higher frequencies of milling equipment at SLO-2.

Clearly, SLO-51/H was the primary, year-round residential site (village) used after 1769. Even with a small excavation sample, the site shows the highest diversity score of any temporal component. It also shows high densities of projectile points, fishing equipment, milling tools, and shell beads. The only other site that has produced mission-period glass beads was SLO-584 (as well as possible mission-era pottery), investigated by Greenwood. This site is situated in an unusual location over 1,000 m inland from the shoreline at an elevation of 230 feet. It may represent a mission refuge or another Late and postcontact settlement showing increased emphasis on inland resources.

Milling Equipment over Time

Ground-stone assemblages from the excavated components can also be used to examine the intensity of the local economy. Basgall (1987) argues that specialized acorn-processing equipment like mortars and pestles can be examined relative to generalized milling equipment like slabs and handstones to determine the relative reliance on acorns. If these functional inferences are accurate, then the diachronic trends suggest a Late Holocene apogee in acorn use along the Pecho Coast (Figure 7.19). Indeed, the trends show a nearly linear increase in the proportion of acorn processing equipment through the Holocene. These findings are also in agreement with regional trends of acorn exploitation (Codding and Jones 2016; Codding et al. 2012; Stevens and McElreath 2015), suggesting an increased reliance on these storable but expensive-to-process carbohydrates.

Discussion

Tentatively, we posit only modest variation in settlement strategies across the 10,000 years of Pecho Coast occupation. The Millingstone/Lower Archaic Period settlement strategy is best considered by viewing the Pecho Coast in tandem with finds from surrounding areas. These suggest three types of settlements: short-term residential sites (seasonal camps) on the shoreline focused on low-level pursuit of shellfish and fish; longer-term residential sites situated inland as represented by SLO-1797 (with a heavy focus on terrestrial plant foods); and resource-procurement locations represented by sites like SLO-1842 near Morro Bay. The latter differs from the other two in that it produced no shell remains or developed midden.

Trade and Exchange

Among the traits that have attracted great attention from scholars of southern California archaeology and prehistory is the exchange of goods, particularly shell beads and, to a lesser degree, obsidian. Abundant and unequivocal evidence from the northern Channel Islands in the form of microblade bead drills and *Olivella* shell-production detritus testify to major production of shell beads on the islands. The degree to which manufacture was exclusively restricted to these insular production centers has long been uncertain as has been the exact means and motivations underlying the conveyance of the beads from the islands to the immediate mainland and beyond. Some California shell beads, recovered from as far away as Idaho

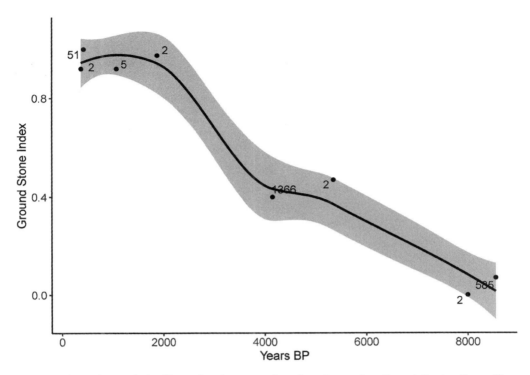

FIGURE 7.19. Ground-stone index illustrating the proportion of mortars and pestles relative to other milling equipment from the excavated assemblages plotted by the component midpoint and fitted using a loess (span=0.75) with 95% confidence intervals.

and New Mexico (Bennyhoff and Hughes 1987; Fitzgerald et al. 2005), speak to long-distance conveyance by such means as group-to-group, down-the-line trade. The exact points of origin within California for the beads found far inland cannot be identified with certainty. Obsidian, on the other hand, is a more definitive marker of long-distance, intergroup connections between the Pecho Coast and elsewhere inasmuch as the nearest sources of this commodity are 275 km to the east and 350 km to the north in the North Coast Ranges (Figure 7.20). Here we consider frequencies of these two commodities over time and discuss patterning relative to the most likely intergroup interactions that they represent.

Obsidian

The total number of obsidian specimens available for the present study is 112, including 16 with source and hydration results reported by Farquhar (2003) from SLO-2 and 96 specimens from six other Pecho sites (Table 7.16). Reports

detailing the technical specifics of the hydration and XRF analyses are available from the original site reports referenced in chapters 3 and 5. Unfortunately, the current sample does not include any findings from Millingstone/Lower Archaic components. Complicating interpretation of the obsidian further are varied opinions on the value/precision of hydration-based dates and multiple alternative schemes for translating hydration readings into calendric ages. In this study we generally eschewed hydration readings as primary data in determining component chronology because multiple studies including one by King (2000) show that hydration readings from coastal environments are inaccurate in terms of calendric time. Nonetheless, obsidian data still need to be considered on some type of temporal scale. Here, we rely on large obsidian samples from well-dated (via radiocarbon) single-components from the greater San Luis Obispo area including one from the Pecho Coast (SLO-9), two from Morro Bay (SLO-14 [Far

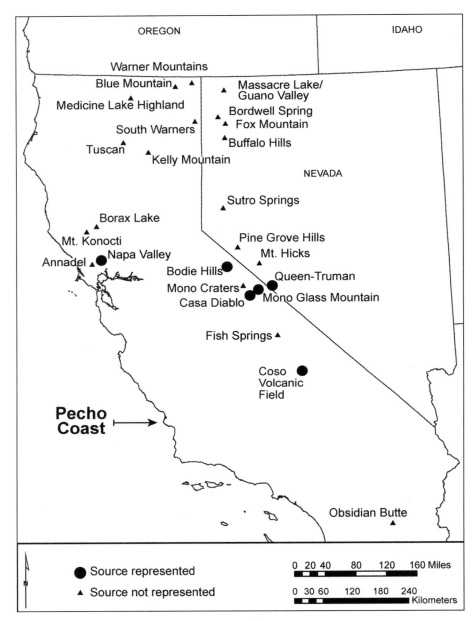

FIGURE 7.20. Obsidian sources represented on the Pecho Coast.

Western Anthropological Research Group 2016; Laurie and Pulcheon 2012] and SLO-165 [Mikkelson et al. 2000]), and SLO-179 near Cambria (Jones and Ferneau 2002). Of these, the most important is probably SLO-14 which has a sample of 45 paired hydration/source readings from a component dated 2100–1900 cal BP. Most of the Coso obsidian hydration readings from SLO-14 (12 of 17) cluster between ca. 3.5 and 4.4 microns; Casa Diablo readings (19 of 28) cluster between 3.4 and 4.6 microns, suggesting that these hydration spans represent the early Middle Period.

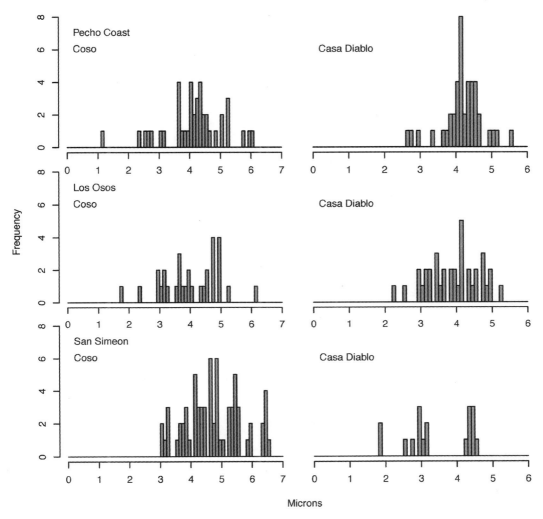

FIGURE 7.21. Obsidian hydration results from key areas of the south-central California coast.

Furthermore, the volumetric density of obsidian from the early Middle Period component at SLO-14 suggests that this may have been a time of heavier obsidian conveyance into the San Luis Obispo County area, and that obsidian samples from many components may be dominated by those from the early Middle Period.

SLO-165 is the most heavily radiocarbon-dated site in San Luis Obispo County with 40 ^{14}C determinations. These show that while the site was witness to some modest occupation during the Millingstone/Lower Archaic and Middle Periods, it is dominated by an Early Period component dating 5700–3400 cal BP. The majority of the Coso readings, however, overlap with SLO-14, suggesting that while the site had only minor Middle Period occupation, most of the obsidian dates to that time. The site does, however, show clusters between 5.2 and 5.7 microns on Coso and 4.8 and 5.6 microns on Casa Diablo which almost certainly predate the Middle Period and help define the micron ranges for the Early Period. Based on the SLO-14 and -165 findings, we place the division between Early and Middle Periods (cal 2600 BP) at 4.8–5.1 microns for both Coso and Casa Diablo obsidians (Figure 7.21).

TABLE 7.16. Summary of the Pecho Coast Obsidian by Component.

Component	Not Analyzed	Coso	Casa Diablo	Mono Glass	Queen	Napa	Warner Mountains	Total	Exc. Volume (m³)	Obsidian/ m³
SLO-51/H Post Contact	0	0	0	0	0	0	0	0	1.2	0.0
SLO-51/H Late	0	5	2	0	0	0	0	7	4.0	1.8
SLO-8 Late	0	0	0	0	0	0	0	0	1.5	0.0
SLO-1366/H	0	0	0	0	0	0	0	0	1.4	0.0
SLO-1370/H	0	0	0	0	0	0	0	0	2.2	0.0
Subtotal	0	5	2	0	0	0	0	7	9.1	0.8
SLO-9 Middle–Late	3	23	27	1	1	1	0	56	34.3	1.6
SLO-5 Late Middle	0	1	0	0	0	0	0	1	10.3	0.1
SLO-10 Middle	6	6	11	0	0	0	0	23	10.5	2.2
Subtotal	9	30	38	1	1	1	0	80	55.1	1.5
SLO-497 Early	0	0	0	0	0	0	0	0	2.3	0.0
SLO-1366/H Early	1	4	1	0	0	0	0	6	7.4	0.8
SLO-1370/H Early	0	2	1	0	0	0	0	3	8.8	0.3
Subtotal	1	6	2	0	0	0	0	9	18.5	0.5
SLO-10 Millingstone	0	0	0	0	0	0	0	0	2.5	0.0
SLO-2*	0	8	7	0	0	0	1	16	*	*
Grand total	10	49	49	1	1	1	1	112	80.3	1.4

*Obsidian recovered via 6 mm (¼ in) mesh not comparable with other sites and not broken down by component.

Seven radiocarbon dates from SLO-9 suggest the site was occupied 1000–700 cal BP. However, Casa Diablo hydration readings (22 of 27) cluster strongly between 3.7 and 4.1 microns; Coso readings (15 of 23) cluster between 3.7 and 4.4 microns. The overlap between the early Middle Period component readings from SLO-14 and the Middle–Late Transition component is problematic and highlights the challenges involved in using obsidian hydration reading for chronological purposes. Fortunately, a Middle–Late Transition component was also recognized at SLO-179 (in addition to a Middle Period occupation) where clusters on Casa Diablo hydration readings and Coso are apparent between 2.4–3.9 and 2.5–4.1, respectively. These readings provide some clarification for the terminus of the Middle–Late Transition Period on the hydration micron scale. We place it at 2.3–2.6 microns for Coso and Casa Diablo obsidians. This temporal framework allows us to evaluate the Pecho Coast obsidian sample.

The Pecho obsidian sample includes 102 specimens for which source was determined. These are dominated by Coso (n=49; 48%) and Casa Diablo (n=49; 48%), with single specimens from Napa, Mono Glass, Queen, and the Warner Mountains in northeastern California. At least for the time periods represented in the current sample (Early–postcontact), obsidian was most commonly received from the Coso and Casa Diablo sources. There is evidence from the Morro Bay area (SLO-626) that suggests Napa obsidian was more numerically abundant during the Early Period (Far Western Anthropological Research Group 2016:304) than it is in the Pecho sample.

In terms of diachronic trends, the Pecho sample mimics larger-scale regional patterns. Findings from the Sudden Flats site in northern Santa Barbara County show that obsidian was arriving on the central coast as early as 10,900 cal BP (Lebow et al. 2014, 2015), but the Cross Creek site and the Pecho Coast show almost no obsidian from Millingstone/Lower Archaic components. A single hydration reading of 8.6 microns from SLO-2 reported by Farquhar (2003) is the only specimen testifying to obsidian conveyance to the Pecho Coast during the early Holocene. Obsidian was being traded to the south-central coast as early as 10,900 years ago, but in seemingly very low quantities.

Obsidian becomes only slightly more visible but is still a minor component of the debitage and tool record on the Pecho Coast during the Early Period as represented by a smattering of readings greater than 5.0 microns. This increase is not as dramatic as once suggested by Jones (1996, 2003), but obsidian is slightly more abundant in the hydration profile between 5 and 6 microns. The combined Early Period components also show an obsidian/m³ value of 0.5 (Table 7.16), with most of it arriving from the two distant eastern Sierran sources of Coso and Casa Diablo (with a slight dominance of Coso). As reflected in the hydration profile, a more compelling increase can be associated with the beginning of the Middle Period when obsidian/m³ increases to 1.5. The highest value for the Pecho Coast is from the Middle Period component at SLO-10 (2.5). The combined obsidian/m³ for the Late Period is lower at 0.8, and also is at least somewhat inflated owing to the fact that at least four of the hydration values from the Late Period levels are more consistent with the Middle Period micron range, and, almost certainly are derived from the early Middle Period component that underlies the Late Period midden at SLO-51/H. The obsidian/m³ value of 0.8 for the Late Period and the local and regional hydration profiles suggest that long-distance obsidian conveyance peaked during the Middle Period (probably the early Middle Period) and was nearly nonexistent during the Late Period.

Beads

Evaluating bead frequencies without grave lots is a potentially problematic exercise because individual graves often yield enormous numbers of beads—far greater than are typically recovered from nongrave midden contexts. Grave lots from the Pecho Coast are limited to those reported by Greenwood (1972) from 66 graves at SLO-2, but the chronology of those burials cannot be established with certainty and the beads themselves are no longer available for study. Consequently, our consideration of beads is restricted to the 385 nonburial-associated loose beads recovered from Pecho Coast middens.

King (1990) suggests that shell beads, in the form of Class L *Olivella* rectangles, appear in the Santa Barbara Channel as early as perhaps 8000 cal BP. Findings from the deserts of southern California indicate that Class A spire-lopped *Olivella* were being conveyed to the interior as early as 10,000 cal BP (Fitzgerald et al. 2005), but their point of origin on the coast is not known. In the San Luis Obispo area in general and the Pecho Coast in particular, there is only meager evidence for use of beads prior to mid-Holocene. No beads can be associated with the Millingstone/Lower Archaic components at SLO-2 or SLO-10, nor from comparably dated components at Morro Bay (e.g., at SLO-165). A single spire-lopped *Olivella* bead was associated with the important Millingstone component at SLO-1797, the Cross Creek Site (Fitzgerald 2000), but this was found only with a substantial excavation volume (> 30 m³). The single burial from SLO-2 associated with the earliest occupation, ca. 10,300 cal BP, had no beads. Three Class L *Olivella* rectangular beads were reported from SLO-165 at Morro Bay, dating ca. 5700 cal BP, but no examples of this type have yet been found at Pecho. Beads become a noticeable (but minor) part of assemblages only at the beginning of the Middle Period when Class G saucers appear for the first time (e.g., at SLO-10). There is nothing to tell us their point of origin, but there is no manufacturing evidence at the sites (SLO-9, -10, -1366/H, -1370/H) where the beads were found. It is likely that they originated from the major production loci in the Santa Barbara Channel, but this has not been established with certainty.

Burials uncovered from SLO-56 at Avila Beach with thousands of beads (D. Jones 2013) complement the Pecho volumetric increase to suggest that the early Middle Period may have been the beginning of major bead importation into what is now San Luis Obispo County. If so, this corresponds with the rise in obsidian exchange that occurred at the same time.

Beads become volumetrically significant on the Pecho Coast, however, only during the Late Period as represented by the large numbers of Class E and K types recovered from precontact and postcontact contexts at SLO-51/H. A comparable volumetric increase dates slightly earlier to the Middle–Late Transition at Morro Bay (Far Western Anthropological Research Group 2016). The recovery of unfinished red abalone beads, at least two bead drills, and possible *Olivella* production detritus indicate that some beads were produced at SLO-51/H on the Pecho Coast, although the contexts and types hint that this was more of a postcontact activity. Bead drills were also reported by Bertrando (1997) and Blake (2010) from precontact, Late Period context at SLO-214. One similar specimen was recovered from SLO-23 (Far Western Anthropological Research Group 2016), and several were reported by Price and colleagues (2009) from SLO-44 in San Luis Obispo. The 12 specimens from SLO-214 were not accompanied by shell production detritus which suggests that bead production could not have been a major activity at that location. Even with some modest on-site manufacture, it is highly unlikely that all or even most of the Late Period beads found at Pecho or Morro Bay were locally produced. Beads seem to have begun to arrive in significant numbers during the Late Period or slightly earlier, and we can surmise that most of them originated from the Channel Islands—although this is not a certainty.

A ramp-up in bead importation and some modest local manufacture during the Middle–Late Transition and Late Period beg for comparison with Chumash bead economies of the Santa Barbara Channel where the timing and intensity of bead production is highly featured in models of emergent sociopolitical complexity. Such models have often been assumed to apply to the northern Chumash-speaking area based on shared linguistics—despite important differences in ecology, material culture, and ethnographically observed sociopolitical complexity between the areas. Following Chagnon (1970), King (1976) suggested that shell beads were parts of resource redistribution networks organized by paramount chiefs in Chumash chiefdoms to level out seasonal and yearly spatial imbalances in food. In a series of papers, Arnold (1992, 2001, 2004) suggested that *Olivella* bead production was one of several craft specializations (the other being sewn-plank canoe construction) that emerged during the climatic crises of the Medieval Climatic Anomaly (Late Middle Period and Middle–Late Transition) under the authority of ruling elites. Arnold essentially argues that the chiefdom form of political organization appeared rather abruptly toward the end of the Middle marked by explosive growth in bead manufacture. Both King and Arnold suggest that beads were a currency that, among other things, was used in exchange for food—most notably for islanders to acquire acorns from the mainland. Fauvelle (2011, 2013), however, showed that such arguments seem largely hyperbolic given the realities of island-mainland transport. Even if they have some validity, they help explain increased production of beads on the islands and their relation to sewn-plank boats, but not the increased conveyance of beads to the northern Chumash area where there were no plank canoes. The northern locales like Pecho and Morro Bay were primarily recipients of beads, not centers of production—despite evidence for some local manufacture. For now, we speculate that the volumetric increase in beads along the Pecho Coast could either represent the initial appearance of Chumash-speaking peoples into what is now San Luis Obispo County, the expansion of an early monetary economic system, or the movement north of powerful Chumashan leaders establishing stronger alliances with northern communities through gifting and reciprocal exchange.

Summary

Seventeen reasonably well-dated components show evidence for distinct variation over time on the Pecho Coast in technology, subsistence, settlement, and exchange. Bolstering Greenwood's (1972) three-part cultural scheme with more than 100 additional radiocarbon determinations, we now divide the local 10,000-year occupational sequence into five major periods

that articulate reasonably well with adjoining regions. We also tentatively identify several subperiod divisions.

Millingstone/Lower Archaic 10,300–5700 cal BP

The period of initial occupation, referred to here as Millingstone/Lower Archaic, dates from 10,300 to 5700 cal BP. The distinctive Millingstone Culture, marked by handstones, milling slabs, and core tools (scraper planes, core hammers, and choppers) has been recognized for over half a century in southern California (Wallace 1954) and is now reasonably well accepted as the predominant cultural pattern in central California for the early Holocene (Fitzgerald and Jones 1999) where it is marked by large sidenotched points. As of 2004, at least 13 sites in the San Luis Obispo area have yielded dates between 10,000 and 5700 cal BP (Fitzgerald 2004; Rosenthal and Fitzgerald 2012), but only Cross Creek SLO-1797 provided a tool assemblage large enough to reveal the Millingstone cultural pattern. On the Pecho Coast, four sites date to this period including SLO-2 which Greenwood (1972) originally used to define the central coastal expression of Millingstone. The more recent findings still leave many aspects of the Millingstone/Lower Archaic Period unclear, but they do provide for some tentative observations.

As a working hypothesis it is reasonable to believe that the distinctive Millingstone tool kit reflects an adaptation heavily focused on plant foods, possibly high-ranking tubers, and that it was related to the warmer, drier climate of the early Holocene (Moratto 1984). Consistent with this, the settlement system seems to have included long-term inland residential bases like Cross Creek, complemented by short-term residential sites like SLO-2 on the coast. The latter function is reflected by low tool diversity (Table 7.17) and high faunal diversity which suggests no major specialization, albeit with a slight emphasis on terrestrial foods (61%) and nearly equal exploitation of deer, rabbits, and marine birds, especially the flightless duck. Shellfish and fish were taken in relatively modest amounts. Marine

TABLE 7.17. Summary of Key Settlement/Subsistence Traits from Pecho Coast Components.

Site	Component	Tool Diversity[1]	Faunal Diversity[1]	% Marine Mammals and Birds	Density (kg/m³) Shell	Density (n/m³) Projectile points	Density (n/m³) Milling Tools	Inferred Function
SLO-51/H	Postcontact	3.211	2.135	49.1	246.7	5.7	1.6	Long-term residential base
SLO-2	Late	2.182	0.928	35.1	—	3.4	1.2	Short-term residential base
SLO-51/H	Late	1.828	1.573	20.8	—	3.0	0.0	Short-term residential base
SLO-1366/H	Late	1.950	—	—	306.1	3.6	0.0	Short-term residential base
SLO-1370/H	Late	—	—	—	1.3	0.9	0.0	—
CA-SLO-9	Middle–Late Transition	2.092	3.202	32.2	38.7	1.3	0.1	Short-term residential base
SLO-2	Middle	1.929	0.970	26.7	—	2.9	0.5	Short-term residential base
SLO-5	Late Middle	1.291	1.927	56.9	125.9	0.8	0.4	Short-term residential base
SLO-10	Middle	2.879	3.171	21.1	108.1	1.1	0.2	Long-term residential base
SLO-497	Terminal Early	—	0.834	3.3	37.7	0.4	0.0	Short-term residential base
SLO-1366/H	Early	2.058	—	21.7	196.2	2.0	0.4	Short-term residential base
SLO-1370/H	Early	1.335	2.140	57.7	4.6	0.5	0.0	Short-term residential base
SLO-2	Initial Early	2.000	2.677	61.5	—	1.8	1.0	Long-term residential base
SLO-10	Millingstone/Lower Archaic	—	—	—	1.6	0.8	0.0	Short-term residential base
SLO-2	Millingstone/Lower Archaic	1.443	3.238	38.6	—	0.6	1.1	Short-term residential base
SLO-585	Millingstone/Lower Archaic	—	3.688	47.5	—	—	—	—

[1] Margalef Diversity score

mammals were insignificant with a small number of sea otters taken. Perhaps the only aspect of this adaptation that has not been emphasized previously is the heavy exploitation of sea birds, especially cormorants and puffins. Cormorants, in particular, have breeding colonies on the Pecho Coast mainland today, so it is reasonable to suspect that such rookeries existed in the past, and that they would have been highly desirable/accessible targets for human predation. While estimates of energetic returns for analogous resources suggest that marine birds (e.g., geese and ducks) were less profitable than rabbits and deer (see Table 2.1), the value of marine bird patches may have been considerably higher when they were concentrated in mainland breeding colonies. The argument here is akin to that made by Hildebrandt and Jones (1992) for marine mammal rookeries. While there is no evidence that seal or sea lion rookeries ever existed on the Pecho Coast, marine bird nesting colonies seem to have been similarly attractive and vulnerable resource concentrations—with the flightless duck being the most vulnerable.

Shellfish exploitation emphasized the California sea mussel as it did throughout the entire sequence at Pecho. However, red abalones represented in a concentration at SLO-10 show large individuals, reaching up to 20 cm in length. The two-sigma date of ca. 7400–7200 cal BP returned from one of the red abalone shells in this concentration falls neatly within the span of 8250–5250 cal BP assigned by Glassow (2016) to red abalone middens on Santa Cruz Island, and there does seem to be a similarity between the Pecho feature and those of the Northern Channel Islands as has been suggested by others (Joslin 2010). As we discuss below, however, the Pecho findings also suggest that the distinctive elements of these red abalone features—the size of the shells and their occurrence in dense concentrations—are limited to the early Holocene. Unlike the Channel Islands, red abalones persist throughout the sequence at Pecho (with the exception of two gaps in directly dated red abalone that itself might be a product of sampling), reflecting the generally cooler waters of central California. However, here we distinguish

the concentrations of large individuals found at Pecho in early Holocene contexts from later, smaller shells recovered individually, not in features. The explanation for the presence of the large red abalone features on Pecho is unclear since they cannot as readily be attributed to cold water temperatures. But, the size of the individuals suggests very sporadic exploitation by humans and other predators (sea otters) which allowed individuals time to grow so large. At a minimum these features seem to reflect a relatively small human population on the coast and possibly a reduced sea otter population as well.

There is no evidence for significant trade to the Pecho Coast before 5700 cal BP, although obsidian profiles from Morro Bay (Far Western Anthropological Research Group 2016) and shell beads from interior California (Fitzgerald et al. 2005) indicate that interregional contacts were being made during this time in California. Indeed, the Millingstone tool kit represented at Pecho was shared across much of southwestern North America during the early Holocene indicating that cultural connections existed. Still, residents of the Pecho Coast were probably fairly isolated, pursuing a generalized, slightly mobile adaptation that featured plant foods and a mix of terrestrial and marine faunal resources with a greater emphasis on inland settlement.

Early Period 5700–2600 cal BP

Changes to the Millingstone lifeway around mid-Holocene have been recognized for nearly a century, although dating the various shifts that mark the transition precisely remains a work in progress. It is important to acknowledge that the Cross Creek Site was generally abandoned ca. 7500 cal BP so that the Millingstone lifeway could actually have come to an end earlier, and the millennia between 7500 and 5700 are not well documented. At Morro Bay there is a distinct gap in the radiocarbon record between ca. 6900 and 5900 cal BP (Far Western Anthropological Research Group 2016). Nonetheless, we here define an Initial Phase of the Early Period beginning at 5700 cal BP which coincides with an increase in both components and radiocarbon dates on the Pecho Coast as well as the central coast in general (Jones et al. 2007). The best expression of this period in the region is at SLO-165 (Morro Bay) which is marked by essentially a single component delineated by more than 40 radiocarbon determinations. At Pecho this phase is represented by the intermediate levels at the multicomponent SLO-2 and the essentially single-component SLO-1370/H.

Many previous scholars have interpreted the mid-Holocene changes on the south-central coast as reflections of increased human population and perhaps an in-migration of people (Jones et al. 2007; Mikkelsen et al. 2000; Warren 1968; among others). At Pecho, the onset of the Early Period (Initial Early) seems to coincide with a shift in settlement that for the first time included both long-term and short-term residential bases, the former represented at SLO-2, where tool diversity increased from the Lower Archaic/Millingstone Period (Table 7.17). Short-term residences are represented by SLO-1370/H which shows a lower tool diversity. Some camps such as the one marked by SLO-1366/H seem to have emphasized shellfish collection. Vertebrate faunal residues show an increase to over 50% reliance on marine taxa, dominated by an even greater focus on marine birds (53% of the combined Early Period remains). Fishing continued to be pursued, but the fish resource remained underutilized. Marine-bird nesting colonies seem to have been the main focus of the coastal subsistence effort which was a continuation from the previous Millingstone/Lower Archaic Period.

Artifact profiles suggest that the portable mortar and pestle appear for the first time, albeit in small numbers. From this, it is inferred that acorn use became more important than it had been previously—although not nearly as much as later in time. We surmise that the two-pronged system of long-term and short-term settlements might at least partially reflect the accumulation of acorn stores at the former which precipitated longer residence at a single location during the year.

Obsidian is slightly more visible in the record during this period, but there is no evidence for major change in interregional conveyance of this commodity or beads.

Middle Period 2600–950 cal BP

The Middle Period shows continued use of a two-pronged settlement strategy with at least one long-term residential base situated at SLO-10 at Spooner's Cove where tool diversity was relatively high. Subsistence residues show multiple signs of intensification related to over-exploitation and a growing human population on the coast. Most notable is a dramatic decline in exploitation of marine birds, led by the disappearance of the flightless duck, the extinction of which, at ca. 2800 cal BP, has been recognized for nearly a decade (Jones, Porcasi, Erlandson, et al. 2008). What can now be further seen from the Pecho fauna is that this was only part of a broader pattern in which marine birds were minimally pursued after 2800–2600 cal BP, almost certainly because accessible mainland and nearshore breeding colonies had been over-exploited and were less abundant. While the more adaptive seabirds like cormorants survived in offshore rookeries, the flightless duck was simply too vulnerable to human exploitation and was hunted into extinction.

Replacing sea birds were lower-ranked sea otters and fish, both of which required greater investments in technology and processing labor. While these resources were exploited during the earlier periods, both show significant increases during the Middle Period (see Figures 7.6, 7.11, and 7.12). A new technology, the circular shell fishhook, accompanies the increase in fishing at Pecho. Some exploitation of otters may have been intended for export since otter pelts were a known ethnographic trade commodity. Furthermore, obsidian increases significantly during this time. Early Middle Period components in particular yield noticeable quantities of obsidian, and hydration profiles show major increases in the micron ranges associated with the Middle Period. Beads in the form of G2/6 *Olivella* saucers become slightly more visible in the record at this time, probably arriving from production loci on the Northern Channel Islands.

Consistent with the other effects of intensification, red abalone shells show a decline in mean size during the Middle Period (see Figure 7.14, Table 7.11) suggesting more frequent harvest by denser human populations.

Middle–Late Transition 950–700 cal BP

Our first excavation on the Pecho Coast in the early 2000s at SLO-9 revealed a Middle–Late Transition component that we have consistently interpreted with reference to medieval droughts (Codding and Jones 2007; Codding et al. 2009, 2010). SLO-9 shows an apogee in rabbits relative to deer, and high frequencies of fish and marine foods which we argued reflect the exigencies of a drought-impoverished terrestrial environment. Certain of these observations still hold, but the larger data base now available for the Pecho Coast and adjoining areas complicates our interpretations. First, we now recognize, based on shell beads, that SLO-9 probably contains an early Middle Period component that is unrepresented in the radiocarbon results. Second, fish bone frequencies from SLO-9 no longer stand above the values from other components as strongly as they did previously with a more limited sample. Third, findings from SLO-5 dated slightly earlier but overlapping with SLO-9 at (1200–880 cal BP two-sigma) seem to show more compelling patterns. Findings from Morro Bay to the north also show order-of-magnitude increases in fish and other marine foods indicating a more pronounced drought-response signal (Jones, Jones, et al. 2017).

Morro Bay shows an enormous increase in aquatic and marine birds (related to the bay's estuarine habitat) and an all-time peak in fish remains. These patterns are not evident on the Pecho Coast. SLO-9 does show an increase in marine birds, but still not at the levels seen during the early Holocene. Cottontail rabbits, however, do show their highest percentage in the Pecho sequence at SLO-9 while deer are extremely low at 4.4%. The combined SLO-5 and -9 fauna also show a 50% representation of marine foods, led primarily by marine mammals. SLO-5 actually shows the highest percentage of marine mammals (44%) from any one component. Combined fish-bone density from SLO-5, -9, and -10 represents the apex in the local sequence—other than the postcontact component at SLO-51/H. Fishing clearly reached its all-time *prehistoric* high on the Pecho Coast sometime between the beginning of the Middle Period and the end of the Middle–Late Transition, but more findings from better-dated components are needed to sort this out further.

Owing to relatively high tool diversity, we tentatively define SLO-9 as a long-term residential base. However, the lack of mortars and pestles and low frequency of milling equipment is not entirely consistent with that characterization because we surmise that long-term bases were associated with acorn storage, processing, and consumption, something which may have been suboptimal or even impossible during this time owing to the medieval droughts.

The situation with obsidian exchange during the Middle–Late Transition is also complicated by the uncertainty surrounding the dating of SLO-9. The site produced an abundance of obsidian, but its hydration profile seems more consistent with the early Middle Period. SLO-5 produced only a single piece of obsidian (0.1 piece/m³). The peak in obsidian conveyance to the Pecho Coast seems to have been sometime during the Middle Period, probably during the early Middle Period.

Multiple examples from SLO-9 and one fragment from SLO-5 show that the bow and arrow reached the Pecho Coast sometime between 1200 and 950 cal BP, but it does not seem to have influenced hunting practices initially given that the most important prey during the late Middle and Middle–Late Transition were rabbits, sea otters, and marine birds that were more readily taken with nets, snares, or possibly harpoons.

Late Period 700–180 cal BP

The Late Period remains somewhat enigmatic for the Pecho Coast in terms of settlement. SLO-51/H seems to have functioned as a long-term residential base complemented by short-term camps at SLO-2, -1366/H, and -1370/H. However, the tool and faunal diversity values for SLO-51/H are low, suggesting that the site was not occupied year-round. Tool diversity is higher for SLO-2, but faunal diversity is considerably lower (Table 7.16). The Late Period adaptation does not seem to have included full sedentism, but rather continued use of both long-term and short-term residential sites.

The faunal record does not show all-time peaks in most resources during the Late Period although deer show a dramatic rebound from 4.4% of the SLO-9 Middle–Late Transition assemblage to 47% of the Late Period. Sea otters were also significant especially at SLO-2, but the percentages are lower than at SLO-5 and -10. Fishing was important based on volumetric density of fish bone at SLO-51/H, but less so than at SLO-10 during the Middle Period. Marine birds show minor increases from the Middle Period but still are far below the levels of the early Holocene.

Obsidian is less visible in Late Period components than earlier ones, and it is fairly apparent that long-distance conveyance of this commodity to the central coast dropped off. However, the defining characteristic of Late Period deposits is the high density of shell beads, mostly in the form of Class E and K variants. The density of beads in Late middens is four times greater than that of any other period. Most if not all of these beads were probably not produced locally but rather originated in the Santa Barbara Channel.

Protohistoric Decline?

In her original interpretations of Obispeño prehistory, Greenwood (1978a:523) suggested that Northern Chumashan territory was already in decline when the Portola expedition came through in 1769. Her view echoes that of King (1978:58) who stated that California Indian societies were more complex during the Protohistoric Period (AD 1500–1770) than they were at the time of contact. Subsequently, the case for Protohistoric plagues and population decline has been made repeatedly (e.g., Erlandson and Bartoy 1996; Preston 1996), particularly for the Chumash area (Erlandson and Bartoy 1995). Greenwood did not elaborate on the basis for her opinion, but it is not unlikely that the apparent drop-off in use of SLO-2 after the Middle Period was a contributing factor. Indeed, our investigations reveal full Late Period occupation only at SLO-51/H. Exactly when and why the focus of settlement shifted to SLO-51/H is not clear, but there is a hint of a peak in the intensity of exploitation of the Pecho Coast and a decline prior to historic contact. Whether the decrease in occupation can be attributed to Protohistoric

diseases or the medieval droughts (or both) cannot at this point be resolved owing to poor chronological resolution.

Postcontact: The Chumash Village of Tstyiwi (CA-SLO-51/H)

Only a single postcontact component was clearly identified on the Pecho Coast, represented by two excavation units at SLO-51/H. While this site was impacted by plowing and shows some mixing, the postcontact component was still reasonably intact, and yielded an enormous quantity of material despite the relatively small excavation sample. Most of the site's glass beads were recovered from the area associated with postcontact occupation, as were all examples of several other postcontact markers including abalone epidermis disks. These glass and shell beads confirm the predominantly postcontact dating of Units 5 and 6 at SLO-51/H.

Many characteristics of the postcontact component distinguish it from all previous occupations at Pecho. More specifically, the site's faunal remains and tools seem to reflect a small population that was constrained in its movements and forced to exploit the immediately adjacent habitats more intensely than before. This was the only investigated site that showed strong evidence for year-round, sedentary habitation as represented by charred plant remains from the hearth-like feature uncovered in Unit 6. The component's tool-diversity score of 3.211 was also the highest of any of the investigated sites.

The most distinctive element of the postcontact occupation at SLO-51/H, however, was the density of fish remains. The volumetric density of fish bones from the wet-screened sample was a staggering 13,511.5 NISP/m^3, easily the highest such value in the current study, and highest known from San Luis Obispo County (see Jones et al. 2016). The dry-screen value of 6,211.4 NISP/m^3 is the single highest value for any dry-screened sample from Monterey, Santa Cruz, or San Luis Obispo Counties. During the postcontact era, fishing became extraordinarily important at the village of Tstyiwi. However, the species profile in the faunal remains (showing very little use of silversides and surfperches) suggests that watercraft was used less frequently and shoreline species, such as pricklebacks, were collected more than in the past—perhaps to maintain a lower profile in the face of the unprecedented historic changes that were taking place nearby.

However, balsas were not given up entirely, and the postcontact component also shows a noticeable increase in marine mammal exploitation (39%) from the Late Period (24%), dominated by sea otters. This is also the only site that shows any use of terrestrial birds (3.7%) including quail, thrush, and robin. Shellfish were also heavily exploited and red abalone shells show an all-time low in diameter indicating intensive local exploitation.

The precontact matrix shows the same high density of beads as the postcontact component.

The recovery of unfinished bead blanks and bead drills indicates that, at a minimum, abalone epidermis disk beads were produced on-site. No obsidian can be associated with the postcontact occupation and it is fairly clear that long-distance exchange connections, already weakened in Late Prehistoric times, were gone altogether.

In the face of the growing Spanish presence, foraging activities seem to have been limited at the village, and people responded by relying more heavily on a restricted foraging area, relying especially on the bounty of adjacent fisheries for subsistence. Full sedentism seems to have emerged for the first time, being imposed on residents of this village by the historic events unfolding around them.

CHAPTER 8

Discussion and Conclusions

Radiocarbon findings reported in 1972 from SLO-2 showed that the Pecho Coast of central California was witness to a 9,000–10,000-year sequence of human occupation, but this evidence was unknown to many archaeological scholars at the time and was questioned or overlooked by others, in part because the dates were so much older than most others from the California shore. Beginning in the 1980s, the dates from SLO-2 were implicated in attempts to argue for a separate coastal migration route into the New World (Paleo-Coastal; Moratto 1984), substantial evidence for which has since accumulated from the Northern Channel Islands (125 km to the south) where a 12,000-year-old coastal adaptation featuring stemmed projectile points, eccentric crescents, and heavy exploitation of sea birds (along with fish and shellfish) is now well documented (Erlandson et al. 2011).

Our investigations over the last 13 years on the Pecho Coast have included acquisition of more radiocarbon dates from SLO-2 and other sites but have not extended the antiquity of the local sequence beyond the 10,000 cal BP threshold established by Greenwood (1972). Indeed, for the region as a whole, only one site, Sudden Flats (SBA-1547, 70 km to the south) has pushed the temporal needle back—extending it to ca. 10,900 ca BP (Lebow et al. 2014, 2015). Closer to Pecho, the Cross Creek Site (SLO-1797, 12 km inland) confirmed the 10,000 cal BP age of local occupations and clarified associated tool assemblages for the local area (Fitzgerald 2000).

Perhaps not surprisingly, the initial Holocene dates from Cross Creek were challenged in terms of how strongly they supported the idea of a coastal migration corridor. Turner (2003) noted the relatively small amount of shell and fish remains recovered from the Cross Creek midden and questioned whether such seemingly insignificant quantities (1.2 kg of shell from 1.9 m³ of recovery volume) reflected a serious marine adaptation. While greater amounts of shell and fish bone were recovered from the basal levels of SLO-2 and from a comparably dated site 65 km to the south (SBA-530, on the Vandenberg coast; Lebow et al. 2007), the question raised by Turner was not unreasonable. Indeed, our evaluation of the components that mark the oldest occupations on the Pecho Coast are somewhat ambiguous in terms of the relative intensity of the marine focus and connections with other terminal Pleistocene/Initial Holocene coastal inhabitants.

Certainly the Millingstone/Lower Archaic components from Pecho reflect people who were collecting shellfish, fishing, and exploiting marine animals. Perhaps the subsistence item that most links them with the Paleo-Coastal tradition is marine birds which were also heavily exploited ca. 12,000 cal BP on Santa Rosa and San Miguel Islands (Erlandson et al. 2011). Both on the islands and at Pecho, this focus seems at least partially related to the relative isolation of these settings which made them well suited for seabird breeding colonies. We argue that the concentrations represented by these rookeries and their accessibility to humans ranked marine-bird patches higher in such settings than the quantitative ethnographic data suggest for hunting waterfowl in other contexts. Exploitation of these resources on the remote, isolated Pecho peninsula represented efficient, marine-focused subsistence. This would be especially true of people who were employing watercraft, although nothing in the subsistence regime represented by the earliest Pecho sites absolutely required a boat. Nonetheless, watercraft of some type was used 12,000 years ago to reach the Northern Channel Islands, so it is reasonable to surmise that people were using boats 2,000 years later on the Pecho Coast mainland. This would have facilitated exploitation of nearshore rocks that served as ideal nesting sites for seabirds.

Not all 9,000- to 10,000-year-old sites on the central coast, however, show a heavy exploitation of sea birds. The basal component at SBA-530 at Vandenberg, for example, showed 92% reliance on cottontail and jack rabbits (combined NISP of 1,443) with sea birds representing less than 1% of the large vertebrates (Lebow et al. 2007). At SLO-2, on the other hand, mule deer were the single most important prey item (37.8%), followed closely by sea birds (32.8%) and then rabbits (18.6%). We attribute this variation, particularly the absence of birds from SBA-530, to differences in habitat. The latter site is not situated on a rocky headland, and may have been farther from quality sea-bird patches. Similarly, the high frequency of rabbit remains at Vandenberg and several of the Pecho sites seems related to coastal chaparral vegetation that was better suited for rabbits than deer.

In addition to the heavy emphasis on deer and rabbits, certain other aspects of the settlement/subsistence patterns associated with the initial Holocene at Pecho and the surrounding areas suggest a greater interest in terrestrial rather than marine resources. Of particular import is the inland setting of both the Cross Creek (12 km) and Sudden Flats (0.4 km) sites, as well as the evidence for prolonged seasonal occupation at the former. The oldest sites identified on the shoreline, on the other hand, at Pecho and

Morro Bay (SLO-812; Far Western Anthropological Research Group 2016) show relatively low tool diversity, suggesting they functioned as seasonal or short-term camps that were used in tandem with more long-term, inland residential bases. Such bases included sites like SLO-1920/H in Paso Robles (Stevens et al. 2004) and SLO-1764 near Arroyo Grande (Lebow et al. 2001). We also interpret the distinctive Millingstone tool kit represented at these sites as a reflection of heavy reliance on edible grass seeds and yucca hearts that would have been more abundant inland, and the latter of which may have provided relatively high returns. Both charred grass seeds and yucca remains were identified at Cross Creek (Jones et al. 2002:224). The core tools in classic Millingstone assemblages, in particular, have long been associated with yucca processing (Kowta 1969). These tools and the plant resources they were used to process also seem consistent with a warmer, drier early Holocene climate.

The Millingstone pattern represented at Pecho can now also be recognized as a local variant of a very widespread complex that extended from the North Coast Ranges (e.g., Crazy Creek [White and Roscoe 1992]) south to San Diego County (Wallace 1954), with components in the San Francisco Bay area and San Joaquin Valley (Fitzgerald and Jones 1999). This distribution seems to support an association between Millingstone and the Hokan language stock (Moratto 1984). Proto-Hokan languages have long been suspected to have been among those spoken by the initial inhabitants of California (Taylor 1961; Moratto 1984). Moratto (1984) associated Pre- or Proto-Hokan with fluted projectile points that are now dated between 13,300 and 12,900 cal BP (Waters and Stafford 2007). Following Taylor (1961), Moratto (1984:547) further suggested that the Millingstone lifeway originated in the deserts of the Great Basin and diffused westward into southern California where it was adopted by the fluted-point big-game hunters who had arrived previously. Millingstone was presumably embraced as an effective adaptation to warming and drying climate. Taylor (1961) suggested that Millingstone was brought into California by actual migrants, but Moratto (1984) felt the process was more one of technological diffusion rather than actual population movement.

At the time of Taylor's writing in 1961, the Chumashan languages were thought to be part of the Hokan stock (Shipley 1978) so the appearance of Millingstone on the coast could be readily interpreted as the arrival of Chumashan-speaking peoples (or perhaps just the arrival of the Millingstone tool kit) from the arid interior. At present, we have nothing other than a single, isolated, fluted projectile point found 20 km to the south at Nipomo (Mills et al. 2005) to suggest that people were present locally before the Millingstone/Lower Archaic Period, although the recently reported Sudden Flats site in Vandenberg Air Force Base to the south, dating 10,900 cal BP, suggests the possibility of a pre-Millingstone Culture that featured microblades. However, the reporting of only five microblades and no microblade cores from a sample of nearly 5,000 pieces of debitage leaves some room for doubt about that specific conclusion. Microblades aside, the large, thin bifaces found at Sudden Flats do not match anything recovered from Cross Creek nor did Sudden Flat produce any handstones or core tools typical of Millingstone. The eccentric crescent reported from the site also is a typological link to Paleo-Coastal sites on the Channel Islands (Erlandson et al. 2011), although crescents are known from at least one Millingstone site to the north in Santa Cruz County (SCR-177; Cartier 1993). Sudden Flats may be testament to a distinctive Paleo-Coastal culture on the mainland that predates and is different from Millingstone. For now, however, the earliest recognizable culture on the Pecho Coast is Millingstone which has never been found on the northern Channel Islands.

Since the earlier models for linguistic prehistory were put forward, Chumashan has been recognized as a linguistic isolate (Golla 2011; Klar 2002), not part of Hokan. This requires some rethinking of the original model. Golla (2011) is now fairly convinced that the earliest languages spoken on the Northern Channel Islands were not Chumashan (though unknown), and that

Chumashan languages did not reach what is now central San Luis Obispo County until 1,000 to 2,000 years ago, replacing an antecedent Hokan language. This would suggest that the Millingstone occupations on Pecho and at Cross Creek represent Hokan, albeit a coastal variant that exploited seabirds and used watercraft. The apparent inland settlement focus of Millingstone seems consistent with an adaptation that was culturally connected to arid interior California. However, red abalones of substantial size were exploited during the Millingstone/Lower Archaic Period, and were deposited in concentrations akin to the "red abalone middens" of the northern Channel Islands.

The end of Millingstone remains somewhat murky inasmuch as radiocarbon profiles show a gap between ca. 6700 and 5800 cal BP. Whether this gap represents the actual disappearance of people from the area in general, a local decline in population, or is simply the product of a limited sample remains unclear. However, a solid signal for human presence is apparent ca. 5700 cal BP. This is the transition referred to as the onset of the Hunting Culture—originally by Rogers (1929) and later by Greenwood (1972). It was described in the Santa Barbara Channel by Harrison and Harrison (1966) and is also recognized on the northern Channel Islands where Glassow (2016) dates it to 5900 cal BP. In keeping with more contemporary chronological nomenclature, we refer to it here as the onset of the Early Period. It is marked by a spike in radiocarbon dates, a slight increase in the variety of coastal settlements (long-term and short-term residential bases), greater frequency of projectile points, and introduction of the mortar and pestle. While previous conceptualizations of the middle Holocene have emphasized the seemingly robust character of these changes, our current findings indicate a significant amount of typological and adaptive continuity. The projectile-point type that dominates assemblages marking the onset of the Early Period, the large side-notched, is the same one found in earlier Millingstone/Lower Archaic components, including at SLO-2 (Greenwood 1972), SLO-1797 (Fitzgerald 2000), and SLO-1756 (Fitzgerald 1997). As Stevens and

McElreath (2015) note, the key change accompanying this transition is essentially additive in nature: mortars and pestles. The rest of the assemblages are essentially carryovers from Millingstone.

Faunal remains from Pecho also show no significant taxonomic change across the Millingstone/Lower Archaic–Early transition, as exploitation of seabirds, rabbits, and deer continued. Fishing shows no major increase nor is there any change in sea mammal exploitation. The biggest change related to subsistence seems to be the shift in settlement that we link to greater use of acorns and longer occupation of residential bases where nuts were stored. This prompted the two-pronged settlement strategy involving long- and short-term (camps) residential sites.

Subsistence continuity is also indicated by the ongoing exploitation of red abalones (more heavily than blacks), with mean sizes of individuals showing no diminution from the previous period. Red abalones seem to have reached substantial age and size during both the Millingstone/Lower Archaic and Early Periods, which must be at least a partial reflection of strong flow in the California Current and high marine productivity between 9000 and 4800 cal BP (Barron and Bukry 2007) as well as limited foraging intensity in the intertidal.

With respect to terrestrial climate, much has been made previously about the relationship between mid-Holocene climatic developments and concomitant cultural changes. Warren (1968) was among the first to suggest that peak Holocene warming caused people to flee the interior deserts of southern California and the Great Basin in favor of the California coast. The appearance of sites like SBA-54 at Goleta, marked by accumulations of large side-notched projectile points and mortars and pestles was thought to represent this cultural intrusion. More recently, Kennett and colleagues (2007) suggested that a severe dry interval between 6300 and 4800 cal BP (within an overall period of aridity 7000–3800 cal BP) caused a movement of people from the deserts to the south coast. Indeed, most regional and synthetic pollen and

TABLE 8.1 Temporal Components over Time, Morro Bay and the Pecho Coast.

Period	Morro Bay	Pecho	Total
Late	17	5	22
Middle–Late	4	1	5
Middle	4	3	7
Early	11	4	15
Millingstone/ Lower Archaic	5	4	9
Total	41	17	58

paleoclimatic schemes envision a peak in temperature and/or aridity between ca. 6000 and 4000 cal BP (e.g., Heusser 1978; Marcott et al. 2013; Viau et al. 2006). Kennett and colleagues (2007) further suggested that dry climate and productive seas stimulated early village development and intensified fishing on the southern Channel Islands although people on the northern Channel Islands were unaffected. For the central coast, Mikkelsen and colleagues (2000) argue that the increased use of SLO-165 at Morro Bay beginning ca. 5700 cal BP represents this same process: people retreating from the arid interior to the central coast.

The findings from Pecho support this scenario, but not unambiguously. Increased human presence is represented by a spike in the radiocarbon date profile that can also be recognized in a combined tally of temporal components from Pecho and Morro Bay (Table 8.1). These increases, along with the apparent change in settlement strategy and adoption of the mortar and pestle, seem consistent with growing numbers of people. Increased exploitation of marine birds and acorns are consistent with economic intensification in the face of growing human populations. However, faunal remains do not show evidence for significant changes. There is no meaningful increase in fishing nor is there evidence for impact on red abalone populations.

Indeed, a more intensive marine-focused lifeway becomes apparent only at the onset of the Middle Period, ca. 2550 cal BP, when the exploitation of seabirds plummeted due to overexploitation of rookeries during the preceding 7,500 years. The extinction of the flightless duck,

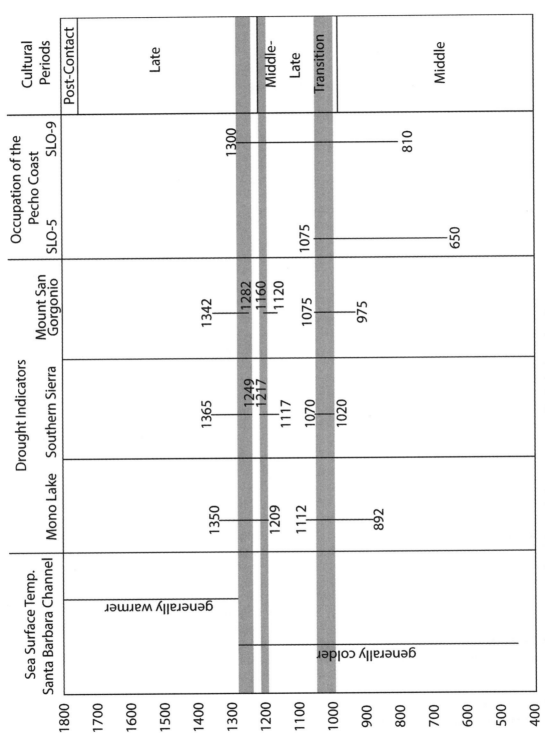

FIGURE 8.1. Summary of climatic conditions and site occupation before and during the Medieval Climatic Anomaly on the Pecho Coast.
Sources: Graunlich (1993), Kennett and Kennett (2000), MacDonald (2007), Stine (1994).

a *fait accompli* by ca. 2800 cal BP, was the most dramatic effect of the long history of exploitation of the seabird breeding colonies. In place of birds, subsistence shows a significant increase in sea otters and fish, the first legitimate evidence for marine intensification. Exploitation of sea otters may have been partially related to the value of their pelts as trade commodities since obsidian from distant eastern California sources shows a marked increase during the early Middle Period. The increase in otters is argued by Hildebrandt and McGuire (2012) to have been motivated primarily by attempts to acquire prestige. We will leave such cases to advance costly signaling interpretations to those authors. Here, we envision the shift from the flightless duck to sea otters as only one aspect of a broader pattern of marine intensification that began during the Middle Period on the Pecho Coast and included increased fishing and, for the first time, noticeable impacts on the size of red abalones. Settlement seems to have continued to involve long-term and short-term residential bases, and full sedentism was not practiced. Findings from nearby Avila Beach show that *Olivella* saucer beads were introduced to the local area by the thousands during the early Middle Period (D. Jones 2012), probably from production loci on the Channel Islands. It is possible that the distinctive changes that mark the Middle Period correlate with the arrival of the Chumashan language into the area, the first of what Golla (2011) suggests were two waves of linguistic intrusion. However, increased production of and general involvement with shell beads is also evident at the same time in the Santa Barbara Channel area where no ethnolinguistic replacement is envisioned.

The end of the Middle Period correlates with the onset of the Middle–Late Transition cultural phase, 950–700 cal BP, which we have consistently correlated with Stine's (1994) Medieval Climatic Anomaly (MCA), a period marked by severe droughts. Studies by Kennett and Kennett (2000) correlated the MCA with intervals of cold sea surface temperatures in the Santa Barbara Channel. However, as our archaeological studies have progressed, it has become necessary to recognize finer chronological resolution in the

climatic sequence and, to the degree possible, evaluate the cultural patterning accordingly. Relying on the sea surface temperatures developed by Kennett and Kennett (2000) for the Santa Barbara Channel and drought chronologies from eastern (Graumlich 1993; Stine 1994) and southern (MacDonald 2007) California shows cold productive ocean waters between AD 450 and 1300, and droughts from AD 1020–1070, 1197–1217, and 1249–1350 (Figure 8.1). Both SLO-5 and SLO-9 were occupied during intervals of cold productive seas and terrestrial drought. However, the bulk of the occupation of SLO-5 took place during the late Middle Period, while the bulk of the occupation at SLO-9 took place during the Middle–Late Transition. Both sites show signs of response to drought although the signal from SLO-5 is stronger. Cottontail rabbits show their highest percentage in the Pecho sequence at SLO-9 while deer are extremely low at 4.4%. SLO-5 shows the highest percentage of marine mammals (44%) in the sequence. The fish-bone density from the SLO-5 wet-screen sample represents the apex in the local sequence—other than the postcontact component at SLO-51/H (and the highly disturbed Late component at SLO-1370/H). Fish-bone density at SLO-10 which was occupied during the Middle and Middle–Late Transition was also very high, and it is clear that fishing reached its all-time prehistoric peak on the Pecho Coast sometime between the beginning of the Middle Period and the end of the Middle–Late Transition. Red abalones from SLO-5 and SLO-9 show their highest volumetric frequency which we interpret as being consistent with cold, productive sea surface temperatures and increased reliance on the marine environment. Mean diameter of red abalone shells remained smaller than those from earlier times. We interpret all of these findings as consistent with foraging populations who were focused on the marine environment in the face of decreased terrestrial productivity during times of severe drought—although the patterning is not as strong as recently recognized at Morro Bay (Far Western Anthropological Research Group 2016; Jones, Jones, et al. 2017), perhaps implying greater resilience of exposed rocky coast ecosystems to drought, or marking a smaller population than compared to the estuarine setting at Morro Bay.

One projectile point fragment from SLO-5 and multiple examples from SLO-9 show that the bow and arrow reached the Pecho Coast sometime between 1000 and 950 cal BP, but the bow does not seem to have influenced hunting practices initially. Given that the most important terrestrial prey at this time were rabbits, the bow might have been beneficial for hunting smaller prey (Tomka 2013).

The Late Period shows declines in almost all quantitative indices associated with Pecho adaptations following the peaks of the Middle and/or Middle–Late Transition. These include fish-bone density (wet-screen), marine mammals, marine birds, and obsidian. Subsistence became slightly less marine-focused and long-distance interregional exchange ended. Settlement continued to feature both long-term and short-term residential sites. The defining characteristic of the Late Period, however, is the high density of shell beads, mostly in the form of Class E and K variants, that probably were not produced locally but, rather, originated from the Santa Barbara Channel. The striking increase in beads could represent either the initial appearance of Chumash-speaking peoples, the second wave of linguistic expansion according to Golla's (2011) model, or attempts to consolidate power by a Chumash leader, like Buchon of the historic period. The marked increase in beads could represent attempts to establish stronger alliances with northern communities through a combination of gifting, reciprocal exchange, and/or forced conquest. Accounts of Buchon consistently associate him with armed entourages and intergroup raiding.

Whether the northern Chumash area was subsequently witness to a protohistoric decline in population (caused by the introduction of European diseases) or whether a population peak was reached toward the end of the Middle Period remains unclear, but the primary focus of occupation seems to have shifted to SLO-51/H during the Late Period. There are multiple signs for a cultural and population peak before contact, but whether the fulcrum point was medieval droughts or Protohistoric disease remains uncertain.

After the arrival of Spanish explorers in 1769 and the establishment of Mission San Luis Obispo de Tolosa in 1772, Chumash-speaking peoples continued to reside at the village of *Tstyiwi* for several decades. Subsistence residues suggest that village inhabitants became fully sedentary at this time, operating within a more limited foraging radius in order to avoid contact with the Spanish who used Avila Beach, 7 km to the east, as their primary port. The tool-diversity score from the postcontact component at SLO-51/H was the highest of any of the investigated sites. Charred plant remains from a feature show strong evidence for year-round site occupation, but the most impressive subsistence shift was one of marine intensification as reflected by the density of fish remains in the postcontact component at SLO-51/H which was greater not only than any site on the Pecho Coast, but any site in San Luis Obispo County.

The postcontact matrix showed the same high density of beads as the precontact component while the recovery of unfinished bead blanks and bead drills indicated that some beads were produced at the village after contact. The lack of obsidian in the postcontact component continued the trend seen previously during the Late Period.

The prehistory of the Pecho Coast is now in sharper focus than ever before. The 10,000-plus-year history of human occupation along the western edge of California represents a microcosm of changes seen across the region: increasing work effort, greater complexity, and dynamic population growth tempered by climatic variability, all ending rather abruptly following Spanish colonization. The unique characteristics of this record also provide evidence for adaptation to local environmental conditions, ranging from the early focus on marine birds to the late circumscription experienced by postcontact populations. As future research continues to refine this story, we hope this monograph provides a detailed summary of what is known so far, just as Greenwood did in 1972.

Glass Beads from the
Ethnographic Village *Tstyiwi* (CA-SLO-51/H)

THAD M. VAN BUEREN

This report analyzes the nine glass beads recovered from CA-SLO-51/H which is associated with the ethnographic Northern Chumash village of *Tstyiwi*. That village name was provided to J. P. Harrington in the early twentieth century by Chumash informants (Greenwood 1972:83). The site was also the location of the Pecho adobe occupied during the Mexican Period (1821–1846). Pecho Creek borders the site on its east side.

Methods

The glass beads were described, classified by type, and measured to capture quantitative data useful for comparative research and cross-dating. Measurements captured the maximum diameter, maximum length, and the maximum diameter of the perforation. Descriptive observations were made regarding bead manufacture methods, shape, glass color and diaphaneity, and the condition of the specimens (e.g., burnt, patinated, fragmentary, etc.).

Glass beads were classified using types originally established by Kidd and Kidd (1970), later supplemented by Karklins (1982). That typology was used because it is the most widely employed system across North America, a matter crucial for understanding the spatial and temporal distribution of these extremely diverse artifacts. Bead shapes were also described using standard terminology following Meighan (1979) to supplement the typological assignments. Because many glass beads in the CA-SLO-51/H collection were covered with a patina, they were wetted to ensure accurate assessment of clarity and color. Clarity is described as either opaque, translucent, or clear when viewed against a strong light source. Color is described in this analysis using numbers assigned in the Pantone® and Munsell® color systems.

Prior regional analyses of glass beads have employed diverse typologies, hindering meaningful comparisons. To overcome that obstacle, matches to glass beads in other collections were predicated on similarities in manufacturing method, color, shape, clarity, size, and condition, all of which may have specific implications for the timing of bead use and their sources of supply and distribution. Matches to other collections were generally made using color photographs and figures or, on a more provisional basis, with published descriptions.

The most secure comparisons to other glass bead assemblages were made with reference to color photographs and published color figures. My own prior studies, color photographs of Clement Meighan's (1979) type collection at the Phoebe Hurst Museum at the University of California in Berkeley, and color figures of collections from other places such as the Hudson's Bay Company settlement at Fort Vancouver, Washington (Ross 1990), supplied the most confident correlations.

Matches were also sought among collections known only through written descriptions and black-and-white images. These latter comparisons

TABLE A.1. Characteristics of Glass Beads from CA-SLO-51/H.

Specimen	Unit	Level (cm)	Type	Description	Color	Pantone Color	Clarity	Shape	Length (mm)	Diam (mm)	Hole (mm)	Remarks
2-3-19	3	0–10	DIIa45	Simple drawn	Blue	543	Clr	Oblate	3.0	3.2	1.2	Pitted; slight patina
2-3-20	3	0–10	DIIa7	Simple drawn	Black	Black	Op	Oblate	2.3	3.2	1.3	Slight patina; burned?
2-6-19	6	0–10	DIIa35	Simple drawn	Blue	283	Op	Oblate	2.1	3.3	1.6	Pitted; heavy patina
2-6-58	6	10–20	DIIa35	Simple drawn	Blue	283	Tr	Oblate	2.3	3.0	1.0	Pitted; moderate patina
2-6-96	6	20–30	DIIa45	Simple drawn	Blue	543	Clr	Oblate	2.5	2.8	0.9	Slight patina
2-6-97	6	20–30	DIIa45	Simple drawn	Blue	543	Clr	Oblate	2.8	3.9	1.7	Pitted; slight patina
2-6-98	6	20–30	DIIa45	Simple drawn	Blue	543	Tr	Oblate	2.5	2.9	1.3	Pitted; moderate patina
2-6-161	6	30–40	DIIa7	Simple drawn	Black	Black	Op	Oblate	2.8	4.3	1.5	Slight patina; burned?
2-6-171	6	30–40	DIIa24	Simple drawn	Green	362	Tr	Oblate	3.9	3.2	1.2	Pitted; moderate patina

were given less weight in this analysis because minor variations in color are often significant and cannot be discerned in the absence of accurate color definitions. Many typologies do not employ verifiable systems for describing minor variations in color. Collections from Hispanic settlements were given particular scrutiny for the entire period prior to the Mexican-American War in 1846. However, other work for the period after the Treaty of Guadalupe Hidalgo was also examined to assess distributions of glass beads in Native American sites (e.g., Van Bueren 1983, 2001) and locations associated with later settlers (e.g., Motz and Schulz 1979).

Glass Beads

A total of nine whole glass beads was recovered from two of the units. They are all simple (single-layer) drawn varieties with oblate forms. Only four types are present, all of them smaller varieties in black, blue, and green colors (Table A.1). The basic manufacturing method is briefly summarized from plentiful literature on the subject (e.g., Kidd 1979; Kidd and Kidd 1970; Karklins 1982).

Drawn beads are made from a gather of molten glass that may have one or more layers. The Type DIIa beads in this assemblage are all simple drawn beads with one layer of glass. Air is blown into the gather through a pontil, a second pontil is attached, and the bubble of glass is pulled into a tube. The tubes are then chopped into short segments and tumbled in heated sand to produce oblate or globular shapes. The color and clarity of the glass was made using various chemical additives designed to produce those specific characteristics. Each bead type is separately described. Correlations are then offered to beads in other collections. The general temporal implications of the assemblage are summarized in a concluding section based on the distribution of these types in other California sites.

Type DIIa7

Description

The two specimens in this collection are opaque black examples with a slight surface patina that is flaking off and some surface pitting that may indicate they were burned. The glass is very dense and does not appear to have a dark olive or deep purple coloration like some related types.

Correlations

Meighan's (1979) type collection contains several glossy black opaque drawn beads with widely varying ages, while the ones from CA-SLO-51/H are pitted and patinated possibly due to burning or natural process. Simple black beads may have been traded over lengthy periods by different partners. The closest correlation is to Meighan's Type 222 which he dates from 1790–1910 in California. This type occurs at several missions, as well as in sites reflecting distribution by the Hudson's Bay Company and during the American Period. This bead tentatively correlates with Gibson's (1976) Type C8a found after 1785 at Mission San Buenaventura (CA-VEN-87/H). A glossy black opaque bead at Fort Vancouver listed as Type 1050 dates between 1829 and 1860 (Hoffman and Ross 1974, 1975; Ross 1976, 1990).

Distribution

Opaque black beads occur at Mission San Jose (CA-ALA-1), Mission Santa Cruz after 1797 (Allen 1998; Bone 1975:Type C8b; Dietz 1983), Mission San Miguel (Van Bueren 2015), and at Missions Santa Inés, San Juan Capistrano, and San Antonio (Diaz 1993:73). They were recovered in Mexican Period burials at CA-YOL-69 (Van Bueren 2005), as well as many later sites including a cremation postdating 1856 at CA-TUO-395 (Van Bueren 1983). It also occurs at sites associated with the Hudson's Bay Company (HBC) including Fort Vancouver (Ross 1990) and sites associated with the Russian American Company (RAC) including Fort Ross (Van Bueren 1991).

Dating

This type was widely distributed in time and thus probably not temporally diagnostic.

DIIa24

Description

A single example of a simple, translucent dark forest-green (Pantone 347/Munsell 10GY2/6) drawn and hot-tumbled oblate spheroid was re-

covered. It has a moderately patinated surface with some pitting that may be natural degradation of the glass by the hydration process.

Correlations

This matches Meighan's (1979) Type 224 and differs from other similar varieties in this color that are made of opaque glass. This is a darker version of Type DIIa28, a variety that is correlated with Gibson's (1976) Type C3a at Mission San Buenaventura (CA-VEN-87/H). The only exact match is an example found at Mission San Miguel dating between 1797 and 1834 or later (Van Bueren 2015). There is a possible correlation with Fort Vancouver Type 1053 dating to 1829–1843, but the match in color is not exact and only a single specimen was recovered there (Ross 1990). A single specimen was also recovered at Fort Ross in a context dating to the Russian occupation from 1812–1842 (Van Bueren 1991).

Distribution

Found at four Channel Island sites, as well as CA-SJO-105, CA-SAC-56, and CA-SIS-262, according to Meighan (1970) who designates this variety as his Type 224. Green translucent beads are mentioned at some mission sites, but the only definite match occurs at Mission San Miguel (Van Bueren 2015). Other incidental occurrences at Fort Ross and Fort Vancouver may differ from this specimen.

Dating

Meighan (1979) suggests this may be an early Spanish type that may predate 1800. The CA-SIS-262 occurrence is an anomaly, suspected to be a different variety. The example from Mission San Miguel is a clear match that fits the Spanish Period distribution for this type.

DIIa35

Description

Two simple opaque sky blue (Pantone 283/Munsell 5PB5/4) drawn oblate spheroid beads were recovered. They have been hot-tumbled and both specimens have a moderate patina with some surface pitting possibly resulting from natural hydration processes.

Correlations

This type matches Meighan's (1979) Type 279. This has no certain correlate at Mission San Buenaventura (Gibson 1976), but it does occur at Mission San Miguel between 1797 and 1834 (Van Bueren 2015). Type 1081 at Fort Vancouver is similar but not a precise match (Ross 1990). It is similar to beads with a shiny appearance found at Fort Ross dated between 1812 and 1842 but may not be a precise match (Van Bueren 1991).

Distribution

This type was found at La Purisima Mission, Mission San Miguel, the neophyte cemetery at the third Mission Santa Clara dating between 1781 and 1818 (Van Bueren 1995), and at CA-HUM-169.

Dating

The limited distribution suggests this is an early type that may have reached California through both the Spanish and Russian American Company between 1800 and the 1830s. RAC fur trapping extended south to the Channel Islands, and some Aleut hunters were captured by Spanish authorities and later released after payment of a ransom that may have included glass beads (Farris 1989:484–485).

DIIa45

Description

Four simple transparent shadow-blue (Pantone 543/Munsell 7.5PB3/4) drawn oblate spheroid beads are the most common type recovered in both Units 3 and 6 at CA-SLO-51/H. Like the other types, these beads were hot-tumbled. They have mild to moderate patina that is flaking off.

Correlations

Correlated with Meighan's (1979) Type 204 and does not appear to have an exact match at Mission San Buenaventura, though Gibson's (1976) Type C1a is similar. There does not appear to be a match at Fort Vancouver (Ross 1990). This type is found at Fort Ross and an associated Pomo village (Van Bueren 1991).

Distribution

This type is primarily associated with Hispanic colonization but also includes examples at Fort Spokane dating between 1810 and 1826 and on the Farallon Islands (SFR-1), reflecting Russian American Company use between 1812 and the 1820s according to Meighan (1979). Among 21 sites that contain this type, according to Meighan, most are in coastal southern California. However, other occurrences include interior sites and CA-SAC-6 and CA-SAC-56 in the north. It is present at La Purisima Mission and may possibly also be one of the types reported at Missions San Antonio, Santa Clara, San Juan Capistrano, and Santa Ines (Diaz 1993).

Dating

The distribution appears consistent with the period from the 1810s into the 1820s, coinciding with the late Spanish Period prior to Mexican independence.

Interpretations

Glass beads provide insights into periods of use, in addition to their implications as signals of social and economic interactions between Native Americans and colonizers. As objects that were valued in a manner similar to traditional beads and ornaments, glass beads may have remained in use for extended periods of time, complicating the interpretation of their temporal significance. The small size of this assemblage and the disturbance processes at this site contribute to the caution warranted in interpreting this collection.

Cross-dating evidence points to a general pattern of distribution and use for most of these glass beads from CA-SLO-51/H weighted toward the late Spanish Period. No research was conducted to ascertain the period of occupation for the Pecho adobe or whether indigenous people may have been employed there after Mexican independence in 1821. However, this assemblage lacks glass-bead types indicative of occupations typical of the Mexican Period or the subsequent American Period (Bennyhoff 1977; Meighan 1979; Silliman 2000).

Types DIIa24, DIIa35, and DIIa45 dominate in pre-1830s contexts, but are not exclusively limited to sites supplied by the Spanish. That fact suggests some of these beads could have reached the local area through other channels such as the Russian American Company. Type DIIa7 is not temporally diagnostic, largely because opaque black beads occur widely through time including in Victorian contexts (Motz and Schulz 1970). It is unclear if the patinated examples at some early sites differ from the glossier varieties distributed more widely in time.

The distribution of imported glass beads and the ongoing production of traditional beads by Native Americans living at this site signal the complex social and economic interactions among the missionaries, secular Hispanic authorities and citizens, and indigenous people. The models used to understand those complex interactions have evolved from early models of acculturation to understandings that recognize each group approached the interactions from their own perspective, negotiating outcomes that had complex meanings (Castillo 1989; Greenwood 1989). Recent studies have favored models that emphasize agency and cultural persistence under the rubric of ethnogenesis. Yet that approach needs to be broadened according to Voss (2015:655) "to identify and investigate those situations in which colonialism and its consequences resulted in ruptures and structural transformations of identity practices."

The production and consumption of glass beads have an underlying economic basis in addition to the social meanings that are implied. Hornbeck (1989) describes the overall trajectory of the economic relations in the California mission system, sketching the initial growth, integration, increasing specialization, and rapid decline of the system between 1769 and 1836. Beads played a crucial role in economic and social interactions among indigenous tribes and also played an important part in interactions with European colonists as described by Gibson (1976) and King (1981, 1988), among others.

A recent study of Mission Santa Clara highlights this economic dimension of bead production and trade, concluding "archaeological assemblages from various temporal and spatial contexts demonstrate that native people contin-

ued to use shell beads throughout the mission period but also incorporated glass beads into local understandings of status and mourning" (Panich 2014:730). Beads were used not only as a medium of exchange arguably comparable to money; they were also buried with the dead. As mortality rates climbed in the historic period due to introduced diseases, there was a growing need for beads used as offerings. Missionaries capitalized on that market by supplying not only glass beads imported from European sources, but also shell beads manufactured by Indian converts.

Although glass beads were manufactured in many countries, the main source of supply for CA-SLO-51/H was likely Murano, Italy. After Mexico lifted its foreign trade ban in 1823, glass beads from other noteworthy sources such as China and Czechoslovakia may have been introduced (Karklins 1982; Liu 1974). The beads arrived through an increasingly diverse array of middlemen. The Russian American Company visited the California coast starting in 1804 and carried out fur trapping as far south as the Channel Islands (Farris 1989). Annual expeditions of fur trappers associated with the Hudson's Bay Company also plied the Central Valley beginning in the 1820s (Hill 1923; Maloney 1945). Those vectors are evident in some of the distinctive distribution patterns noted for specific types of glass beads. American ships also regularly plied the California coast, contributing to the diversity of glass beads that missionaries obtained in exchange for hides and tallow. Those beads were in turn used to mediate exchanges with Indian converts.

Some sources suggest local tribes valued glass beads above those they manufactured themselves (Hemert-Engart and Teggart 1910:139). One aspect of the attraction may simply be the diversity of bead colors and forms. The novel bead forms and colors also may have been valued for their scarcity or association with powerful new trading partners. Glass bead colors may be fruitfully compared with the patterns found at missions and other native villages, offering clues about relative valuation, availability, ethnic preferences, and other factors.

References Cited

Allen, Rebecca
1998   *Native Americans at Mission Santa Cruz, 1791–1834: Interpreting the Archaeological Record.* Perspectives in California Archaeology 5, Institute of Archaeology, University of California, Los Angeles.

Bennyhoff, James A.
1977   The Ethnography of the Plains Miwok. *Center for Archaeological Research at Davis Publication* 5. University of California, Davis.

Bone, Kenneth J.
1975   A Preliminary Analysis of Beads from Mission San Jose, Alameda County, California. Manuscript on file, Robert Lowie Museum of Anthropology, University of California, Berkeley.

Castillo, Ed D.
1989   The Native Response to the Colonization of California. In *Archaeological and Historical Perspectives on the Spanish Borderlands West*, edited by David H. Thomas, pp. 377–394. Smithsonian Institution, Washington, DC.

Costello, Julia G., and David Hornbeck
1989   Alta California: An Overview. In *Archaeological and Historical Perspectives on the Spanish Borderlands West*, edited by David H. Thomas, pp. 303–331. Smithsonian Institution, Washington, DC.

Diaz, Christine
1993   Beads from the Cross: A Comparative Analysis of Glass Bead Assemblages from Four Spanish California Missions. Senior honor's thesis, Department of Anthropology, California State University, San Bernardino.

Deetz, James
1963   Archaeological Investigations at La Purisima Mission. *Archaeological Survey Annual Report* 5:163–208. University of California, Los Angeles.

Dietz, Stephen A.
1983   *Final Report of Archaeological Investigations at Mission San Jose (CA-ALA-1).* Northwest Information Center, California Historical Resources Information System, Sonoma State University, Rohnert Park.

Farris, Glenn J.
1989   The Russian Imprint on the Colonization of California. In *Archaeological and Historical Perspectives on the Spanish Borderlands West*,

edited by David H. Thomas, pp. 481–497. Smithsonian Institution, Washington. DC.

Gibson, R. O.
1976   A Study of Beads and Ornaments from the San Buenaventura Mission Site (VEN-87). In *The San Buenaventura Mission Plaza Project Archaeological Survey Report*, edited by Roberta S. Greenwood, pp. 78–166. Report on file, Redevelopment Agency of the City of Ventura, California.

Greenwood, Roberta S.
1972   *9000 Years of Prehistory at Diablo Canyon, San Luis Obispo County, California.* San Luis Obispo County Archaeological Society Occasional Papers no. 7.
1989   The California Ranchero: Fact and Fancy. In *Archaeological and Historical Perspectives on the Spanish Borderlands West*, edited by David H. Thomas, pp. 451–465. Smithsonian Institution, Washington, DC.

Hemert-Engart, A. von, and F. J. Teggart (editors)
1910   The Narrative of the Portola Expedition of 1769–1770. *Publication of the Academy of Pacific Coast History* 1(4):9–159. University of California Press, Berkeley.

Hill, Joseph J.
1923   *Ewing Young in the Fur Trade of the Far Southwest, 1822–1834.* Koke-Tiffany Company, Eugene, Oregon.

Hoffman, J. J., and Lester A. Ross
1974   *Fort Vancouver Excavations VIII: Fur Store.* Submitted to the National Park Service, Portland, Oregon.
1975   *Fort Vancouver Excavations IX: Indian Trade Store.* Submitted to the National Park Service, Portland, Oregon.

Hoover, Robert L., and Julia G. Costello (editors)
1985   Excavations at Mission San Antonio, 1976–1978. *Institute of Archaeology Monograph* 26. University of California, Los Angeles.

Hornbeck, David
1989   Economic Growth and Change at the Missions of Alta California, 1769–1846. In *Archaeological and Historical Perspectives on the Spanish Borderlands West*, edited by David H. Thomas, pp. 423–433. Smithsonian Institution, Washington, DC.

Karklins, Karlis
1982   Guide to the Description and Classification of Glass Beads. *History and Archaeology* 59. Parks Canada, Hull, Quebec, Canada.

Kidd, Kenneth E.

1979   Glass Bead-Making from the Middle Ages to the Early 19th Century. *History and Archaeology* 30. National Historic Sites Service, Ottawa.

Kidd, Kenneth E., and Martha A. Kidd

1970   A Classification System for Glass Beads for the Use of Field Archaeologists. *Canadian Historic Sites Occasional Papers in Archaeology and History* 1. National Historic Sites Service, Ottawa, Canada.

King, Chester

1981   The Evolution of Chumash Society: A Comparative Study of Artifacts Used in Social System Maintenance in the Santa Barbara Channel Region before AD 1804. PhD dissertation, University of California, Davis. University Microfilms, Ann Arbor, Michigan.

1988   *Beads from Excavations at the Santa Barbara Presidio*. Report to Woodward-Clyde Consultants, Oakland, California.

Liu, Robert K.

1975   Chinese Glass Beads and Ornaments. *Bead Journal* 1(3):13–28.

Maloney, Alice B.

1945   *Fur Brigade to the Bonaventura: John Work's California Expedition 1832–1833 for the Hudson's Bay Company*. California Historical Society, San Francisco.

Meighan, Clement

1979   Glass Trade Beads in California. Manuscript on file, Lowie Museum of Anthropology, University of California, Berkeley.

Motz, Lee, and Peter D. Schulz

1970   European "Trade" Beads from Old Sacramento. *California Archaeological Reports* 19:49–68. California Department of Parks and Recreation, Sacramento.

1979   *European "Trade" Beads from Old Sacramento*. California Department of Parks and Recreation, Sacramento.

Panich, Lee M.

2014   Native American Consumption of Shell and Glass Beads at Mission Santa Clara de Asís. *American Antiquity* 79(4):730–748.

Ross, Lester A.

1976   *Fort Vancouver, 1829–1860: A Historical Archaeological Investigation of the Goods Imported and Manufactured by the Hudson's Bay Company*. Submitted to the National Park Service, Washington, DC.

1990   Trade Beads from Hudson's Bay Company Fort Vancouver (1829–1860), Vancouver, Washington. *Beads* 2:29–67.

Silliman, Stephen W.

2000   Colonial Worlds, Indigenous Practices: The Archaeology of Labor on a 19th-Century California Rancho. PhD dissertation, University of California, Berkeley. University Microfilms, Ann Arbor, Michigan.

Van Bueren, Thad M.

1983   Archaeological Perspectives on Central Sierra Miwok Culture Change during the Historic Period. Unpublished Master's thesis, Department of Anthropology, San Francisco State University, San Francisco.

1991   Analysis of Glass Beads Associated with the Activities of the Russian American Company in California. Manuscript in the author's possession.

1995   Glass Beads. In *Archaeological Investigations at the Third Location of Mission Santa Clara de Asis: The Murguia Mission, 1781–1818*, by Mark G. Hylkema, pp. 80–85. California Department of Transportation, Oakland.

2005   Glass Beads. In *Final Report: Archaeological Evaluation and Mitigative Data Recovery at CA-YOL-69, Madison Aggregate Plant, Yoloy County, California*, by Randy S. Wiberg, pp. 11.1–11.9. Holman and Associates, San Francisco.

2015   *An Analysis of Beads Recovered from the Neophyte Quadrangle at San Miguel Mission, California*. Submitted to Greenwood and Associates, Pacific Palisades, California.

Voss, Barbara L.

2015   What's New? Rethinking Ethnogenesis in the Archaeology of Colonialism. *American Antiquity* 80:655–670.

Charred Plant Remains from CA-SLO-51/H

ERIC WOHLGEMUTH AND ANGELA ARPAIA

This report documents charred plant remains recovered from three flotation samples, comprising 21.4 liters of sediment, processed from California Polytechnic State University–San Luis Obispo investigations at postcontact Native American archaeological site SLO-51/H, along the Pecho Coast west of Avila Beach. All flotation samples were collected from Unit 6. Two are from Feature 1, and the last is from the deepest level sampled (40–50 centimeters). The focus is on identification and interpretation of charred seed and fruit remains; wood charcoal was not attempted.

Background

Recent archaeobotanical studies from around Morro Bay and at Avila Beach 15 kilometers north and four kilometers east of SLO-51, respectively, provide ample context to interpret the SLO-51 findings. The Morro Bay findings are from seven archaeological sites spanning most of the last 5,000 years. The trajectory of plant use in the Morro Bay area begins in the Early Period, as no useful data were obtained from the Millingstone Period, and focuses on residential bases from the Early Period, Middle–Late Transition, and Late Period. The Early Period data from SLO-23 and SLO-165 suggest a relatively balanced use of a variety of plant foods, including acorns. But plant foods appear to have been less important in native diets relative to shellfish, and there is no evidence of intensive plant food gathering and processing that characterizes later occupations beginning in the Middle–Late Transition. The Middle Period is not as well

understood since the only component sampled at SLO-14 appears to be a short-term seasonal camp that does not provide a full picture of plant use. Plant foods appear to have been more important relative to shellfish than at the Early Period residential bases, but the lack of data from a more residential Middle Period site limits our understanding of broad patterns of plant use available for all other phases. The Middle–Late Transition Period assemblage at SLO-457 is squarely focused on acorns, with very little other plant foods, and reflects the commitment to acorns as a staple food, with attendant intensive gathering and processing, known from ethnographic reports for California (e.g., Kroeber 1925:814–815). The Late Period residential component at SLO-23 highlights not only continued intensive acorn use, but intensive use of small seeds, the latter also reflected at Late Period seasonal camp SLO-626. Further, both Late Period sites show diversification of nut resources, with bay nut increasing somewhat from prior periods (Wohlgemuth 2016).

The intensification of acorn use around Morro Bay by at least the Middle–Late Transition, and small seeds in the Late Period, contrasts with the lack of evidence for plant food intensification in dry interior reaches of the central coast, or only until the Mission Period (Stevens et al. 2013; Wohlgemuth 2004). Even farther inland, acorn use became more intensive by at least the Middle–Late Transition in the Cuyama River canyon, but small seed intensification did not arise in the Cuyama locality until the protohistoric or historic era (Wohlgemuth

TABLE B.1. Density per Liter of Charred Plant Remains from CA-SLO-51/H.

Unit			6	6	6
Depth (centimeters)			40–60	40–60	40–50
Feature			1	1	—
Sample Number			1	2	7
Volume (liters)			7	10	4.4

Taxon	Common Name				
Nutshell					
Pinus sabiniana	Gray pine	ct	0.1	0.3	0.2
		mg	0.4	1.8	0.8
Prunus ilicifolia	Islay	ct	35.0	32.5	15.0
		mg	19.8	13.5	7.3
Quercus sp.	Acorn	ct	207.1	226.4	184.8
		mg	70.6	73.4	62.2
Umbellularia californica	Bay	ct	2.4	6.4	12.5
		mg	1.8	3.1	4.5
Total Dietary Nutshell		ct	244.8	265.6	212.5
		mg	92.6	91.8	74.8
Berry pit					
Arctostaphylos sp.	Manzanita	ct	3.0	1.6	0.2
		mg	1.6	2.5	1.3
Small seed					
Amsinckia sp.	Fiddleneck	ct	—	0.2	2.7
Bromus sp.	Brome grass	ct	15.0	3.4	23.5
Calandrinia sp.	Red maids	ct	7.1	4.3	3.0
Chenopodium berlandieri	Pitseed goosefoot	ct	2.9	2.0	6.1
Chenopodium sp.	Goosefoot	ct	1.4	0.7	2.3
Clarkia sp.	Farewell to spring	ct	—	—	2.3
Deschampsia sp.	Hairgrass	ct	—	3.0	—
Galium sp.	Bedstraw	ct	—	—	0.9
Hordeum sp.	Native barley	ct	5.7	1.3	—
Lepidium sp.	Peppergrass	ct	—	—	1.5
Madia sp.	Tarweed	ct	1.7	1.0	4.1
Phacelia sp.	Phacelia	ct	0.6	—	—
Phalaris sp.	Maygrass	ct	1.4	0.9	0.9
Plantago sp.	Plantain	ct	0.3	0.7	—
Poa sp.	Bluegrass	ct	2.9	—	3.0
Ranunculus sp.	Buttercup	ct	—	—	2.3
Schoenoplectus sp.	Tule	ct	1.7	—	—
Asteraceae	Sunflower family	ct	10.3	8.7	23.5
Brassicaceae	Mustard family	ct	1.4	—	—
Chenopodiaceae	Goosefoot	ct	7.1	—	—
Fabaceae	Bean family	ct	17.1	22.6	15.2
Fabaceae Z	Unidentified bean	ct	0.3	—	—
Malvaceae	Mallow family	ct	—	0.2	—
Poaceae caryopses	Grass family	ct	2.4	4.7	21.2
Poaceae fragments	Grass family	ct	172.3	193.9	207.6
Unidentified embryo		ct	2.9	10.8	33.0
Unidentified seed		ct	1.6	—	—
Unidentified seed fragments		ct	54.9	9.3	77.8
Total identified to genus		ct	55.6	36.8	84.8
Total identified to family		ct	266.6	266.9	352.3
Cultigen					
Cultivated grain fragments		ct	0.4	—	0.5
Hordeum vulgare	Barley	ct	0.1	—	0.7
Triticum sp.	Wheat	ct	0.1	0.1	0.2
Miscellaneous					
Acorn attachment disk		ct	0.1	0.9	—
Brodiaea sp.	Blue dicks	ct	—	—	0.5
Non-grain pieces		ct	11.4	2.2	6.4
Unidentified wood charcoal		mg	8361.3	3733.4	2404.1

2014). The contrasting archaeobotanical sequences reinforce findings from central California, where the most favored areas (the San Francisco Bay Area and Sacramento Valley) have a much deeper and more complex record of plant food intensification than more marginal places like the Sierra Nevada foothills and outer coast (Wohlgemuth 2004).

Also germane is the robust plant remains assemblage from Middle Period residential base SLO-56 in Avila Beach only four kilometers distant (Jones and Mikkelsen 2012). The SLO-56 data, from a similar habitat to SLO-51/H, will elucidate change in plant use from the Middle to the postcontact Periods. The SLO-56 data may also help fill the Middle Period gap in the Morro Bay sequence.

Methods

Flotation was conducted by William Stillman, using a manual tub technique used to process hundreds of samples in northern and central California (Wohlgemuth 1989). Buoyant light fraction is collected using 40 mesh/inch (0.4 mm) screen, and heavy fraction washed through 1 mm (window screen) mesh. Inasmuch as recovery effectiveness measured at other sites ranges from 85–95% of dense nutshell and berry pits, and more than 98% of small seeds, only the buoyant light fraction material was sorted for charred plant remains.

All sorting and identification of light fraction constituents was done by Angela Arpaia and verified by Eric Wohlgemuth. Light fraction was size-sorted using 2 mm, 1 mm, 0.7 mm, and 0.5 mm mesh. All seed and fruit remains were removed from the sorted portions of samples. Nutshell fragments were sorted only to the 0.7 mm grade, while small seeds were sorted to the 0.5 mm grade. Unidentified nongrain pieces (not wood charcoal, nutshell, or seeds) were sorted only from the 2 mm grade, and wood charcoal was sorted from the 2 mm and 1 mm grades. While all segregated constituents were counted, fragments of nutshell and wood charcoal were weighed to 0.1 mg. Constituents were stored in translucent, hard-plastic centrifuge tubes with acid-free paper tags denoting site trinomial, sample number, size grade, and a constituent code type. All items of a single type or taxon were stored (in separate centrifuge tubes for each provenience and size grade) in 2 mil plastic bags with acid-free paper labels. All tags were labeled with #2 pencil.

Results

The sorting effort identified 562 dietary nutshell fragments of four genera. Also identified were 786 small seeds (identified to plant family, of which 175 were identified to 19 genera), two *Brodiaea*-type corms, 11 manzanita berry pits, and 12 Eurasian cultigen grains, including 4 barley and 3 wheat (Table B.1). This robust sample (total number of identified specimens of 1,373) comprises a very useful comparative collection in understanding long-term subsistence trends in the region. The charred plant remains identified at SLO-51/H are consistent with those found previously in Morro Bay and at Avila Beach, and for the most part with central California ethnobotanies (Table B.2). These are clearly cultural residues of ancient Native Californian subsistence activities. One clear exception is bedstraw, which was not a food plant, but possibly used in bedding, or the spiny seeds unintentionally brought to the site in clothing or animal fur.

Interestingly, gray-pine nutshell is present in all three samples, albeit in low frequency, and was probably regularly brought to the site and eaten. But the nearest gray pine are some 15–17 kilometers to the northeast (Calflora 2016; Griffin and Critchfield 1976:89), so the results indicate logistical gathering from distant patches, exchange with other social groups living in those patches, or both. Table B.3 shows the similarity of plant taxa identified at SLO-51/H to SLO-56 and sites around Morro Bay.

We can identify key plant foods by their occurrence in quantity in all three samples. Islay (wild cherry pit) and especially acorn nutshell are very common, along with seeds of brome, fescue, red maids, goosefoot, and clover, as well as nightshade berries. These were probably the most important plant foods eaten at SLO-51/H. Tarweed and maygrass seeds are also found in all samples but at lower frequency, suggesting their regular use as well, if not as intensively as the others.

TABLE B.2. Ethnobotanical Resources in the Vicinity of CA-SLO-51/H.

Taxon	Common Name	Growth Habit[a]	Habitats[a]	Ethnographic Use[b]	Seed Seasonal Availability[b]	Disturbance Follower?[c]
Amsinckia sp.	Fiddleneck	Herb	Open grasslands	None noted	Late spring	Yes
Arctostaphylos sp.	Manzanita	Shrub	Dry slopes and hills	Berry eaten	Summer (fall)	??
Brodiaea sp.	Brodiaea	Herb	Shaded areas or open grasslands	Root eaten	Late spring/summer	Yes
Bromus sp.	Brome grass	Grass	Varied	Seed eaten	Late spring	Yes
Calandrinia sp.	Red maids	Herb	Open, disturbed places	Seed eaten	Spring	Yes
Chenopodium sp.	Goosefoot	Herb	Open, disturbed or saline areas	Seeds, leaves eaten	Spring or summer	Yes
Clarkia sp.	Farewell to spring	Herb	Shaded areas or open grasslands	Seed eaten	Late spring	Yes
Deschampsia sp.	Hairgrass	Grass	Seasonal wetlands, vernal pools	None noted	Summer	??
Galium sp.	Bedstraw	Herb	Shaded areas	Leaf used for medicine	Late spring/summer	No
Hordeum sp.	Wild barley	Grass	Varied; open grasslands	Seed eaten	Late spring	Yes
Hordeum vulgare	Cultivated barley	Crop	Cultivated fields	Grain eaten	Late spring	Yes
Lepidium sp.	Peppergrass	Herb	Grasslands	Whole plant eaten	Late spring	Yes
Madia sp.	Tarweed	Herb	Varied, grasslands	Seed eaten	Summer (fall)	Yes
Phacelia sp.	Phacelia	Herb	Varied	None noted	Late spring	Yes
Phalaris sp.	Maygrass	Grass	Moist places	None noted	Summer	??
Pinus sabiniana	Gray pine	Tree	Dry slopes and flats	Nut eaten	Summer (green), fall (ripe)	??
Plantago sp.	Plantain	Herb	Open, disturbed places	None noted	Spring or summer	Yes
Poa sp.	Bluegrass	Grass	Moist places	Seed eaten	Summer	Yes
Prunus ilicifolia	Islay	Shrub	Dry slopes and hills	Pit eaten	Fall	??
Quercus sp.	Oak	Tree	Varied	Nut eaten	Fall	??
Ranunculus sp.	Buttercup	Herb	Varied, moist areas	Seed eaten	Late spring	No
Schoenoplectus sp.	Tule	Herb	Marshes, wet areas	Seed eaten, stems for textiles	Summer	??
Solanum sp.	Nightshade	Shrub	Moist shady areas	Berry eaten	Summer	??
Trifolium sp.	Clover	Herb	Grasslands	Leaves, seed eaten	Spring	Yes
Triticum sp.	Wheat	Crop	Cultivated fields	Grain eaten	Late spring	Yes
Umbellularia californica	Bay	Tree	Moist canyons, riparian zones	Nut eaten	Fall	??
Vulpia sp.	Fescue grass	Grass	Dry open places, grasslands	Seed eaten	Late spring	Yes

[a] Munz 1968; Hickman 1993.
[b] Barrett and Gifford 1933; Bocek 1984; Chesnut 1902; Dubois 1935; Duncan 1963; parentheses indicate secondary season.
[c] Sources: Stebbins 1965; Timbrook, Johnson and Earle 1982; and personal communications, Michael Barbour, John Menke, Grady Webster, Jon E. Keeley, and Fred Hrusa.

Seasonality Indicators

SLO-51/H has a wide range of charred plant taxa which ripen in the full range of seasons that plants can be gathered. Four fall-ripening nut crops are present, along with six genera of small seeds and berry pits that reflect summer gathering, and 11 spring-ripening small seed genera. If we focus on the key plant foods, the full range of seasonal indicators is also included, with fall nuts (acorn and islay), vernal seeds (brome, red maids, clover, and fescue), and summer seeds (goosefoot) and berries (nightshade). The plant data suggest SLO-51/H was occupied at least from spring through the fall nut harvest. Additionally, the high frequency of nuts and small seeds suggests intensive occupation typical of a year-round village community.

Eurasian Cultivators

While only in low numbers, the presence of Eurasian cultigens in all three flotation samples from SLO-51/H is intriguing. Cultigens have been found in several postcontact Native American archaeological sites in California where they are clearly in context (Wohlgemuth 2004), suggesting the SLO-51/H wheat and barley could have been obtained from Spanish explorers or from contact with mission agricultural communes. However, SLO-51/H has been used as a wheat and barley field for decades, if not more than a century. This raises the issue of whether the charred cultigens in flotation samples might be recent or historic-era farming contaminants, and not actually associated with the postcontact Native community.

There are multiple reasons to believe the cultigens are actually in context. First, no other Eurasian plant seeds were found in the flotation samples. Cultigens in postcontact Native American archaeological sites are invariably found with Eurasian weeds, notably filaree and mallow (Wohlgemuth 2004). Second, as noted in *Results* above, all other plant taxa identified in the SLO-51/H flotation samples are typical finds in California Native American sites, and most are well-documented foods. It is much more complex to argue that the cultigens are contaminants while all other taxa are not, than to conclude that

the cultigens are also in context. Third, at least two flotation samples are from an intact feature that was clearly used by Native Americans. Lingering doubts about the association of the cultigens could be resolved by AMS radiocarbon dating of the grains themselves.

Middle and Postcontact Period Plant Use at SLO-51/H and SLO-56

Table B.4 shows plant-use indices for SLO-51/H, SLO-56, and sites around Morro Bay. The proportion of acorn to all dietary nutshell and the ratio of acorn (mg) to small seeds (count, identified to genus) have been used to monitor acorn intensification, while the ratio of small seeds to wood charcoal has been used to augment the acorn:small-seed ratio to track small-seed intensification (Wohlgemuth 2004). Around Morro Bay, while changes in the acorn:small-seed ratio do seem to reflect acorn intensification, declining Late Period acorn proportion instead shows diversification in nut use (Wohlgemuth 2016). Interestingly, the acorn proportion for both SLO-51/H and SLO-56 is much lower than any site around Morro Bay. This is probably due to more productive stands of islay and bay than around Morro Bay. The slight increase in acorn proportion at SLO-51/H from the SLO-56 value is probably not significant, particularly since only three flotation samples were analyzed from each site.

Both SLO-51/H and SLO-56 have relatively high acorn:small-seed ratios, exceeding all sites at Morro Bay except Middle–Late Transition SLO-457. The decline in the ratio by nearly 40% from SLO-56 to SLO-51/H is consistent with similar findings throughout central California that index increased reliance on small seeds after the Middle Period (Wohlgemuth 2004). The high ratio at residential base SLO-56 suggests acorn intensification at least at one Middle Period site in coastal San Luis Obispo County, providing a better context than contemporaneous seasonal camp SLO-14 by Morro Bay.

The low small-seed:wood-charcoal ratio at SLO-56 is consistent with low levels found prior to the Late Period at Morro Bay, mirroring findings there that suggest small seeds

TABLE B.3. Mean Density per Liter of Charred Plant Remains from Morro Bay, SLO-51, and SLO-56.

Site			Early				Middle		M–L Trans[d]	Late		Post-Contact
		SLO-23	SLO-165[b]	SLO-165[c]	SLO-458	SLO-14	SLO-165	SLO-56	SLO-457	SLO-626	SLO-23	SLO-51
Volume (liters)		102.3	81.8	nd	48.2	36.8	12.4	23.1	16.0	17.7	43.4	21.4
Number of Samples		14	5	>7	4	9	1	3	4	4	5	3
Number of Identified Specimens[a]		508	152	682	23	102	165	364	317	104	1,315	1,373
Nutshell												
Quercus sp. — Acorn	mg	1.9	0.41	—	0.008	0.53	2.4	4.3	5.0	0.4	21.7	68.7
Umbellularia californica — Bay	mg	0.11	0.02	—	—	0.07	0.2	—	0.01	0.1	0.9	3.1
Prunus ilicifolia — Islay	mg	—	—	—	—	0.01	—	2.3	—	0.005	—	13.5
Pinus sabiniana — Gray pine	mg	—	—	12	—	0.01	—	—	—	—	0.4	1.0
Total Dietary Nutshell	mg	2.0	0.42	12	0.008	0.63	2.6	6.5	5.06	0.4	23.0	86.4
Marah sp. — Wild cucumber	mg	0.06	0.06	—	—	0.05	—	0.3	0.1	0.1	0.6	—
Berry pit												
Arctostaphylos sp. — Manzanita	mg	0.3	0.1	—	—	0.08	1.7	—	0.3	0.1	—	1.8
Morella californica — Wax myrtle	ct	—	—	—	—	—	—	—	6.2	0.3	—	—
Small seed												
Amsinckia sp. — Fiddleneck	ct	—	0.01	—	—	—	—	—	—	—	0.1	1.0
Atriplex sp. — Saltbush	ct	0.02	—	—	—	—	—	—	—	—	—	—
Bromus sp. — Brome grass	ct	—	—	—	—	—	—	0.2	—	—	0.4	14.0
Calandrinia sp. — Red maids	ct	0.02	—	—	—	—	—	0.2	0.07	—	0.3	4.8
Chenopodium cf. desiccatum — Aridland goosefoot	ct	—	—	—	—	—	—	0.4	—	—	4.8	—
Chenopodium sp. — Goosefoot	ct	0.61	0.02	3	—	—	0.2	0.6	—	—	17.0	5.1
Clarkia sp. — Farewell to spring	ct	0.02	—	—	0.02	—	0.3	0.2	—	—	0.1	0.8
Claytonia sp. — Miners lettuce	ct	—	—	—	—	—	—	—	—	—	0.2	—
Deschampsia sp. — Hairgrass	ct	—	—	—	—	—	0.1	0.1	—	—	—	1.0
Elymus sp. — Wild rye	ct	—	—	3	—	—	—	—	—	—	—	—
Eriogonum sp. — Wild buckwheat	ct	—	—	—	—	—	—	—	—	0.1	—	—
Erodium sp.[e] — Filaree	ct	—	—	—	—	—	0.1	0.1	—	—	—	—
Galium sp. — Bedstraw	ct	—	—	—	—	—	—	0.1	—	0.2	—	0.3

Hemizonia sp.	Tarweed	ct	0.01	0.05	9	—	—	0.4	0.1	—	—	—	—
Hordeum sp.	Wild barley	ct	—	—	25	—	—	—	0.1	—	—	—	2.3
Lepidium sp.	Peppergrass	ct	—	—	2	—	—	—	—	—	—	—	0.5
Lotus sp.	Bird's foot	ct	—	—	—	—	0.05	—	—	—	0.2	—	—
Lupinus sp.	Lupine	ct	0.01	—	—	—	—	—	—	—	—	—	—
Madia sp.	Tarweed	ct	0.05	—	1	—	—	0.7	0.2	—	—	0.2	2.3
Phacelia sp.	Phacelia	ct	0.03	0.01	—	—	—	0.2	—	—	0.1	0.1	0.2
Phalaris sp.	Maygrass	ct	0.01	0.06	2	—	0.02	0.2	0.2	—	0.1	0.2	1.1
Plantago sp.	Plantain	ct	—	0.01	—	—	—	—	—	—	—	—	0.3
Potamogeton sp.	Pondweed	ct	—	—	—	—	—	—	—	—	—	0.1	—
Rumex sp.	Dock	ct	—	—	1	—	—	—	—	—	—	—	—
Salvia sp.	Sage	ct	0.48	0.02	46	—	—	0.2	—	—	—	1.8	—
Scirpus sp.	Tule	ct	—	—	—	—	—	—	—	—	—	0.5	0.6
Trifolium sp.	Clover	ct	—	0.02	—	—	—	0.2	0.4	—	—	0.03	3.6
Vulpia sp.	Fescue	ct	—	0.03	—	—	—	0.2	0.3	—	—	0.5	14.2
Apiaceae	Carrot family	ct	—	—	—	—	—	0.1	0.1	—	—	—	—
Asteraceae	Sunflower family	ct	0.04	0.08	10	0.02	0.09	0.9	0.1	0.2	0.1	0.6	14.1
Fabaceae	Bean family	ct	0.04	0.05	—	0.04	0.08	1.7	0.2		0.8	0.4	18.3
Lamiaceae	Mint family	ct	0.01	—	—	—	0.08	—	—	0.07	0.3	1.8	—
Poaceae fragments	Grass family	ct	0.2	0.9	571	0.02	0.35	2.7	3.6	0.2	1.2	8.0	200.7
Total identified to genus		ct	1.3	0.2	89	0.02	0.07	2.3	2.6	0.07	0.7	21.6	59.0
Total identified to family		ct	1.6	1.3	670	0.12	0.68	7.6	6.5	0.6	2.9	32.4	295.2
Miscellaneous													
Brodiaea sp.	Blue dicks	ct	0.01	—	—	—	0.03	—	0.2	—	—	—	0.2
Clarkia sp. capsule	Farwell to spring	ct	0.01	0.002	—	—	—	nd	—	—	—	—	—
Hesperoyucca whipplei	Yucca leaf fragment	ct	—	nd	1	—	0.05	nd	—	—	—	0.05	—
Unidentified wood charcoal		mg	194.3	nd	—	6.3	23.9	nd	867.6	125.5	46.0	1075.6	4832.9

[a] Nuts, berry pits, and small seeds identified to family.
[b] Mikkelsen et al. 2000 (small seeds sorted to 0.7 mm grade—all others sorted to 0.5 mm).
[c] Hammett 1991—raw counts, not densities.
[d] Middle–Late Transition.
[e] Introduced taxon.
nd: data not available.

TABLE B.4. Plant Indices from Morro Bay, SLO-51/H, and SLO-56.

Site	Early		Middle		M/L Trans[a]	Late		Post-Contact
	SLO-23	SLO-165	SLO-14	SLO-56	SLO-457	SLO-626	SLO-23	SLO-51/H
Acorn % of Dietary Nutshell	100.0%	98.4%	97.6%	71.4%	100.0%	84.5%	93.6%	79.8%
Acorn: Small Seeds	0.70	0.22	0.28	2.10	7.51	0.14	0.72	1.30
Small Seeds: Wood Charcoal	0.017	nd	0.02	0.007	0.007	0.097	0.031	0.017

[a] Middle–Late Transition; nd—data not available.

were not important until the Late Period. The small-seed:wood-charcoal ratio at SLO-51/H is more than twice as high as the SLO-56 value, confirming greater reliance on small seeds than in the Middle Period. However, while the SLO-51/H ratio exceeds or equals all pre-Late Period values at Morro Bay, it is substantially less than both Late Period sites there. This probably is due to excellent preservation of wood charcoal at SLO-51/H depressing the ratio, as small-seed frequency is nearly three times higher than at Late Period SLO-23 (Table B.3). Small seeds were clearly intensively used in the postcontact period at SLO-51/H.

The presence of cultigens (apparently) in context with the robust native plant food debris at SLO-51/H is noteworthy. Some postcontact Native American sites, notably mission neophyte contexts, mark much less use of low-ranked native small seeds when cultivated grains became staple foods (Wohlgemuth and Arpaia 2016). The paucity of cultigens at SLO-51/H, paired with the highest frequency of small seeds found to date in coastal San Luis Obispo County demonstrating that small seeds were still very important, suggests that Eurasian cultigens were rarely available and not relied upon as important foods. Instead, cultigens may have been rarely available from mission sources, perhaps even used as a prestige food.

Conclusions

Analysis of three flotation samples from SLO-51/H, two from Feature 1, documents a charred-plant assemblage of abundant native food plant debris and a few Eurasian wheat and barley grains. The native plant remains are wholly consistent with findings from the San Luis Obispo coast and central California (Wohlgemuth 2004, 2016), documenting occupation of the site from spring through fall, and probably year-round. The absence of Eurasian weeds commonly found in association with crop grains suggests the latter are in context rather than contaminants from farm fields.

Comparative data from nearby SLO-56 and more distant sites around Morro Bay suggest that acorn use intensified by the Middle Period in the Avila Beach area. Gaps in the Morro Bay sequence had obscured the inception of acorn intensification, previously documented only as far back as the Middle–Late Transition (Wohlgemuth 2016). The SLO-56 data suggest that intensified use of acorns at least in part underwrote the intensive Middle Period occupation there. Late Period small-seed intensification previously seen in the Morro Bay sequence clearly extended into the postcontact period at SLO-51/H. Cultigens provided at best a minor contribution to subsistence, with native food plants, including low-ranked small seeds, retaining primary importance.

References Cited

Barrett, S. A., and E. W. Gifford

1933   *Miwok Material Culture*. Bulletin of the Public Museum of the City of Milwaukee Vol. 2, No. 4. Cannon Printing Company, Milwaukee, Wisconsin.

Bocek, Barbara R.

1984   Ethnobotany of Costanoan Indians, California, Based on Collections by John Harrington. *Economic Botany* 38(2):240–255.

Calflora

2016   Distribution of *Pinus sabiniana* (Gray Pine) in California. Electronic document, http://www/calflora.org, accessed September 10, 2016.

Chesnut, Victor King

1902   Plants Used by the Indians of Mendocino County, California. *Contributions from the U.S. National Herbarium* 7(3):295–422.

DuBois, Cora A.

1935   Wintu Ethnography. *University of California Publications in American Archaeology and Ethnology* 26:1–147. Berkeley.

Duncan, John Whitfield

1963   Maidu Ethnobotany. Unpublished Master's thesis, Department of Anthropology, California State University, Sacramento.

Griffin, James R., and William B. Critchfield

1976   *The Distribution of Forest Trees in California*. USDA Forest Service Research Paper PSW – 82/1972. Berkeley.

Hickman, James C. (editor)

1993   *The Jepson Manual: Higher Plants of California*. University of California Press, Berkeley.

Jones, Deborah, and Patricia Mikkelsen

2012   *Archaeological Monitoring and Excavation for Water and Sewer Upgrades to the San Luis Bay Inn at CA-SLO-56, Avila Beach, San Luis Obispo County, California*. Submitted to San Miguelito Mutual Water Company, Avila Beach, California.

Kroeber, A. L.

1925   *Handbook of the Indians of California*. Smithsonian Institution, Bureau of American Ethnology Bulletin, 78. Reprinted (1976) Dover Publications, New York.

Munz, Philip A.

1968   *A California Flora and Supplement*. University of California Press, Berkeley.

Stebbins, G. Ledyard

1965   Colonizing Species of the Native California Flora. In *The Genetics of Colonizing Species*, edited by H. G. Baker and G. L. Stebbins, pp. 173–191. Academic Press, New York.

Stevens, Nathan E., Philip Kaijankoski, and Sharon Waechter

2013   *Cultural Resource National Register: Eligibility Assessments of Eleven Selected Locations at Camp Roberts Military Training Facility, Monterey and San Luis Obispo Counties, California*. Far Western Anthropological Research Group, Inc., Davis, California. Submitted to California Army National Guard, Mather, California.

Timbrook, Jan, John R. Johnson, and David D. Earle

1982   Vegetation Burning by the Chumash. *Journal of California and Great Basin Anthropology* 4(2):163–186.

Wohlgemuth, Eric

1989   Appendix H: Archaeobotanical Remains. *Prehistory of the Sacramento River Canyon, Shasta County, California*, edited by M. E. Basgall and W. R. Hildebrandt. University of California, Davis.

2004   The Course of Plant Food Intensification in Native Central California. PhD dissertation, University of California, Davis.

2014   Change and Stability in Plant Use in the Cuyama River Canyon. In Volume I: *Synthesis: Cuyama Valley, A Corridor to the Past*. Submitted to Caltrans District 05, San Luis Obispo, California.

2016   Charred Plant Remains from the Morro Bay Locality. In *Archaeological Investigations for the Los Osos Wastewater Project, San Luis Obispo County, California*, by Patricia Mikkelsen, Deborah Jones, William R. Hildebrandt, and Terry L. Jones. Submitted to San Luis Obispo County Department of Public Works.

Wohlgemuth, Eric, and Angela Arpaia

2016   Neophyte Plant Use at Mission Santa Clara. Presented at the 50th Annual Meeting of the Society for California Archaeology, Ontario, California.

Radiocarbon Dates

SiteNo	Trinom	Unit	LabNo	Depth_cm	Material	Species
2	CA-SLO-2	S4/W9	UCLA-1686A	320–330	Bone	*Homo sapiens*
2	CA-SLO-2	N1/W5	GAK-02044	290	Shell	*Halitois rufescens*
2	CA-SLO-2	NES4W9	BETA-192961	330–340	Shell	*Collisella* sp.
2	CA-SLO-2	N1W4	SR-6833	290–300	Bone	*Chendytes lawi*
2	CA-SLO-2	S1W12	BETA-197950	280–290	Shell	*Mytilus californianus*
2	CA-SLO-2	NES4W9	BETA-192962	330–340	Shell	*Mytilus californianus*
2	CA-SLO-2	N1E4	BETA-216555	260–270	Bone	*Odocoileus hemionus*
2	CA-SLO-2	S4/W2	BETA-206363	120–130	Bone	*Chendytes lawi*
2	CA-SLO-2	N10W1	BETA-192956	80–90	Shell	*Mytilus californianus*
2	CA-SLO-2	S1W1	BETA-170138	180–190	Shell	*Hinnites* sp.
2	CA-SLO-2	N1W1	BETA-170137	200–210	Shell	*Halitois rufescens*
2	CA-SLO-2	N4W2	BETA-197949	250–260	Shell	*Mytilus californianus*
2	CA-SLO-2	N4W4	BETA-170139	220–230	Shell	*Tivela stultorum*
2	CA-SLO-2	NE1/8N1W22	BETA-216558	240–250	Shell	*Tegula* sp.
2	CA-SLO-2	S1W1	BETA-192957	200–210	Shell	*Balanus* sp.
2	CA-SLO-2	S4W2	BETA-206360	230–240	Shell	*Balanus* sp.
2	CA-SLO-2	S1 W12	BETA-204130	160–170	Shell	*Cryptochiton stelleri*
2	CA-SLO-2	S1 W12	BETA-204132	290–300	Shell	*Balanus* sp.
2	CA-SLO-2	N1W4	BETA-197947	290–300	Shell	*Balanus* sp.
2	CA-SLO-2	N4W1	BETA-216556	250–260	Bone	*Odocoileus hemionus*
2	CA-SLO-2	S1W1	BETA-216559	140–150	Shell	*Balanus* sp.
2	CA-SLO-2	N1W5	BETA-192960	170–180	Shell	*Mytilus californianus*
2	CA-SLO-2	N10 W13	BETA-204129	110–120	Shell	*Mytilus californianus*
2	CA-SLO-2	N4W2	BETA-206358	30–40	Shell	*Mytilus californianus*
2	CA-SLO-2	N10W13	BETA-206359	70–80	Shell	*Mytilus californianus*
2	CA-SLO-2	N1 W5	BETA-204126	60–70	Shell	*Mytilus californianus*
2	CA-SLO-2	S1W12	BETA-204128	90–100	Shell	*Cryptochiton stelleri*
2	CA-SLO-2	N10W4	BETA-192959	130–140	Shell	*Balanus* sp.
2	CA-SLO-2	N10W12	BETA-192958	30–40	Shell	*Mytilus californianus*
2	CA-SLO-2	N7W14	BETA-216557	0–10	Shell	*Tegula* sp.
2	CA-SLO-2	S4W1	BETA-197951	110–120	Shell	*Mytilus californianus*
2	CA-SLO-2	N4W5	UCLA-1686B	120	Bone	*Homo sapiens*
2	CA-SLO-2	N4W2	BETA-197948	20–30	Shell	*Saxidomus nuttalli*
2	CA-SLO-2	N1W1	BETA-197946	40–50	Shell	*Tegula* sp.
5	CA-SLO-5	DCNR3	?	Surface	Shell	*Haliotis* sp.
5	CA-SLO-5	DCNR3	BETA-242069	Surface	Shell	*Haliotis* sp.
5	CA-SLO-5	8	BETA-358279	60–70	Shell	*Haliotis cracherodi*
5	CA-SLO-5	8	BETA-358277	10–20	Shell	*Haliotis rufescens*

Conventional 14CAge	Cal1Sig Max	Cal1Sig Mid	Cal1Sig Min	Cal2Sig Max	Cal2Sig Mid	Cal2Sig Min	Reference
9480+175	11130	10822	10513	11238	10744	10250	Greenwood 1972
9780+260	10661	10384	10106	11066	10342	9617	Greenwood 1972
8620+50	8991	8888	8784	9060	8867	8674	Jones et al. 2008
8355+25	8575	8515	8454	8622	8514	8405	Jones et al. 2008
8340+40	8571	8499	8426	8625	8504	8383	Jones et al. 2008
8300+50	8537	8465	8392	8594	8472	8349	Jones et al. 2008
7110+40	7968	7925	7882	8006	7932	7857	Jones et al. 2008
7510+40	7736	7679	7622	7807	7690	7573	Jones et al. 2008
6740+90	7081	6950	6819	7182	6941	6700	Jones et al. 2008
6560+80	6834	6731	6628	6941	6721	6501	Farqhuar 2003
6090+80	6292	6224	6156	6395	6193	5990	Farqhuar 2003
5700+40	5873	5791	5709	5906	5773	5639	Jones et al. 2008
5600+80	5749	5665	5580	5888	5685	5482	Farqhuar 2003
5550+40	5659	5617	5574	5731	5630	5528	Jones et al. 2008
5220+120	5435	5242	5048	5569	5218	4867	Jones et al. 2008
5150+40	5274	5160	5046	5305	5137	4969	Jones et al. 2008
5130+40	5261	5147	5032	5295	5124	4952	Jones et al. 2008
5120+40	5253	5139	5025	5289	5116	4942	Jones et al. 2008
5040+40	5057	4972	4887	5228	5033	4837	Jones et al. 2008
3260+40	3559	3504	3448	3576	3482	3388	Jones et al. 2008
3270+40	2787	2751	2714	2860	2769	2678	Jones et al. 2008
2880+90	2349	2244	2139	2516	2266	2015	Jones et al. 2008
2360+40	1708	1634	1560	1798	1657	1516	Jones et al. 2008
2170+40	1508	1430	1352	1549	1423	1297	Jones et al. 2008
2140+40	1472	1398	1324	1525	1403	1281	Jones et al. 2008
2130+70	1491	1393	1295	1555	1403	1250	Jones et al. 2008
2100+40	1399	1345	1291	1498	1379	1259	Jones et al. 2008
1870+80	1246	1144	1042	1298	1116	934	Jones et al. 2008
1740+100	1132	1017	901	1245	1007	769	Jones et al. 2008
1690+40	992	946	900	1061	942	823	Jones et al. 2008
1660+90	1009	904	799	1147	926	705	Jones et al. 2008
1010+85	978	889	800	1169	953	736	Greenwood 1972
1020+40	444	371	298	483	376	268	Jones et al. 2008
940+100	420	287	153	494	247	0	Jones et al. 2008
1950+130	1272	1223	1174	1299	1211	1123	Jones et al. 2015
1880±50	1233	1150	1067	1277	1135	992	Jones et al. 2015
1860±30	1183	1122	1060	1250	1125	1000	Jones et al. 2015
1820±30	1161	1097	1033	1216	1087	957	Jones et al. 2015

SiteNo	Trinom	Unit	LabNo	Depth_cm	Material	Species
5	CA-SLO-5	1	BETA-358276	50–60	Shell	*Haliotis rufescens*
5	CA-SLO-5	8	BETA-358278	34	Shell	*Haliotis rufescens*
5	CA-SLO-5	1	BETA-358275	0–10	Shell	*Haliotis cracherodi*
5	CA-SLO-5	8	BETA-358280	80–90	Shell	*Haliotis rufescens*
7	CA-SLO-7	3	BETA-23797	130–140	Shell	*Mytilus californianus*
7	CA-SLO-7	3	BETA-26685	90–100	Shell	*Mytilus californianus*
7	CA-SLO-7	3	BETA-26055	110–120	Shell	*Mytilus californianus*
7	CA-SLO-7	3	BETA-26684	70–80	Shell	*Mytilus californianus*
7	CA-SLO-7	4	WSU-3785	30–40	Shell	*Mytilus californianus*
7	CA-SLO-7	4	WSU-3787	70–80	Shell	*Mytilus californianus*
7	CA-SLO-7	4	WSU-3786	50–60	Shell	*Mytilus californianus*
7	CA-SLO-7	4	WSU-3789	110–120	Shell	*Mytilus californianus*
7	CA-SLO-7	4	WSU-3788	90–100	Shell	*Mytilus californianus*
7	CA-SLO-7	4	WSU-3784	10–20	Shell	*Mytilus californianus*
8	CA-SLO-8	C	WSU-3808	40–50	Shell	*Mytilus californianus*
8	CA-SLO-8	A	BETA-23798	30	Shell	*Haliotis rufescens*
9	CA-SLO-9	1	BETA-199103	80–90	Shell	*Mytilus californianus*
9	CA-SLO-9	5	BETA-198052	10–20a	Shell	*Balanus*
9	CA-SLO-9	4	BETA-199104	30–40	Shell	*Mytilus californianus*
9	CA-SLO-9	4	BETA-198051	70–80	Shell	*Mytilus californianus*
9	CA-SLO-9	4	BETA-198050	10–20a	Shell	*Mytilus californianus*
9	CA-SLO-9	5	BETA-198053	80–90	Shell	*Mytilus californianus*
9	CA-SLO-9	4	BETA-199105	30–40	Shell	*Mytilus californianus*
10	CA-SLO-10	4	BETA-223299	120–130	Shell	*Haliotis rufescens*
10	CA-SLO-10	3	BETA-263856	50–60	Shell	*Mytilus californianus*
10	CA-SLO-10	3	BETA-263857	120–130	Shell	*Mytilus californianus*
10	CA-SLO-10	NA	GA-1202-4	60–70	Shell	?
10	CA-SLO-10	NA	GA-1202-2	80–90	Shell	?
10	CA-SLO-10	NA	GA-1202-3	0–10	Shell	?
51	CA-SLO-51	1	BETA-424264	90–100	Shell	*Mytilus californianus*
51	CA-SLO-51	4	BETA-424267	10–20	Shell	*Mytilus californianus*
51	CA-SLO-51	4	BETA-424268	40–50	Shell	*Haliotis rufescens*
51	CA-SLO-51	1	BETA-424266	40–50	Shell	*Mytilus californianus*
51	CA-SLO-51	5 Auger	BETA-421352	100–120	Shell	*Mytilus californianus*
51	CA-SLO-51	1	BETA-424265	10–20	Shell	*Mytilus californianus*
51	CA-SLO-51	5	BETA-421353	10–20	Shell	*Mytilus californianus*
51	CA-SLO-51	5	BETA-421355	30–40	Shell	*Mytilus californianus*
51	CA-SLO-51	5	BETA-421354	20–30	Shell	*Haliotis rufescens*
58	CA-SLO-58	1	BETA-466814	40–50	Shell	*Mytilus californianus*
58	CA-SLO-58	2	BETA-466815	50–60	Shell	*Haliotis rufescens*
58	CA-SLO-58	3	BETA-466816	90–100	Shell	*Mytilus californianus*
58	CA-SLO-58	1	BETA-466817	10–20	Shell	*Mytilus californianus*
58	CA-SLO-58	2	BETA-466818	30–40	Shell	*Mytilus californianus*
58	CA-SLO-58	1	BETA-466819	20–30	Shell	*Haliotis rufescens*
61	CA-SLO-61	CS3	BETA-297987	60–70	Shell	*Mytilus or Haliotis*

Conventional ^{14}CAge	Cal1Sig Max	Cal1Sig Mid	Cal1Sig Min	Cal2Sig Max	Cal2Sig Mid	Cal2Sig Min	Reference
1810±030	1148	1076	1004	1185	1068	950	Jones et al. 2015
1790±30	1122	1050	977	1173	1052	930	Jones et al. 2015
1780±30	1102	1035	967	1168	1046	924	Jones et al. 2015
1700±30	998	954	910	1059	968	876	Jones et al. 2015
3530+80	3179	3056	2932	3318	3070	2822	Breschini and Haversat 1988
3040+90	2669	2500	2330	2731	2500	2268	Breschini and Haversat 1988
2970+80	2484	2389	2294	2677	2412	2146	Breschini and Haversat 1988
1640+60	957	887	816	1048	891	733	Breschini and Haversat 1988
1070+90	835	744	653	927	744	560	Breschini and Haversat 1988
910+65	661	598	535	721	609	496	Breschini and Haversat 1988
800+90	617	542	467	667	523	378	Breschini and Haversat 1988
800+90	617	542	467	667	523	378	Breschini and Haversat 1988
670+70	495	411	326	537	406	275	Breschini and Haversat 1988
610+90	473	375	277	524	334	144	Breschini and Haversat 1988
940+90	692	616	540	790	641	491	Breschini and Haversat 1988
1050+70	480	391	301	521	391	260	Breschini and Haversat 1988
1720+40	1042	980	917	1114	999	883	Codding and Jones 2007
1670+80	1012	923	833	1137	934	730	Codding and Jones 2007
1610+40	921	856	790	967	850	733	Codding and Jones 2007
1570+60	908	822	736	960	817	673	Codding and Jones 2007
1510+80	881	776	671	938	783	628	Codding and Jones 2007
1510+80	881	776	671	938	783	628	Codding and Jones 2007
1470+40	774	721	667	861	751	640	Codding and Jones 2007
6810+50	7139	7040	6941	7187	7027	6867	Herein
2700+70	2141	2041	1940	2288	2072	1856	Herein
2520+40	1892	1833	1773	1967	1831	1695	Herein
1940+60	1278	1216	1154	1332	1192	1051	Dallas 1994
1430+70	755	697	638	875	713	550	Dallas 1994
240+60	0	0	0	0	0	0	Dallas 1994
2610 ± 30	1990	1931	1872	2064	1940	1816	Herein
1320 ± 30	649	600	551	674	598	521	Herein
1050 ± 30	461	394	326	492	391	289	Herein
1020 ± 30	437	369	301	476	376	275	Herein
910 ± 30	297	272	246	377	256	134	Herein
820 ± 30	252	167	81	277	139	0	Herein
800 ± 30	242	121	0	267	134	0	Herein
740 ± 30	125	63	0	236	118	0	Herein
610 ± 30	0	0	0	0	0	0	Herein
3570 ± 30	4151	4118	4084	4228	4108	3988	Herein
1590 ± 30	1532	1473	1414	1552	1478	1404	Herein
3470 ± 30	3826	3740	3654	3836	3739	3641	Herein
3570 ± 30	3898	3867	3836	3966	3850	3733	Herein
1780 ± 30	1724	1676	1628	1816	1715	1613	Herein
2040 ± 30	2036	1993	1949	2110	2007	1904	Herein
4730±40	4705	4611	4517	4800	4616	4432	Price et al. 2012

SiteNo	Trinom	Unit	LabNo	Depth_cm	Material	Species
61	CA-SLO-61	CS2	BETA-297984	0–10	Shell	*Mytilus* or *Haliotis*
61	CA-SLO-61	CS3	BETA-297986	0–10	Shell	*Mytilus* or *Haliotis*
61	CA-SLO-61	CS2	BETA-297983	30–40	Shell	*Mytilus* or *Haliotis*
61	CA-SLO-61	CS2	BETA-297985	60–70	Shell	*Mytilus* or *Haliotis*
61	CA-SLO-61	CS3	BETA-297988	30–40	Shell	*Mytilus* or *Haliotis*
497	CA-SLO-497	1	BETA-293076	40–50	Shell	*Haliotis*
497	CA-SLO-497	Auger 1	BETA-25345	90–105	Shell	?
497	CA-SLO-497	2	BETA-293077	20–30	Shell	*Haliotis*
497	CA-SLO-497	Auger 1	BETA-25346	25–30	Shell	?
497	CA-SLO-497	2	BETA-293078	70–80	Shell	*Haliotis*
585	CA-SLO-585	N12W6	GAK-02040	200	Shell	*Haliotis rufescens*
585	CA-SLO-585	N11W6	BETA-197953	210–220	Shell	*Mytilus californianus*
585	CA-SLO-585	N14W7	GAK-02043	120–130	Shell	*Haliotis rufescens*
585	CA-SLO-585	N14W7	GAK-02042	160–170	Shell	*Haliotis rufescens*
585	CA-SLO-585	N10W1	BETA-197952	110–120	Shell	*Saxidomus nuttali*
585	CA-SLO-585	N8W1	GAK-02041	160	Shell	*Haliotis rufescens*
585	CA-SLO-585	N14W8	BETA-204127	80–90	Shell	*Haliotis cracherodii*
585	CA-SLO-585	N14W7	BETA-206362	60–70	Shell	*Mytilus californianus*
585	CA-SLO-585	N11W6	BETA-206361	40–50	Shell	*Mytilus californianus*
585	CA-SLO-585	N11W6	BETA-197954	30–40	Shell	*Mytilus californianus*
1366	CA-SLO-1366/H	NA	BETA-284547	Surface	Shell	*Mytilus californianus*
1366	CA-SLO-1366/H	5	BETA-312939	118	Shell	*Haliotis rufescens*
1366	CA-SLO-1366/H	5	BETA-312940	120–130	Shell	*Haliotis rufescens*
1366	CA-SLO-1366/H	1	BETA-312941	50–60	Shell	*Mytilus californianus*
1366	CA-SLO-1366/H	NA	BETA-242070	Surface	Shell	*Mytilus californianus*
1366	CA-SLO-1366/H	1	BETA-312938	10–20	Shell	*Mytilus californianus*
1366	CA-SLO-1366/H	NA	BETA-242071	20	Shell	*Haliotis*
1370	CA-SLO-1370/H	2	BETA-285159	40–50	Shell	*Saxidomus nuttalli*
1370	CA-SLO-1370/H	NA	BETA-210896	Lower	Shell	?
1370	CA-SLO-1370/H	2	BETA-285160	80–90	Shell	*Haliotis rufescens*
1370	CA-SLO-1370/H	5	BETA-285162	90–100	Shell	*Mytilus californianus*
1370	CA-SLO-1370/H	4	BETA-285161	30–40	Shell	*Haliotis rufescens*
1370	CA-SLO-1370/H	NA	BETA-247460	Not Reported	Shell	?
1370	CA-SLO-1370/H	NA	BETA-210897	Upper	Shell	?
1370	CA-SLO-1370/H	2	BETA-285158	10–20	Shell	*Haliotis rufescens*
1451	CA-SLO-1451/H	NA	BETA-210895	Buried Midden	Shell	*Haliotis*
1451	CA-SLO-1451/H	NA	CAMS-150599	Not Reported	Shell	*Limpet*
1452	CA-SLO-1452/H	NA	BETA-233050	Not Reported	Shell	*Haliotis*
1453	CA-SLO-1453	NA	BETA-233051	Not Reported	Shell	*Haliotis*
1455	CA-SLO-1455	NA	CAMS150598	Not Reported	Shell	Clam
1458	CA-SLO-1458	NA	CAMS-150596	Not Reported	Shell	*Haliotis*
1459	CA-SLO-1459	NA	CAMS-150595	Not Reported	Shell	*Haliotis*
1460	CA-SLO-1460	NA	CAMS-150594	Not Reported	Shell	*Haliotis*
1461	CA-SLO-1461	NA	CAMS-150593	Not Reported	Shell	*Haliotis*
1466	CA-SLO-1466	NA	BETA-284548	Not Reported	Shell	*Haliotis*

Conventional ^{14}CAge	Cal1Sig Max	Cal1Sig Mid	Cal1Sig Min	Cal2Sig Max	Cal2Sig Mid	Cal2Sig Min	Reference
4550±40	4429	4360	4290	4514	4365	4216	Price et al. 2012
4540±30	4416	4352	4287	4498	4358	4218	Price et al. 2012
4410±40	4256	4171	4085	4366	4180	3994	Price et al. 2012
4340±40	4149	4065	3980	4238	4073	3908	Price et al. 2012
3480±30	3059	2988	2917	3142	2994	2846	Price et al. 2012
5600±50	5730	5661	5591	5849	5707	5565	Herein
3500+90	3157	3015	2872	3308	3035	2762	Barter 1988
3410±40	2964	2895	2826	3055	2905	2755	Herein
3140+100	2734	2590	2445	2836	2578	2320	Barter 1988
2910±40	2344	2311	2278	2438	2293	2147	Herein
8820+260	9467	9135	8803	9774	9118	8461	Greenwood 1972
8470+40	8753	8667	8580	8894	8710	8526	Jones et al. 2009
7930+240	8356	8110	7864	8593	8111	7628	Greenwood 1972
7780+220	8174	7948	7722	8397	7973	7549	Greenwood 1972
7630+40	7864	7801	7737	7927	7799	7671	Jones et al. 2009
5510+180	5757	5589	5421	5978	5595	5212	Greenwood 1972
5260+40	5395	5332	5269	5452	5330	5208	Jones et al. 2009
3430+40	2993	2919	2844	3074	2923	2771	Jones et al. 2009
1100+40	494	455	416	522	417	311	Jones et al. 2009
1000+40	426	356	286	472	366	259	Jones et al. 2009
6850+60	7163	7071	6979	7243	7067	6890	Codding et al. 2013
5770±30	5908	5872	5836	5966	5848	5729	Codding et al. 2013
4720±30	4686	4600	4514	4786	4610	4434	Codding et al. 2013
4390±30	4225	4151	4076	4295	4140	3984	Codding et al. 2013
4120+40	3857	3776	3694	3929	3778	3627	Codding et al. 2013
3000±30	2476	2405	2334	2604	2453	2302	Codding et al. 2013
610+40	0	0	0	0	0	0	Codding et al. 2013
5470+70	5603	5532	5460	5703	5514	5324	Hadick et al. 2012
5420+40	5569	5506	5442	5593	5458	5322	Price et al. 2006
5390+60	5563	5463	5362	5593	5443	5293	Hadick et al. 2012
5310+40	5446	5372	5297	5514	5389	5263	Hadick et al. 2012
4750+80	4797	4653	4509	4843	4623	4403	Hadick et al. 2012
4340+40	4149	4065	3980	4238	4073	3908	PricePC
3780+60	3446	3379	3312	3548	3374	3199	Price et al. 2006
1200+60	555	516	477	637	530	423	Hadick et al. 2012
2560+50	1948	1879	1810	2034	1875	1716	Price et al. 2006
2550±30	1922	1867	1812	1984	1861	1737	PricePC
640±50	0	0	0	88	44	0	PricePC
750±50	139	70	0	257	129	0	PricePC
655±30	0	0	0	65	33	1	PricePC
710+/35	74	37	0	141	71	0	PricePC
640±30	0	0	0	49	35	21	PricePC
720±30	91	46	0	144	72	0	PricePC
675+35	0	0	0	118	59	0	PricePC
1395±30	689	662	634	739	655	570	PricePC

Obsidian Hydration and Source Results

Site	CatNo	Depth	Source	SubSource	Rim	Error	Reference
CA-SLO-5	9-12a	30–40	Coso	West Sugarloaf	3.2	0.1	Jones et al. 2015
CA-SLO-9	1-14a	10–20	Coso	West Sugarloaf	3.7	0.1	Codding et al. 2009
CA-SLO-9	1-14b	10–20	Casa Diablo	Lookout Mt	4.0	0.1	Codding et al. 2009
CA-SLO-9	3-5	0–10	Casa Diablo	Lookout Mt	4.0	0.1	Codding et al. 2009
CA-SLO-9	3-31	40–50	Coso	West Sugarloaf	4.4	0.1	Codding et al. 2009
CA-SLO-9	4-20	10–20	Coso	NA	3.9	0.1	Codding et al. 2009
CA-SLO-9	4-65	70–80	Coso	West Sugarloaf	4.1	0.1	Codding et al. 2009
CA-SLO-9	6-3	0–10	Coso	West Sugarloaf	4.0	0.0	Codding et al. 2009
CA-SLO-9	6-10	10–20	Coso	West Sugarloaf	3.7	0.1	Codding et al. 2009
CA-SLO-9	6-11	10–20	Coso	West Sugarloaf	4.2	0.1	Codding et al. 2009
CA-SLO-9	6-23	30–40	Coso	West Sugarloaf	6.1	0.1	Codding et al. 2009
CA-SLO-9	6-31	100–110	Coso	NA	4.4	0.1	Codding et al. 2009
CA-SLO-9	6-60A	70–80	Coso	NA	2.6	0.1	Codding et al. 2009
CA-SLO-9	6-60B	40–50	Coso	NA	5.1	0.1	Codding et al. 2009
CA-SLO-9	6-78	—	Grimes Canyon Fused Shale	Fused	NM±	NM	Codding et al. 2009
CA-SLO-9	3-42	70–80	Coso	NA	6.0	0.1	Codding et al. 2009
CA-SLO-9	3-45	80–90	Casa Diablo	Lookout Mt	3.7	0.1	Codding et al. 2009
CA-SLO-9	3-47	90–100	Coso	NA	3.7	0.1	Codding et al. 2009
CA-SLO-9	21a	20–30	Casa Diablo	Lookout Mt	4.1	0.1	Codding et al. 2009
CA-SLO-9	21b	20–30	Casa Diablo	Lookout Mt	4.5	0.1	Codding et al. 2009
CA-SLO-9	21c	20–30	Coso	NA	4.4	0.1	Codding et al. 2009
CA-SLO-9	33	40–50	Casa Diablo	Sawmill Ridge	3.8	0.1	Codding et al. 2009
CA-SLO-9	21a	10–20	Casa Diablo	Lookout Mt	3.0	0.1	Codding et al. 2009
CA-SLO-9	21b	10–20	Coso	NA	1.2	0.1	Codding et al. 2009
CA-SLO-9	60b	50–60	Coso	NA	2.8	0.1	Codding et al. 2009
CA-SLO-9	19	20–30	Casa Diablo	Lookout Mt	3.9	0.1	Codding et al. 2009
CA-SLO-9	21	30–40	Napa Valley	NA	NA	±	Codding et al. 2009
CA-SLO-9	51	70–80	Napa Valley	NA	1.7	0.1	Codding et al. 2009
CA-SLO-9	14-1	0–10	Casa Diablo	Sawmill Ridge	4.7	0.1	Codding et al. 2009
CA-SLO-9	14-10	10–20	Casa Diablo	Lookout Mt	4.2	0.1	Codding et al. 2009
CA-SLO-9	14-11	10–20	Coso	NA	4.7	0.1	Codding et al. 2009
CA-SLO-9	20-40	30–40	Casa Diablo	Lookout Mt	5.2	0.1	Codding et al. 2009
CA-SLO-9	21-1	0–10	Casa Diablo	Lookout Mt	4.6	0.1	Codding et al. 2009
CA-SLO-9	21-31	40–50	Casa Diablo	Lookout Mt	4.6	0.1	Codding et al. 2009
CA-SLO-9	21-32	40–50	Casa Diablo	Lookout Mt	5.1	0.1	Codding et al. 2009
CA-SLO-9	21-48	70–80	Casa Diablo	Lookout Mt	4.6	0.1	Codding et al. 2009

Site	CatNo	Depth	Source	SubSource	Rim	Error	Reference
CA-SLO-9	22-11	0–10	Casa Diablo	Lookout Mt	4.3	0.1	Codding et al. 2009
CA-SLO-9	22-22	10–20	Coso	NA	4.3	0.1	Codding et al. 2009
CA-SLO-9	22-49	40–50	Casa Diablo	Lookout Mt	4.4	0.1	Codding et al. 2009
CA-SLO-9	14-20	40–50	Queen	NA	4.2	0.1	Codding et al. 2009
CA-SLO-9	15-4	0–10	Casa Diablo	Lookout Mt	4.2	0.1	Codding et al. 2009
CA-SLO-9	15-21	20–30	Grimes Canyon Fused Shale	NA	NM±	NM	Codding et al. 2009
CA-SLO-9	16-2	0–10	Casa Diablo	Lookout Mt	4.4	0.1	Codding et al. 2009
CA-SLO-9	16-3	0–10	Casa Diablo	Sawmill Ridge	4.2	0.1	Codding et al. 2009
CA-SLO-9	16-30	30–40	Coso	NA	4.5	0.1	Codding et al. 2009
CA-SLO-9	16-32	30–40	Casa Diablo	Lookout Mt	4.4	0.1	Codding et al. 2009
CA-SLO-9	17-17	20–30	Mono Glass Mt	NA	4.4	0.1	Codding et al. 2009
CA-SLO-9	18-4	10–20	Casa Diablo	Lookout Mt	5.0	0.1	Codding et al. 2009
CA-SLO-9	18-5	10–20	Casa Diablo	Lookout Mt	4.5	0.1	Codding et al. 2009
CA-SLO-9	18-22	30–40	Casa Diablo	Lookout Mt	4.2	0.1	Codding et al. 2009
CA-SLO-9	18-23	30–40	Coso	West Sugarloaf	4.3	0.1	Codding et al. 2009
CA-SLO-9	18-24	30–40	Coso	NA	5.3	0.1	Codding et al. 2009
CA-SLO-9	18-34	50–60	Casa Diablo	Lookout Mt	4.6	0.1	Codding et al. 2009
CA-SLO-9	19-21	30–40	Coso	NA	5.3	0.1	Codding et al. 2009
CA-SLO-9	19-22	30–40	Casa Diablo	Lookout Mt	4.5	0.1	Codding et al. 2009
CA-SLO-9	19-28	40–50	Coso	NA	4.6	0.1	Codding et al. 2009
CA-SLO-9	20-11	0–10	Casa Diablo	Lookout Mt	4.7	0.1	Codding et al. 2009
CA-SLO-10	Surf1	Surf	Casa Diablo	Lookout Mt	3.4	0.1	Herein
CA-SLO-10	1-23	20–30	Coso	NA	4.9	0.1	Herein
CA-SLO-10	2-13	10–20	Casa Diablo	Lookout Mt	2.7	0.1	Herein
CA-SLO-10	2-48	60–70	Coso	NA	4.4	0.1	Herein
CA-SLO-10	2-49	60–70	Casa Diablo	Lookout Mt	4.2	0.1	Herein
CA-SLO-10	3-31a	30–40	Coso	NA	4.2	0.1	Herein
CA-SLO-10	3-31b	30–40	Casa Diablo	Lookout Mt	3.9	0.1	Herein
CA-SLO-10	3-31c	30–40	Casa Diablo	Lookout Mt	4.1	0.1	Herein
CA-SLO-10	3-31d	30–40	Casa Diablo	Lookout Mt	4.3	0.1	Herein
CA-SLO-10	3-46a	50–60	Coso	West Sugarloaf	4.1	0.1	Herein
CA-SLO-10	3-46b	50–60	Casa Diablo	Lookout Mt	4.1	0.1	Herein
CA-SLO-10	3-46c	50–60	Coso	NA	4.1	0.1	Herein
CA-SLO-10	3-46d	50–60	Casa Diablo	Lookout Mt	4.1	0.1	Herein
CA-SLO-10	3-78	80–90	Casa Diablo	Lookout Mt	4.2	0.1	Herein
CA-SLO-10	3-80	80–90	Coso	NA	4.3	0.1	Herein
CA-SLO-10	4-21	30–40	Casa Diablo	Lookout Mt	4.2	0.1	Herein
CA-SLO-10	5-17	10–20	Casa Diablo	Lookout Mt	4.2	0.1	Herein
CA-SLO-51/H	2-1-13	0–10	Coso	West Sugarloaf	2.4	0.1	Herein
CA-SLO-51/H	2-1-66	20–30	Coso	West Sugarloaf	4.5	0.1	Herein
CA-SLO-51/H	2-2-14	0–10	Coso	West Sugarloaf	3.1	0.1	Herein
CA-SLO-51/H	2-2-30	10–20	Casa Diablo	Lookout Mt	4.4	0.1	Herein
CA-SLO-51/H	2-3-50	20–30	Casa Diablo	Sawmill Ridge	2.8	0.1	Herein
CA-SLO-51/H	2-3-32	10–20	Coso	West Sugarloaf	3.8	0.1	Herein
CA-SLO-51/H	2-4-20	0–10	Coso	West Sugarloaf	3.7	0.1	Herein

Site	CatNo	Depth	Source	SubSource	Rim	Error	Reference
CA-SLO-1366	1--6	0–10	Coso	Sugarloaf Mt	5.1	0.1	Codding et al. 2013
CA-SLO-1366	2--22	30–40	Coso	West Sugarloaf	5.3	0.1	Codding et al. 2013
CA-SLO-1366	3--5	0–10	Coso	West Sugarloaf	4.6	0.1	Codding et al. 2013
CA-SLO-1366	3--14	20–30	Casa Diablo	Lookout Mt	4.5	0.1	Codding et al. 2013
CA-SLO-1366	3--22	30–40	Coso	West Sugarloaf	5.8	0.1	Codding et al. 2013
CA-SLO-1370	4-36	50–60	Casa Diablo	Lookout Mt	5.6	0.1	Hadick et al. 2012
CA-SLO-1370	6-15a	30–40	Coso	West Sugarloaf	4.1	0.1	Hadick et al. 2012
CA-SLO-1370	6-15b	30–40	Coso	West Sugarloaf	2.7	0.1	Hadick et al. 2012

Beads from the Pecho Coast

Site	Specimen No.	Unit	Depth (cm)	Length (mm)	Width /Diameter (mm)	Perforation (mm)
CA-SLO-5	8	1	10–20	—	—	1.5
CA-SLO-5	17	4	10–20	—	—	1.9
CA-SLO-5	14	5	20–30	—	7.5	—
CA-SLO-5	72	8	40–50	—	—	1.3
CA-SLO-5	73	8	40–50	—	—	1.3
CA-SLO-5	75	8	40–50	—	—	1.4
CA-SLO-5	87	8	50–60	—	—	1.2
CA-SLO-5	100	8	60–70	9.2	5.8	3.7 × 1.2
CA-SLO-5	101	8	70–80	—	—	—
CA-SLO-5	107	8	70–80	10.2	6.5	5.4 × 3.04
CA-SLO-5	117	8	80–90	—	—	1.2
CA-SLO-5	45	CS8	40–50	4.9	5.5	1.0
CA-SLO-9	P1387-1-19	1	20–30	—	6.7	2.3
CA-SLO-9	P1387-1-31	1	30–40	11.9	8.5	5.9 × 3.2
CA-SLO-9	P1387-3-7	3	0–10	—	5.8	1.3
CA-SLO-9	P1387-3-8	3	0–10	9.5	6.8	4.7 × 2.5
CA-SLO-9	P1387-3-48	3	90–100	—	5.3	2.1
CA-SLO-9	P1387-4-38	4	40–50	13.2	8.8	4.9 × 3.1
CA-SLO-9	P1387-4-39	4	40–50	6.8	5.8	4.4 × 2.9
CA-SLO-9	P1387-4-54b	4	50–60	11.6	6.2	5.1 × 2.3
CA-SLO-9	P1387-5-2	5	0–10	—	6.6	1.8
CA-SLO-9	P1387-5-19	5	0–10	—	6.0	1.5
CA-SLO-9	P1387-5-20	5	0–10	—	5.1	1.4
CA-SLO-9	P1387-5-9	5	10–20	—	5.1	1.6
CA-SLO-9	P1387-5-21	5	10–20	—	5.4	1.7
CA-SLO-9	P1387-5-22	5	20–30	—	5.4	1.6
CA-SLO-9	P1387-5-32	5	30–40	—	7.3	1.9
CA-SLO-9	P1387-5-49	5	70–80	—	7.1	1.9
CA-SLO-9	P1387-5-48	5	70–80	13.6	7.5	6.8 × 2.4
CA-SLO-9	P1387-5-62	5	0–25	12.8	9.1	5.5 × 2.8
CA-SLO-9	P1387-5-61	5	0–100	12.8	8.6	4.6 × 2.9
CA-SLO-9	P1387-6-7	6	10–20	8.5	6.1	5.0 × 2.3
CA-SLO-9	P1387-6-24	6	30–40	—	4.8	1.6
CA-SLO-9	P1387-6-32	6	40–50	—	4.7	2.1
CA-SLO-9	P1387-6-33	6	40–50	12.4	8.1	6.9 × 2.9
CA-SLO-9	P1387-6-34	6	40–50	8.2	6.1	4.8 × 2.1

Thickness (mm)	Curvature (mm)	Material	Type	Condition/Comment
1.3	1.3	Olivella	G1	
0.9	1.5	Olivella	G2a	
1.4	2.8	Limpet	Limpet Ring	
0.8	1.2	Olivella	G1	
1.1	1.6	Olivella	G2a	
0.9	1.6	Olivella	G2a	
0.5	1.1	Olivella	G1	
1.2	2.3	Limpet	Limpet Ring	
1.6	1.9	Limpet	Limpet Ring	
0.7	1.6	Limpet	Limpet Ring	
0.9	1.0	Olivella	G1	
1.0	1.2	Mussel	Bead Blank	
1.5	1.9	Olivella	G2a	Complete
1.1	3.0	Limpet	N/A	Complete
0.9	1.5	Olivella	G2a	Broken edge
0.9	2.0	Limpet	N/A	Complete
1.0	1.7	Olivella	G2a	Complete
0.8	3.9	Limpet	N/A	Complete
1.1	1.7	Limpet	N/A	Complete
1.7	2.3	Limpet	N/A	Complete
1.1	1.9	Olivella	G2a	Complete
1.1	1.8	Olivella	G2a	Complete
0.9	1.3	Olivella	G2a	Broken edge
0.9	1.5	Olivella	G2a	Complete
0.9	1.4	Olivella	G2a	Complete
1.0	1.7	Olivella	G2a	Complete
1.1	1.5	Olivella	G2b	Complete
1.0	1.9	Olivella	G2b	Complete
1.8	3.4	Limpet	N/A	Complete
1.7	3.9	Limpet	N/A	Complete
1.8	3.7	Limpet	N/A	Complete
1.2	1.9	Limpet	N/A	Complete
2.1	2.9	Olivella	K1	Complete
1.5	1.3	Steatite	Disk	Complete
2.9	3.9	Limpet	N/A	Complete
1.7	2.5	Limpet	N/A	Complete

Site	Specimen No.	Unit	Depth (cm)	Length (mm)	Width /Diameter (mm)	Perforation (mm)
CA-SLO-9	P1387-6-35	6	40–50	9.8	5.7	4.2 × 1.4
CA-SLO-9	P1387-6-45	6	50–60	10.8	5.6	—
CA-SLO-9	P1387-7-6a	7	0–10	—	5.2	1.6
CA-SLO-9	P1387-7-6b	7	0–10	—	6.9	2
CA-SLO-9	P1387-7-6c	7	0–10	6.9	6.5	3.2 × 1.8
CA-SLO-9	P1387-7-6d	7	0–10	13.7	8.7	5.2 × 1.7
CA-SLO-9	P1387-7-6e	7	0–10	11.6	9.1	4.8 × 2.4
CA-SLO-9	P1387-7-6f	7	0–10	13.9	11.1	5.5 × 2.6
CA-SLO-9	P1387-7-14a	7	10–20	5.7	4.2	2.7 × 1.5
CA-SLO-9	P1387-7-14b	7	10–20	11.0	7.5	5.8 × 2.5
CA-SLO-9	P1387-7-32	7	30–40	—	3.7	1.2
CA-SLO-9	P1387-7-50	7	60–70	12.7	9.1	3.9 × 4.8
CA-SLO-9	P1387-7-56a	7	70–80	14.8	10.5	5.4 × 2.8
CA-SLO-9	P1387-7-56b	7	70–80	12.0	7.7	5.8 × 1.8
CA-SLO-9	P1387-7-67	7	0–20	12.3	8.9	5.4 × 2.1
CA-SLO-9	P1387-8-1	8	0–10	—	5.7	1.9
CA-SLO-9	P1387-8-17a	8	10–20	7.5	4.8	2.8 × 2.2
CA-SLO-9	P1387-8-17b	8	10–20	10.5	7.9	4.9 × 3.9
CA-SLO-9	P1387-8-17c	8	10–20	13.4	9.3	5.0 × 2.9
CA-SLO-9	P1387-8-17d	8	10–20	13.6	9.4	7.4 × 3.2
CA-SLO-9	P1387-8-37	8	40–50	9.4	6.9	5.5 × 2.8
CA-SLO-9	P1387-8-38	8	40–50	—	8.6	4.9
CA-SLO-9	P1387-8-69	8	0–30	8.8	5.5	5.4 × 2.0
CA-SLO-9	P1387-8-68	8	0–50	10.6	8.7	6.6 × 2.4
CA-SLO-9	P1387-9-2	9	0–10	15.3	9.1	5.7 × 2.3
CA-SLO-9	P1387-9-10	9	10–20	10.5	6.8	5.0 × 2.1
CA-SLO-9	P1387-9-20	9	20–30	13.1	9.6	5.9 × 3.6
CA-SLO-9	P1387-9-42	9	0–40	12.7	8.7	6.6 × 3.6
CA-SLO-9	P1387-10-8	10	0–10	3.5	6.2	—
CA-SLO-9	P1387-10-20	10	10–20	11.0	8.1	5.7 × 2.4
CA-SLO-9	P1387-10-35	10	40–50	—	4.5	1.5
CA-SLO-9	P1387-10-37	10	40–50	15.0	9.1	6.8 × 4.9
CA-SLO-9	P1387-10-54a	10	40–50	9.7	7.9	5.4 × 1.7
CA-SLO-9	P1387-10-54b	10	40–50	13.8	8.6	5.4 × 2.4
CA-SLO-9	P1387-10-54c	10	40–50	14.0	10.8	5.5 × 2.5
CA-SLO-9	P1387-10-80	10	70–80	13.5	8.3	6.8 × 2.5
CA-SLO-9	P1387-11-1	11	0–10	12.5	8.1	6.1 × 2.7
CA-SLO-9	P1387-11-24	11	20–30	—	7.6	2.2
CA-SLO-9	P1387-11-39	11	40–50	—	5.6	1.8
CA-SLO-9	P1387-12-9	12	10–20	12.3	7.5	6.2 × 2.3
CA-SLO-9	P1387-13-6	13	10–20	12.6	8.3	6.3 × 1.9
CA-SLO-9	P1387-13-4	13	0–10	10.3	6.5	4.8 × 2.2
CA-SLO-9	P1387-14-9b	14	10–20	9.5	6.4	2.2 × 4.3
CA-SLO-9	P1387-14-13	14	20–30	18.9	10.8	2.92
CA-SLO-9	P1387-15-11b	15	10–21	12.3	7.3	2.8 × 6.5

Thickness (mm)	Curvature (mm)	Material	Type	Condition/Comment
1.2	2.4	Limpet	N/A	Complete
1.8	—	Limpet	N/A	Broken
1.2	1.5	Olivella	G2a	Broken edge
0.9	2.5	Olivella	G2a	Complete
0.9	2.9	Limpet	N/A	Complete
1.3	3.0	Limpet	N/A	Complete
1.6	3.6	Limpet	N/A	Complete
2.5	5.3	Limpet	N/A	Complete
0.9	1.6	Limpet	N/A	Squared edges
1.9	3.3	Limpet	N/A	Complete
0.9	1.1	Olivella	G1	Complete
4.4	4.5	Limpet	N/A	Complete
1.7	4.6	Limpet	N/A	Broken edge
1.2	4.0	Limpet	N/A	Complete
1.4	3.6	Limpet	N/A	Complete
1.2	1.6	Olivella	G2a	Complete
2.0	2.5	Limpet	N/A	Squared edges
2.6	3.1	Limpet	N/A	Squared edges
1.6	3.4	Limpet	N/A	Complete
2.2	4.3	Limpet	N/A	Complete
1.5	2.8	Limpet	N/A	Complete
1.2	1.3	Olivella	G3	Complete
1.5	1.7	Limpet	N/A	Complete
1.1	3.6	Limpet	N/A	Broken end
1.5	4.2	Limpet	N/A	Complete
0.9	2.1	Limpet	N/A	Complete
1.6	4.2	Limpet	N/A	Broken edge
1.1	2.0	Limpet	N/A	Complete
1.5	—	Limpet	N/A	Broken in half
1.4	3.2	Limpet	N/A	Broken edge
1.2	2.6	Olivella	K1	Complete
1.9	3.2	Limpet	N/A	Broken edge
1.6	4.0	Limpet	N/A	Broken edge
2.7	3.9	Limpet	N/A	Broken edge
1.8	5.7	Limpet	N/A	Broken edge
2.2	3.8	Limpet	N/A	Broken edge
1.5	2.8	Limpet	N/A	Complete
1.5	2.4	Olivella	G2b	Complete
1.0	1.7	Olivella	G2a	Broken edge
1.0	3.3	Limpet	N/A	Complete
1.9	3.4	Limpet	N/A	Complete
1.2	2.2	Limpet	N/A	Complete
1.2	2.1	Limpet	N/A	Broken edge
—	—	Olivella	A1c	Complete
1.3	2.2	Limpet	N/A	Complete

Site	Specimen No.	Unit	Depth (cm)	Length (mm)	Width /Diameter (mm)	Perforation (mm)
CA-SLO-9	P1387-15-11c	15	10–22	10.2	5.9	2.4 × 5.1
CA-SLO-9	P1387-15-20	15	20–30	8.8	5.3	2.6 × 3.8
CA-SLO-9	P1387-16-31	16	30–40	14.5	9.3	2.7 × 7.2
CA-SLO-9	P1387-16-38a	16	30–40	—	6.5	2.2
CA-SLO-9	P1387-16-38b	16	30–40	—	5.1	1.6
CA-SLO-9	P1387-16-39a	16	30–40	13.2	9.6	2.4 × 6.4
CA-SLO-9	P1387-17-18	17	20–30	7.7	4.8	2.6
CA-SLO-9	P1387-17-28	17	30–40	—	4.6	1.6
CA-SLO-9	P1387-17-35	17	50–60	—	5.0	1.9
CA-SLO-9	P1387-17-56	17	Back Dirt	—	5.0	1.3
CA-SLO-9	P1387-17-57a	17	Back Dirt	13.8	8.8	4.1 × 5.7
CA-SLO-9	P1387-18-13	18	10–20	—	4.1	1.4
CA-SLO-9	P1387-19-12	19	10–20	9.6	6.5	1.9 × 4.7
CA-SLO-9	P1387-21-10	21	10–20	—	5.1	1.5
CA-SLO-9	P1387-21-26	21	30–40	—	5.6	1.5
CA-SLO-9	P1387-22-10	22	0–10	10.9	6.6	5.4 × 1.7
CA-SLO-9	P1387-22-20a	22	10–20	6.7	4.3	3.5 × 1.4
CA-SLO-9	P1387-22-20b	22	10–20	7.3	4.6	2.4
CA-SLO-9	P1387-22-46	22	30–40	—	3.9	1.9
CA-SLO-51/H	SLO-51/H-2-1-17	1	0–10		7.7	2.5
CA-SLO-51/H	SLO-51/H-2-1-18	1	0–10		5.5	2.0
CA-SLO-51/H	SLO-51/H-2-1-19	1	0–10	9.9	6.8	3.3
CA-SLO-51/H	SLO-51/H-2-1-35	1	10–20	20.2	11.7	2.4
CA-SLO-51/H	SLO-51/H-2-1-38	1	10–20		4.2	1.3
CA-SLO-51/H	SLO-51/H-2-1-39	1	10–20		3.9	1.6
CA-SLO-51/H	SLO-51/H-2-1-61	1	20–30		4.3	2.0
CA-SLO-51/H	SLO-51/H-2-1-62	1	20–30		3.4	1.3
CA-SLO-51/H	SLO-51/H-2-1-63	1	20–30		3.0	1.3
CA-SLO-51/H	SLO-51/H-2-1-76	1	30–40			
CA-SLO-51/H	SLO-51/H-2-1-77	1	30–40		3.9	1.7
CA-SLO-51/H	SLO-51/H-2-1-80	1	30–40	5.1	3.4	2.1
CA-SLO-51/H	SLO-51/H-2-1-81	1	40–50	6.7	9.6	3.8
CA-SLO-51/H	SLO-51/H-2-1-82	1	40–50		4.8	1.4
CA-SLO-51/H	SLO-51/H-2-2-16	2	0–10		3.3	1.3
CA-SLO-51/H	SLO-51/H-2-2-18	2	0–10	14.9	9.1	1.8
CA-SLO-51/H	SLO-51/H-2-2-20	2	0–10		4.1	1.5
CA-SLO-51/H	SLO-51/H-2-2-21	2	0–10		4.5	1.3
CA-SLO-51/H	SLO-51/H-2-2-22	2	0–10		2.8	1.7
CA-SLO-51/H	SLO-51/H-2-2-23	2	0–10		2.8	1.5
CA-SLO-51/H	SLO-51/H-2-2-24	2	0–10		4.2	0.9
CA-SLO-51/H	SLO-51/H-2-2-25	2	0–10		2.7	1.6
CA-SLO-51/H	SLO-51/H-2-2-31	2	10–20		3.6	1.3
CA-SLO-51/H	SLO-51/H-2-2-32	2	10–20		3.2	1.3
CA-SLO-51/H	SLO-51/H-2-2-33	2	10–20		3.9	1.9
CA-SLO-51/H	SLO-51/H-2-2-44	2	20–30		4.0	1.8

Thickness (mm)	Curvature (mm)	Material	Type	Condition/Comment
1.1	1.7	Limpet	N/A	Broken edge
1.1	2.0	Limpet	N/A	Broken edge
1.9	3.8	Limpet	N/A	Broken edge
1.1	2.1	*Olivella*	G2a	Complete
1.0	1.6	*Olivella*	G2a	Complete
1.9	2.8	Limpet	N/A	Broken edge
—	—	*Olivella*	A1a	Complete
1.1	1.1	*Olivella*	G2a	Complete
1.3	1.5	*Olivella*	G2a	Complete
0.7	1.3	*Olivella*	K1	Complete
1.7	2.2	Limpet	N/A	Broken edge
1.5	2.2	*Olivella*	K1	Complete
1.3	2.1	Limpet	N/A	Broken edge
1.2	1.5	*Olivella*	G2a	Complete
0.8	1.6	*Olivella*	G2a	Complete
1.4	2.6	Limpet	N/A	Broken edge
0.8	1.4	Limpet	N/A	Broken edge
—	—	*Olivella*	A1a	Complete
0.7	1.0	*Olivella*	G1	Complete
1.3	4.1	*Olivella*	E1b1	
1.9	3.0	*Olivella*	K1	
0.8		*Olivella*	A1b	
1.3		*Olivella*	A1c	
1.2	2.4	*Olivella*	K1	
1.5	0.9	*Olivella*	G1	
1.9	1.9	*Olivella*	K1	
2.1	2.1	*Olivella*	K1	
1.7	1.8	*Olivella*	K1	
		shell	limpet ring	limpet ring
0.9	1.2	*Olivella*	G1	
		Olivella	A1a	
3.3		steatite	steatite	steatite
1.0	1.5	*Olivella*	G1	
1.9		*Olivella*	K2	
		Olivella	A1b	
2.3	2.3	*Olivella*	K1	
1.6	2.6	*Olivella*	K1	
2.4	2.3	*Olivella*	K3	
1.6	1.7	*Olivella*	K3	
0.8	1.1	*Olivella*	H1b	
1.9	2.1	*Olivella*	K3	
1.8	1.8	*Olivella*	K2	
1.1	1.1	*Olivella*	K2	
1.5	1.4	*Olivella*	K2	
2.8		Shell	clam disk	wrapped fibers

Site	Specimen No.	Unit	Depth (cm)	Length (mm)	Width /Diameter (mm)	Perforation (mm)
CA-SLO-51/H	SLO-51/H-2-2-45	2	20–30		4.1	1.7
CA-SLO-51/H	SLO-51/H-2-2-46	2	20–30		3.9	1.2
CA-SLO-51/H	SLO-51/H-2-2-51	2	30–40		9.9	2.1
CA-SLO-51/H	SLO-51/H-2-2-52	2	30–40			
CA-SLO-51/H	SLO-51/H-2-2-53	2	30–40			
CA-SLO-51/H	SLO-51/H-2-2-54	2	30–40	17.8	9.9	1.6
CA-SLO-51/H	SLO-51/H-2-2-55	2	30–40	19.5	11.3	2.7
CA-SLO-51/H	SLO-51/H-2-2-61	2	40–50			
CA-SLO-51/H	SLO-51/H-2-2-62	2	40–50	21.6	12.6	5.1
CA-SLO-51/H	SLO-51/H-2-3-19	3	0–10			
CA-SLO-51/H	SLO-51/H-2-3-20	3	0–10			
CA-SLO-51/H	SLO-51/H-2-3-21	3	0–10		5.0	1.3
CA-SLO-51/H	SLO-51/H-2-3-22	3	0–10		3.9	1.4
CA-SLO-51/H	SLO-51/H-2-3-23	3	0–10		4.5	1.9
CA-SLO-51/H	SLO-51/H-2-3-24	3	0–10	17.3	10.0	1.8
CA-SLO-51/H	SLO-51/H-2-3-26	3	10–20		4.5	1.6
CA-SLO-51/H	SLO-51/H-2-3-27	3	10–20		4.1	1.8
CA-SLO-51/H	SLO-51/H-2-3-28	3	10–20		5.0	2.3
CA-SLO-51/H	SLO-51/H-2-3-29	3	10–20		3.9	1.4
CA-SLO-51/H	SLO-51/H-2-3-30	3	10–20		4.3	1.9
CA-SLO-51/H	SLO-51/H-2-3-40	3	0–20			
CA-SLO-51/H	SLO-51/H-2-3-43	3	20–30		6.3	2.0
CA-SLO-51/H	SLO-51/H-2-3-44	3	20–30			
CA-SLO-51/H	SLO-51/H-2-3-45	3	20–30		4.3	1.0
CA-SLO-51/H	SLO-51/H-2-3-46	3	20–30	16.3	8.3	1.5
CA-SLO-51/H	SLO-51/H-2-3-67	3	30–40		7.8	1.9
CA-SLO-51/H	SLO-51/H-2-3-68	3	30–40		4.5	1.8
CA-SLO-51/H	SLO-51/H-2-3-69	3	30–40		5.5	1.9
CA-SLO-51/H	SLO-51/H-2-3-70	3	30–40		4.4	1.4
CA-SLO-51/H	SLO-51/H-2-3-71	3	30–40			
CA-SLO-51/H	SLO-51/H-2-3-95	3	40–50		3.8	1.2
CA-SLO-51/H	SLO-51/H-2-3-96	3	40–50		4.5	2.2
CA-SLO-51/H	SLO-51/H-2-4-11	4	0–10		4.9	1.8
CA-SLO-51/H	SLO-51/H-2-4-12	4	0–10		3.4	1.5
CA-SLO-51/H	SLO-51/H-2-4-13	4	0–10		5.2	1.6
CA-SLO-51/H	SLO-51/H-2-4-30	4	10–20	11.3	7.2	2.2
CA-SLO-51/H	SLO-51/H-2-4-31	4	10–20	18.5	11.9	1.7
CA-SLO-51/H	SLO-51/H-2-4-32	4	10–20		4.5	1.4
CA-SLO-51/H	SLO-51/H-2-4-40	4	20–30			
CA-SLO-51/H	SLO-51/H-2-4-41	4	20–30		3.6	1.4
CA-SLO-51/H	SLO-51/H-2-4-64	4	30–40			
CA-SLO-51/H	SLO-51/H-2-4-67	4	30–40		5.0	1.5
CA-SLO-51/H	SLO-51/H-2-4-68	4	30–40		4.2	1.6
CA-SLO-51/H	SLO-51/H-2-4-69	4	30–40		3.1	1.6
CA-SLO-51/H	SLO-51/H-2-4-77	4	40–50		9.3	2.6

Thickness (mm)	Curvature (mm)	Material	Type	Condition/Comment
0.9	1	*Olivella*	G1	
1.2	1.4	*Olivella*	G1	
2.2	4.1	*Olivella*	E1a	
		shell	limpet ring	limpet ring
		shell	limpet ring	limpet ring
		Olivella	A1c	
		Olivella	A1c	
		shell	limpet ring	limpet ring
		Olivella	A1a	
		glass	trade	blue w/ pat.
		glass	trade	black w/ pat.
2.5	2.7	*Olivella*	K1	
2.5	2.3	*Olivella*	K1	
2.2	1.6	*Olivella*	K1	
		Olivella	A4c	
2.3	2.3	*Olivella*	K1	
2.8	2.8	steatite	steatite	steatite
2.5	2.5	*Olivella*	K1	
2.3	2.3	*Olivella*	K1	
2.4	2.5	*Olivella*	K1	
		shell	limpet ring	limpet ring
1.7	3.0	*Olivella*	E1a	
		Fish bone	vert	vert
1.1	1.2	*Olivella*	H1b	
		Olivella	A1b	
1.9	3.1	*Olivella*	E1a	
0.9	1.1	*Olivella*	G1	
2.0	2.3	*Olivella*	K1	
0.9	1.2	*Olivella*	G1	
		Shell	abalone nacre	abalone nacre
2.3	1.6	*Olivella*	K1	
1.9		steatite	steatite	steatite
2.4	1.4	*Olivella*	K1	
1.9	1.8	*Olivella*	K2	
1.7		shell	clam disk	burnt, previously mistaken as steatite
		Olivella	A1b	
		Olivella	A4c	
0.9	1.3	*Olivella*	G1	
		shell	limpet ring	limpet ring
1.9	2.3	*Olivella*	K2	
		shell	dentalium	possible bead
2.0	2.0	shell	clam disk	clam
2.1	1.9	*Olivella*	K1	
1.6	1.7	*Olivella*	K2	
1.4	3.9	*Olivella*	E1b2	

Site	Specimen No.	Unit	Depth (cm)	Length (mm)	Width /Diameter (mm)	Perforation (mm)
CA-SLO-51/H	SLO-51/H-2-5-14	5	0–10		6.4	1.9
CA-SLO-51/H	SLO-51/H-2-5-15	5	0–10		10.9	2.4
CA-SLO-51/H	SLO-51/H-2-5-16	5	0–10		8.5	3.1
CA-SLO-51/H	SLO-51/H-2-5-17	5	0–10		4.2	1.8
CA-SLO-51/H	SLO-51/H-2-5-19	5	0–10		2.7	1.5
CA-SLO-51/H	SLO-51/H-2-5-20	5	0–10		3.8	1.5
CA-SLO-51/H	SLO-51/H-2-5-22	5	0–10		3.6	1.7
CA-SLO-51/H	SLO-51/H-2-5-23	5	0–10		3.4	1.8
CA-SLO-51/H	SLO-51/H-2-5-25	5	0–10		10.8	2.5
CA-SLO-51/H	SLO-51/H-2-5-36	5	10–20		4.5	1.3
CA-SLO-51/H	SLO-51/H-2-5-37	5	10–20		8.6	2.3
CA-SLO-51/H	SLO-51/H-2-5-40	5	10–20		10.5	2.4
CA-SLO-51/H	SLO-51/H-2-5-41	5	10–20			
CA-SLO-51/H	SLO-51/H-2-5-45	5	10–20		8.6	2.1
CA-SLO-51/H	SLO-51/H-2-5-47	5	10–20		10.3	2.8
CA-SLO-51/H	SLO-51/H-2-5-50	5	10–20			
CA-SLO-51/H	SLO-51/H-2-5-51	5	10–20		3.9	1.5
CA-SLO-51/H	SLO-51/H-2-5-52	5	10–20		4.2	1.8
CA-SLO-51/H	SLO-51/H-2-5-54	5	10–20		3.5	1.7
CA-SLO-51/H	SLO-51/H-2-5-55	5	10–20			
CA-SLO-51/H	SLO-51/H-2-5-57	5	10–20		3.8	1.6
CA-SLO-51/H	SLO-51/H-2-5-61	5	10–20	8.1	4.9	0.8
CA-SLO-51/H	SLO-51/H-2-5-71	5	20–30		3.6	1.5
CA-SLO-51/H	SLO-51/H-2-5-73	5	20–30		4.3	1.8
CA-SLO-51/H	SLO-51/H-2-5-74	5	20–30		2.8	1.5
CA-SLO-51/H	SLO-51/H-2-5-85	5	20–30		3.1	1.9
CA-SLO-51/H	SLO-51/H-2-5-83	5	20–30		4.4	1.5
CA-SLO-51/H	SLO-51/H-2-5-84	5	20–30			
CA-SLO-51/H	SLO-51/H-2-5-88	5	20–30		4.4	1.8
CA-SLO-51/H	SLO-51/H-2-5-90	5	20–30		4.2	1.2
CA-SLO-51/H	SLO-51/H-2-5-92	5	20–30		4.2	1.6
CA-SLO-51/H	SLO-51/H-2-5-99	5	20–30		4.5	1.1
CA-SLO-51/H	SLO-51/H-2-5-98	5	20–30			
CA-SLO-51/H	SLO-51/H-2-5-100	5	20–30		3.2	1.7
CA-SLO-51/H	SLO-51/H-2-5-103	5	20–30		4.5	2.2
CA-SLO-51/H	SLO-51/H-2-5-104	5	20–30		4.8	1.4
CA-SLO-51/H	SLO-51/H-2-5-109	5	20–30	23.9	13.4	2.2
CA-SLO-51/H	SLO-51/H-2-5-113	5	20–30	17.7	11.6	2.8
CA-SLO-51/H	SLO-51/H-2-5-115	5	20–30	5.3	5.8	3.7
CA-SLO-51/H	SLO-51/H-2-5-116	5	20–30	18.5	10.0	3.8
CA-SLO-51/H	SLO-51/H-2-5-117	5	20–30	9.6	6.7	2.0
CA-SLO-51/H	SLO-51/H-2-5-120	5	30–40		8.0	2.5
CA-SLO-51/H	SLO-51/H-2-5-121	5	30–40		3.4	1.8
CA-SLO-51/H	SLO-51/H-2-5-122	5	30–40		6.3	2.9
CA-SLO-51/H	SLO-51/H-2-5-123	5	30–40		3.5	1.9

Thickness (mm)	Curvature (mm)	Material	Type	Condition/Comment
3.0	3.2	*Olivella*	E1a1	
2.0	4.4	*Olivella*	E2a	
3.9	2.5	*Olivella*	E1a	
1.9	2.4	*Olivella*	K1	
1.7	1.9	*Olivella*	K3	
1.2	1.4	*Olivella*	K2	
1.6	1.8	*Olivella*	K2	
1.6		steatite	steatite	steatite
2.7	4.7	*Olivella*	C2	
0.7	0.9	*Olivella*	G1	
1.6	3.1	*Olivella*	G2	
2.7	5.0	*Olivella*	E2a1	
		shell	limpet ring	limpet ring
3.9	3.4	*Olivella*	E2a1	
1.6	3.8	*Olivella*	E2a1	
		steatite	steatite	steatite
1.0	1.3	*Olivella*	G1	
1.3	1.2	*Olivella*	G1	
1.7	1.7	*Olivella*	K2	
		shell	abalone ep.	red abalone
1.8	1.9	*Olivella*	K2	
		Olivella	A1a	
1.2	1.4	*Olivella*	G1	
1.3	1.7	*Olivella*	K1	
2.0	1.9	*Olivella*	K3	
1.7	1.8	*Olivella*	K2	
2.1	2.5	*Olivella*	K1	
		Shell	Abalone ep.	red abalone
1.2	1.5	*Olivella*	G1	
1.7	1.5	*Olivella*	K1	
1.5	1.5	*Olivella*	G1	
1.2	1.3	*Olivella*	H1a	
		Fish Bone	vert	vert
1.7	1.5	*Olivella*	K2	
2.1	2.3	*Olivella*	K1	
2.3	2.3	*Olivella*	K1	
		Olivella	A1c	
		Olivella	A4c	
		Olivella	B3	
		Olivella	A5c	
		Olivella	A1b	
1.2	3.3	*Olivella*	E1b	
1.7	1.7	*Olivella*	K2	
1.9	3.9	*Olivella*	E1a	
1.3		steatite	steatite	steatite

Site	Specimen No.	Unit	Depth (cm)	Length (mm)	Width /Diameter (mm)	Perforation (mm)
CA-SLO-51/H	SLO-51/H-2-5-124	5	30–40		2.8	1.9
CA-SLO-51/H	SLO-51/H-2-5-125	5	30–40		6.7	2.3
CA-SLO-51/H	SLO-51/H-2-5-126	5	30–40	17.9	10.9	4.5
CA-SLO-51/H	SLO-51/H-2-5-127	5	30–40		3.1	1.2
CA-SLO-51/H	SLO-51/H-2-5-128	5	30–40		9.0	4.7
CA-SLO-51/H	SLO-51/H-2-5-129	5	30–40		11.1	2.0
CA-SLO-51/H	SLO-51/H-2-5-130	5	30–40		4.0	1.5
CA-SLO-51/H	SLO-51/H-2-5-131	5	30–40		6.5	1.9
CA-SLO-51/H	SLO-51/H-2-5-132	5	30–40		3.8	1.2
CA-SLO-51/H	SLO-51/H-2-5-133	5	30–40		3.9	1.3
CA-SLO-51/H	SLO-51/H-2-5-134	5	30–40		3.6	1.5
CA-SLO-51/H	SLO-51/H-2-5-135	5	30–40		4.3	1.4
CA-SLO-51/H	SLO-51/H-2-5-136	5	30–40		4.2	1.4
CA-SLO-51/H	SLO-51/H-2-5-137	5	30–40		4.8	1.1
CA-SLO-51/H	SLO-51/H-2-5-138	5	30–40		3.9	1.4
CA-SLO-51/H	SLO-51/H-2-5-139	5	30–40		3.4	1.5
CA-SLO-51/H	SLO-51/H-2-5-140	5	30–40		4.7	1.6
CA-SLO-51/H	SLO-51/H-2-5-141	5	30–40		3.5	1.4
CA-SLO-51/H	SLO-51/H-2-5-142	5	30–40		3.5	1.6
CA-SLO-51/H	SLO-51/H-2-5-143	5	30–40		3.5	1.5
CA-SLO-51/H	SLO-51/H-2-6-1	6	0–10		3.1	1.3
CA-SLO-51/H	SLO-51/H-2-6-2	6	0–10		7.5	2.5
CA-SLO-51/H	SLO-51/H-2-6-3	6	0–10		3.3	2.0
CA-SLO-51/H	SLO-51/H-2-6-4	6	0–10			
CA-SLO-51/H	SLO-51/H-2-6-7	6	0–10		4.2	1.9
CA-SLO-51/H	SLO-51/H-2-6-8	6	0–10		3.3	1.9
CA-SLO-51/H	SLO-51/H-2-6-10	6	0–10		4.4	1.7
CA-SLO-51/H	SLO-51/H-2-6-11	6	0–10		3.7	1.6
CA-SLO-51/H	SLO-51/H-2-6-12	6	0–10		5.2	1.5
CA-SLO-51/H	SLO-51/H-2-6-13	6	0–10		10.3	2.4
CA-SLO-51/H	SLO-51/H-2-6-14	6	0–10		3.7	1.5
CA-SLO-51/H	SLO-51/H-2-6-15	6	0–10		4.5	1.0
CA-SLO-51/H	SLO-51/H-2-6-16	6	0–10		6.3	3.0
CA-SLO-51/H	SLO-51/H-2-6-17	6	0–10		2.9	1.5
CA-SLO-51/H	SLO-51/H-2-6-18	6	0–10		11.5	2.6
CA-SLO-51/H	SLO-51/H-2-6-19	6	0–10			
CA-SLO-51/H	SLO-51/H-2-6-21	6	0–10		4.5	1.8
CA-SLO-51/H	SLO-51/H-2-6-22	6	0–10		2.8	1.4
CA-SLO-51/H	SLO-51/H-2-6-29	6	0–10			
CA-SLO-51/H	SLO-51/H-2-6-31	6	0–10			
CA-SLO-51/H	SLO-51/H-2-6-48	6	10–20			
CA-SLO-51/H	SLO-51/H-2-6-51	6	10–20		12.4	2.0
CA-SLO-51/H	SLO-51/H-2-6-52	6	10–20			
CA-SLO-51/H	SLO-51/H-2-6-53	6	10–20		3.9	1.5
CA-SLO-51/H	SLO-51/H-2-6-54	6	10–20			

Thickness (mm)	Curvature (mm)	Material	Type	Condition/Comment
1.9	1.6	*Olivella*	K3	
1.4	3.4	*Olivella*	E1a	
		Olivella	A1c	
1.6	1.7	*Olivella*	K2	
2.1	4.7	*Olivella*	E3a	
1.1	4.5	*Olivella*	E2a1	
0.8	1.0	*Olivella*	G1	
2.3	3.8	*Olivella*	E1a	
0.8	1.25	*Olivella*	G1	
1.6	1.77	*Olivella*	K2	
1.4	1.41	*Olivella*	K2	
1.8	2.4	*Olivella*	K1	
0.8	1.18	*Olivella*	G1	
1.2	1.49	*Olivella*	H1a	
0.8	1.07	*Olivella*	G1	
1.5	1.59	*Olivella*	K2	
2.4	2.56	*Olivella*	K1	
1.8	1.63	*Olivella*	K2	
1.5	1.6	*Olivella*	K2	
1.7	1.59	*Olivella*	K2	
1.7	1.82	*Olivella*	K2	
1.7	3.2	*Olivella*	E1a	
2.1	2.1	*Olivella*	K1	
		steatite	steatite	
1.3	1.3	*Olivella*	G1	
1.7		steatite	steatite	
1.9	1.9	Abalone	Abalone ep	
0.9	1.12	*Olivella*	G1	
2.4	2.53	*Olivella*	K1	
4.5	4.45	*Olivella*	E2a1	
2.2	2.02	*Olivella*	K1	
1.2	1.64	*Olivella*	H1b	
0.8	0.89	*Olivella*	G3a	
1.7	1.67	*Olivella*	K3	
4.9	4.83	*Olivella*	E3a	
		Glass	trade	
2.5	2.6	*Olivella*	K1	
1.7	1.63	*Olivella*	K3	
		Shell	barnacle	
		Shell	limpet ring	
		Shell	dentalium	
3.0	5.42	*Olivella*	E3a	
		Shell	limpet ring	
2.1	2.07	*Olivella*	K1	
		Shell	dentalium	

Site	Specimen No.	Unit	Depth (cm)	Length (mm)	Width /Diameter (mm)	Perforation (mm)
CA-SLO-51/H	SLO-51/H-2-6-56	6	10–20		4.1	1.4
CA-SLO-51/H	SLO-51/H-2-6-57	6	10–20		3.1	1.4
CA-SLO-51/H	SLO-51/H-2-6-59	6	10–20		5.5	2.1
CA-SLO-51/H	SLO-51/H-2-6-60	6	10–20		3.4	1.4
CA-SLO-51/H	SLO-51/H-2-6-61	6	10–20		3.7	1.7
CA-SLO-51/H	SLO-51/H-2-6-62	6	10–20		3.9	1.2
CA-SLO-51/H	SLO-51/H-2-6-63	6	10–20		3.3	1.5
CA-SLO-51/H	SLO-51/H-2-6-65	6	10–20		3.9	1.3
CA-SLO-51/H	SLO-51/H-2-6-66	6	10–20		4.3	1.6
CA-SLO-51/H	SLO-51/H-2-6-67	6	10–20		7.4	2.8
CA-SLO-51/H	SLO-51/H-2-6-68	6	10–20			
CA-SLO-51/H	SLO-51/H-2-6-69	6	10–20			
CA-SLO-51/H	SLO-51/H-2-6-70	6	10–20			
CA-SLO-51/H	SLO-51/H-2-6-71	6	10–20			
CA-SLO-51/H	SLO-51/H-2-6-76	6	0–20		5.3	2.2
CA-SLO-51/H	SLO-51/H-2-6-79	6	20–30		3.7	1.3
CA-SLO-51/H	SLO-51/H-2-6-78	6	20–30	7.1	4.7	1.9
CA-SLO-51/H	SLO-51/H-2-6-80	6	20–30		4.2	1.7
CA-SLO-51/H	SLO-51/H-2-6-83	6	20–30		3.2	1.5
CA-SLO-51/H	SLO-51/H-2-6-84	6	20–30		3.3	1.6
CA-SLO-51/H	SLO-51/H-2-6-85	6	20–30		3.9	1.4
CA-SLO-51/H	SLO-51/H-2-6-86	6	20–30			
CA-SLO-51/H	SLO-51/H-2-6-87	6	20–30		5.0	0.9
CA-SLO-51/H	SLO-51/H-2-6-88	6	20–30		3.4	1.7
CA-SLO-51/H	SLO-51/H-2-6-89	6	20–30		4.3	1.2
CA-SLO-51/H	SLO-51/H-2-6-90	6	20–30		3.5	1.2
CA-SLO-51/H	SLO-51/H-2-6-91	6	20–30		2.7	1.4
CA-SLO-51/H	SLO-51/H-2-6-92	6	20–30		4.2	2.3
CA-SLO-51/H	SLO-51/H-2-6-93	6	20–30			
CA-SLO-51/H	SLO-51/H-2-6-94	6	20–30		2.7	1.7
CA-SLO-51/H	SLO-51/H-2-6-95	6	20–30		3.0	
CA-SLO-51/H	SLO-51/H-2-6-96	6	20–30			
CA-SLO-51/H	SLO-51/H-2-6-97	6	20–30			
CA-SLO-51/H	SLO-51/H-2-6-98	6	20–30			
CA-SLO-51/H	SLO-51/H-2-6-99	6	20–30		3.7	1.2
CA-SLO-51/H	SLO-51/H-2-6-100	6	20–30		3.3	1.7
CA-SLO-51/H	SLO-51/H-2-6-101	6	20–30		3.8	1.4
CA-SLO-51/H	SLO-51/H-2-6-102	6	20–30		3.9	1.4
CA-SLO-51/H	SLO-51/H-2-6-103	6	20–30		9.4	2.8
CA-SLO-51/H	SLO-51/H-2-6-105	6	20–30	17.0	9.6	2.1
CA-SLO-51/H	SLO-51/H-2-6-106	6	20–30		3.7	1.6
CA-SLO-51/H	SLO-51/H-2-6-107	6	20–30		3.3	1.6
CA-SLO-51/H	SLO-51/H-2-6-108	6	20–30		4.5	1.6
CA-SLO-51/H	SLO-51/H-2-6-109	6	20–30		3.0	1.7
CA-SLO-51/H	SLO-51/H-2-6-110	6	20–30		3.7	1.8

Thickness (mm)	Curvature (mm)	Material	Type	Condition/Comment
1.9		*Olivella*	K1	
1.8		*Olivella*	K2	
2.4	2.9	*Olivella*	K1	
1.7		*Olivella*	K2	
1.7	1.8	*Olivella*	K1	
1.7		Steatite	steatite	steatite
1.8	1.8	*Olivella*	k3	
0.8	1.2	*Olivella*	G1	
0.8	1.2	*Olivella*	G1	
0.7	2.2	Fish Bone	vert	vert
		Fish Bone	vert	vert
		Fish Bone	vert	vert
		Fish Bone	vert	vert
		Shell	Abalone ep.	red abalone
2.8	2.8	*Olivella*	K1	
1.7	1.7	*Olivella*	K2	
		Olivella	A1a	
1.3	1.7	*Olivella*	G1	
1.2	1.1	*Olivella*	G1	
1.9	1.9	*Olivella*	K2	
1.3	1.3	*Olivella*	G1	
		shell	mussel	mussel
1.5	1.7	*Olivella*	H2	
1.3	0.3	*Olivella*	K2	
0.8	1.1	*Olivella*	G1	
0.7	1.0	*Olivella*	G1	
2.1	2.0	*Olivella*	K3	
0.7	1.1	*Olivella*	G1	
		Shell	abalone ep.	red abalone
2.0	1.9	*Olivella*	K3	
		Olivella	K1	
		Glass		
		Glass		
		Glass		
0.8	1.0	*Olivella*	G1	
1.1	2.1	*Olivella*	K2	
2.1	2.1	*Olivella*	K1	
1.4	1.5	*Olivella*	G1	
3.8	4.1	*Olivella*	E2a1	
		Olivella	A4c	
1.8	1.8	*Olivella*	K2	
1.8	1.8	*Olivella*	K2	
0.9	1.3	*Olivella*	G1	
2.1	2.1	*Olivella*	K3	
1.7	1.8	*Olivella*	K2	

Site	Specimen No.	Unit	Depth (cm)	Length (mm)	Width /Diameter (mm)	Perforation (mm)
CA-SLO-51/H	SLO-51/H-2-6-111	6	20–30		3.2	1.6
CA-SLO-51/H	SLO-51/H-2-6-112	6	20–30		4.4	1.7
CA-SLO-51/H	SLO-51/H-2-6-113	6	20–30		4.3	1.5
CA-SLO-51/H	SLO-51/H-2-6-114	6	20–30		4.8	0.9
CA-SLO-51/H	SLO-51/H-2-6-115	6	20–30		3.2	1.7
CA-SLO-51/H	SLO-51/H-2-6-123	6	20–30			
CA-SLO-51/H	SLO-51/H-2-6-130	6	30–40		3.3	1.5
CA-SLO-51/H	SLO-51/H-2-6-131	6	30–40			
CA-SLO-51/H	SLO-51/H-2-6-132	6	30–40			
CA-SLO-51/H	SLO-51/H-2-6-134	6	30–40	19.5	11.0	2.9
CA-SLO-51/H	SLO-51/H-2-6-143	6	30–40		4.2	1.9
CA-SLO-51/H	SLO-51/H-2-6-144	6	30–40		4.2	1.5
CA-SLO-51/H	SLO-51/H-2-6-145	6	30–40			
CA-SLO-51/H	SLO-51/H-2-6-146	6	30–40		3.4	1.7
CA-SLO-51/H	SLO-51/H-2-6-147	6	30–40		4.8	1.7
CA-SLO-51/H	SLO-51/H-2-6-148	6	30–40		3.9	1.6
CA-SLO-51/H	SLO-51/H-2-6-149	6	30–40		3.7	1.5
CA-SLO-51/H	SLO-51/H-2-6-150	6	30–40		10.4	2.2
CA-SLO-51/H	SLO-51/H-2-6-151	6	30–40			
CA-SLO-51/H	SLO-51/H-2-6-152	6	30–40		6.9	2.1
CA-SLO-51/H	SLO-51/H-2-6-153	6	30–40		9.3	2.2
CA-SLO-51/H	SLO-51/H-2-6-161	6	30–40			
CA-SLO-51/H	SLO-51/H-2-6-162	6	30–40		3.8	1.8
CA-SLO-51/H	SLO-51/H-2-6-164	6	30–40	17.08	8.9	2.1
CA-SLO-51/H	SLO-51/H-2-6-165	6	30–40		2.9	1.9
CA-SLO-51/H	SLO-51/H-2-6-166	6	30–40		4.4	1.9
CA-SLO-51/H	SLO-51/H-2-6-167	6	30–40		9.2	2.3
CA-SLO-51/H	SLO-51/H-2-6-168	6	30–40		3.7	2.4
CA-SLO-51/H	SLO-51/H-2-6-170	6	30–40		4.1	1.5
CA-SLO-51/H	SLO-51/H-2-6-171	6	30–40			
CA-SLO-51/H	SLO-51/H-2-6-172	6	30–40		4.1	1.5
CA-SLO-51/H	SLO-51/H-2-6-173	6	30–40			
CA-SLO-51/H	SLO-51/H-2-6-174	6	30–40		3.6	1.6
CA-SLO-51/H	SLO-51/H-2-6-175	6	30–40		4.5	1.7
CA-SLO-51/H	SLO-51/H-2-6-177	6	30–40		3.5	2.1
CA-SLO-51/H	SLO-51/H-2-6-178	6	30–40		4.7	1.6
CA-SLO-51/H	SLO-51/H-2-6-179	6	30–40		N/A	N/A
CA-SLO-51/H	SLO-51/H-2-6-186	6	40–50	18.48	10.1	1.5
CA-SLO-51/H	SLO-51/H-2-6-187	6	40–50		4.7	1.6
CA-SLO-51/H	SLO-51/H-2-6-188	6	40–50		4.3	1.9
CA-SLO-51/H	SLO-51/H-2-6-189	6	40–50		3.6	1.8
CA-SLO-51/H	SLO-51/H-2-6-190	6	40–50		4.3	1.4
CA-SLO-51/H	SLO-51/H-2-6-191	6	40–50			
CA-SLO-51/H	SLO-51/H-2-6-192	6	40–50		4.4	1.2
CA-SLO-51/H	SLO-51/H-2-6-195	6	40–50		5.1	1.7

Thickness (mm)	Curvature (mm)	Material	Type	Condition/Comment
1.2	1.4	*Olivella*	K2	
1.0	1.3	*Olivella*	G1	
0.8	1.1	*Olivella*	G1	
1.1	1.5	*Olivella*	H1a	
1.2	1.4	*Olivella*	K2	
		Shell	dentalium	
1.9		Steatite	steatite	steatite
		Shell	abalone ep.	red abalone
		Shell	limpet ring	limpet ring
		Olivella	A1c	
1.5	1.4	*Olivella*	K1	
1.1	1.2	*Olivella*	G1	
		Fish Bone	vert	vert
1.8	1.8	*Olivella*	K2	
1.5	1.5	*Olivella*	G1	
1.2	1.4	*Olivella*	G1	
1.1	1.4	*Olivella*	G1	
3.8	4.3	*Olivella*	E2a1	
		Shell	abalone ep.	red abalone
2.2	3.8	*Olivella*	E1a1	
2.2	4.6	*Olivella*	E2a	
		Glass	trade	
1.8	1.8	*Olivella*	K2	
		Olivella	A1b	
1.8	1.8	*Olivella*	K3	
1.2	1.4	*Olivella*	G1	
3.9	4.2	*Olivella*	E2a1	
3.4	3.4	Bone	indeterminant	indeterminate bone
1.6	1.6	*Olivella*	G1	
		Glass	trade	
1.7	1.7	*Olivella*	K1	
		Shell	Abalone ep.	Red
1.9	1.8	*Olivella*	K2	
1.3	1.4	*Olivella*	G1	
3.6		Steatite	steatite	steatite
1.2	1.4	*Olivella*	G1	
N/A	N/A	*Olivella*	H	
		Olivella	A1c	
1.1	1.4	*Olivella*	G1	
1.2	1.3	*Olivella*	G1	
1.7	1.7	*Olivella*	K2	
1.5	1.6	*Olivella*	K1	
		Shell	abalone ep.	red abalone ep.
1.5	1.6	*Olivella*	G1	
2.2	2.6	*Olivella*	K1	

Site	Specimen No.	Unit	Depth (cm)	Length (mm)	Width /Diameter (mm)	Perforation (mm)
CA-SLO-51/H	SLO-51/H-2-6-197	6	40–50			
CA-SLO-51/H	SLO-51/H-2-6-198	6	40–50			
CA-SLO-51/H	SLO-51/H-2-6-202	6	40–50		7.1	2.4
CA-SLO-51/H	SLO-51/H-2-6-203	6	40–50		2.6	1.2
CA-SLO-51/H	SLO-51/H-2-6-204	6	40–50		3.5	1.8
CA-SLO-51/H	SLO-51/H-2-6-206	6	40–50		3.4	1.7
CA-SLO-51/H	SLO-51/H-2-6-214	6	40–50		4.8	1.3
CA-SLO-51/H	SLO-51/H-2-6-215	6	40–50		4.5	1.9
CA-SLO-51/H	SLO-51/H-2-6-216	6	40–50		3.8	1.6
CA-SLO-51/H	SLO-51/H-2-6-218	6	40–50		4.6	1.2
CA-SLO-51/H	SLO-51/H-2-S-1	20S/45W		17.8	11.3	4.8
CA-SLO-51/H	SLO-51/H-2-S-2	50S/10W			6.7	2.4
CA-SLO-51/H	SLO-51/H-2-S-3	5S/25W		12.0	7.8	3.6
CA-SLO-51/H	SLO-51/H-2-S-4	5S/15W		20.5	12.1	2.6
CA-SLO-51/H	SLO-51/H-2-S-5	5S/50W		18.5	10.1	1.5
CA-SLO-51/H	SLO-51/H-2-S-6	10S/40W				
CA-SLO-51/H	SLO-51/H-2-S-7	10S/0W			4.3	1.8
CA-SLO-51/H	SLO-51/H-2-S-8	10S/5W			10.6	2.2
CA-SLO-51/H	SLO-51/H-2-S-9	10S/35W			6.9	2.1
CA-SLO-51/H	SLO-51/H-2-S-11	15S/20W		21.3	11.7	5.8
CA-SLO-51/H	SLO-51/H-2-S-12	15S/25W		20.5	11.1	1.5
CA-SLO-51/H	SLO-51/H-2-S-10	10S/35W			2.7	1.4
CA-SLO-51/H	SLO-51/H-2-S-14	15S/40W			4.0	1.5
CA-SLO-51/H	SLO-51/H-2-S-15	10S/45W		18.3	12.3	7.4
CA-SLO-51/H	SLO-51/H-2-S-17	25S/10W			13.1	2.7
CA-SLO-51/H	SLO-51/H-2-S-18	25S/15W		20.1	12.7	4.1
CA-SLO-51/H	SLO-51/H-2-S-20	25S/35W			4.4	2.4
CA-SLO-51/H	SLO-51/H-2-S-21	25S/40W			11.1	2.2
CA-SLO-51/H	SLO-51/H-2-S-22	25S/50W			8.5	2.3
CA-SLO-51/H	SLO-51/H-2-S-23	30S/40W			3.3	1.7
CA-SLO-51/H	SLO-51/H-2-S-25	35S/50W		18.9	11.3	1.7
CA-SLO-51/H	SLO-51/H-2-S-26	40S/10W		12.5	10.4	4.2
CA-SLO-51/H	SLO-51/H-2-S-27	40S/35W			8.4	3.2
CA-SLO-51/H	SLO-51/H-2-S-28	45S/20W		21.5	12.7	1.5
CA-SLO-51/H	SLO-51/H-2-S-29	45S/20W		9.1	6.8	3.6
CA-SLO-51/H	SLO-51/H-2-S-30	50S/40W			4.1	1.5
CA-SLO-51/H	SLO-51/H-2-S-31	50S/35W			4.6	1.2
CA-SLO-51/H	SLO-51/H-2-S-32	55S/40W		16.9	10.4	3.7
CA-SLO-51/H	SLO-51/H-2-S-33	55S/25W		19.4	11.3	3.1
CA-SLO-51/H	SLO-51/H-2-S-34	55S/10W			3.9	1.3
CA-SLO-51/H	SLO-51/H-2-S-35	55S/20W		16.9	9.7	1.5
CA-SLO-51/H	SLO-51/H-2-S-36	55S/20W				
CA-SLO-51/H	SLO-51/H-2-S-37	0N/15W		20.8	11.8	2.7
CA-SLO-51/H	SLO-51/H-2-S-40	10N/20W		17.4	10.4	1.8
CA-SLO-51/H	SLO-51/H-2-S-41	10N/40W			7.8	2.3

Thickness (mm)	Curvature (mm)	Material	Type	Condition/Comment
		bone	indeterminate	indeterminate bone
		bone	epidermis bead	red abalone
1.7	2.6	*Olivella*	G2	
1.4	1.3	*Olivella*	K3	
1.7	1.7	*Olivella*	K2	
1.9	1.9	*Olivella*	K2	
1.1	1.6	*Olivella*	G1	
1.1	1.2	*Olivella*	G1	
1.2	1.2	*Olivella*	G1	
0.9	1.4	*Olivella*	G1	
		Olivella	A1c	
3.7	3.2	*Olivella*	E1a	
		Olivella	A1b	
		Olivella	A1c	
		Olivella	A1c	
		shell	limpet	limpet ring
1.7	1.6	*Olivella*	K2	
3.3	3.9	*Olivella*	E2a1	
3.6	3.9	*Olivella*	E1a	
		Olivella	A1c	
		Olivella	A1c	
1.1	1.0	*Olivella*	K3	
1.9	2.1	*Olivella*	K2	
		Olivella	A1c	
3.0	5.5	*Olivella*	E3a	
		Olivella	A1c	
2.6	2.6	*Olivella*	K1	
2.8	3.8	*Olivella*	E2a1	
2.3	2.5	*Olivella*	G2	
1.7	1.8	*Olivella*	K2	
		Olivella	A1c	
		Olivella	A1c	
2.9	3.0	*Olivella*	E1a2	
		Olivella	A1c	
		Olivella	A1b	
0.8	1.2	*Olivella*	G1	
1.3	1.6	*Olivella*	G1	
		Olivella	A1c	
		Olivella	A1c	
2.2	2.3	*Olivella*	K1	
		Olivella	A1c	
		shell	limpet	limpet ring
		Olivella	A1c	
		Olivella	A1c	
3.2	3.5	*Olivella*	E1a	

Site	Specimen No.	Unit	Depth (cm)	Length (mm)	Width /Diameter (mm)	Perforation (mm)
CA-SLO-51/H	SLO-51/H-2-S-42	15N/25W			14.1	
CA-SLO-51/H	SLO-51/H-2-S-43	15N/45W		18.7	11.8	2.8
CA-SLO-51/H	SLO-51/H-2-S-45	20N/20W		21.6	12.8	5.6
CA-SLO-51/H	SLO-51/H-2-S-46	20N/20W		20.2	11.6	3.1
CA-SLO-51/H	SLO-51/H-2-S-47	25N/20W		20.2	12.2	4.3
CA-SLO-51/H	SLO-51/H-2-S-48	30N/30W		18.5	10.9	3.3
CA-SLO-51/H	SLO-51/H-2-S-49	No Prov.			8.9	2.3
CA-SLO-51/H	SLO-51/H-2-S-50	15S/35W				
CA-SLO-51/H	SLO-51/H-2-CS-1	SS#6	1/4			
CA-SLO-51/H	SLO-51/H-2-CS-7	SS#3	1/8		4.6	1.7
CA-SLO-51/H	SLO-51/H-2-CS-52	SS#6	1/8		4.0	1.4
CA-SLO-51/H	SLO-51/H-2-CS-53	SS#6	1/8			
CA-SLO-51/H	SLO-51/H-2-CS-72	SS#7	1/8			
CA-SLO-51/H	SLO-51/H-2-CS-69	SS#7	1/8		4.6	1.9

Thickness (mm)	Curvature (mm)	Material	Type	Condition/Comment
		Olivella	O4	
		Olivella	A1c	
		Olivella	A1c	
		Olivella	A1c	
		Olivella	A1c	
		Olivella	A1c	
5.4	5.0	*Olivella*	E2a1	
		shell	limpet	limpet ring
		shell	clam disk	clam disk
1.0	1.3	*Olivella*	G1	
1.1	1.3	*Olivella*	G1	
		bone	vert	fish bone
		bone	vert	fish bone
1.6	1.6	*Olivella*	G1	

Projectile Points from the Pecho Coast

Site	Specimen	Unit	Depth (cm)	Weight (g)	Length (mm)	Width (mm)	Thickness (mm)	Neck width (mm)
CA-SLO-5	-1-22	2	30–40	3.6	40.8	23.4	6.0	—
CA-SLO-5	-1-96	8	60–70	0.3	11.3	9.9	2.9	—
CA-SLO-5	-1-30	5	30–40	6.0	29.0	28.3	9.4	—
CA-SLO-5	-1-57	5	70–80	3.3	27.0	20.6	7.5	—
CA-SLO-5	-1-40	8	0–10	6.7	27.8	21.6	11.2	—
CA-SLO-5	-1-18a	2	20–30	4.7	26.3	20.4	6.5	—
CA-SLO-5	-1-21a	4	20–30	0.6	15.5	12.5	4.4	—
CA-SLO-5	-1-16a	5	20–30	3.1	21.5	20.0	7.3	—
CA-SLO-9	P1387-1-15	1	10–20	4.6	37.3	19.3	8.0	—
CA-SLO-9	P1387-1-35	1	40–50	7.0	40.3	24.4	7.8	—
CA-SLO-9	P1387-1-54	1	0–40	2.9	15.7*	27.7	8.1	—
CA-SLO-9	P1387-2-1	2	0–10	5.6*	35.9*	22.1*	9.2*	—
CA-SLO-9	P1387-2-2	2	0–10	3.7	36.1	17.6	7.7	14.0
CA-SLO-9	P1387-2-8	2	10–20	0.6*	14.6*	10.9*	4.5*	—
CA-SLO-9	P1387-2-25	2	30–40	1.2*	20.8*	13.8*	6.3*	—
CA-SLO-9	P1387-3-25	3	30–40	1.5*	27.1*	14.1	5.4*	—
CA-SLO-9	P1387-4-21	4	10–20	8.4*	41.7*	20.9	8.6	16.7 & 17.2
CA-SLO-9	P1387-4-66	4	70–80	4.0*	32.9	17.5	7.8	11.7
CA-SLO-9	P1387-5-29	5	30–40	6.5	61.9	16.1	6.9	14.4
CA-SLO-9	P1387-5-53	5	70–80	3.6*	32.8*	19.3	6.4	14.4
CA-SLO-9	P1387-6-48	6	50–60	0.6*	14.8*	15.5*	4.2*	—
CA-SLO-9	P1387-6-63	6	70–80	11.7	63.8	24.9	8.9	19.5
CA-SLO-9	P1387-7-16	7	20–30	1.8*	23.8*	14.9*	5.1*	—
CA-SLO-9	P1387-7-31	7	30–40	0.5*	23.1*	10.3*	2.6	—
CA-SLO-9	P1387-8-12	8	10–20	1.1*	26.6	11.1	4.7	—
CA-SLO-9	P1387-8-14	8	10–20	5.2*	24.3*	26.6*	8.5*	—
CA-SLO-9	P1387-9-1b	9	0–10	4.0*	35.5*	14.7*	8.3	—
CA-SLO-9	P1387-9-49	9	50–60	2.9*	32.2*	20.0	5.7*	—
CA-SLO-9	P1387-9-6	9	0–10	7.6*	32.9*	23.3	9.9	—
CA-SLO-9	P1387-10-6b	10	0–10	0.7*	14.9*	10.2*	4.3*	—
CA-SLO-9	P1387-10-17	10	10–20	3.0*	33.2*	17.6	5.0	—
CA-SLO-9	P1387-10-44	10	30–40	3.1*	27.6*	18.0	5.7	—
CA-SLO-9	P1387-10-45	10	30–40	0.5*	11.5*	11.2*	4.9*	—
CA-SLO-9	P1387-10-79	10	70–80	0.8*	13.8*	11.0*	5.3*	—
CA-SLO-9	P1387-11-11	11	10–20	4.2	38.1	18.3	7.0	16.5
CA-SLO-9	P1387-11-14	11	20–30	3.3*	26.5*	18.9*	7.0	—

* An asterisk indicates an incomplete measurement.

Basal width (mm)	Material	Description/Comment	Type	Citation
—	Monterey chert	Midsection, basal break	Lanceolate	Jones et al. 2015
—	Monterey chert	Tip	Small leafed-shaped	Jones et al. 2015
—	Monterey chert	Basal fragment	Contracting stemmed	Jones et al. 2015
—	Monterey chert	Tip	Indeterminate	Jones et al. 2015
—	Monterey chert	Basal fragment	Contracting stemmed	Jones et al. 2015
—	Monterey chert	Basal fragment	Indeterminate	Jones et al. 2015
—	Monterey chert	Tip fragment	Indeterminate	Jones et al. 2015
—	Monterey chert	Basal fragment	Indeterminate	Jones et al. 2015
17.4	Monterey chert	Complete	Small leaf-shaped	Codding et al. 2009
—	Monterey chert	Complete	Contracting stemmed	Codding et al. 2009
—	Monterey chert	Medial fragment	Indeterminate	Codding et al. 2009
—	Monterey chert	fragment	Indeterminate	Codding et al. 2009
5.5	Monterey chert	Complete, reworked	Contracting stemmed	Codding et al. 2009
—	Monterey chert	Tip, fragment	Indeterminate	Codding et al. 2009
—	Monterey chert	Tip, fragment	Indeterminate	Codding et al. 2009
—	Monterey chert	Basal fragment	Contracting stemmed	Codding et al. 2009
—	Monterey chert	Broken tip and base	Double side-notched	Codding et al. 2009
6.8	Monterey chert	Reworked, minor fragment missing	Contracting stemmed	Codding et al. 2009
8.1	Monterey chert	Complete	Contracting stemmed	Codding et al. 2009
12.9	Monterey chert	Basal fragment	Contracting stemmed	Codding et al. 2009
—	Monterey chert	Tip, fragment	Indeterminate	Codding et al. 2009
18.9	Shale	Complete	Contracting stemmed	Codding et al. 2009
—	Monterey chert	Tip, fragment	Indeterminate	Codding et al. 2009
—	Monterey chert	Medial fragment	Indeterminate	Codding et al. 2009
7.7*	Monterey chert	Fragment, tip	Small leaf-shaped	Codding et al. 2009
—	Monterey chert	Fragment	Indeterminate	Codding et al. 2009
—	Franciscan chert	Fragment	Small leaf-shaped	Codding et al. 2009
—	Monterey chert	Fragment, fire affected	Contracting stemmed	Codding et al. 2009
—	Monterey chert	Tip fragment	Indeterminate	Codding et al. 2009
—	Monterey chert	Tip, fragment	Indeterminate	Codding et al. 2009
—	Monterey chert	Fragment	Small leaf-shaped	Codding et al. 2009
—	Monterey chert	Fragment	Small leaf-shaped	Codding et al. 2009
—	Monterey chert	Tip fragment	Indeterminate	Codding et al. 2009
—	Monterey chert	Tip, fragment	Indeterminate	Codding et al. 2009
—	Monterey chert	Reworked	Contracting stemmed	Codding et al. 2009
—	Franciscan chert	End fragment	Indeterminate	Codding et al. 2009

Site	Specimen	Unit	Depth (cm)	Weight (g)	Length (mm)	Width (mm)	Thickness (mm)	Neck width (mm)
CA-SLO-9	P1387-11-15	11	20–30	2.4	34.1	15.5	6.0	—
CA-SLO-9	P1387-12-5	12	10–20	4.3*	35.4*	17.7	6.3	—
CA-SLO-9	P1387-12-20	12	20–30	6.0*	25.6*	24.9	7.9	16.3
CA-SLO-9	P1387-12-23	12	30–40	3.1*	20.9*	18.2	7.2*	—
CA-SLO-9	P1387-13-19	13	20–30	8.1	28.6*	29.8*	9.0*	—
CA-SLO-9	P1387-13-20	13	20–30	9.1	53.4	29.4	7.9	21.8
CA-SLO-9	P1387-14-5	14	0–10	2.3	23.9	17.7	6.2	11.4
CA-SLO-9	P1387-15-5	15	0–10	0.6	14.5	17.7	3.1	8.3
CA-SLO-9	P1387-16-10	16	0–10	2.7	21.0	18.7	4.1	—
CA-SLO-9	P1387-17-51	17	Back Dirt	4.0	39.5	19.7	6.2	—
CA-SLO-9	P1387-17-52	17	Back Dirt	3.5	39.5	16.6	6.2	—
CA-SLO-9	P1387-17-53	17	Back Dirt	4.1	22.0	25.0	5.2	—
CA-SLO-9	P1387-18-9	18	10–20	5.2	40.5	33.2	5.2	18.7
CA-SLO-9	P1387-19-18	19	20–30	26.0	63.5	34.3	13.5	—
CA-SLO-9	P1387-21-14	21	20–30	4.0	41.6	16.6	5.2	—
CA-SLO-9	P1387-21-44	21	60–70	2.0	28.1	20.8	5.1	—
CA-SLO-10	Surface 1	S	Surface	2.0	18.2*	20.4*	5.7	—
CA-SLO-10	1-8	1	0–10	1.2	15.2	14.6	4.8	—
CA-SLO-10	1-17	1	10–20	3.0	32.7	19.0	5.9	—
CA-SLO-10	1-62a	1	80–90	5.8	36.9	18.6	9.2	—
CA-SLO-10	1-68a	1	40–50	0.8	11.9*	14.9*	4.7*	—
CA-SLO-10	1-63	1	80–90	10.0	46.1	26.8	8.1	—
CA-SLO-10	1-74	1	100–110	8.0	50.3	20.0	11.2	—
CA-SLO-10	2-6	2	0–10	4.0	52.1	16.5	6.4	—
CA-SLO-10	2-68	2	100–110	3.7	37.2	19.1	5.5	—
CA-SLO-10	3-6a	3	0–10	0.9	—	—	—	—
CA-SLO-10	4-83	4	50–60	6.0	36.1	23.9*	6.8	15.9*
CA-SLO-10	5-17	5	10–20	2.4	23.9*	21.5	5.8	—
CA-SLO-10	5-72a	5	90–100	0.3	—	—	—	—
CA-SLO-10	5-94	5	130–140	10.0	41.9*	32.3	8.0	19.3
CA-SLO-51/H	1-26	1	0–10	12.1*	49.9*	27.9	8.9	—
CA-SLO-51/H	1-40	1	10–20	0.5	11.6*	13.0	3.3	—
CA-SLO-51/H	1-57	1	20–30	0.9	22.9	12.1	3.7	—
CA-SLO-51/H	1-86	1	40–50	1.6	17.0*	15.9	4.7	—
CA-SLO-51/H	1-93	1	40–50	3.0*	17.1*	20.8*	8.8	—
CA-SLO-51/H	2-64	2	40–50	4.5	27.3*	27.0	4.3	—
CA-SLO-51/H	2-67	2	40–50	0.5	17.9	8.2	3.4	—
CA-SLO-51/H	3-54	3	20–30	1.5	21.8	14.5	4.3	
CA-SLO-51/H	3-63	3	30–40	1.6	23.5*	13.7	4.7	—
CA-SLO-51/H	3-91	3	40–50	3.2	22.5	21.2	8.9	
CA-SLO-51/H	3-92	3	40–50	0.5	12.2*	13.3	3.9	—
CA-SLO-51/H	4-22	4	0–10	0.8	11.0*	14.9	3.8	—
CA-SLO-51/H	5-60	5	10–20	1.1	22.4*	14.8	3.8	—

Basal width (mm)	Material	Description/Comment	Type	Citation
—	Monterey chert	Reworked	Contracting stemmed	Codding et al. 2009
—	Monterey chert	Broken tip and base	Small leaf-shaped	Codding et al. 2009
22.5*	Franciscan chert	Fragment, base	Large side-notched	Codding et al. 2009
—	Monterey chert	Broken tip and base	Small leaf-shaped	Codding et al. 2009
—	Franciscan chert	Fragment	Indeterminate	Codding et al. 2009
6.5	Monterey chert	Broken tip, reworked	Contracting stemmed	Codding et al. 2009
—	Monterey chert	Broken tip and base	Contracting stemmed	Codding et al. 2009
—	Monterey chert	Midsection	Contracting stemmed	Codding et al. 2009
—	Monterey chert	Midsection	Indeterminate	Codding et al. 2009
—	Monterey chert	Complete	Contracting stemmed	Codding et al. 2009
—	Monterey chert	Near complete, broken base	Contracting stemmed	Codding et al. 2009
—	Monterey chert	Broken Tip	Indeterminate	Codding et al. 2009
—	Monterey chert	Complete, pot lidded	Contracting stemmed	Codding et al. 2009
—	Basalt	Tip, broken base	Indeterminate	Codding et al. 2009
—	Monterey chert	Near complete, broken tip	Small leaf-shaped	Codding et al. 2009
—	Franciscan chert	Broken Base	Indeterminate	Codding et al. 2009
—	Obsidian	Basal fragment	Concave base	Herein
—	Monterey chert	Base	Contracting stemmed	Herein
—	Monterey chert	Broken tip	Contracting stemmed	Herein
—	Monterey chert	Mostly complete	Contracting stemmed	Herein
—	Monterey chert	Base	Indeterminate	Herein
—	Monterey chert	Tip?	Indeterminate	Herein
—	Monterey chert	Complete, reworked	Contracting stemmed	Herein
—	Monterey chert	Shouldered, complete	Lanceolete	Herein
—	Monterey chert	Complete, reworked	Small leaf-shaped	Herein
—	Monterey chert	Tip	Indeterminate	Herein
—	Monterey chert	Mostly complete	Large side-notched	Herein
—	Obsidian	Mostly complete, tip broken	Concave base	Herein
—	Monterey chert	Tip	Indeterminate	Herein
—	Franciscan chert	Mostly complete, tip broken	Large side-notched	Herein
—	Monterey chert	Midsection	Contracting-Stemmed	Jones et al. 2017
—	Monterey chert	Tip	Indeterminate	Jones et al. 2017
—	Monterey chert	Mostly complete	Desert side-notched	Jones et al. 2017
—	Monterey chert	Base	Canalino/coastal cottonwood	Jones et al. 2017
—	Monterey chert	Tip	Indeterminate	Jones et al. 2017
—	Monterey chert	Base fragment	Concave base	Jones et al. 2017
—	Monterey chert	Base	Canalino/coastal cottonwood	Jones et al. 2017
	Monterey chert	Base	Arrow point	Jones et al. 2017
—	Monterey chert	Missing tip	Small leaf-shaped	Jones et al. 2017
	Monterey chert	Tip	Indeterminate	Jones et al. 2017
—	Franciscan chert	Tip	Indeterminate	Jones et al. 2017
—	Monterey chert	Midsection	Indeterminate	Jones et al. 2017
—	Monterey chert	Missing tip	Desert side-notched	Jones et al. 2017

Site	Specimen	Unit	Depth (cm)	Weight (g)	Length (mm)	Width (mm)	Thickness (mm)	Neck width (mm)
CA-SLO-51/H	5-65	5	10–20	2.1	27.8	12.4+	6.1	—
CA-SLO-51/H	5-66	5	10–20	1.3	23.5*	13.9	6.4	—
CA-SLO-51/H	5-67	5	100–20	3.6	24.1	25.1	6.4	
CA-SLO-51/H	5-80	5	20–30	0.5	9.6*	15.0	3.8	—
CA-SLO-51/H	5-150	5	30–40	1.6	18.6	12.1	5.1	—
CA-SLO-51/H	5-158	5	30–40	0.1	8.9*	12.3	3.1	—
CA-SLO-497	P1759-1-3	1	0–10	21.1	56.1	34.5	13.7	17.1
CA-SLO-1366	1-1	1	0–10	4.7	34.4	19.2	7.9	18.8
CA-SLO-1366	1-2	1	0–10	7.1*	31.0*	33.2	8.2	21.9
CA-SLO-1366	1-10	1	10–20	7.6*	47.9*	23.1*	8.3*	—
CA-SLO-1366	1-48	1	90–100	5.1	33.2	26.7	6.8	15.3
CA-SLO-1366	2-2b	2	0–10	5.6*	28.6*	31.4*	—	8.5
CA-SLO-1366	2-24	2	30–40	0.9*	13.7*	2.1*	6.3*	—
CA-SLO-1366	2-29b	2	40–50	0.5*	18.0*	19.0*	5.5*	—
CA-SLO-1366	2-35	2	50–60	5.6*	31.9*	25.7	8.1	22.9
CA-SLO-1366	2-48	2	60–70	5.5*	39.4*	26.3*	6.8*	—
CA-SLO-1366	2-58	2	70–80	4.8*	27.3*	28.6	6.1	—
CA-SLO-1366	2-68	2	100–110	2.3*	20.3*	21.8*	5.9*	—
CA-SLO-1366	2-77	2	0–130	5.4	42.0	25.6	5.9	17.1
CA-SLO-1366	3-1	3	0–10	0.7*	17.9*	10.0	3.4	—
CA-SLO-1366	3-18	3	20–30	0.8*	14.6*	13.4*	5.6*	—
CA-SLO-1366	3-26	3	40–50	1.8*	26.7*	18.4*	5.7*	—
CA-SLO-1366	3-31	3	0–40	1.1*	22.8*	18.4*	6.1*	—
CA-SLO-1366	3-40	3	60–70	8.3	53.3	28.0	7.9	17.3
CA-SLO-1366	3-56	3	90–100	2.6*	24.1*	21.9*	6.4*	—
CA-SLO-1366	4-13	4	20–30	4.7*	24.2*	21.9*	11.2	—
CA-SLO-1366	5-47	5	80–90	1.5*	16.4*	15.9*	8.2*	—
CA-SLO-1370	4-58	4	0–100	4.1	36.3	17.5	7.4	—
CA-SLO-1370	6-20a	6	40–50	2.5	27.4	17.2	5.9	—
CA-SLO-1370	6-20b	6	40–50	0.4	15.8	10.5	3.1	—
CA-SLO-1370	6-43	6	0–10	6.2	—	22.9	10.2	—
CA-SLO-1370	7-24	7	50–60	7.4	38.8	24.1	8.9	—
CA-SLO-1370	7-36	7	70–80	0.5	14.2	15.1	5.7	—

Basal width (mm)	Material	Description/Comment	Type	Citation
—	Monterey chert	Nearly complete	Small leaf-shaped	Jones et al. 2017
—	Monterey chert	Tip	Indeterminate	Jones et al. 2017
	Monterey chert	Tip	Indeterminate	Jones et al. 2017
—	Monterey chert	Base	Desert side-notched	Jones et al. 2017
—	Monterey chert	Tip	Indeterminate	Jones et al. 2017
—	Monterey chert	Base	Desert side-notched	Jones et al. 2017
—	Monterey chert	Complete	Contracting stemmed	Herein
12.1	Monterey chert	Complete, reworked	Contracting stemmed	Codding et al. 2013
13.2	Monterey chert	Base	Contracting stemmed	Codding et al. 2013
—	Monterey chert	End	Indeterminate	Codding et al. 2013
7.7	Monterey chert	Complete, reworked	Contracting stemmed	Codding et al. 2013
NA	Franciscan chert	Base	Contracting stemmed	Codding et al. 2013
—	Monterey chert	End	Indeterminate	Codding et al. 2013
—	Monterey chert	Tip	Indeterminate	Codding et al. 2013
5	Monterey chert	Base	Contracting stemmed	Codding et al. 2013
26.3*	Monterey chert	Complete	Concave base	Codding et al. 2013
28.6	Monterey chert	Base	Indeterminate	Codding et al. 2013
16.8	Franciscan chert	Base	Square stem?	Codding et al. 2013
25.6	Monterey chert	Complete	Large side-notched	Codding et al. 2013
—	Monterey chert	Midsection	Indeterminate arrow	Codding et al. 2013
—	Monterey chert	End	Indeterminate	Codding et al. 2013
—	Monterey chert	Tip	Indeterminate	Codding et al. 2013
—	Monterey chert	End	Indeterminate	Codding et al. 2013
4.5	Monterey chert	Complete	Contracting stemmed	Codding et al. 2013
—	Monterey chert	End	Indeterminate	Codding et al. 2013
10.1	Franciscan chert?	Base	Contracting stemmed?	Codding et al. 2013
—	Monterey chert	End	Indeterminate	Codding et al. 2013
—	Chert	Complete, reworked	Contracting stemmed	Hadick et al. 2012
—	Chert	Tip	Indeterminate	Hadick et al. 2012
—	Chert	Tip	Indeterminate	Hadick et al. 2012
—	Chert	Midsection	Indeterminate	Hadick et al. 2012
—	Chert	End	Indeterminate	Hadick et al. 2012
—	Chert	Tip	Indeterminate	Hadick et al. 2012

References Cited

All about Birds
2017   https://www.allaboutbirds.org/guide
        /search/. Accessed July 20, 2017.

Anderson, R. Scott, Ana Ejarque, Johnathan Rice,
Susan J. Smith, and Clayton G. Lebow
2015   Historic and Holocene Environmental
        Change in the San Antonio Creek Basin,
        Mid-coastal California. *Quaternary Research*
        83:273–286.

Anderson, R. Scott, and Roger D. Stillick
2013   800 Years of Vegetation Change, Fire, and
        Human Settlement in the Sierra Nevada,
        California. *The Holocene* 23:838–847.

Andrefsky, William, Jr.
1998   *Lithics*. Cambridge University Press,
        Cambridge, United Kingdom.

Andrews, Allen H., Ken W. Gobalet, and Terry L.
Jones
2003   Reliability Assessment of Season-of-Capture
        Determination from Archaeological
        Otoliths. *Bulletin of the Southern California
        Academy of Sciences* 100:66–78.

Antevs, Ernst
1948   Climatic Changes and Pre-White Man.
        University of Utah Bulletin 38:168–191.
1953   On Division of the Last 20,000 Years.
        *University of California Archaeological
        Survey Reports* 22:5–8.
1955   Geologic-Climatic Dating in the West.
        American Antiquity 20:317–335.

Applegate, Richard N.
1974   Chumash Placenames. *The Journal of
        California Anthropology* 1:186–205.
1975   An Index of Chumash Placenames. In
        Papers on the Chumash. San Luis Obispo
        County Archaeological Society Occasional
        Paper 9:21–46.

Arnold, Jeanne E.
1992   Complex Hunter-Gatherer-Fishers of
        Prehistoric California: Chiefs, Specialists,
        and Maritime Adaptations of the Channel
        Islands. *American Antiquity* 57:60–84.

Arnold, Jeanne E. (editor)
2001   *The Origins of a Pacific Coast Chiefdom: The
        Chumash of the Channel Islands*. University
        of Utah Press, Salt Lake City.
2004   *Foundations of Chumash Complexity*. Cotsen
        Institute of Archaeology, University of Cali-
        fornia, Los Angeles.

Bamforth, Douglas
1991   Technological Organization and Hunter-
        Gatherer Land Use. *American Antiquity*
        56:219–235.

Barlow, Kevin R., and Melissa Heck
2002   More on Acorn Eating during the Natu-
        fian: Expected Patterning in Diet and the
        Archaeological Record of Subsistence. In
        *Hunter-Gatherer Archaeobotany: Perspectives
        from the Northern Temperate Zone*, edited
        by Sarah L. R. Mason and Jon G. Hather,
        pp. 128–145. Taylor and Francis, New York.

Barron, John A., and David Bukry
2007   Development of the California Current
        during the Past 12,000 Years Based on
        Diatoms and Silicoflagellates. *Palaeo-
        geography, Palaeoclimatology, Palaeoecology*
        248:313–338.

Barter, Eloise
1988   *Statewide Resource Management Project:
        Montaña de Oro State Park*. Report on file,
        California Department of Parks and Rec-
        reation, Sacramento.

Basgall, Mark E.
1987   Resource Intensification among Hunter-
        Gatherers: Acorn Economies in Prehistoric
        California. *Research in Economic Anthropol-
        ogy* 9:21–52.

Bayham, Frank E.
1979   Factors Influencing the Archaic Pattern of
        Animal Utilization. *Kiva* 44:219–235.

Béarez, Philippe, Felipe Fuentes-Mucherl, Sandra
Rebolledo, Diego Salazar, and Laura Olguín
2016   Billfish Foraging along the Northern Coast
        of Chile during the Middle Holocene

(7400–5900 cal BP). *Journal of Anthropological Archaeology* 41:185–195.

Bell, Arran M.

2009   On the Validity of Archaeological Shellfish Metrics in Coastal California. Unpublished Master's thesis, Department of Anthropology, California State University, Chico.

Bennyhoff, James A., and Richard E. Hughes

1987   Shell Bead and Ornament Exchange Networks between California and the Western Great Basin. *Anthropological Papers of the American Museum of Natural History* 64:79–175.

Bernard, Julia L.

2001   The Origins of Open-Ocean and Large Species Fishing in the Chumash Region of Southern California. Unpublished Master's thesis, Department of Anthropology, University of California, Los Angeles.

Bertrando, Ethan

1997   *Cultural Resource Subsurface Evaluation (Phase 2) of the Powell Parcel (CA-SLO-214) APN: 038-711-010 (B. 1) EI Morro Avenue, Los Osos, CA.* Bertrando and Bertrando Research Consultants, San Luis Obispo, California. Prepared for Michael Powell, Los Osos, California. Copies available from California Historic Resources Information System, Central Coast Information Center, University of California, Santa Barbara.

2006   Hunter-Gatherers in the Morro Bay Watershed 3,650 Years Ago: Settlement, Subsistences, and Technology during an Archaeological Point in Time. *Proceedings of the Society for California Archaeology* 19:211–219.

Bertrando, Ethan, and Douglas Harro

1997   Correlations between Lithic Raw Material Quality and Availability and the Formation of Flaked Stone Tool Assemblages: Examples from the Chorro Valley, San Luis Obispo County. *Proceedings of the Society for California Archaeology* 10:123–130.

Bertrando, Ethan B., and Valerie A. Levulett (editors)

2004   Emerging from the Ice Age—Early Holocene Occupations on California's Central Coast: A Compilation of Research in Honor of Roberta S. Greenwood. San Luis Obispo County Archaeological Society Occasional Papers no. 17. San Luis Obispo.

Binford, Lewis W.

1980   Willow Smoke and Dogs' Tails: Hunter-Gatherer Settlement Systems and Archaeo-logical Site Formation. *American Antiquity* 45:4–20.

Bird, Douglas W., and Rebecca B. Bird

1997   Delayed Reciprocity and Tolerated Theft: The Behavioral Ecology of Food-Sharing Strategies. *Current Anthropology* 38:49–78.

2000   The Ethnoarchaeology of Juvenile Foragers: Shellfishing Strategies among Meriam Children. *Journal of Anthropological Archaeology* 19:461–476.

Bird, Douglas W., and James F. O'Connell

2006   Behavioral Ecology and Archaeology. *Journal of Archaeological Research* 14:143–188.

Blake, Michelle

2010   Drill Baby Drill: An Analysis of Late Period Chumash Microdrills from CA-SLO-214. Unpublished Master's thesis, Sonoma State University, Rohnert Park, California.

Bolton, Herbert E. (editor)

1930   *Anza's California Expeditions.* 5 volumes. University of California Press, Berkeley.

Boone, Christie M.

2012   Integrating Zooarchaeology and Modeling: Trans-Holocene Fishing in Monterey Bay, California. Unpublished PhD dissertation, Department of Anthropology, University of California, Santa Cruz.

Braje, Todd J.

2007   Geographic and Temporal Variability of Middle Holocene Red Abalone Middens on San Miguel Island, California. *Journal of California and Great Basin Anthropology* 27:153–164.

2016   *Shellfish for the Celestial Empire: The Rise and Fall of Commercial Abalone Fishing in California.* University of Utah Press, Salt Lake City.

Braje, Todd J., and Jon M. Erlandson

2016   California's Red Abalone (*Haliotis rufescens*) Middens: Comment on Glassow. *American Antiquity* 81:591–592.

Braje, Todd J., Torben C. Rick, and Jon M. Erlandson

2017   The Forest or the Trees: Interpreting Temporal Changes in California Mussel Shell Sizes. *Quaternary International* 427:243–245.

Breschini, Gary S., and Trudy Haversat

1980   *Preliminary Archaeological Report and Archaeological Management Recommendations for CA-MNT-170, on Pescadero Point, Monterey County, California.* Archaeological Consulting, Salinas, California. Copies available from Northwest Archaeological Information Center, Department of Anthropology, Sonoma State University, Rohnert Park, California.

1983   *A Cultural Resources Overview of the Coast and Coast-Valley Study Areas.* Archaeological Consulting, Salinas. Copies available from Bureau of Land Management, Bakersfield, California.

1985   *Archaeological Test Excavation at CA-SLO-10, Montaña de Oro State Park, San Luis Obispo County, California.* Archaeological Consulting, Salinas. Manuscript on file at the California Historic Resources Information System, Central Coast Information Center, University of California, Santa Barbara.

1988   *Archaeological Investigations at CA-SLO-7 and CA-SLO-8, Diablo Canyon, San Luis Obispo County, California.* Archives of California Prehistory 28. Coyote Press, Salinas.

1995   *Archaeological Evaluation of CA-MNT-234, at the Site of the Proposed Moss Landing Marine Laboratory, Moss Landing, Monterey County, California.* Archaeological Consulting, Salinas, California. Copies available from Northwest Archaeological Information Center, Sonoma State University, Rohnert Park, California.

2000   *Archaeological Radiocarbon Dating of a Portion of CA-MNT-103, Monterey, Monterey County, California.* Archaeological Consulting, Salinas, California. Copies available from Northwest Archaeological Information Center, Sonoma State University, Rohnert Park, California.

Bronk Ramsey, Christopher

2009   Bayesian Analysis of Radiocarbon Dates. *Radiocarbon* 51:337–360.

2013   OxCal version 4.2.4. University of Oxford Radiocarbon Accelerator Unit. Computer Program.

Broughton, Jack M., Michael D. Cannon, Frank E. Bayham, and David A. Byers

2011   Prey Body Size and Ranking in Zooarchaeology: Theory, Empirical Evidence, and Applications from the Northern Great Basin. *American Antiquity* 76:403–428.

Broughton, Jack M., E. P. Martin, Brian McEneaney, Thomas Wake, and Dwight. D. Simons

2015   Late Holocene Anthropogenic Depression of Sturgeon in San Francisco Bay, California. *Journal of California and Great Basin Anthropology* 35:3–27.

Brown, Alan K.

1967   The Aboriginal Population of the Santa

Barbara Channel. *University of California Archaeological Survey Reports* 69:1–99. Berkeley.

2001   *A Description of Distant Roads: Original Journals of the First Expedition into California, 1769–1770.* San Diego State University Press, San Diego, California.

Byers, David A., and Jack M. Broughton

2004   Holocene Environmental Change, Artiodactyl Abundances, and Human Hunting Strategies in the Great Basin. *American Antiquity* 69:235–256.

Calflora

2016   Distribution of *Pinus sabiniana* (Gray Pine) in California. Electronic document, http://www/calflora.org, accessed September 10, 2016.

Carpenter, Kimberley, William Hildebrandt, Deborah Jones, Rebecca Kellewan, Sharon Waechter, Mike Taggart, and Maggie Trumbly

2010   *Draft Report Historic Properties Management Plan for the Diablo Canyon Power Plant in San Luis Obispo County, California.* Far Western Anthropological Research Group, Davis, California. Copies available from Pacific Gas and Electric Company, Sacramento.

Carpenter, Tim, David Nicholson, and David W. Zeanah

2007   *Archaeological Evaluations of Twelve Prehistoric Properties on Camp San Luis Obispo and Camp Roberts, San Luis Obispo, California.* Archaeological Research Center, Institute of Archaeology and Cultural Studies, Department of Anthropology, California State University, Sacramento. Submitted to Military Department, California Army National Guard, Sacramento, California.

Cartier, Robert R.

1993   *The Scotts Valley Site: CA-SCR-177.* Santa Cruz Archaeological Society, Santa Cruz.

Casteel, Richard W.

1972   Some Biases in the Recovery of Archaeological Faunal Remains. *Proceedings of the Prehistoric Society* 38:382–388.

Chagnon, Napoleon A.

1970   Ecological and Adaptive Aspects of California Shell Money. *Annual Reports of the University of California Archaeological Survey* 12:1–25. University of California, Los Angeles.

Chaput, Michelle A., and Konrad Gajewski

2016   Radiocarbon Dates as Estimates of Ancient

Human Population Size. *Anthropocene* 15:3–12.

Charnov, Eric L., Gordon H. Orians, and Kim Hyatt
1976 Ecological Implications of Resource Depression. *American Naturalist* 110:247–259.

Chavez, Francisco P., John Ryan, Salvador E. Lluch-Cota, and Miguel Niquen
2003 From Anchovies to Sardines and Back: Multidecadal Change in the Pacific Ocean. *Science* 299:217–221.

Chipping, Dave H.
1987 *The Geology of San Luis Obispo County: A Brief Description and Field Guide.* Self-published, San Luis Obispo, California.

Codding, Brian F., and Douglas W. Bird
2015 Behavioral Ecology and the Future of Archaeological Science. *Journal of Archaeological Science* 56:9–20.

Codding, Brian F., and Terry L. Jones
2006 *The Middle–Late Transition on the Central California Coast: Archaeological Salvage at CA-SLO-9, Montaña de Oro State Park, San Luis Obispo County, California.* Manuscript on file at the California Historic Resources Information System, Central Coast Information Center, University of California, Santa Barbara.
2007 History and Behavioral Ecology during the Middle–Late Transition on the Central California Coast: Findings from the Coon Creek Site, CA-SLO-9, San Luis Obispo County. *Journal of California and Great Basin Anthropology* 27:23–49.
2010 Levels of Explanation in Behavioral Ecology: Understanding Seeming Paradoxical Behavior along the Central California Coast. *California Archaeology* 2:77–91.
2013 Environmental Productivity Predicts Colonization, Migration, and Demographic Patterns in Prehistoric California. *Proceedings of the National Academy of Science* 110:14569–14573.
2016 External Impacts on Internal Dynamics: Effects of Paleoclimatic and Demographic Variability on Acorn Exploitation along the Central California Coast. In *The Archaeology of Human-Environment Interactions*, edited by Daniel Contreras, pp. 195–210. Routledge, Oxford.

Codding, Brian F., Douglas W. Bird, and Terry L. Jones
2012 A Land of Work: Foraging Behavior and

Ecology. In *Contemporary Issues in California Archaeology*, edited by Terry L. Jones and Jennifer Perry, pp. 115–132. Left Coast Press, Walnut Creek, California.

Codding, Brian F., Rebecca B. Bird, and Douglas W. Bird
2011 Provisioning Offspring and Others: Risk–Energy Trade-offs and Gender Differences in Hunter–Gatherer Foraging Strategies. *Proceedings of the Royal Society of London B: Biological Sciences* 278:2502–2509.

Codding, Brian F., Terry L. Jones, and Judith F. Porcasi
2010 Explaining Prehistoric Variation in the Abundance of Large Prey: A Zooarchaeological Analysis of Deer and Rabbit Hunting along the Pecho Coast of Central California. *Journal of Anthropological Archaeology* 29:47–61.

Codding, Brian F., Amber M. Barton, Emily J. Hill, Elise Wheeler, Nathan Stevens, and Terry L. Jones
2009 *The Middle–Late Transition on the Central California Coast: Final Report on Salvage at CA-SLO-9, Montaña de Oro State Park, San Luis Obispo County, California.* Occasional Papers of the San Luis Obispo Archaeological Society no. 19.

Codding, Brian F., Terry L. Jones, Roshanne S. Bakhtiary, Samantha Law, Judith F. Porcasi, and Ken Gobalet
2013 *Archaeological Investigations at Tom's Pond (CA-SLO-1366/H), Diablo Canyon Lands, San Luis Obispo County, California: Draft Final Report of the 2011 Cal Poly Field School and Mitigation Program.* Submitted to Pacific Gas and Electric Company, Walnut Creek, California.

Cohen, Mark N.
1977 *The Food Crisis in Prehistory: Overpopulation and the Origin of Agriculture.* Yale University Press, New Haven.

Cole, Kenneth L., and Geng-Wu Liu
1994 Holocene Paleoecology of an Estuary on Santa Rosa Island, California. *Quaternary Research* 41:326–335.

Colligan, Kaely R., Adrian R. Whitaker, and William R. Hildebrandt
2015 Where the Pavement Ends: An Assessment of the Near Absence of *Haliotis rufescens* in the Archaeological Record on Alta California's North Coast. *California Archaeology* 7:33–57.

Cook, Edward R., Connie A. Woodhouse, C. Mark Eakin, David M. Meko, and David W. Stahle
2004   Long-Term Aridity Changes in the Western United States. *Science* 306:1015–1018.

Cook, Emma Frances
2016   Pitted Stones: An Experimental Analysis. Unpublished senior thesis, California Polytechnic State University, San Luis Obispo.

Cook, Emma, Terry L. Jones, and Brian F. Codding
2017   The Function of Pitted Stones: An Experimental Evaluation. *Journal of California and Great Basin Anthropology* 37:220–231.

Cooper, William Skinner
1967   *Coastal Dunes of California, Memoir 104.* The Geological Society of America, Boulder, Colorado.

Dallas, Herb, Jr.
1994   *Preliminary Results of Archaeological Testing at CA-SLO-10, at the Spooner Cove, in Montaña de Oro State Park.* Report on file, California Department of Parks and Recreation, Sacramento.

Dansgaard, W., and S. J. Johnsen
1993   Evidence for General Instability of Past Climate from a 250-kyr Ice-Core Record. *Nature* 364:218–220.

Davenport, Demorest, John R. Johnson, and Jan Timbrook
1993   The Chumash and the Swordfish. *Antiquity* 67:257–272.

Davis, Betty S.
1981   *Indian, Sea Otter and Shellfish Interrelationships.* Society for California Occasional Papers 3:33–41.

Davis, Owen K.
1999   Pollen Analysis of Tulare Lake, California: Great Basin-like Vegetation in Central California during the Full-Glacial and Early Holocene. *Review of Palaeobotany and Palynology* 107:249–257.

Davis, Owen K., and Michael J. Moratto
1988   Evidence for a Warm Dry Early Holocene in the Western Sierra Nevada of California: Pollen and Plant Macrofossil Analysis of Dinkey and Exchequer Meadows. *Madroño* 35:132–149.

Davis-King, Shelly
1991   *Archaeological Survey on Portions of the North Property Coastal Shelf, Diablo Canyon Nuclear Power Plant, San Luis Obispo County, California.* Submitted to Pacific Gas and Electric Company, San Francisco.

Davis-King, Shelly, and Scott Williams
1992   *Archaeological Survey on Portions of Diablo Canyon Nuclear Power Plant, North Property Coastal Shelf, San Luis Obispo County, California (Second Field Season).* Submitted to Pacific Gas and Electric Company, San Francisco.

Denardo, Carol, and R. Texier
2007   *National Register of Historic Places Nomination Form for the Rancho Canada de los Osos y Pecho y Islay Prehistoric Archaeological Site District, San Luis Obispo County, California.* Garcia and Associates. Copies available from Pacific Gas and Electric Company, Sacramento.

Dietz, Stephen A., and Thomas L. Jackson
1981   *Report of Archaeological Excavations at Nineteen Archaeological Sites for the Stage 1 Pacific Grove–Monterey Consolidation Project of the Regional Sewerage System.* Archaeological Consulting and Research Services, Santa Cruz. Copies available from Northwest Archaeological Information Center, Department of Anthropology, Sonoma State University, Rohnert Park, California.

Dills, Charles E.
1981   *Halcyon Bay: An Ancient Estuary.* Society for California Archaeology Occasional Papers 3: 43–48. California State University, Fullerton.

Engelhardt, Zephyrin
1963   *Mission San Luis Obispo in the Valley of the Bears.* W. T. Genns, Santa Barbara.

Erlandson, Jon M.
1991   Early Maritime Adaptations on the Northern Channel Islands. In *Hunter-Gatherers of Early Holocene Coastal California,* edited by Jon M. Erlandson and Roger H. Colten, pp. 101–111. Cotsen Institute of Archaeology, University of California, Los Angeles.

1994   *Early Hunter-Gatherers of the California Coast.* Plenum Press, New York.

2001   The Archaeology of Aquatic Adaptations: Paradigms for a New Millennium. *Journal of Archaeological Research* 9:287–350.

2013   Channel Island Amol Points: A Stemmed Paleocoastal Point Type from Santa Rosa Island, California. *California Archaeology* 5:105–122.

Erlandson, Jon M., and Kevin Bartoy
1995   Cabrillo, the Chumash, and Old World Diseases. *Journal of California and Great Basin Anthropology* 17:153–173.

1996   Protohistoric California: Paradise or Pandemic? *Proceedings of the Society for California Archaeology* 9:304–309.

Erlandson, Jon M., Todd J. Braje, Kristina M. Gill, and Michael H. Graham

2015   Ecology of the Kelp Highway: Did Marine Resources Facilitate Human Dispersal from Northeast Asia to the Americas? *The Journal of Island and Coastal Archaeology* 10:392–411.

Erlandson, Jon M., Douglas J. Kennett, B. Lynn Ingram, Dan. A. Guthrie, Donald P. Morris, Mark A. Tveskov, G. James West, and Philip L. Walker

1996   An Archaeological and Paleontological Chronology for Daisy Cave (CA-SMI-261), San Miguel Island, California. *Radiocarbon* 38:355–373.

Erlandson, Jon M., and Torben C. Rick

2002   Late Holocene Cultural Developments along the Santa Barbara Coast. In *Catalysts to Complexity: Late Holocene Societies of the California Coast*, edited by Jon M. Erlandson and Terry L. Jones, pp. 166–182. Cotsen Institute of Archaeology, University of California, Los Angeles.

Erlandson, Jon M., Torben C. Rick, Todd J. Braje, Molly Casperson, Brendan Culleton, Brian Fulfrost, Tracy Garcia, Daniel A. Guthrie, Nicholas Jew, Douglas J. Kennett, Madonna L. Moss, Leslie A. Reeder, Craig Skinner, Jack Watts, and Lauren Willis

2011   Paleoindian Seafaring, Maritime Technologies, and Coastal Foraging on California's Channel Islands. *Science* 331:1181–1185.

Erlandson, Jon M., Torben C. Rick, Todd J. Braje, A. Steinberg, and Rene L. Vellanoweth

2008   Human Impacts on Ancient Shellfish: A 10,000 Year Record from San Miguel Island, California. *Journal of Archaeological Science* 35:2144–2152.

Erlandson, Jon M., Torben C. Rick, Terry L. Jones, and Judy F. Porcasi

2007   One If by Land, Two If by Sea: Who Were the First Californians? In *California Prehistory: Colonization, Culture, and Complexity*, edited by T. L. Jones and K. A. Klar, pp. 53–62. Altimira, New York.

Erlandson, Jon M., and Michael A. Glassow (editors)

1997   *Archaeology of the California Coast during the Middle Holocene.* Cotsen Institute of Archaeology, University of California, Los Angeles.

Fages, Pedro

1972   [1775] *A Historical, Political, and Natural Description of California by Pedro Fages,* *Soldier of Spain*, translated by Herbert Ingram Priestley. University of California Press, Berkeley.

Farquhar, Jennifer M.

2003   *Organization of Flaked Stone Technology and Settlement Mobility on the South Central Coast of California: A Perspective from Diablo Canyon and Point Sal.* Unpublished Master's thesis, Department of Anthropology, California State University, Sacramento.

Farquhar, Jennifer M., Ryan T. Brady, Tom Garlinghouse, and John Ellison

2014   Draft Report Archaeological Assemblage Analysis and National Register of Historic Places Eligibility Determination for Three Locations at Camp San Luis Obispo: CA-SLO-534, CA-SLO-536, and CA-SLO-1839, San Luis Obispo County, California. On file, California Army National Guard, Camp San Luis Obispo, California.

Farris, Glenn

1994   Spanish Accounts of the Obispeño. In *Toward a Prehistory of Morro Bay: Phase II Archaeological Investigations for the Highway 41 Widening Project, San Luis Obispo County, California*, edited by Terry L. Jones, Kathleen Davis, Glen Farris, Steven D. Grantham, Teresa W. Fung, and Betty Rivers, pp. 11–14. Caltrans, San Luis Obispo. Copies available from the California Historic Resources Information System, Central Coast Information Center, University of California, Santa Barbara.

Far Western Anthropological Research Group

2016   *Archaeological Investigations for the Los Osos Wastewater Project, San Luis Obispo County, California.* Submitted to Department of Public Works, County of San Luis Obispo, San Luis Obispo, California. Copies available from Central Coast Information Center, University of California, Santa Barbara.

Fauvelle, Mikael

2011   Mobile Mounds: Asymmetrical Exchange and the Role of the Tomol in the Development of Chumash Complexity. *California Archaeology* 3:141–158.

2013   Evaluating Cross-Channel Exchange in the Santa Barbara Region: Experimental Data on Acorn Processing and Transport. *American Antiquity* 78:790–808.

Ferneau, Jennifer A.

1998   Late Holocene Shellfish Exploitation on the Northern San Luis Obispo Coast, California.

Unpublished Master's thesis, Department of Anthropology, Sonoma State University, Rohnert Park, California.

Fitch, John

1972 Fish Remains, Primarily Otoliths from CA-SLO-2, Diablo Canyon. In *9000 Years of Prehistory at Diablo Canyon, San Luis Obispo County, California*, edited by Roberta S. Greenwood, pp. 101–120. Occasional Paper no. 7, San Luis Obispo County Archaeological Society, San Luis Obispo, California.

Fitzgerald, Richard T.

1997 *Archaeological Data Recovery at the Salinas River Crossing Site, CA-SLO-1756, San Luis Obispo County, California*. Garcia and Associates, San Anselmo. Copies available from South Central Archaeological Information Center, Department of Anthropology, University of California, Santa Barbara.

2000 *Cross Creek: An Early Holocene/Millingstone Site*. California State Water Project, San Luis Obispo County Archaeological Society Coastal Branch Series Paper 12. San Luis Obispo, California.

2004 9000 Years of Prehistory and Beyond: A Survey of the Early Holocene Sites of the Central Coast of California Discovered since Diablo Canyon. In *Emerging from the Ice Age: Early Holocene Occupations on the California Central Coast, A Compilation of Research in Honor of Roberta Greenwood*, edited by E. Bertrando and V. A. Levulett, pp. 5–16. San Luis Obispo County Archaeological Society.

Fitzgerald, Richard T., and Terry L. Jones

1999 The Milling Stone Horizon Revisited: New Perspectives from Northern and Central California. *Journal of California and Great Basin Anthropology* 21:65–93.

2003 On the Weight of the Evidence from Cross Creek: A Reply to Turner. *American Antiquity* 68:396–399.

Fitzgerald, Richard T., Terry L. Jones, and Adella Schroth

2005 Ancient Long Distance Trade in Western North America: New AMS Radiocarbon Dates from Southern California. *Journal of Archaeological Science* 32:423–434.

Flores Fernandez, Carola

2017 Importance of Small-Scale Paleo-oceanographic Conditions to Interpret Changes in Size of California Mussel (*Mytilus californianus*), Late Holocene, Santa Cruz Island, California. *Quaternary International* 427:137–150.

Gamble, Lynn

2008 *The Chumash World at European Contact: Power, Trade, and Feasting among Complex Hunter-Gatherers*. University of California Press, Berkeley.

Gause, Seana L. S.

2002 Ecology and Prey Characteristics of Fish Species Found in the Vicinity of San Simeon Reef. In *Prehistory at San Simeon Reef: Archaeological Data Recovery at CA-SLO-179 and -267, San Luis Obispo County, California*, edited by T. L. Jones and J. A. Ferneau, pp. 409–427. San Luis Obispo County Archaeological Society Occasional Papers no. 16.

Geiger, Maynard, and Clement C. Meighan

1976 *As the Padres Saw Them: California Indian Life and Customs as Reported by the Franciscan Missionaries, 1813–1815*. Santa Barbara Mission Archive-Library, Santa Barbara.

Gerdes, Gene L., and Bruce M. Browning

1974 *Natural Resources of Morro Bay: Their Status and Future*. Coastal Wetland Series no. 8. State of California Department of Fish and Game.

Giambastiani, Mark A.

2004 Prehistoric Obsidian Use on the Volcanic Tableland and Its Implications for Settlement Patterns and Technological Change in the Western Great Basin. Unpublished PhD dissertation, Department of Anthropology, University of California, Davis.

Gibson, Robert O.

1983 Ethnography of the Salinan People: A Systems Approach. Unpublished Master's thesis, Department of Anthropology, California State University, Hayward.

1988 Preliminary Results of Shell Bead Analysis for CA-SLO-877, Cayucos, San Luis Obispo County, California. *Archives of California Prehistory* 23:65–75.

1991 *The Chumash*. Chelsea House Publishers. New York.

Gibson, Robert O., and Henry C. Koerper

2000 AMS Radiocarbon Dating of Shell Beads and Ornaments from CA-ORA-378. *Journal of California and Great Basin Anthropology* 20:342–352.

Gifford, Edward W.

1940 Californian Bone Artifacts. *University of California Anthropological Records* 3:153–237.

Gifford-Gonzalez, D., David B. Damrosch, Debra R. Damrosch, John Pryor, and Robert L. Thunen

1985   The Third Dimension in Site Structure: An Experiment in Trampling and Vertical Dispersal. *American Antiquity* 50:803–818.

Gifford-Gonzalez, Diane, Seth D. Newsome, Paul L. Koch, Thomas P. Guilderson, Josh J. Snodgrass, and Rob K. Burton

2005   Archaeofaunal Insights on Pinniped-Human Interactions in the Northeastern Pacific. In *The Exploitation and Cultural Importance of Marine Mammals, 9th ICAZ Conference*, edited by Gregory Monks, pp. 19–38. Vol. 7. Oxbow Books, Oxford.

Gilliland, L. E.

1985   Proximate Analysis and Mineral Composition of Traditional California Native Foods. Unpublished Master's thesis, Department of Nutrition Science, University of California, Davis.

Gilreath, Amy

1989   Flaked Stone Analysis. In *Prehistory of the Sacramento River Canyon, Shasta County, California*, by M. E. Basgall and W. R. Hildebrandt, pp. A1–A85. Center for Archaeological Research at Davis Publications no. 9.

Glassow, Michael A.

1979   An Evaluation of Models of Ineseño Chumash Subsistence and Economics. *Journal of California and Great Basin Anthropology* 1:155–161.

1993a   Changes in Subsistence on Marine Resources through 7,000 Years of Prehistory on Santa Cruz Island. In *Archaeology on the Northern Channel Islands of California*, edited by Michael A. Glassow, pp. 75–90. Archives of California Prehistory 34. Coyote Press, Salinas.

1993b   The Occurrence of Red Abalone Shells in Northern Channel Island Archaeological Middens. In *Third California Island Symposium, Recent Advances in Research on the California Islands*, edited by F. G. Hochberg, pp. 567–576. Santa Barbara Museum of Natural History, Santa Barbara, California.

1996   *Purisimeno Chumash Prehistory Maritime Adaptations along the Southern California Coast*. Harcourt Brace College Publishers, Fort Worth, Texas.

1997   Middle Holocene Cultural Development in the Central Santa Barbara Channel Region. In *The Archaeology of the California Coast during the Middle Holocene*, edited by

Jon M. Erlandson and Michael A. Glassow, pp. 73–90. Cotsen Institute of Archaeology, University of California, Los Angeles.

2015   Chronology of Red Abalone Middens on Santa Cruz Island, California, and Evidence for Subsistence and Settlement Change. *American Antiquity* 80:745–759.

2016   Reply to Braje and Erlandson. *American Antiquity* 81:593–594.

Glassow, Michael A., Heather B. Thakar, and Douglas J. Kennett

2012   Red Abalone Collecting and Marine Water Temperature during the Middle Holocene Occupation of Santa Cruz Island, California. *Journal of Archaeological Science* 39:2574–2582.

Glassow, Michael A., Larry R. Wilcoxon, and Jon M. Erlandson

1988   Cultural and Environmental Change during the Early Period of Santa Barbara Channel Prehistory. In *The Archaeology of Prehistoric Coastlines*, edited by Geoffrey Bailey and John Parkington, pp. 64–77. Cambridge University Press, Cambridge.

Gobalet, Kenneth W.

2001   A Critique of Faunal Analysis: Inconsistency among Experts in Blind Tests. *Journal of Archaeological Science* 28:377–386.

Golla, Victor

2011   *California Indian Languages*. University of California Press, Berkeley.

Gordon, Elizabeth A.

1993   Screen Size and Differential Faunal Recovery: A Hawaiian Example. *Journal of Field Archaeology* 20:453–460.

Grant, Campbell

1978   Chumash Introduction. In *California*, edited by R. F. Heizer, pp. 505–508. Handbook of California Indians, Vol. 8, W. C. Sturtevant, general editor. Smithsonian Institution, Washington, DC.

Graumlich, Lisa J.

1993   A 1000-Year Record of Temperature and Precipitation in the Sierra Nevada. *Quaternary Research* 39:249–255.

Green, Kate Erickson

2016   *An Archaeological Study of the Pecho Creek Adobe Site, San Luis Obispo County, California*. Report on file, Pacific Gas and Electric Company, Sacramento.

Greenwood, Roberta S.

1972   *9000 Years of Prehistory at Diablo Canyon, San Luis Obispo County, California*. San

Luis Obispo County Archaeological Society Occasional Papers no. 7.

1978a Obispeño and Purisimeño Chumash. In *California*, edited by R. F. Heizer, pp. 520–523. Handbook of California Indians, Vol. 8, W. C. Sturtevant, general editor. Smithsonian Institution, Washington, DC.

1978b *Archaeological Assessment of CA-SLO-2, Diablo Canyon, San Luis Obispo County.* Report prepared for Pacific Gas and Electric Company, San Francisco, California.

2004 Diablo Canyon Revisited. In *Emerging from the Ice Age: Early Holocene Occupations on the Central California Coast*, edited by Ethan Betrando and Valerie A. Levulett, pp. 1–4. San Luis Obispo County Archaeological Society Occasional Papers no. 17.

Gremillion, Kristen J.
2002 Foraging Theory and Hypothesis Testing in Archaeology: An Exploration of Methodological Problems and Solutions. *Journal of Anthropological Archaeology* 21:142–164.

2004 Seed Processing and the Origins of Food Production in Eastern North America. *American Antiquity* 69:215–233.

Griffin, James R., and William B. Critchfield
1976 The Distribution of Forest Trees in California. USDA Forest Service Research Paper PSW – 82/1972. Berkeley, California.

Groza, Randy. G.
2002 An AMS Chronology for Central California *Olivella* Shell Beads. Unpublished Master's thesis, Department of Anthropology, California State University, San Francisco.

Groza, Randy, Jeffrey Rosenthal, Jon Southon, and Randy T. Milliken
2011 A Refined Shell Bead Chronology for Central California. *Journal of California and Great Basin Anthropology* 31:135–154.

Hadick, Kacey, Terry L. Jones, Erica Cerles, Danielle Krauss, Samantha Kuri, Lauren May, Robbie Munoz, and Morgan Roth
2012 *Final Report on the Cal Poly 2009 Archaeological Field Class Investigation at CA-SLO-1370/H, Point Buchon, San Luis Obispo County, California.* Report prepared for Pacific Gas and Electric Company, Walnut Creek. Copies available from the California Historic Resources Information System, Central Coast Information Center, University of California, Santa Barbara.

Hale, Micah J.
2001 Technological Organization of the Milling-stone Patterns in Southern California. Unpublished Master's thesis, California State University, Sacramento.

Hall, Clarence A.
1973 Geology of the Arroyo Grande 15-Minute Quadrangle, San Luis Obispo County, California. Map Sheet 24, California Division of Mines and Geology.

Harrison, William M., and Edith S. Harrison
1966 An Archaeological Sequence for the Hunting People of Santa Barbara, California. In *UCLA Archaeological Survey Annual Report* 8, pp. 1–89. Department of Anthropology, University of California, Los Angeles.

Haversat, Trudy, and Gary S. Breschini
2014 AMS Radiocarbon Dating of *Olivella* G1 Beads in Central California. *California Archaeology* 6:304–308.

Headlee, Larry A.
1966 Geology of the Coastal Portion of the San Luis Range, San Luis Obispo County, California. Unpublished Master's thesis, Department of Geology, University of Southern California.

Heizer, Robert F. (editor)
1952 California Indians Linguistic Records: The Mission Indian Vocabularies of H. W. Henshaw. *Anthropological Records* 15:1–84. University of California, Berkeley.

1955 California Indians Linguistic Records: The Mission Indian Vocabularies of Alphonse Pinart. *Anthropological Records* 15:1–84. University of California, Berkeley.

1975 Chumash Place Names Lists: Compilations by A. L. Kroeber, C. Hart Merriam, and H. W. Henshaw. Archaeological Research Facility, Department of Anthropology, Berkeley, California.

Heusser, Linda E.
1978 Pollen in the Santa Barbara Basin, California: A 12,000 Year Record. *Geological Society of America Bulletin* 89:673–678.

1995 Pollen Stratigraphy and Paleoecologic Interpretation of the 160-K.Y., edited by J. P. Kennett, J. G. Balduaf, and M. Lyle. Records from Santa Barbara Basin, Hole 893A. *Proceedings of the Ocean Drilling Program, Scientific Results*, 146:265–277.

1998 Direct Correlation of Millennial-Scale Changes in Western North American Vegetation and Climate with Changes in the California Current System over the Past ~60 kyr. *Paleoceanography* 13:252–262.

Heusser, Linda E., and F. Sirocko
1997 Millennial Pulsing of Environmental Change in Southern California from the Past 24 k.y.: A Record of Indo-Pacific ENSO events? *Geology* 25:243–246.

Hildebrandt, William R.
2004 *Xonxon'ata, in the Tall Oaks: Archaeology and Ethnohistory of a Chumash Village in the Santa Ynez Valley.* Santa Barbara Museum of Natural History Contributions in Anthropology no. 2.

Hildebrandt, William R., and Terry L. Jones
1992 Evolution of Marine Mammal Hunting: A View from the California and Oregon Coasts. *Journal of Anthropological Archaeology* 11:360–401.

Hildebrandt, William R., and Kelly R. McGuire
2003 Large Game Hunting, Gender-Differentiated Work Organization and the Role of Evolutionary Ecology in California and Great Basin Prehistory. *American Antiquity* 68: 790–792.
2012 A Land of Prestige. In *Contemporary Issues in California Archaeology*, edited by Terry L. Jones and Jennifer Perry, pp. 133–151. Left Coast Press, Walnut Creek, California.

Hildebrandt, William R., Kelly R. McGuire, and Jeffrey S. Rosenthal
2010 Human Behavioral Ecology and Historical Contingency: A Comment on the Diablo Canyon Archaeological Record. *American Antiquity* 75:679–688.

Holson, John
1986 *Archaeological Resources Located on Parcel P, Diablo Canyon, San Luis Obispo County, California.* Report prepared for Pacific Gas and Electric Company, Walnut Creek, California. Copies available from the California Historic Resources Information System, Central Coast Information Center, University of California, Santa Barbara.

Hoover, Robert L.
1975 *Notes on Northern Chumash Ecology and Settlement Patterns.* Robert E. Schenk Archives of California Archaeology Paper no. 75, San Francisco State University.

Hoover, Robert L., and William B. Sawyer
1977 *Los Osos Junior High School Site 4-SLO-214.* San Luis Obispo County Archaeological Society Occasional Papers no. 11.

Hubbs, Carl L.
1967 A Discussion of the Geochronology and Archaeology of the California Islands. In *Proceedings of the Symposium on the Biology of the California Islands*, edited by Ralph N. Philbrick, pp. 337–342. Santa Barbara Botanic Gardens, Santa Barbara.

Hudson, Travis, and Thomas C. Blackburn
1979 *The Material Culture of the Chumash Interaction Sphere.* Vol. 1, *Food Procurement and Transportation.* Ballena Press and the Santa Barbara Museum of Natural History, Los Altos, California.
1983 *The Material Culture of the Chumash Interaction Sphere.* Vol. 2, *Food Preparation and Shelter.* Ballena Press, Palo Alto, California.
1985 *The Material Culture of the Chumash Interaction Sphere.* Vol. 3, *Clothing, Ornamentation, and Grooming.* Ballena Press, Palo Alto, California.
1986 *The Material Culture of the Chumash Interaction Sphere.* Vol. 4, *Ceremonial Paraphernalia, Games, and Amusements.* Ballena Press, Palo Alto, California.
1987 *The Material Culture of the Chumash Interaction Sphere.* Vol. 5, *Manufacturing Processes, Metrology, and Trade.* Ballena Press, Palo Alto, California.

Ingram, B. Lynn, and John R. Southon
1996 Reservoir Ages in Eastern Pacific Coastal and Estuarine Waters. *Radiocarbon* 38:573–582.

James, Steven R.
1997 Methodological Issues Concerning Screen Size Recovery Rates and Their Effects on Archaeofaunal Interpretations. *Journal of Archaeological Science* 24:385–397.

Jameson, Everett Williams, Jr., and Hans J. Peeters
1988 *California Mammals.* University of California Press, Berkeley.

Jazwa, Christopher S., Douglas J. Kennett, and Bruce Winterhalder
2013 The Ideal Free Distribution and Settlement History at Old Ranch Canyon, Santa Rosa Island. In *California's Channel Islands: The Archaeology of Human-Environment Interactions*, edited by Christopher S. Jazwa and Jennifer E. Perry, pp. 75–96. University of Utah Press, Salt Lake City.

Jochim, Michael A.
1988 Optimal Foraging and the Division of Labor. *American Anthropologist* 90:130–135.

Johnson, John R., Tomas W. Stafford Jr., H. O. Ajie, and Don P. Morris
2002 Arlington Springs Revisited. *Proceedings of the 5th California Islands Symposium*, edited by D. R. Browne, K. L. Mitchell, and

H. W. Chaney, pp. 541–545. Santa Barbara Museum of Natural History, Santa Barbara, California.

Jones, Debbie A.

2012   *Archaeological Monitoring and Excavation for Water and Sewer Upgrades to the San Luis Bay Inn at CA-SLO-56, Avila Beach, San Luis Obispo County, California.* Copies available from the California Historic Resources Information System, Central Coast Information Center, University of California, Santa Barbara.

Jones, Debbie A., Patricia A. Mikkelsen, and William R. Hildebrandt

2004   Prehistoric Occupations on Ancient Halcyon Bay/Estuary: Excavation Results from CA-SLO-832, and -1420. In *Emerging from the Ice Age: Early Holocene Occupations on the California Central Coast*, edited by Ethan Betrando and Valerie A. Levulett, pp. 71–80. San Luis Obispo County Archaeological Society Occasional Papers no. 17.

Jones, Debbie A., D. Craig Young, and William R. Hildebrandt

2002   *Prehistoric Occupations on Ancient Halcyon Bay/Estuary: Excavations at Sites CA-SLO-832 and -1420, Pismo Beach, California.* San Luis Obispo County Archaeological Society Occasional Papers no. 15.

Jones, Terry L.

1992   Settlement Trends along the California Coast. In *Essays on the Prehistory of Maritime California*, edited by Terry L. Jones, pp. 1–37. Center for Archaeological Research at Davis, Publication no. 10. University of California, Davis.

1993   Big Sur: A Keystone in Central California Culture History. *Pacific Coast Archaeological Society Quarterly* 29(1):1–78.

1996   Mortars, Pestles, and Division of Labor in Prehistoric California: A View from Big Sur. *American Antiquity* 61:243–264.

2003   Prehistoric Human Ecology of the Big Sur Coast, California. *Contributions of the University of California Archaeological Research Facility* no. 61. Berkeley.

Jones, Terry L., and Brian F. Codding

2010   Historical Contingencies, Issues of Scale, and Flightless Hypotheses: A Response to Hildebrandt et al. *American Antiquity* 75:689–699.

2011   Sampling Issues in Evaluations of Diet and Diversity: Lessons from Diablo Canyon.

In *Exploring Methods of Faunal Analysis: Perspectives from California Archaeology*, edited by Michael A. Glassow and Terry L. Joslin, pp. 187–198. Cotsen Institute Press, University of California, Los Angeles.

Jones, Terry L., and Jennifer A. Ferneau

2002   *Prehistory at San Simeon Reef: Archaeological Data Recovery at CA-SLO-179 and -267, San Luis Obispo County, California.* San Luis Obispo County Archaeological Society Occasional Papers no. 16.

Jones, Terry L., Richard T. Fitzgerald, Douglas J. Kennett, Charles H. Miksicek, John L. Fagan, John Sharp, and Jon M. Erlandson

2002   The Cross Creek Site (CA-SLO-1797) and Its Implications for New World Colonization. *American Antiquity* 67:213–230.

Jones, Terry L., and Jefferson W. Haney

1997   *Archaeological Evaluation of CA-MNT-521, Fort Hunter Liggett, Monterey County, California.* Garcia and Associates, San Anselmo, California. Copies available from Northwest Archaeological Information Center, Department of Anthropology, Sonoma State University, Rohnert Park, California.

Jones, Terry L., and Kathryn A. Klar

2005   Diffusionism Reconsidered: Linguistic and Archaeological Evidence for Prehistoric Polynesian Contact with Southern California. *American Antiquity* 70:457–484.

2012   A Land Visited: Reviewing the Case for Polynesian Contact in Southern California. In *Contemporary Issues in California Archaeology*, edited by Terry L. Jones and Jennifer Perry, pp. 217–235. Left Coast Press, Walnut Creek, California.

Jones, Terry L., and Jennifer R. Richman

1995   On Mussels: *Mytilus californianus* as a Prehistoric Resource. *North American Archaeologist* 16:33–58.

Jones, Terry L., and Georgie Waugh

1995   *Central California Coastal Prehistory: A View from Little Pico Creek.* Cotsen Institute of Archaeology, University of California, Los Angeles.

Jones, Terry L., David Knight, and Brian F. Codding

2015   *Archaeological Investigations at CA-SLO-5, Diablo Canyon Lands, San Luis Obispo County, California: Final Report of the 2013 Cal Poly Field School and Mitigation Program.* Report prepared for Pacific Gas and Electric Company, Walnut Creek. Copies available from the California Historic

Resources Information System, Central
Coast Information Center, University of
California, Santa Barbara.

Jones, Terry L., Deborah A. Jones, Kacey Hadick,
Kenneth W. Gobalet, Judith Porcasi, and William R.
Hildebrandt

2017   The Morro Bay Fauna: Evidence for a
        Medieval Drought Refugium on the Central
        California Coast. *American Antiquity*
        82:203–222.

Jones, Terry L., Gary Brown, L. Mark Raab, Janet
McVickar, Geoff Spaulding, Douglas J. Kennett,
Andrew York, and Philip L. Walker

1999   Environmental Imperatives Reconsidered:
        Demographic Crises in Western North
        America during the Medieval Climatic
        Anomaly. *Current Anthropology* 40:137–156.

Jones, Terry L., Kathleen Davis, Glenn Farris,
Steven D. Grantham, Teresa W. Fung, and Betty J.
Rivers

1994   *Toward a Prehistory of Morro Bay: Phase II
        Archaeological Investigations for the Highway
        41 Widening Project, San Luis Obispo County,
        California.* On file, California Department of
        Transportation, San Luis Obispo, California.

Jones, Terry. L., Richard T. Fitzgerald, and Judy F.
Porcasi

2009   The Cross Creek–Diablo Canyon Complex
        of South Central California: Mid-latitude
        Pacific Foragers at the Pleistocene-Holocene
        Boundary. *Journal of North Pacific Prehistory*
        2:169–202.

Jones, Terry L., Kenneth W. Gobalet, Patricia
Mikkelsen, Kacey Hadick, William R. Hildebrandt,
and Deborah A. Jones

2016   Prehistoric Fisheries of Morro Bay, San
        Luis Obispo County, California. *Journal of
        California and Great Basin Anthropology*
        36:119–146.

Jones, Terry L., Judy F. Porcasi, Jon M. Erlandson,
Herb Dallas Jr., Thomas A. Wake, and Rae
Schwaderer

2008a   The Protracted Holocene Extinction of
        California's Flightless Sea Duck (*Chendytes
        lawi*) and Its Implications for the Pleisto-
        cene Overkill Hypothesis. *Proceedings of the
        National Academy of Science* 105:4105–4108.

Jones, Terry L., Judith F. Porcasi, Jereme Gaeta, and
Brian F. Codding

2008b   The Diablo Canyon Fauna: A Coarse-
        Grained Record of Trans-Holocene Foraging
        from the Central California Mainland Coast.
        American Antiquity 73:289–316.

Jones, Terry L., Judy F. Porcasi, Kenneth W. Gobalet,
and Leroy T. Laurie

2004   CA-SLO-215, A Late Milling Stone Site
        at Morro Bay, San Luis Obispo County,
        California. In *Out of the Ice Age: Papers
        in Honor of Roberta Greenwood*, edited by
        E. Bertrando and V. Levulett, pp. 57–70. San
        Luis Obispo County Archaeological Society
        Occasional Papers no. 17.

Jones, Terry L., Douglas J. Kennett, James A.
Kennett, and Brian F. Codding

2008   Seasonal Stability in Late Holocene Shellfish
        Harvesting on the Central California Coast.
        Journal of Archaeological Science 35:2286–
        2294.

Jones, Terry L., Brendan J. Culleton, Shawn Larson,
Sarah Mellinger, and Judith F. Porcasi

2011   Toward a Prehistory of the Southern Sea
        Otter (*Enhydra lutris nereis*). In *Human and
        Marine Ecosystems: Archaeology and Histori-
        cal Ecology of Northeastern Pacific Seals, Sea
        Lions, and Sea Otters*, edited by T. Rick and
        T. Braje, pp. 243–272. University of Cali-
        fornia Press, Berkeley.

Jones, Terry L., Sebastian C. Garza, Judith F. Porcasi,
and Jereme W. Gaeta

2009   Another Trans-Holocene Sequence from
        Diablo Canyon: New Faunal and Radio-
        carbon Findings from CA-SLO-585, San
        Luis Obispo County, California. *Journal of
        California and Great Basin Anthropology*
        29:19–31.

Jones, Terry L., Nathan E. Stevens, Debbie A. Jones,
Richard T. Fitzgerald and Mark G. Hylkema

2007   The Central Coast: A Midlatitude Milieu. In
        *California Prehistory: Colonization, Culture,
        and Complexity*, edited by T. L. Jones and
        K. A. Klar, pp 125–148. AltaMira Press,
        New York.

Jones, Terry L., Brian F. Codding, Emma Cook,
Kelly Fischer, Kaya Wiggins, Madison Hames, Tori
Mau, Marley Ochoifeoma, Stephen Page, Shalini
Quattlebaum, Lucy Simpson, Jack Webb, and Emma
Wright

2017   *Archaeological Investigations at the Chu-
        mash Village of Tstyiwi: Final Report on the
        2015 Cal Poly Field School at CA-SLO-51/H,
        PG&E Diablo Canyon South Ranch, San Luis
        Obispo County, California.* San Luis Obispo
        County Archaeological Society Occasional
        Papers no. 21.

Joslin, Terry L.

2006   Late Prehistoric Coastal Adaptations along

the San Simeon Reef, San Luis Obispo County, California. Unpublished Master's thesis, Department of Anthropology, University of California, Santa Barbara.

2010   Middle and Late Holocene Hunter-Gather Adaptations to Coastal Ecosystems along the southern San Simeon Reef, California. Unpublished PhD dissertation, Department of Anthropology, University of California, Santa Barbara.

Karklins, Karlis
2012   Guide to the Description and Classification of Glass Beads Found in the Americas. *Journal of the Society of Bead Researchers* 24:62–90.

Kelly, Robert
1983   Hunter-Gather Mobility Strategies. *Journal of Anthropological Research* 39:277–306.

1988   The Three Sides of a Biface. *American Antiquity* 53:717–734.

Kelly, Robert L., Todd A. Surovell, Bryan N. Shuman, and Geoffrey M. Smith
2013   A Continuous Climatic Impact on Holocene Human Population in the Rocky Mountains. *Proceedings of the National Academy of Sciences* 110:443–447.

Kennedy, Michael A.
2005   An Investigation of Hunter-Gatherer Shellfish Foraging Practices: Archaeological and Geochemical Evidence from Bodega Bay, California. Unpublished PhD dissertation, Department of Anthropology, University of California.

Kennett, Douglas J.
2005   *The Island Chumash: Behavioral Ecology of a Maritime Society*. University of California Press, Berkeley.

Kennett, Douglas J., and James P. Kennett
2000   Competitive and Cooperative Responses to Climate Instability in Coastal Southern California. *American Antiquity* 65:379–395.

Kennett, Douglas J., James P. Kennett, Jon M. Erlandson, and Kevin G. Cannariato
2007   Human Responses to Middle Holocene Climate Change on California's Channel Islands. *Quaternary Science Reviews* 26: 351–367.

Kennett, James P., and B. Lynn Ingram
1995   A 20,000-Year Record of Ocean Circulation and Climate Change from the Santa Barbara Basin. *Nature* 377:510–514.

Kidd, Kenneth E., and Martha A. Kidd
1970   *A Classification System for Glass Beads for the Use of Field Archaeologists*. Canadian Historic Sites Occasional Papers in Archaeology and History no. 1. National Historic Sites Service, Ottawa, Canada.

King, Chester D.
1969   Approximate 1760 Chumash Village Locations and Populations (Map). *Annual Reports of the University of California Archaeological Survey* 11:3. Los Angeles.

1971   Chumash Intervillage Economic Exchange. *The Indian Historian* 4:30–43.

1975   The Names and Locations of Historic Chumash Villages, assembled by Thomas Blackburn. *Journal of California Anthropology* 2:171–179.

1976   Chumash Intervillage Economic Exchange. In *Native Californians: A Theoretical Retrospective*, edited by Lowell John Bean and Thomas C. Blackburn, pp. 289–318. Ballena Press, Ramona, California.

1978   Protohistoric and Historic Archaeology. In *California*, edited by R. F. Heizer, pp. 58–68. Handbook of California Indians, Vol. 8, W. C. Sturtevant, general editor. Smithsonian Institution, Washington, DC.

1982   The Evolution of Chumash Society: A Comparative Study of Artifacts Used in Social System Maintenance in the Santa Barbara Channel Region before AD 1804. Unpublished PhD dissertation, Department of Anthropology, University of California, Davis.

1990   *Evolution of Chumash Society: A Comparative Study of Artifacts Used for Social System Maintenance in the Santa Barbara Channel Region before AD 1804*. Garland Publishing, New York.

King, Thomas F.
1970   *Avila Beach: Descriptive Data and Hypotheses from the Excavation of 1929*. Archives of California Archaeology no. 1. Society for California Archaeology, San Francisco.

King, Jerome H.
2000   Re-Examining Coso Obsidian Hydration Rates. Paper presented at the 2000 meeting of the Society for California Archaeology, Riverside, California.

Klar, Kathryn
1975   Pismo and Nipomo: Two Northern Chumash Placenames. *Names* 23:26–30.

1977a   Obispeno (Northern Chumash) Placenames from the John P. Harrington Notes. San Luis Obispo County Archaeological Society Occasional Paper 11:51–54.

1977b Topics in Historical Chumash Grammmar. Unpublished PhD dissertation, Department of Linguistics, University of California, Berkeley.

1991 Precious beyond the Power of Money to Buy, John P. Harington's Fieldwork with Rosario Cooper. *Anthropological Linguistics* 33:379–391.

2002 The Island Chumash Language: Implications for Interdisciplinary Work. In *Proceedings of the Fifth California Islands Symposium: 29 March to 1 April, 1999*, edited by David R. Browne, Kathryn L. Mitchell, and Henry W. Chaney, pp. 654–658. Santa Barbara Museum of Natural History.

Klar, Kathryn A., and Terry L. Jones

2005 Linguistic Evidence for a Prehistoric Polynesia–Southern California Contact Event. *Anthropological Linguistics* 47:369–400.

Klein, Richard G., and Teresa E. Steele

2013 Archaeological Shellfish Size and Later Human Evolution in Africa. *Proceedings of the National Academy of Science* 110: 10910–10915.

Kowta, Mark

1969 *The Sayles Complex: A Late Milling Stone Assemblage from Cajon Pass and the Ecological Implications of Its Scraper Planes.* University of California Publications in Anthropology 6. University of California Press, Berkeley.

Krieger, Daniel E.

1990 *Looking Backward into the Middle Kingdom: San Luis Obispo County.* Nature Books, San Luis Obispo, California.

Kroeber, Alfred L.

1925 *Handbook of the Indians of California.* Smithsonian Institution, Bureau of American Ethnology Bulletin no. 78. Reprinted (1976) Dover Publications, New York.

Kuchler, A. Will

1977 The Map of the Natural Vegetation of California. Appendix of *Terrestrial Vegetation of California.* California Native Plant Society Special Publication no. 9. Sacramento.

Landberg, Leif C. W.

1965 *The Chumash Indians of Southern California.* Southwest Museum Papers no. 19. Southwest Museum, Los Angeles.

Langenwalter, Paul E., Brenda Bowser, and Richard W. Huddleston

1988 Appendix I Vertebrate Animal Remains from CA-SLO-7 and CA-SLO-8, Diablo Canyon, San Luis Obispo County, California. In *Archaeological Investigations at CA-SLO-7 and CA-SLO-8, Diablo Canyon, San Luis Obispo County, California*, edited by Gary S. Breschini and Trudy Haversat, pp. 65–82. *Archives of California Prehistory* 28. Coyote Press, Salinas.

Langenwalter, Paul E., and Richard W. Huddleson

1991 Vertebrate Remains from CA-MNT-129, A Late Period Coastal Abalone Processing Site on the Monterey Peninsula. *Archives of California Prehistory* 33:45–60.

Laurie, Leroy, and Andrew Pulcheon

2012 *Archaeological Monitoring and Data Recovery at CA-SLO-14 for the Broderson Avenue Waterline Installation Project, Los Osos, San Luis Obispo County, California.* LSA Associates, Inc., San Luis Obispo. Prepared for Golden State Water Company, Los Osos, California.

Lebow, Clayton G., Douglas R. Harro, and Rebecca L. McKim

2016 *The Archaeology and Rock Art of Swordfish Cave.* University of Utah Press, Salt Lake City.

Lebow, Clayton G., Rebecca L. McKim, Douglas R. Harro, Ann M. Munns, and Carole Denardo

2007 *Littoral Adaptations throughout the Holocene: Archaeological Investigations at the Honda Beach Site (CA-SBA-530).* Manuscript on file at the California Historic Resources Information System, Central Coast Information Center, University of California, Santa Barbara.

Lebow, Clayton G., Douglas R. Harro, Rebecca L. McKim, Charles M. Hodges, Ann M. Munns, Erin A. Enright, and Leeann G. Haslouer

2014 *The Sudden Flats Site: A 10,910–10,600-Year-Old Coastal Shell Midden on Vandenberg Air Force Base, Santa Barbara County, California.* Applied EarthWorks, Inc., Lompoc, California. Submitted to 30th Civil Engineer Squadron, Installation Management Flight, Environmental Section, Environmental Assets (30 CES/CEIEA), Vandenberg AFB, California.

2015 The Sudden Flats Site, a Pleistocene/Holocene Transition Shell Midden on California's Central Coast. *California Archaeology* 7:265–294.

Lebow, C., M. C. Baloian, D. R. Harro, R. L. McKim, C. Denardo, J. Onken, E. Romanski, and B. A. Price

2001 *Final Report of Archaeological Investigations*

for Reaches 5B and 6 Coastal Branch Aqueduct, Phase II. Applied Earth Works Inc., Fresno, California. Submitted to Central Coast Water Authority, Buellton, California. Copies available from California Department of Water Resources, Sacramento.

Lindstrom, Susan

1996 Great Basin Fisherfolk: Optimal Diet Breadth Modeling the Truckee River Aboriginal Subsistence Fishery. In *Prehistoric Hunter-Gatherer Fishing Strategies*, edited by Mark G. Plew, pp. 114–179. Boise State University Press, Boise, Idaho.

Love, Milton

2011 *Certainly More Than You Want to Know About the Fishes of the Pacific Coast: A Postmodern Experience*. Really Big Press, Santa Barbara.

MacArthur, Robert and Eric Pianka

1966 On Optimal Use of a Patchy Environment. *The American Naturalist* 100:603–609.

Magurran, Anne E.

1988 *Ecological Diversity and Its Measurement*. Princeton University Press, Princeton, New Jersey.

Marcott, Shaun, Jeremy D. Shakun, Peter U. Clark, and Alan C. Mix

2013 A Reconstruction of Regional and Global Temperature for the Past 11,300 Years. *Science* 339:1198–1201.

McCarthy, Helen

1993 A Political Economy of Western Mono Acorn Production. Unpublished PhD dissertation, Department of Anthropology, University of California, Davis.

MacDonald, Glen M,

2007 Severe and Sustained Drought in Southern California and the West: Present Conditions and Insights from the Past on Causes and Impacts. *Quaternary International* 173–174: 87–100.

McKenzie, Dustin

2007 Experimental Fishing Methods on the Northern Channel Islands: Testing the Relative Productivity of Bone Gorges and Incurving Shell Fishhooks. Unpublished Master's thesis, Department of Anthropology, University of California, Santa Barbara.

McGuire, Kelly R., and William R. Hildebrandt

1994 The Possibilities of Women and Men: Gender and the California Millingstone Horizon. *Journal of California and Great Basin Anthropology* 16:41–59.

2005 Re-Thinking Great Basin Foragers: Prestige Hunting and Costly Signaling during the Middle Archaic Period. *American Antiquity* 70:695–712.

McLendon, Sally, and John R. Johnson

1999 *Cultural Affiliation and Lineal Descent of Chumash Peoples in the Channel Islands and Santa Monica Mountains*. 2 vols. Prepared for the Archaeology and Ethnography Program, National Park Service, Washington, DC. Santa Barbara Museum of Natural History, Santa Barbara, California.

Meighan, Clement

1979 Glass Trade Beads in California. Manuscript on file, Lowie Museum of Anthropology, University of California, Berkeley.

Mensing, Scott A.

1998 560 Years of Vegetation Change in the Region of Santa Barbara, California. *Madrono* 45:1–11.

Merriam, C. Hart

1955 *Studies of California Indians*. University of California Press, Berkeley.

1968 *Village Names in Twelve California Mission Records*. University of California Archaeological Survey Reports 74. Berkeley.

Merriam, Clinton Hart, Zenaida Merriam Talbot, and Robert Fleming Heizer

1974 Boundary Descriptions of California Indian Stocks and Tribes. California Indian Library Collections, Sacramento.

Mikkelsen, Patricia, William R. Hildebrandt, and Debbie A. Jones

2000 *Prehistoric Adaptations on the Shores of Morro Bay Estuary: Excavations at Site CA-SLO-165, Morro Bay, California*. San Luis Obispo County Archaeological Society Occasional Papers no. 14.

Miller, Bruce W.

1988 *Chumash: A Picture of Their World*. Sand River Press, Los Osos, California.

Milliken, Randy T., and John R. Johnson

2005 *An Ethnogeography of Salinan and Northern Chumash: 1769 to 1810*. Report prepared for Caltrans District 5. Far Western Anthropological Research Group, Davis. Copies available from California Department of Transportation, San Luis Obispo.

Milliken, Randy, and Al Schwitalla

2012 *California and Great Basin* Olivella *Shell Bead Guide: A Diagnostic Type Guide in Memory of James A. Bennyhoff*. Left Coast Press, Walnut Creek, California.

Mills, Wayne, Michael F. Rondeau, and Terry L. Jones
2005   A Fluted Point from Nipomo, San Luis Obispo County, California. *Journal of California and Great Basin Anthropology* 25:68–74.

Moratto, Michael J.
1984   *California Archaeology*. Academic Press, New York.

Morgan, Anthony, Linda Scott Cummings, and James L. Rudolph
1991   Paleoenvironmental Change. In *Western Chumash Prehistory: Resource Use and Settlement in the Santa Ynez River Valley*, edited by C. F. Woodman, J. L. Rudolph, and T. P. Rudolph, pp. 65–102. Science Applications International Corporation, Santa Barbara, California. Prepared for the Unocal Corporation. Submitted to US Army Corps of Engineers, Los Angeles, California.

Motz, Lee, and Peter D. Schulz
1979   *European "Trade" Beads from Old Sacramento*. Report on file, California Department of Parks and Recreation, Sacramento.

Orme, Anthony R.
1990   The Instability of Holocene Coastal Dunes: The Case of the Morro Dunes, California. In *Coastal Dunes: Form and Process*. Edited by Karl Nordstrom, Norbert Psuty, and Bill Carter, pp. 315–333. John Wiley & Sons, Chichester, England.

Osborn, Alan
1977   Strandloopers, Mermaids, and Other Fairy Tales: Ecological Determinants of Marine Resource Utilization—The Peruvian Case. In *For Theory Building in Archaeology*, edited by Lewis R. Binford, pp. 157–205. Academic Press, New York.

Page, L. M., H. Espinosa-Perez, L. T. Findley, C. R. Gilbert, R. N. Lea, N. E. Mandrake, R. L. Mayden, and J. S. Nelson
2013   Common and Scientific Names of Fishes from the United States, Canada, and Mexico. Seventh Edition. American Fisheries Society Special Publication no. 34.

Peros, Matthew C., Samuel E. Munoz, Konrad Gajewski, and André E. Viau
2010   Prehistoric Demography of North America Inferred from Radiocarbon Data. *Journal of Archaeological Science* 37:656–664.

Peterson, Roger Tory
1990   *Western Birds*. Houghton Mifflin, Boston.

Phillips, Philip, and Gordon R. Willey
1953   Method and Theory in American Archaeology: An Operational Basis for Cultural-Historical Integration. *American Anthropologist* 55:615–633.

Pilling, Arnold R.
1948   *Archaeological Site Record for CA-SLO-51*. On file at the California Historic Resources Information System, Central Coast Information Center, University of California, Santa Barbara.
1951   The Surface Archaeology of the Pecho Coast, San Luis Obispo County, California. *The Masterkey* 25:196–200.

Pisias, Nicholas G., A. C. Mix, and Linda Heusser
2001   Millennial Scale Climate Variability of the Northeast Pacific Ocean and Northwest North America Based on Radiolaria and Pollen. *Quaternary Science Reviews* 20:1561–1576.

Pohorecky, Zenon S.
1976   *Archaeology of the South Coast Ranges of California*. Contributions of the University of California Archaeological Research Facility no. 34. University of California, Berkeley.

Porcasi, Judith F.
2008   Subsistence Patterns of Prehistoric Coastal California: Investigating Variations of Early Maritime Adaptation. Unpublished PhD dissertation, University of Leicester, England.

Powell, John Wesley
1891   *Indian Linguistic Families of America North of Mexico*. 7th Annual Report of the Bureau of American Ethnology for the Years 1885–1886. Washington, DC.

Preston, William
1996   Serpent in Eden: Dispersal of Foreign Diseases into Pre-Mission California. *Journal of California and Great Basin Anthropology* 18:3–37.

Price, Barry A.
2008   *Archaeological Site Monitoring and Condition Assessment, Diablo Canyon Power Plant North Ranch Study Area*. Applied EarthWorks, Inc., San Luis Obispo, California. Prepared for Pacific Gas and Electric Company, Sacramento.

Price, Barry, and Maggie Trumbly
2009   *Cultural Resources Overview for the Diablo Relicensing Feasibility Study, San Luis Obispo, Monterey, Fresno, Kings and Kern*

Counties, California. Technical Report prepared by Pacific Gas and Electric Company and Applied Earthworks.

Price, Barry A., Randy Baloian, and Jay B. Lloyd

2006   *Cultural Resources of Pacific Gas and Electric Company's Diablo Canyon North Ranch Property, San Luis Obispo County, California.* Report on file at the California Historic Resources Information System, Central Coast Information Center, University of California, Santa Barbara.

Price, Barry A., Marc Linder, Douglas R. Harro, Rebecca L. McKim, Leeann Haslouer, Ann Munns, and Mary Clark Baloian

2009   *A Snapshot of Protohistoric Northern Chumash: Data Recovery at CA-SLO-44.* Applied EarthWorks, Inc., San Luis Obispo, California. Prepared for Tenet Healthcare Corporation, Santa Ana, California. Draft manuscript on file, Applied Earthworks, San Luis Obispo, California.

Price, Barry A., Ann M. Munns, Georgeanna Hawley, Terry L. Joslin, Douglas R. Harro, and Rebecca L. McKim

2012   *A Slice of Time at Diablo Canyon: Archaeological Sampling at CA-SLO-61, San Luis Obispo County, California.* Applied Earth-Works, Inc., San Luis Obispo, California. Prepared for Pacific Gas and Electric Company, Sacramento.

R Core Team

2016   R: A Language and Environment for Statistical Computing. R Foundation for Statistical Computing, Vienna, Austria. https://www.R-project.org/, accessed February 19, 2018.

Raab, L. Mark

1992   An Optimal Foraging Analysis of Prehistoric Shellfish Collecting on San Clemente Island, California. *Journal of Ethnobiology* 12:63–80.

Raab, L. Mark, Jim Cassidy, Andrew Yatsko, and William J. Howard

2009   *California Maritime Archaeology: A San Clemente Island Perspective.* AltaMira Press, New York.

Raff, Jennifer, and Deborah A. Bolnick

2014   Palaeogenomics: Genetic Roots of the First Americans. *Nature* 506:162–163.

Rasmussen, Morten, Sarah L. Anzick, Michael R. Waters, Pontus Skoglund, Michael DeGiorgio, Thomas W. Stafford Jr., Simon Rasmussen, Ida Moltke, Anders Albrechtsen, Shane M. Doyle, G. David Poznik, Valborg Gudmundsdottir, Rachita Yadav, Anna-Sapfo Malaspinas, Samuel Stockton White V, Morten E. Allentoft, Omar E. Cornejo, Kristiina Tambets, Anders Eriksson, Peter D. Heintzman, Monika Karmin, Thorfinn Sand Korneliussen, David J. Meltzer, Tracey L. Pierre, Jesper Stenderup, Lauri Saag, Vera M. Warmuth, Margarida C. Lopes, Ripan S. Malhi, Søren Brunak, Thomas Sicheritz-Ponten, Ian Barnes, Matthew Collins, Ludovic Orlando, Francois Balloux, Andrea Manica, Ramneek Gupta, Mait Metspalu, Carlos D. Bustamante, Mattias Jakobsson, Rasmus Nielsen, and Eske Willerslev

2014   The Genome of a Late Pleistocene Human from a Clovis Burial Site in Western Montana. *Nature* 505:225–229.

Raven, Michelle M.

1990   The Point of No Diminishing Returns: Hunting and Resource Decline on Boigu Island, Torres Strait. Unpublished PhD dissertation, Department of Anthropology, University of California, Davis.

Reimer, Paula J., Edouard Bard, Alex Bayliss, J. Warren Beck, Paul G. Blackwell, Christopher Bronk Ramsey, Caitlin E. Buck, Hai Cheng, R. Lawrence Edwards, Michael Friedrich, Pieter M. Grootes, Thomas P. Guilderson, Haflidi Haflidason, Irka Hajdas, Christine Hatté, Timothy J. Heaton, Dirk L. Hoffmann, Alan G. Hogg, Konrad A. Hughen, K. Felix Kaiser, Bernd Kromer, Sturt W. Manning, Mu Niu, Ron W. Reimer, David A. Richards, E. Marian Scott, John R. Southon, Richard A. Staff, Christian S. M. Turney, and Johannes Van DerPlicht

2013   IntCal13 and Marine13 Radiocarbon Age Calibration Curves 0–50,000 Years Cal BP. *Radiocarbon* 55:1869–1887.

Rick, John W.

1987   Dates as Data: An Examination of the Peruvian Preceramic Radiocarbon Record. *American Antiquity* 52:55–73.

Rick, Torben C., Rene L. Vellanoweth, Jon M. Erlandson, and Douglas J. Kennett

2002   On the Antiquity of the Single-Piece Shell Fishhook: AMS Radiocarbon Evidence from the Southern California Coast. *Journal of Archaeological Science* 29:933–942.

Rick, Torben, Robert DeLong, Jon M. Erlandson, Todd Braje, Terry L. Jones, Douglas J. Kennett, Thomas Wake, and Phillip Walker

2009   A Trans-Holocene Archaeological Record of Guadalupe Fur Seals (*Arctocephalus townsendi*) on the California Coast. *Marine Mammal Science* 25:487–502.

Rick, Torben, Robert DeLong, Jon M. Erlandson, Todd Braje, Terry L. Jones, Jeanne E. Arnold, Matthew Des Lauriers, William R. Hildebrandt, Douglas J. Kennett, Rene L. Vellanoweth, and Thomas A. Wake

2012   Where Were the Northern Elephant Seals? Holocene Archaeology and Biogeography of *Mirounga angustirostris*. *The Holocene* 21:1159–1166.

Ricketts, Edward Flanders

1985   *Between Pacific Tides.* 5th edition. Stanford University Press, Stanford, California.

Riddell, Frances A.

1966   *An Archaeological Reconnaissance of the Diablo Creek Vicinity, San Luis Obispo County, California.* Report prepared for Pacific Gas and Electric. Copies on file California Department of Parks and Recreation, Sacramento.

Rivers, Betty J.

1994   The Mission Responses of Fray Luis Antonio Martinez. *Toward a Prehistory of Morro Bay: Phase II Archaeological Investigations for the Highway 41 Widening Project, San Luis Obispo County, California,* edited by T. L. Jones, K. Davis, and G. Farris, pp. 16–18. California Department of Transportation, Sacramento.

2000   *A Line through the Past: Historic and Ethnographic Background for the Branch Canal.* California State Water Project, Coastal Branch Series Paper no. 1. San Luis Obispo County Archaeological Society.

Rogers, David Banks

1929   *Prehistoric Man of the Santa Barbara Coast.* Museum of Natural History, Santa Barbara, California.

Rosenthal, Jeffery S., and Richard T. Fitzgerald

2012   The Paleo-Archaic Transition in Western California. In *On the Brink, Transformations in Human Organization and Adaptation at the Pleistocene–Holocene Boundary in North America,* edited by C. Britt Bousman and Bradley J. Vierra. Texas A&M University Press, College Station.

Ross, Lester A.

1990   Trade Beads from Hudson's Bay Company Fort Vancouver (1829–1860), Vancouver, Washington. *Beads* 2:29–67.

Running, S. W.

2012   Home Numerical Terradynamic Simulation Group Modeling and Monitoring Ecosystem Function at Multiple Scales. http://www .ntsg.umt.edu/project/mod17. Accessed December 31, 2016.

Salls, Roy A.

1988   Prehistoric Fisheries of the California Bight. Unpublished PhD dissertation, Archaeology Program, University of California, Los Angeles.

Schaffer, Brian S., and Julia L. J. Sanchez

1994   Comparison of ⅛-Inch and ¼-Inch Mesh Recovery of Controlled Samples of Small- to Medium-Sized Mammals. *American Antiquity* 59:525–530.

Schumacher, Paul

1875   Ancient Graves and Shell Heaps of California. *Smithsonian Institution Annual Report for 1874.* Washington, DC.

Shipley, William F.

1978   Native Languages of California. In *California,* edited by R. F. Heizer, pp. 80–90. *Handbook of California Indians,* Vol. 8, W. C. Sturtevant, general editor. Smithsonian Institution, Washington, DC.

Simenstad, Charles A., James A. Estes, and Karl W. Kenyon

1978   Aleuts, Sea Otters, and Alternative Stable State Communities. *Science* 200:403–411.

Simms, Steven R.

1987   *Behavioral Ecology and Hunter-Gatherer Foraging: An Example from the Great Basin.* British Anthropological Reports no. 381.

Skinner, Elizabeth J.

1986   Analysis of Flaked Stone Recovered during the Crane Valley Hydroelectric Project Testing Program. In *Cultural Resources of the Crane Valley Hydroelectric Project Area,* Vol. 3, Pt. 2, edited by S. K. Goldberg, pp. 419–594. Report on file at the State Office of Historic Preservation, Sacramento.

1990   Flaked Stone Analysis. In *Archaeological Excavations at Sites CA-MNO-574, CA-MNO-577, CA-MNO-578, and CA-MNO-833: Stoneworking in Mono County, California.* Infotec Research Incorporated. Manuscript on file, Office of Cultural Studies, Environmental Division, California Department of Transportation, Sacramento.

Slowikowski, Kamil

2016   ggrepel: Repulsive Text and Label Geoms for 'ggplot2'. R package.

Smith, Eric Alden

1991   *Inujjuamiunt Foraging Strategies: Evolution-*

ary Ecology of an Arctic Hunting Economy. A. de Gruyter, New York.

Stahl, Peter W.

1996 The Recovery and Interpretation of Microvertebrate Bone Assemblages from Archaeological Contexts. *Journal of Archaeological Method and Theory* 3:31–75.

Stevens, Nathan E.

2012 Technological Plasticity and Cultural Evolution along the Central Coast of California. Unpublished PhD dissertation, University of California, Davis.

Stevens, Nathan E., and Brian F. Codding

2009 Inferring the Function of Flaked Stone Projectile Points from the Central Coast of Alta California. *California Archaeology* 1:7–28.

Stevens, Nathan E., and Jelmer Eerkens

2012 Understanding Obsidian Movement and Hydration Dating on the Central Coast. Paper presented at the Society for California Archaeology, 46th Annual Meeting, San Diego.

Stevens, Nathan E., Richard T. Fitzgerald, Nancy Farrell, Mark A. Giambastiani, Jennifer M. Farquhar, and Dayna Tinsley

2004 *Archaeological Test Excavations at Santa Ysabel Ranch, Paso Robles, San Luis Obispo County, California.* Cultural Resource Management Services, Paso Robles, California. Submitted to Weyrich Development, LLC, Paso Robles, California. Copies available from California Historic Resources Information System, Central Coast Information Center, University of California, Santa Barbara.

Stevens, Nathan E., and Richard McElreath

2015 When Are Two Tools Better than One? Mortars, Millingslabs, and the California Acorn Economy. *Journal of Anthropological Archaeology* 37:100–111.

Stine, Scott

1994 Extreme and Persistent Drought in California and Patagonia during Mediaeval Time. *Nature* 369:546–549.

Strudwick, Ivan

1995 The Multifunctional Pitted Stones of Central California and Their Use in Marine Mammal Shell Processing. *Proceedings of the Society for California Archaeology* 8:141–166.

Stuiver, Minze, Paula J. Reimer, and R. Reimer

2016 CALIB Radiocarbon Calibration Version 7.1. http://calib.qub.ac.uk/calib/, accessed February 19, 2018.

Surdam, Ronald C., and Clarence A. Hall Jr.

1984 Diagenesis of the Miocene Obispo Formation, Coast Range California. Special Publications of the Society of Economic Paleontologists and Mineralogists. http://archives.datapages.com/data/sepm_sp/fg2/Diagenesis_of_the_Miocene.htm. Accessed February 26, 2018.

Surovell, Todd A., Judson Byrd Finley, Geoffrey M. Smith, P. Jeffrey Brantingham, and Robert Kelly

2009 Correcting Temporal Frequency Distributions for Taphonomic Bias. *Journal of Archaeological Science* 36:1715–1724.

Taylor, Alexander S.

1860–1863 The Indianology of California. In *California Farmer and Journal of Useful Sciences*, vols. 13–20. February 22, 1860–October 30, 1863.

Taylor, W. W.

1961 Archaeology and Language in Western North America. *American Antiquity* 27:71–81.

Thakar, Heather B., Michael A. Glassow, and Carol Blanchette

2017 Reconsidering Evidence of Human Impacts: Implications of Within-Site Variation of Growth Rates in *Mytilus californianus* along Tidal Gradients. *Quaternary International* 427:151–159.

Thomas, David H.

1969 Great Basin Hunting Patterns: A Quantitative Method for Treating Faunal Remains. *American Antiquity* 34:392–401.

2008 *Native American Landscapes of St. Catherines Island, Georgia.* American Museum of Natural History, New York.

Tomka, Steve A.

2013 The Adoption of the Bow and Arrow: A Model Based on Experimental Performance Characteristics. *American Antiquity* 78:553–569.

Turner, Christy G., III

2003 Three Ounces of Sea Shells and One Fish Bone Do Not a Coastal Migration Make. *American Antiquity* 68:391–395.

Ugan, Andrew

2005 Does Size Matter? Body Size, Mass Collecting, and Their Implications for Understanding Prehistoric Foraging Behavior. *American Antiquity* 70:75–89.

United States Soil Conservation Service

1977 *Soil Survey of San Luis Obispo County.* U.S. Soil Conservation Service, Washington, DC.

Van Bueren, Thad M.

1983   Archaeological Perspectives on Central
        Sierra Miwok Culture Change during the
        Historic Period. Unpublished Master's
        thesis, Department of Anthropology, San
        Francisco State University, San Francisco.

Viau, A. E., K. Gajewski, M. C. Sawada, and P. Fines

2006   Millennial-Scale Temperature Variations
        in North America during the Holocene.
        Journal of Geophysical Research 111, D09102,
        doi:10.1029/2005JD006031.

Wagner, H. R.

1924   The Voyage to California of Sebastian Rodri-
        guez Cermeño in 1595. *California Historical
        Society Quarterly* 3:3–24.

Wallace, William J.

1954   The Little Sycamore Site and the Early Mill-
        ing Stone Cultures of Southern California.
        American Antiquity 20:112–123.

Warren, Claude N.

1964   Cultural Change and Continuity on the San
        Diego Coast. Unpublished PhD dissertation,
        Department of Anthropology, University of
        California, Los Angeles.

1967   The Southern California Milling Stone Hori-
        zon: Some Comments. *American Antiquity*
        32:233–236.

1968   Cultural Tradition and Ecological Adapta-
        tion on the Southern California Coast. In
        *Archaic Prehistory in the Western United
        States*, edited by C. Irwin-Williams, pp. 1–14.
        Contributions in Anthropology 1(3). Eastern
        New Mexico University Paleo-Indian Insti-
        tute, Portales.

Warren, Claude N., Delbert L. True, and A. A. Eudey

1960   Early Gathering Complexes of Western San
        Diego County: Results and Interpretations
        of an Archaeological Survey. *University of
        California, Los Angeles, Archaeological Sur-
        vey Annual Report* 1960–1961:1–106.

Waters, Michael R., and Thomas W. Stafford Jr.

2007   Redefining the Age of Clovis: Implications
        for the Peopling of the Americas. *Science*
        315:1122–1126.

West, James G., Wallace Woolfenden, James A.
Wanket, and Scott Anderson

2007   Late Pleistocene and Holocene Environ-
        ments. In *California Prehistory: Coloniza-
        tion, Culture, and Complexity*, edited by T. L.
        Jones and K. Klar, pp. 11–34. AltaMira Press,
        Walnut Creek, California.

Whitaker, Adrian R.

2008   Incipient Aquaculture in Prehistoric

California?: Long-Term Productivity and
Sustainability vs. Immediate Returns for the
Harvest of Marine Invertebrates. *Journal of
Archaeological Science* 35:1114–1123.

2009   Are Deer Really Susceptible to Resource
        Depression? Modeling Deer *(Odocoileus
        hemionus)* Populations under Human Pre-
        dation. *California Archaeology* 1:93–108.

2010   Prehistoric Behavioral Depression of
        Cormorant *(Phalacrocorax* spp.) on the
        Northern California Coast. *Journal of Ar-
        chaeological Science* 37:2562–2571.

Whitaker, Adrian R., and Brian F. Byrd

2012   Boat-Based Foraging and Discontinuous
        Prehistoric Red Abalone Exploitation along
        the California Coast. *Journal of Anthropolog-
        ical Archaeology* 31:196–214.

2014   Social Circumscription, Territoriality, and
        the Late Holocene Intensification of Small-
        Bodied Shellfish along the California Coast.
        *The Journal of Island and Coastal Archaeol-
        ogy* 9:150–168.

White, Greg G.

1989   *A Report of Archaeological Investigations
        at Eleven Native American Coastal Sites,
        MacKerricher State Park, Mendocino County,
        California.* Report prepared for the Cali-
        fornia Department of Parks and Recreation,
        Sacramento. Copies available from North-
        west Information Center, Sonoma State
        University, Rohnert Park, California.

White, Greg G., and James Roscoe

1992   *Results of Test Excavations at Crazy Creek
        Falls (CA-LAK-1682) and Serpentine Camp
        (CA-LAK-1683), Crazy Creek Valley, Lake
        County, California.* Report on file, Northwest
        Archaeological Information Center, Sonoma
        State University, Rohnert Park, California.

Wickham, Hadley

2009   ggplot2: Create Elegant Data Visualisations
        Using the Grammar of Graphics. R package.

Wilcoxon, Larry R.

1988   *Final Report Results of a Cultural Resources
        Evaluation for the North Property Access
        Road, Diablo Canyon Power Plant, San Luis
        Obispo County, California.* Report on file at
        the California Historic Resources Infor-
        mation System, Central Coast Information
        Center, University of California, Santa
        Barbara.

Winterhalder, Bruce, Douglas J. Kennett, M. N.
Grote, and J. Bartruff

2010   Ideal Free Settlement on California's Northern Channel Islands. *Journal of Anthropological Archaeology* 29:469–490.

Wohlgemuth, Eric
2004   The Course of Plant Food Intensification in Native Central California. Unpublished PhD dissertation, University of California, Davis.

Woodward, Jim
1987   *Pecho Coast Archaeology: A Survey Update.* Report on file California Department of Parks and Recreation, Sacramento.

Yamada, Sylvia Behrens, and Erin E. Peters
1988   Harvest Management and the Growth and Condition of Submarket Size Mussels, *Mytilus californianus. Aquaculture* 74: 293–299.

Zohar, Irit, and Miriam Belmaker
2005   Size Does Matter: Methodological Comments on Sieve Size and Species Richness in Fishbone Assemblages. *Journal of Archaeological Science* 32:635–641.

Index

Note: pages numbers printed in *italics* refer to figures, illustrations, or tables.